Bryan Cummins • John Steckley

Full Circle
First Nations of Canada

Third Edition

Cover Art: Pearson Learning Solutions

Previously published as:

Full Circle: Canada's First Nations, Second Edition
by John L. Steckley and Bryan D. Cummins
Copyright © 2008, 2001 by Pearson Education Canada
Published by Prentice Hall
Toronto, Ontario

Pearson Learning Solutions, 501 Boylston Street, Suite 900, Boston, MA 02116
A Pearson Education Company
www.pearsoned.com

8   17

000200010271740492

LF/KE

ISBN 10: 1-269-44153-1
ISBN 13: 978-1-269-44153-7

Full Circle

To my mother, Frances Anne (Cooper) Cummins,
who was always so supportive. And to my students—past, present, and future—
who inspire me and have given me the greatest job in the world.—B.C.

To my mother, Margaret Lawson Kerton,
who long knew this day would come—J.S.

Brief Contents

Contents

Chapter Twenty-Four: Native Governance 269

Chapter Twenty-Five: Undoing the Past 281

Preface

As we write this second edition of *Full Circle*, there is a confrontation occurring in Caledonia, in Southern Ontario, near the Six Nations reserve. Like so many similar issues, it is a matter of Aboriginal rights and the way they should be interpreted. But it is also an issue of lack of knowledge. Reading editorials, listening to politicians' speeches, following readers' comments in online versions of the major newspapers in Canada, we cannot help but be struck, once again, by the wall that separates Aboriginal and non-Aboriginal peoples in Canada. This wall disables the two groups from truly seeing, learning from, and living in peace with each other.

No one introductory textbook can bring down the entire wall. Such a book would have to be thousands of pages long. But a step on the path of knowledge involves realizing that there is so much information that needs to be conveyed. The interwoven stories of Aboriginal peoples in Canada cannot be taught in one course. The political, educational, and general cultural structures of ignorance need to be understood before they can be dismantled, and years of teaching and learning are required.

This being said, *Full Circle* is an attempt to poke some holes in that wall. We have tried to achieve this through several means. Of key importance is the incorporation of Aboriginal voices into the text. This begins with an acknowledgment of the fact that there is no one Aboriginal experience; instead, there are many. There are many different languages still spoken in Canada. There are traditional stories that share some principles but hold meanings unique to different peoples. There are elders and there are young people with unique visions. There are men who, since contact, have often been separated from women by sexist laws, primarily the Indian Act. There are women who have had to fight to be respected by governments, non-Aboriginal peoples, the men in their communities, and each other. There are communities that have suffered dislocation from traditional lands, and those who have greater continuity in their sense of place. While the reserve experience has to be articulated, urban voices need to be heard as well. Most Aboriginal people now live, work, or spend significant parts of their lives in urban areas and have experiences that need to be spoken and heard.

Our hope is that this book starts readers on the path of learning that enables them to take more steps and make their own contributions to tearing down the wall of ignorance that blinds people, both Aboriginal and non-Aboriginal, in this country.

Instructor's Supplement

To assist with this learning process, the second edition of *Full Circle* is accompanied by a Test Item File. This supplement is available for downloading from a password-protected section of Pearson Education Canada's online catalogue (vig.pearsoned.ca). See your local sales representative for details and access.

Acknowledgments

I thank my colleague in Golden Lake, Kirby Whiteduck, for sharing his insights and expertise. I also thank my research assistant, Ms. Mithra Dubey, for always being prompt, diligent, and thorough; and Dave Lafleche, for his interest and enthusiasm. Last, my family has been an invaluable source of support. Pauline Lore and Frances Cummins—my late mother-in-law and mother, respectively—were always encouraging and are missed. A special thank you goes to Tricia, who is always there.

Bryan Cummins

While many individuals helped with this work, the first thanks are reserved for my mother, Margaret Lawson Kerton, who always believed in me as a writer. Thanks also to my colleagues at Humber College, particularly Gina Antonacci, who helped us get started, and Wayson Choy, whose experience and reassuring confidence in my ability helped get the first edition of the book finished. I thank my students for their genuine interest in the project (rather than just sucking up to their teacher). My dogs Egwene and Cosmo are thanked for their distractions and their companionship. Last, I thank my wife, Angelika (Angie), whose support is never praised enough.

John Steckley

We would both like to acknowledge the contributions of Russ Blackbird, James Pardy, and Jim Silverstone, whose reviews provided great insight into shaping the first edition of this text. For their feedback on the second edition, we would like to thank the following reviewers:

Steven Boddington, *Athabasca University*
Louis Hill, *Wilfrid Laurier University*
Barbara Wilkes, *University of Calgary*

We once again thank all those at Pearson Education Canada who helped us publish the first edition of *Full Circle*; however, second editions have their own challenges. For this, we would like to acknowledge and thank Christine Cozens for patiently listening to our long list of complaints and helping us get the second edition started. Next, we wish to acknowledge the work of Rachel Stuckey for keeping us on track and on schedule. Thanks also go to Amanda Wesson for guiding us through the production process with new technology, and to our copyeditor Nancy Mucklow, whose great attention to detail was challenged by all those native-language terms. Finally, we thank those members of the team with whom we didn't have the pleasure of working directly.

chapter one

Oral Traditions

INTRODUCTION

Before Europeans came to this country, the Aboriginal peoples of Canada recorded their laws and history and taught their lessons orally. They did not have or feel the need to write them down. Father Paul Ragueneau, a Jesuit missionary who lived among the Huron in the first half of the seventeenth century, wrote the following around 1646 on what he early learned about oral traditions. The source is the *Jesuit Relations* (JR), a valuable collection of reports written by the Jesuits back to their superiors in France:

> The elders of the country were assembled this winter for the election of a very celebrated Captain [i.e., leader or chief]. They are accustomed, on such occasions, to relate the stories which they have learned regarding their ancestors, even those most remote, so that the young people, who are present and hear them, may preserve the memory thereof, and relate them in their turn, when they shall have become old. They do this in order thus to transmit to posterity the history and the annals of the country—striving, by this means, to supply the lack of writing and of books, which they have not. They offer, to the person from whom they desire to hear something, a little bundle of straws a foot long, which serve them as counters for calculating the numbers, and for aiding the memory of those present, distributing in various lots these same straws, according to the diversity of the things which they relate (JR30:61).

This chapter will examine several traditional Native stories. When you read the stories presented, keep in mind that they are only parts of much fuller stories, that they are translated from more meaningful versions in their original languages, and that in being written they lose a lot. You don't get the tone and expression of the storyteller, nor do you see the way he or she might act out parts of the story. In effect, you are getting a cheap imitation. Further, you will see in the stories a mixture of the sacred and the humourous almost simultaneously. Some of the jokes may not seem all that funny to you, but you must realize that humour requires a common context. Think about times that you have tried to explain a funny part of a movie to people who did not see the movie. They probably didn't laugh like you did. Finally, keep in mind that one significant purpose of these stories is to teach—and you (and even the authors of this book) often do not have enough understanding to get the full benefits of what the stories have to teach.

TRUTH AND STORIES

All cultures respond to a human need to explain how it is that things are the way that they are. But human beings cannot know all the answers. When people tell stories about the past, they can point their stories in the direction of truth as it makes sense to them; but there is no absolute truth that we can arrive at as a final destination. What happened five minutes ago is open to different interpretation and debate, let alone in centuries past. Basil Johnston, an Anishinabe scholar and author of 20 books, defined this kind of truth in his article, "One Generation from Extinction" (Johnston 1991). He wrote that when an Anishinabe person says that someone is telling the truth, the person uses the term *w'daeb-awae,* an Ojibwe term for a particular concept of truth. This does not just mean that what that someone has said is true:

> It is at the same time a philosophical proposition that, in saying, a speaker casts his words and his voice only as far as his vocabulary and his perception will enable him. In so doing the tribe was denying that there was absolute truth; that the best a speaker could achieve and a listener expect was the highest degree of accuracy. Somehow that one expression "w'daeb-awae" set the limits of a single statement as well as setting limits on all speech. (Johnston 1991:12)

People who thus followed the rule of restricting what they say to what they actually knew would be respected by their listeners:

> Of that man or woman they would say "w'daeb-awae." Better still, people would want to hear the speaker again and by so doing bestow upon the speaker the opportunity to speak, for ultimately it is the people who confer the right of speech by their audience. In order to understand a people, you must try to see their truth (Johnston 1991:12).

Cree Oral Tradition: *Âtalohkâna* and *Tipâcimôwina*

There are different types of stories, with different amounts of stress on what is important in terms of such factors as teaching, entertainment, and an attempt to get at what "actually happened."

C. Douglas Ellis learned from listening to Cree Elders living by the west coast of James Bay that they had two basic kinds of stories, expressed in Swampy Cree as **âtalohkâna** (usually translated as legends) and **tipâcimôwina** (singular, *tipâcimôwin*; typically translated as stories, news, historical narratives, or personal experiences).

Âtalohkâna (for an example, see Box 1-1) are often stories that take place at a time when the world was changing into the world we know today. The main figures are cultural heroes, usually individuals who are tricksters such as *Weesakechahk* or *Chahkabesh*, animals who can readily talk to humans, or spirits who give advice to humans. The trickster figure has a number of different counterparts across Canada: *Glooscap* of the Mi'kmaq, *Nanabush* of the Ojibwa, *N'api* of the Blackfoot, and *Coyote* or *Raven* among the peoples of British Columbia.

BOX 1-1	Where Does the Name "Turtle Island" Come From?

You might have heard people talking or writing about North America as "Turtle Island." That expression comes from an origin story shared by several North American peoples. The story that is told below is one version held by the Wyandot people, descendants of the Petun and Huron (both known among themselves as Wendat people), who lived in southern Ontario until the 1650s. This version was told originally in Wyandot in 1912 by Catherine Johnson. Her translator was Mary Kelley.

When the story begins, there are two worlds. One, which is in the sky, is inhabited by a small number of people. The other, which is covered with water, is inhabited by animals.

> Several brothers and sisters were living together. The only meal they had every day consisted of a single basket of corn, the daily yield of their corn-patch.

> Tired of thus gathering the corn for every meal, the young woman thought to herself one day, "Now, maybe, the easiest way is to cut the stalks [and gather the ears once and for all]." So she cut down the corn stalks and gathered them all. Her brothers, in their grief, spoke to her

and said, "You have spoilt everything and ruined our subsistence! You have wasted it all!" They dropped her through a hole into the ocean.

Wild geese were roaming about on the waters. Their leader exclaimed, "A body is falling from above. Let us all gather close together!" And the woman from above fell gently upon the backs of the Geese, as they were all assembled together. One of them spoke after a while and said, "We are getting tired. Let someone else now take our place." The Turtle, emerging from under the waters, said, "It is I, the next!" And the body of the woman fallen from above now rested upon the Turtle's back.

Then the Toad went [down] and came back with a mouthful of dirt. She gave the dirt to the woman fallen from above, saying, "Do this! Sprinkle it about at arm's length where you lie." The Toad meant her to sprinkle the [grains of] earth all around her. So the woman did; and the land grew around her. She rose and began to walk about the new land . . . . (Barbeau 1915).

According to the Wendat story, North Americans now live on the Turtle's back.

Weesakechahk (from which is derived the English term "whisky jack," referring to the gray or Canada jay) stories often have him trying to fool someone in an attempt to get food. In the end, he usually gets tricked himself. In the often-told story of the "Shut Eye Dance," Weesakechahk cons birds such as geese, loons, and ducks to dance a dance in which they keep their eyes shut. As they dance, he knocks them over the head. Eventually, one of the birds (a loon in one version) finds out what is happening and warns the others. For its efforts, the loon receives the flattened shape it has today. Weesakechahk himself gets tricked in the end. He puts the birds he can't eat head-first into the sand with their feet sticking out. The next morning he discovers that people have come and have stolen his birds, leaving only the feet, so he didn't earlier suspect a thing.

BOX 1-2	The Meaning of *Pâstâmowin*

You can see something in the meaning of *pâstâmowin* by seeing how the root "pâstâ" is used in other words:

pâstâh: bring evil on s.o. [someone], cast an evil spell on s.o.

pâstâho: utter s.t. [something], which brings evil or bad luck on oneself

pâstâm: speak so as to bring evil on s.o.

pâstân: put pressure on s.o./s.t. to the point of cracking

pâstin: crack s.o./s.t. (e.g., an egg) while holding it (Ellis 1995).

Another Cree trickster figure, Chahkabesh, is small, only one hand high in some stories. He lives with his older sister and is very curious, which often gets him in trouble. As with all tricksters, the world changes because of his adventures. In the last story of the cycle, Chahkabesh ignores his sister's warning not to look at the full moon, looks anyways, and is drawn in by the moon forever. The Cree believe we can see his face there today.

Another kind of story that fits into the *âtalohkâna* type is the **pâstâmowin** (plural, *pâstâmowina*), that is, speaking ill of sacred things, blasphemy that brings retribution (see Box 1-2). These stories are about what can happen if you break the rules by which a "good person" lives. In one such story, a man makes fun of someone else, ridiculing him for being bitten by a rabbit. He ends up being bitten to death by rabbits.

The equivalents of the *âtalohkâna* among other North American peoples focus on a variety of subjects, of which origins is a common theme. The following stories are two examples, one from the Peigan of Alberta, and the other from the Dogrib of the Northwest Territories.

Peigan Tradition: Old Man, the River, and the Origin of Death

N'api [Old Man] created the first Peigan woman and child out of clay. They walked down to the river where N'api told them who he was. What resulted was both comical and sad.

The woman asked N'api whether or not they would live forever. N'api replied that he had not ever thought about that before, and so he came up with a plan. He would take a piece of dried buffalo dung and throw it in the river. If it floated, when people die, they would come back to life after four days. But if it sank, they would die and not return to life. He threw the buffalo chip in the water, and it floated. However, the woman tried the same trick with a stone, saying:

"No, I will throw this stone in the river; if it floats we will always live, if it sinks people must die, that they may always be sorry for each other." The woman threw the stone into the water, and it sank. "There," said Old Man, "you have chosen. There will be an end to them." (Sanders and Peek 1973:38)

Not long afterwards, the woman's child died. She cried a great deal, and said to N'api: "Let us change this. The law that you first made, let that be a law." He said: "Not so. What is made law must be law. We will undo nothing that we have done. The child is dead, but it cannot be changed. People will have to die." (Sanders and Peek 1973:38)

The Origin Story of the Dogrib

The following is an English version of the story of the origin of the Dogrib, as recorded by Emile Petitot in 1891. The woman who marries the dog in this story is a Yellowknife.

> [A] *Tatsanottine* [Yellowknife] woman . . . was dwelling with her two brothers N. of Great Slave lake. One day a strong and handsome stranger arrived, who, on the proposal of the brothers, took her for his wife. Waking in the middle of the wedding night she found her husband gone and heard an animal crunching bones at the fireplace . . . . The same thing happened the next night. The bride and her brothers lighted torches, but found no animal. On the third night one of the brothers hurled a stone axe in the corner whence the noise of gnawing proceeded. A cry of agony was heard, and when a torch was lighted a great black dog was seen twitching in the death throes. As the human husband did not reappear, the brothers chased forth their sister because she had married a dog-man, a sorcerer, a Tlingit. She wandered into [a] treeless desert . . . where in the course of time she brought forth a litter of puppies, which she kept hidden in a bag of reindeer skin. When they could run alone she was astonished to find on her return from hunting, prints of infants' feet in the ashes. Hiding one day, she saw the little dogs leap from the bag, becoming handsome children as soon as they reached the light. She ran and pulled the string of the bag, but not before three succeeded in jumping back in the dark hole. Two boys and two girls were kept forcibly in the daylight, and these became the progenitors of the *Thlingchadinne* [Dogrib] (Hodge 1971a:454).

Tipâcimôwin

Tipâcimôwina are historical narratives. The following is a *tipâcimôwin* called "How Ghost River got its name." Peoples living on both sides of James Bay tell this story. The Iroquois and the Cree were fighting each other, and the Cree had a shaman who could predict when the Iroquois would arrive at a particular place:

> So the People prepared . . . to lie in wait for the Iroquois for them to drift downstream. And they killed many then by doing this, having foreseen where they would lie in wait for them. They also took many as slaves.

> And that is the reason why Ghost River is today called by that name, Ghost River (Ellis 1995:177).

For both Native and non-Native historians, a *tipâcimôwin* can be a tremendous source of information. Thanadelthur ("Marten Jumping" or "Shaking") was an eighteenth-century Chipewyan woman who escaped capture by the Cree. She was also instrumental in linking her people with the fur trade, perhaps saving them from being totally defeated by the Cree. The written record of the time did not tell us her name, much of what she thought, and other important aspects of her story. However, her story has been preserved in oral tradition, and she is remembered as a hero to her people. In 1879, more than 150 years after Thanadelthur died, Chipewyan Alexis Enna-azè told Thanadelthur's story to have it written down, filling in many of the gaps. The story of the powerful Dogrib man (see Box 1-3) is another such *tipâcimôwin*.

BOX 1-3   The Story of the Powerful Old Dogrib Man

The Dogrib became quite active in the fur trade during the nineteenth century. A good indication of their attitude towards some of the traders working for the Hudson's Bay Company (HBC) can be seen in the following tale told by Vital Thomas, a Dogrib storyteller, in 1966.

It begins with a group of Dogrib travelling a long way to a post to ask for credit for much-needed supplies, only to be turned down by a stingy company clerk. Credit was often necessary for northern Natives to be able to trap, even to survive, and the HBC often used it to create Native indebtedness. As the group returned home empty-handed, they came across a second group, who had among them a wise and spiritually powerful old man. He was asked to help them, and he agreed. The old Dogrib man started to sing "Hey hey, Pale Man! hey hey" and worked his arms down into the earth, about half the length of his arms. Then he said, "Here is the man we have been talking about" and hauled the HBC clerk up out of the ground as far as his armpits.

Then he began to rub his hands over the man's head as if he was pulling or cupping up water. All of a sudden he clapped his hands loudly and said, "Here it is! I got his mind right here in my hands!" And the Hudson's Bay man sank back through the earth. "He had gone home now without his mind. We got to hurry to get there. We got to do our trading fast and [come] right back because I can't hold his mind very long" (Nabokov 1991:47–8).

Perhaps the most important role of a *tipâcimôwin* or any Native story lies in the fact that it teaches without lecturing, allowing the listeners to learn what they can. This is well described by Mohawk writer Patricia Monture-Angus:

The tradition of oral history as a method of sharing the lessons of life with children and young people . . . had the advantage that the Elders told us stories. They did not tell us what to do or how to do it or figure out the world for us—they told us a story about their experience, about their life or their grandfather's or grandmother's or auntie's or uncle's life. It is in this manner that Indian people are taught independence as well as respect, because you have to do your own figuring for yourself (Monture-Angus 1995:11).

The Great Law of Peace: An Iroquois Oral Tradition

A good example of an oral tradition and the benefits that such might hold to a people is what is known in Mohawk as **Gayanerengo:wa** ("it is a great good"), known in English as the Great Law of Peace. This story is a tradition that probably has lasted about 550 years. It is hard to put a precise date on it. Most writers estimate it originated from 1420 to 1550. Some say that it originated in 1451 and others say 1536, based on a reference in some versions to an eclipse of the sun. There was such an eclipse in 1451 and again in 1536.

The archaeology of southern Ontario can also lend insight into the period of time from which the Great Law of Peace dates, a good example of how archaeology and oral tradition can be used to reinforce each other (not an unusual thing). During this period, the population of southern Ontario peaked. Communities were clustering into what can be called tribal units. There is ample evidence of war. Some villages were surrounded with multiple rows of palisades. Bones dug up from that period often show signs of violent death. It was within such a conflict-ridden social environment that the Great Law of Peace arose.

The following is a very basic outline of what the story is about. Keep in mind that the authors learned about what goes into this story primarily from written versions (for an example, see Box 1-4) and have never heard the story told in an Iroquoian language. Their knowledge, therefore, can only be partial, and is far from complete.

Great Law of Peace: Storyline

A woman and her adult daughter were worried about the warfare that surrounded them, so they went to live on their own, apart from any community. According to most versions, they settled somewhere around the Bay of Quinte, at the eastern end of the northern shore of Lake Ontario. The nation to which these two women belonged varies according to source, but most people now believe that it was the Wendat. To the daughter was born a boy called Deganawida, a name for which there is no translation, and which no Iroquois has used since. He is often referred to as the Peacemaker, since his grandmother had a vision in which the Creator expressed that her grandson would bring peace to his people.

When the boy grew up, he decided to share with the five warring Iroquoian tribes living to the south of him the vision of peace he had carried since childhood. He went first to the Mohawk. In one Mohawk community, he was accepted by the peace chief, whom he named Hiawatha (sometimes translated as "He makes wampum"). Hiawatha spoke for him and helped to bring about the acceptance of the Peacemaker's vision, both with the Mohawk and with the others (see also Box 1-5 on page 8).

After the Mohawk accepted the vision, the two men went separately to speak with the neighbouring Oneida. Around that time, tragedy struck Hiawatha. His three daughters died. In mourning, he created strings of wooden beads that resembled shell-bead wampum. The Oneida invited him to their community using their copy of his wooden wampum. This is

BOX 1-4   The Gibson Manuscript

To get some sense of how long an oral tradition can be, consider the Gibson manuscript, the only complete written version of the Great Law of Peace recorded in one of the languages of the league. It was dictated by Chief John A. Gibson to the anthropologist Alexander A. Goldenweiser in 1912. His mother was Seneca of the Turtle clan, so when he was of appropriate age, he received the Seneca sachem name of *Skanyatai:yo?* ("Handsome Lake"). His father was Onondaga, with the sachem name of Thadodaho. Chief Gibson was linguistically gifted. It is said that he was equally fluent in Cayuga and Onondaga, could speak Seneca, Oneida, and some Tuscarora, and sometimes performed rituals in Mohawk. His dictation of the Great Law of Peace, in Onondaga, took up 514 handwritten pages (with no translation). When it was finally published in 1995 with a translation, it was 701 pages long.

BOX 1-5   The Song of Hiawatha

In 1855, Henry Wadsworth Longfellow wrote a famous poem called "The Song of Hiawatha." In that poem, Longfellow made Hiawatha an Ojibwa hero, living "by the shores of Gitche Gumee" (Ojibwe for "large lake," referring to Lake Superior), where "stood the Wigwam" (Algonquian term for "house") "of Nokomis" (Ojibwe for "grandmother"). This mix-up of languages and locations is comparable to writing about a great German hero named Napoleon who lived in Berlin in the home of his Oma (German for "grandmother")!

sometimes said to have been the origin of using wampum for this purpose. The Oneida were convinced that the Peacemaker's message was the path they should take.

The biggest obstacle to the Peacemaker's dreams was the shaman/war leader of the Onondaga, named Thadodaho. Therefore, the Peacemaker arranged that the Onondaga, the middle of the five nations, was the last visited. There, Thadodaho was approached not only by the Peacemaker and Hiawatha, but also by the four other nations who had accepted the vision. The Cayuga were convinced, followed by the Seneca, although the war leaders of the Seneca had not accepted the Peacemaker's message of peace.

The Peacemaker had to face some spiritual challenges along the way. For example, before he could make it to the major community of the Onondaga, he had to cross a lake. It is said that three times Thadodaho tried to use sorcery to create a storm on the lake, blowing back the Peacemaker's canoe. Three times the Peacemaker faced the challenge and calmed the waters of the lake.

At the eventual meeting of the five nations, the Peacemaker spelled out how the people would be brought together in one confederacy, or league. They would be divided into two **moieties** (from the French word for half): one, referred to as the "fathers" (sometimes the "older brothers"), would be made up of the Mohawk, Seneca, and Onondaga; the other, referred to in council as the "sons" (less often as the "younger brothers"), would be made up of the Oneida and the Cayuga. The chiefs would sit in council with the "fathers" on one side of the fire and the "sons" at the other.

They also decided that issues would be resolved through consensus, as opposed to majority vote. When an issue was to be discussed, it would first be presented to the Mohawk chiefs. They were to talk about it and arrive at some kind of consensus. The Mohawk would pass on their consensus decision to the Seneca, who would then discuss the issue by themselves and try to arrive at a consensus: ideally, one in support of what the Mohawk had decided. The two groups would then appoint a speaker to take this view "across the hearth or fire" to the Oneida, after which the issue would be taken to the Cayuga, who would deal with it as the others had. If there were two different opinions coming from the Mohawk and the Seneca, the "sons" had to consider both. Finally, the "sons" would give their view, ideally a consensus, to the Mohawk, who would take it to the Onondaga. The Onondaga would ratify the agreement. If there was a split opinion, then the Onondaga were responsible for breaking the tie or for suggesting a new compromise to be discussed by the others.

The council of the confederacy thus formed was to be made up of 50 chiefs or **sachems** (an Algonquian word now in English). The Onondaga would have 14 sachems, the Cayuga 10, the Mohawk and the Oneida nine each, and the Seneca eight. Because there was no voting, however, this arrangement was more an honouring distribution than one that gave differing degrees of power. The Onondaga were further honoured by being named the Fire-keepers, meaning that they would host the meetings of the council. The Seneca war chiefs, who were finally convinced to accept the Peacemaker's vision, were honoured by being named the Doorkeepers, controlling access to the meetings of the council.

Also established through the Great Law of Peace was the Condolence Council, which used the invitation wampum first employed with Hiawatha. The Condolence Council is the most complex ceremony of the league, lasting anywhere from six to eight hours. Its purpose is to mourn a sachem's death and to "raise up" his successor.

The Great Law also established symbols of the confederacy. Their collective name would be based on the noun root *nonhs*, meaning "house," combined either with the verb root *yonni*, meaning "to be extended, finished, whole," or the verb root *onni*, meaning "to make." The name would then be (in Seneca) *Hotinnonhysyonni*, "they are of the extended house," or *Hotinnonhson:ni:h*, "they build a house." At that same time, the new confederates planted a great white pine tree of peace, burying their weapons with the roots, symbolizing that the five nations would not fight each other. Each nation also brought an arrow that would be part of a group bound together by sinew, to show that they were stronger together than they were apart.

In 2006, the number of people reporting themselves as being Aboriginal was 1,172,790, representing 3.8% of the Canadian population. Currently, there are 617 First Nation communities, which represent more than 50 nations of cultural groups and 50 Aboriginal languages. Over half (54%) of Aboriginal people live in urban areas (http://www.aadncaandc. gc.ca/eng/1100100013791/1100100013795).

The provincial and territorial distribution of Aboriginal peoples is as follows:

Province/Territory	Number	Percentage
Canada	1,172,790	100
Newfoundland and Labrador	23,450	2
Prince Edward Island	1,730	0.1
Nova Scotia	24,175	2
New Brunswick	17,655	2
Québec	108,430	9
Ontario	242,496	21
Manitoba	175,395	15
Saskatchewan	141,890	12
Alberta	188,365	16
British Columbia	196,075	17
Yukon	7,580	0.6
Northwest Territories	20,635	2
Nunavut	24,920	2

(http://www.aadncaandc.gc.ca/eng/1100100013791/1100100013795)

Native Individuals 1-1

Chahkabesh: A mythical figure, said to be only one hand high, found in a number of traditional Cree stories.

John A. Gibson: A Seneca/Onondaga man whose recitation of the Great Law of Peace has helped to preserve that important oral document.

Hiawatha: Mohawk man who aided Deganawida the Peacemaker in bringing the Great Law of Peace to his people.

Deganawida the Peacemaker: A man thought to be Huron/Wendat whose visions led to the development of the Great Law of Peace and thereby the Confederacy of the Iroquois.

Weesakechahk: A mythical figure, the culture hero/trickster in many Cree stories.

KEY TERMS

âtalohkâna (Cree)

Gayanerengo:wa (Mohawk)

moieties

pâstâmowin (Cree)

sachems

tipâcimôwina (Cree)

CONTENT QUESTIONS

1. How did Basil Johnston define "truth"?
2. What is the origin of the name "Turtle Island"?
3. What is the Great Law of Peace?
4. How are *âtalohkâna* and *tipâcimôwina* different?
5. How did the Dogrib get their name?

WEBLINKS

www.ainc-inac.gc.ca/ch/rcap/index_e.html
The Royal Commission on Aboriginal Peoples Report includes a discussion of the importance of language and oral tradition for Natives in Canada. The complete RCAP Report can be found at www.ainc-inac.gc.ca/ch/rcap/sg/sgmm_e.html.

www.ilhawaii.net/~stony/loreindx.html
Over 100 stories and legends of various North American Native groups have been compiled at the Native American Lore Index Page.

chapter two

The Peopling of the Americas

INTRODUCTION

As we saw from the story of Turtle Island, and as we will see in the discussion of the Huron word -*ondcch*- in Chapter 3, it is part of traditional beliefs for the Aboriginal people to say that they began life in the Americas, that they have been here "from time immemorial." It is similar to the set of beliefs set down in the book of Genesis in the Bible. Like Genesis, these stories are part of the covenant that the people hold with the spirit world, and with the Creator, guiding people who want to lead a good, spiritual life on the right path. You don't have to share the beliefs to know that the covenant must be respected.

But while respecting the covenant and agreeing that Natives are the First Nations of the Americas by thousands of years, anthropologists do not agree with the notion of special creation of people in the Americas. What they believe begins with evolution. Scientific evidence demonstrates that from perhaps six or seven million years ago, to about 1.8 million years ago, our ancestors and their cousins lived in Africa. At some point, humans left Africa to travel east to Georgia (in Eastern Europe), Indonesia, and China. They later populated the world. No one people was created separately. According to science, Natives could not have emerged first in the Americas; they had to get here from somewhere else.

Long ago, anthropologists noticed that the Aboriginal peoples of the Americas were similar in several ways to certain peoples living in Asia. Among the shared traits are straight black hair, relatively little facial or body hair, very infrequent baldness, brown skin, broad faces, and prominent cheekbones (which, some Native writers have said, "jokingly," came from leaning on their hands waiting for their treaty rights to be respected). Some Native groups also have the **epicanthic fold** of the upper eyelid, identified as "looking Asian," and share the so-called shovel-shaped incisors found among early humans and contemporary populations in East Asia.

THE BERING STRAIT THEORY

How did Aboriginal people get to the Americas from Asia? Anthropologists have traditionally looked to the Ice Age and its effects on the Bering Strait that now separates Siberia from Alaska by 90 km (or 55 miles). The last Ice Age, referred to in North America
as the Wisconsin Ice Age, lasted from 75,000 to 10,000 years ago, with some warming periods. During the colder periods of the Ice Age, a large amount of the world's
moisture was locked up in the glaciers and ice sheets. As a result, ocean levels dropped
by more than 90 metres. The Bering Strait became a land bridge, known as Beringia,
some 1,600 kilometres wide north to south. Large land mammals (mastodons, extra
large bison, camels, and sloths) moved across the bridge, and people followed them. The
optimal time for entry was just before and just after the height of glaciation (24,000–
22,000 B.C. and 10,000–8000 B.C.), when the climate was sufficiently cold for Beringia
to be dry and warm enough to permit a large, ice-free corridor from one continent to
the other. There were huge continental glaciers on both sides: the Cordilleran was centred over the Rocky Mountains, while the Laurentide—about 2,900 metres thick at its
maximum—was centred over Hudson Bay. Unable to cross ice through the continent,
the travellers would most likely have taken a Pacific coast route south. Unfortunately,
archaeological signs of their trip along the west coast of North America are few, as what
was the coast during the Ice Age is underwater now; the melt from the ending of the Ice
Age drowned the sites of their first stopping points and settlements. This west coast theory
is supported by linguistics. By far the greatest variety of Native languages in Canada and
the United States exists on the West Coast.

   The biggest questions for anthropologists lie in how long ago Native people came to
the Americas and in how many waves. The traditional anthropological theory held that
there were two waves of migration, "Indians" and "Inuit," and that the former group came
here about 12,000 years ago. The artefact from their material culture that identified them to
archaeologists was the **Clovis point**, named after the site in New Mexico where the points
were first discovered. Clovis points are long spear points that are fluted or grooved on each
side enabling them to be hafted onto a wooden shaft. Clovis points date from between 12,700
and 13,200 years ago. It was long believed by anthropologists that these were part of the
material culture of the first peoples arriving in the Americas, but there is evidence to the contrary. Recently for example, in the Paisley Caves in Oregon, there have been found Western
Stemmed spear points, so named after the stem at the dull end of the spear point that is hafted
to the wooden shaft, that date from a similar period, from 12,960 to 13,230 years ago. This
points to there being two early cultural traditions, and therefore at least two different peoples
coming to the Americas at about the same time. Even earlier (at least 14,600 years ago) is
the Monte Verde site, in Chile, at which was found a 60 foot long tent-like structure, framed
with logs and planks and covered with hide from mastodons and the ancestors of llamas.

KENNEWICK MAN AND THE BOAT PEOPLE

Much of contemporary anthropological research suggests that Aboriginal peoples came to
the New World in four waves. The discovery of the Kennewick Man focused attention on
a first wave of migrants and suggested that they were different from the others.

On July 28, 1996, two college students found some bones in Kennewick, Washington, by the shores of the Columbia River. The physical anthropologist who first saw the skeleton thought the bones to be of a White settler, as the skull had a long head and a narrow and projecting face, as opposed to the more usual rounded head and wider and flatter face of Aboriginal people. It wasn't very long before it was discovered that the skeleton was much older than initially thought, between 9300 to 9600 years old.

This individual, dubbed Kennewick Man (he was a man of some 45 to 50 years of age when he died) has touched off a number of controversies. One is the question of who "owns" the bones. The Native American Graves Protection and Repatriation Act of 1990 allows for ancestral remains connected with a particular people to be reburied. Five nations of the American Northwest Coast have pursued a court case to have the bones repatriated. Scientists see this as a unique opportunity to study early Native history. But, as Armand Minthorn, a religious leader of the Umatilla people, states, "We already know our history . . . . It is passed on to us through our Elders and through our religious practices" (Minthorn 1996).

In December 2005, a study of 81 early skulls (7500 to 11,000 years old) from Lagoa Santa in central Brazil was published. The authors noted that while more modern Aboriginal people had skulls shaped more like the inhabitants of modern North Asia (for example, having broad, relatively flat faces), the more ancient skulls resemble more closely those of the Aborigines of Australia and of the Melanesians (Pacific island people) (Neves & Hubbe 2005). The Melanesians speak Austronesian languages, whose speakers travelled by boat to such far-flung places as Madagascar off the southeast coast of Africa, Samoa, Hawaii, Easter Island, and New Zealand. Could they have also travelled to the Americas by boat?

Similarly, Kennewick Man is said to resemble the Ainu. The Ainu are the indigenous people of Japan, living in that country and in the islands immediately to the north of it for thousands of years before Japanese speakers moved in an estimated 2000 years ago. The Ainu look different from the Japanese newcomers in a number of ways; for example, the Ainu are relatively hairy. Natives of the Northwest Coast are known to have been hairier than Natives elsewhere in North America. Some Ainu customs are shared with Northwest Coast peoples, including making clothing out of bark (well processed with boiling and pounding) and singing death songs. The boat trip to North America may not have been all that difficult. The Japan Current has been known to take fishermen's net floats across the relatively narrow northern Pacific to the Northwest Coast.

Much needs to be discovered and explained before the boat traveller theory, for at least the first wave of the peopling of the Americas, can be considered to be proved, however.

If the first wave was from Japan or Melanesia, the second wave became the ancestors of most of the Aboriginal people of the Americas. The third wave could have been the Athapaskan speakers. Linguistically, the Athapaskans have tones as part of their words, as is typical of languages such as Mandarin, Cantonese, and Vietnamese on the Pacific Coast of Asia. Recent research has revealed that Athapaskan languages appear to be related to the Siberian language Ket. The fourth wave were possibly the ancestors of the Inuit.

EARLY PERIODS OF NATIVE HISTORY

In *A History of the Native People of Canada: Volume I (10,000–1,000 B.C.)*, one of the most influential archaeologists in Canada, J.V. Wright, Curator Emeritus of the Canadian

Museum of Civilization, laid out what he felt were the first 9000 years of Native history in Canada. As it represents, more or less, the orthodox archaeological view, it will be discussed as showing how archaeologists have set up these early periods.

What Wright sets up as Period I is 12,000 to 10,000 B.P. The material cultures of these times, known as Palaeo-Indian and Northwest Palaeo-Arctic, stretch across Canada with sites in the Yukon, the Prairies, Ontario, and Nova Scotia. The Northwest Palaeo-Arctic shares some features with what is called Dyuktai culture in Siberia, the latter dating back at least to 18,000 B.P. The shared features include wedge-shaped core tools (i.e., tools made out of the core of a rock, not the flakes that are broken off), microblades (i.e., flakes struck from a core of rock), bifacial knives (i.e., knives with a blade on both sides), and burins (stone tools for working with antler and bone).

Period II is set from 10,000 to 6000 B.P., representing what is conventionally called the Early Archaic (10,000 to 8000 B.P.) and Middle Archaic (8000 to 6000 B.P.). It was a time when new weapons technology (i.e., the "atlatl" or spear thrower) was applied to changing and localized environments, with fewer megafauna (i.e., big mammals) being hunted. In their material culture, at least, people began to change.

One important point should be made here. As archaeologists often say, the stone tools cannot talk. We cannot know what languages their makers spoke. At this stage, it is difficult to make firm connections between material cultural traditions that bear the names that archaeologists give them and the peoples who live in Canada now. Human history shows that people don't usually stay in the same place for thousands of years—people move. Migrations are often spoken of in the traditional stories of the peoples. The Anishinabe people, for example, speak of moving west into Quebec, Ontario, and the Prairies, from a place by the Atlantic.

By the time of Wright's Period III (6000 to 3000 B.P.), more connections can be made. There is a good chance that the Middle Maritime culture of this period provided the ancestors for the Algonquian speakers of the Atlantic provinces and Quebec. Some have argued that the contemporary Middle Great Lakes–St. Lawrence culture may have been ancestral to at least some of the Iroquoian speakers of the contact period, although this connection is far from proven. A much better case can be made for the Middle Shield culture becoming the Cree, Ojibwa, Innu, and possibly the Beothuk.

As we will see in Chapter 9, "The Plains," there was a great deal of disruption in that area after contact, with the introduction of the horse and the gun, and moving peoples in and out of the Prairie provinces. However, the Blackfoot and possibly some of the Siouan peoples may have at least some of their origins in the Middle Plains culture in Saskatchewan. The Middle Plateau culture east of the Rocky Mountains has been linked with at least the Shuswap, currently in the Plateau region. There seems to be more continuity in the Northwest Coast, with probably most of the current peoples descending from ancestors in the Early West Coast culture of this period, as can also be said for the Middle Northwest Interior culture and the Athapaskan speakers of the Western Subarctic. Although there were technological innovations and migrations in the Arctic (see Chapter 5), the current Inuit have as their primary ancestors at least some of the groups forming the Early Palaeo-Eskimo culture.

HISTORY, PREHISTORY, AND THE MYTH OF THE "NEW COUNTRY"

Traditionally, non-Native historians made a distinction between "history" and "prehistory." History was a period of time recorded by writing and written about by historians trained in the analysis of written documents. Of course, this would be European writing for Canada. Prehistory was a period of time recorded through archaeology and through the oral traditions of the people. History books, then, tended to have short, cursory, introductory sections on prehistory, while the history was the focus. This is misleading. It creates the illusion, which the authors have heard, and no doubt the readers have heard as well, that this is a "new country." A similar illusion maintains that Native people have only been on this land for "a few hundred years," an expression used more than a few times by politicians opposing Native peoples fighting for their rights, and even by judges who have denied that Natives have rights. One of the authors has asked the following question of students taking Introduction to Anthropology and Canada's Native Peoples courses:

How long have Native people been on this land?

a) 500 years

b) 500 to 1000 years

c) 1000 to 5000 years

d) More than 10,000 years

It is no longer surprising to have students believing the second and even the first answer is right, when it is "d" that is correct. Before you read this chapter, which answer would you have given? As a short assignment, students have been asked to ask this question of five people, record their answers, and then record their response to the right answer. Many students have reported not only that relatively few of the people asked gave the right answer, but that some even defended, with heated arguments, the rightness of their wrong answer, sometimes claiming they had read it somewhere.

Consider what would be the impression in the teaching of Canadian history if the distinction between prehistory and history was eliminated and there was an attempt to give an equal balance to all periods of history. If you live in Ontario, your history is at least 10,000 years long. How much of your history is Native history alone? The first Europeans came to Ontario a little less than 400 years ago. Do the math. At least 96 percent of your history is Native history before the coming of Europeans. Think of it like this: if there were an Ontario history textbook with ten chapters, each chapter depicting an equal percentage of history, then the first nine chapters would be Native history alone, as would be most of the tenth and final chapter. If you want to learn your history, you need to learn about Natives first.

KEY TERMS

Clovis point   epicanthic fold

CONTENT QUESTIONS

1. What is the Bering Strait Theory?
2. Who is Kennewick Man?
3. Why can't we find some of the earliest sites on the West Coast?

WEBLINKS

www.kennewick-man.com/index.html
This site is constantly updated and presents a balanced picture of Kennewick Man.

www.washington.edu/burkemuseum/kman/ancientpeoples.php
The Burke Museum of Natural History and Culture, in Seattle, has a good online presentation of the Bering Strait Theory.

chapter three

Connections to the Land

INTRODUCTION

It is hard to express in a few pages the Native connection with this land, a connection forged over thousands of years of living here. It can be seen, a bit, in ancient sacred sites, such as the 40-tonne Majorville Medicine Wheel in the Plains that dates back 5000 years (see Chapter 9), or Mnjikaning, the 4500-year-old fish weir that gave Toronto its name (see Box 3-1).

Months of the Year

The connection can also be seen in the terms the different peoples have for the months of the year, which are so much more connected with what is happening all around them than the terms that French and English speakers use. Consider the following translations of Native words for two different months:

April
Abenaki: Sugar Moon
Maliseet: Arrival of Spring Moon
Mi'kmaq: Egg-Laying (i.e., of waterfowl)
Ojibwe: Sucker Moon
Huron: Pickerel Come
Mohawk: Leaves Are Leaking a Little
Blackfoot: Frog Moon
Moose Cree: Goose Moon

August
Abenaki: Eating Moon
Maliseet: Feather Shedding Moon
Mi'kmaq: Young Birds Are Fledged
Ojibwe: Blackberry Moon
Huron: Corn Is Made
Mohawk: Time of Freshness, Newness
Blackfoot: When Choke Cherries Ripen
Moose Cree: (Geese) Flying Up Moon

BOX 3-1   Toronto: Poles in Water

Some 4500 years ago, people wanting to catch fish in the fast-moving waters flowing between Lake Couchiching and Lake Simcoe in southern Ontario came up with a smart idea. They put cedar poles in the water to build a fish weir or trap, thereby fencing in the fish. Some of those poles are still in the water. The first name written down for this fish weir appeared in the Huron language in the 1600s. The Huron referred to Lake Simcoe as **Ouentaronk**, "poles that cross." Later that century, the Mohawk moved into the area. The earliest rendition of their name for the lake was **Lac Tar8nteau**, "trees or poles in water," a name later written as "Toronto."[1] By the end of that century, the Ojibwa, who had long known about the site and had visited it as allies of the Huron, moved into the area and took over the site. The name they gave to the fish weir and surrounding area is written today as **Mnjikaning**, "at the [fish] fence."

According to Ojibwa oral traditions, the fish weir site had significance beyond that of being merely a place where food could be obtained. It was a sacred place. According to one modern Ojibwa writer:

People came great distances to spend time at this good place. They would help fix the Fish Fence. They came with their wounds and soreness looking for the healing powers of our medicine people. They came with their bad feelings looking for good therapy. Ceremonies were held often. More and more people came to spend some time at this good clean place. Lots of food. Lots of good talk about the future. It was a nice safe place to spend some time. People came from further away just to stay awhile. (Douglas n.d.:8)

Much of this meaning was lost when the Ojibwa began to be inundated with non-Natives. The Ojibwa people who lived in the area were divided into several bands living separately from each other. The local Ojibwa community came to be known as Rama. Today, there is a strong move to protect the site and have it serve as a centre of revitalization of traditions and identity, a sacred place once more. In 1993, the Rama community officially declared its name to be Mnjikaning.

Everything Gets Used: The Caribou

The way that Native groups completely used particular resources supplied by the land, such as the caribou and the bison, reveals their link with the resources provided by the land. The following is paraphrased from Chapter 5; for a similar description of bison, see Chapter 9:

> Caribou hair is hollow, trapping air, thus making it ideal for insulation, softness and lightness, ideal for clothing, footwear, tents, bedding, blankets, and bags. It has been calculated that fifty caribou were required to meet the needs of each person for a single year, with eight to eleven skins per person for clothing and twenty to thirty skins for tent coverings (Wright 1995:425).

E.S. Burch provides a good description of the use of other parts of the caribou:

> Excellent thread can be made from their back sinew, and components of tools, weapons and utensils can be manufactured from their antlers and bones. People who consume all of the meat, viscera, stomach contents (rich in vitamin C), and fat of caribou are able to satisfy all of their nutritional requirements. If caribou are available in sufficient numbers at appropriate times of year, and if they are fully utilized, they can provide for the total subsistence requirements of a human population. (Burch 1995:129)

Ondech(r)a and [Y]andarachrio: The Huron Speak of the Country

The connection to the land can especially be seen in how the peoples themselves talk about or use the words that mean "country," "bush," or "land." Look at the meanings of the following two Huron/Wendat nouns for land, as recorded in seventeenth- and eighteenth-century French-Huron dictionaries (Steckley 1993:18–21). These early records demonstrate that this type of speaking is traditional to Natives—it is not a politically correct, New Age way of speaking.

The noun stem -**ondech(r)**- was the most often used word for "country." It is derived from the verb -**onde**-, meaning "to have as one's country" (Potier 1920:408). When used with the verb root -**ndionk**-, "to be skilled, able," it had the following meaning:

ondechandionk /to be able, capable on the land/

être bon piéton, être homme de voyage /to be a good pedestrian, traveller/ (Potier 1920:293)

The noun -**ondech**- did not just refer to the physical entity "country, earth," but also to the religious beliefs and practices of the Huron (collectively called **ondech(r)a**), as they were believed to have come out of the earth where they lived. In the following entry, using the verb root -**nde,ar**- meaning "to rise, raise," we see that a person could be referred to as being drawn out of the earth or the country when he or she was born:[2]

atiaondechandera /she rose up, lifted up in the country/

c'est la qu'elle vint au monde /it is there where she came into the world. (Potier 1920:181)

In the following dictionary entry, the noun -**ondech**- is used with the verb root -**inde**- "to drag, draw" (literally meaning "dragged from the country") to mean something such as "since the beginning of time" when referring to the practice of carrying a corpse in a traditional burial ceremony:

on,8atondechinde on,8ahoarinnenha8i

/we draw, drag it from the country, we carry the corpse/

nous avons cette sorte de danse depuis le commencement, la naissance, l'origine de notre pais /we have had this kind of dance since the commencement, the birth, the origin of the country/. (Potier 1920:323)

Ondech(r)a also meant "country" in the political sense. Political leaders were sometimes referred to as **Hennondecha** ("they, country"). Part of the ceremony designed to bring about reconciliation when a Huron had killed another was referred to as **xondaie onsahon-dechari**, "this is that which rejoins the country."

The noun **-ndarach(r)-** is derived from the verb root **-ndare-**, "to dwell, exist" (Potier 1920:280). By itself, it was usually used to mean "dwelling, residence, habitation." The use of the expression "First Nation(s)" is new to the English language but is an old concept among Native people.

The seventeenth-century Huron used **-ndarach(r)-** in combination with the verb root **-io-**, meaning "to be large, good, great" to express the notion of a people being the original or first people in an area. This can be clearly seen in the following examples, including **[y]andarachrio**:

,andarachrio

être les maîtres habitans, les vrais, le/s/ naturels, les 1re habitants; les originaires par opposition à d'autres qui viennent ensuite se joindre à ces /to be the master inhabitants, the true, the native, the first inhabitants; the natives in opposition to the others who came afterwards to join with these first ones (Potier 1920:280)

Les sauvages sont les vrays et naturels habitants de ce pais /The "savages" are the true and native inhabitants of this country/

and

on,8e n'on,8e daat endarachrio dex'ondechate

/humans who are humans are the very good, great ones in their dwelling place, this country/ (FH1693)

It should be noted that in the last entry, **on,8e n'on,8e** ("humans who are human") is a term used by speakers of Iroquoian languages to refer specifically to Iroquoian peoples and more generally to Natives as opposed to non-Natives.

ENDNOTES

1. The character "8" represents a sound close to "oo" in English, and was used in the old Jesuit spelling of the word Tar8nteau.

2. The character "," represents a sound similar to that represented by "y" in English.

KEY TERMS

[y]andarachrio (Huron)   on,8e n'on,8e (Ongwehon:we; Huron)
-ondech- (Huron)

CONTENT QUESTIONS

1. What does the word "Toronto" mean and what does that meaning refer to?
2. What is the significance of the Toronto site in terms of Native connection to the land?
3. In what ways can the caribou supply the needs of the people?
4. How are Native language names for months of the year different from those in English?
5. What do the noun stems **-ondech(r)-** and **-ndarach(r)-** mean and how are these meanings different from the nearest English equivalents?

WEBLINKS

http://ncseonline.org/NAE
The website known as "Native Americans and the Environment" is a good starting point for environmental issues. Under the "Internet" area of the website you can find an annotated list of other helpful Weblinks.

www.fnen.org
This is the website of the First Nations Environmental Network, a Canadian organization with a focus on environmental activism.

www.ankn.uaf.edu/curriculum/Articles/BarnhardtKawagley/Indigenous_Knowledge. html
The Alaska Native Knowledge Network's Web page on Indigenous Knowledge Systems provides information about traditional ecological knowledge and sustainable resource planning.

FIGURE 3-1   Aboriginal Language and Cultural Divisions

LANGUAGE FAMILIES

1. Eyak
2. Ahtena
3. Nabesna
4. Bellabella
5. Bellacoola
6. Chilcotin
7. Kwakuitl
8. Lillooet
9. Thompson, Okanagan
10. Sanpoil
11. Spokan
12. Coeur d'Alene
13. Yakima
14. Columbia
15. Klikitat
16. Twana
17. Cowichan
18. Nootka
19. Quileute
20. Quinault
21. Kalispel
22. Nitinat
23. Comox
24. Klallam

Source: Courtesy of Oxford University Press.

chapter four

Native Languages

MISCONCEPTIONS ABOUT NATIVE LANGUAGES

For a long time, many misconceptions concerning Native languages have existed in history books, in classrooms, and in people's minds. There are few areas that Canadians are more ignorant about. The first part of this chapter deals with three main misconceptions about Native languages.

Misconception 1: All Native Languages Are Related

Imagine you were a child looking up the following words in a dictionary:

chipmunk: n., small squirrel of N. Amer. [Indian name *achitamon*] (Morehead and Morehead 1972:78)
totem: n., tribal badge or emblem, usually an animal . . . [N. Amer. Ind., hereditary emblem] (385)
moccasin: n., Amer. Ind. soft shoe . . . [N. Amer. Ind.] (255)
skunk: n., small N. American animal like a weasel, which defends itself by emitting an evil-smelling fluid . . . [N. Amer. Ind. *segankw*] (352)

Reading this, and knowing no better, you would assume that "North American Indian" is a language. People frequently speak and write as if there were only one Aboriginal language. Individuals are said to be "speaking Indian." As we have just seen, dictionaries and books about place names tell us that a term is "an Indian word for" something. This would seem to be a smaller part of a larger stereotype that "all Indians are the same."

Imagine if a Blackfoot speaker wrote that "three" or "trois" is "European for" **nioók-ska**. Yet, as the terms for that number sound alike in almost all European languages, that statement is more true than to say that any word "is Indian for" anything. There is greater language variety in Native Canada than there is in Europe. As we will see, there are 11 Aboriginal language families and isolates spoken in Canada, as opposed to only three in Europe: Indo-European, which includes the vast majority of all European languages; Finno-Ugric, which includes Finnish, Hungarian, and a small number of other languages; and Basque, which stands alone.

Aboriginal Languages: Number of Speakers According to the 2011 Census

Algonquian Languages

Algonquin	1,755
Atikamekw	5,915
Cree	83,475
Malecite	485
Michif	645
Mi'kmaq	8,030
Innu	10,965
Ojibwe	19,275
Oji-Cree	10,180

Athabaskan Languages

Beaver	360
Carrier	1,525
Chilcotin	930
Dene/Chipewyan	11,860
Dogrib (Tlicho)	2,080
Gwich'in	370
Hare	225
Kaska (Nahani)	295
Sarcee	165
Sekani	65
Slavey	1,595
Tahltan	125
Northern Tutchone	205
Southern Tutchone	205

Eskimo-Aleut

Inuktitut	34,110
Inuinnaqtun	410
Inuvialuktun	625

Haida | 75

Iroquoian

Cayuga	240
Mohawk	545
Oneida	180

Kutenai | 105

Salishan

Halkomelem	570
Lillooet	305
Okanagan	365
Shuswap	680
Squamish	65
Straits	170
Thompson	435

Sioiuan

Dakota	1,160
Nakota	3,155

Tlingit | 130

Tsimshian

Gitksan	925
Nisga'a	615
Tsimshian	275

Wakashan

Nuu-chah-nulth	320
Haisla	160
Heiltsuk	95
Kwak'wala	495

Native Language Families

What do we mean by language family? A **language family** is a group of languages that have been shown to be related. How is that relationship demonstrated? Linguists look at commonalities in the way words are constructed (**morphology**) and the way they are put together into sentences (**syntax**). For example, all Iroquoian languages have five different conjugations of verbs and nouns, based on the set of forms the pronominal prefixes take. Table 4-1 demonstrates how the Huron language works.

Linguists also look for cognates. **Cognates** are words, or roots of words, that sound similar, have similar meanings, and ultimately come from the same word. Table 4-2 shows the following cognate terms in Algonquian languages for "fish," as well as for specific fish, all believed to have originated from a single word for fish. When there is a

TABLE 4-1   Five Huron Conjugations

Conjugation	Huron Term	Pronominal Prefix	English
a-stem	skwatatiak	skw-	you (plural) talk
	ontatiak	on-	they (indefinite) talk
Consonant stem	skwahiaton	skwa-	you (pl.) write
	ehiaton	e-	they (indef.) write
e-stem	skwehieras	skw-	you (pl.) remember
	ayehieras	ay-	they (indef.) remember
Yen-/i-stem	skwentenrha	skw(en)-	you (pl.) have pity
	aitenrha	a(i)-	they (indef.) have pity
o-stem	tsoritha	ts-	you (pl.) season it
	ayoritha	ay-	they (indef.) season it

TABLE 4-2   Some Cognates in the Algonquian Language Family

Language	Root	Term for Fish	Terms for Specific Fish	
East Cree	-name-	names	namekush	lake trout
			nameu	sturgeon
			namepii	white or red sucker
Ojibwe	-nme-		nmegos	lake trout, brown trout
			nme	sturgeon
			nmebin	sucker, carp
Abenaki	-nama-	namas	namagw	lake trout
Delaware	-name-	namées	_____	_____
Blackfoot	-mii-	mamii	sisákkoomii	Dolly Varden trout

long list of cognates between two languages, then it can be said that the two languages are related.

The 11 Aboriginal language families in Canada range in size from large families encompassing many separate languages (e.g., Algonquian) to **language isolates**, that is, languages with no close relatives (e.g., Kutenai). The map of these language families shows a peculiar pattern.

Other language families have their own specific regions. The **Eskimoan** language family goes right across our northern shores. **Iroquoian** is found in Ontario and Quebec. In the Prairie provinces, there are three language families: **Algonquian**, **Siouan**, and **Athapaskan**. British Columbia breaks the mould. It has eight different language families, six of which exist in no other province (see Box 4-1).

Box 4-1   Native Languages and Their Families

Language Family	Language	Location in Canada
Algonquian	Abenaki	Quebec
	Blackfoot	Alberta
	Cree	Quebec to Alberta
	Delaware	Ontario
	Innu	Quebec and Labrador
	Maliseet	New Brunswick
	Mi'kmaq	Atlantic Provinces and Quebec
	Ojibwe (Odawa, Algonquin, Saulteaux)	Quebec to British Columbia
	Potawatomi	Ontario
Athapaskan	Beaver	Alberta and British Columbia
	Carrier (Dakelh)	British Columbia
	Chilcotin	British Columbia
	Chipewyan	Manitoba, Saskatchewan, Alberta, N.W.T.
	Dogrib	N.W.T.
	Gwich'in	Yukon
	Han	Yukon
	Hare	N.W.T.
	Kaska	Yukon
	Sarcee	Alberta
	Sekani	British Columbia
	Slavey	N.W.T.
	Tagish [recently extinct]	Yukon
	Tahltan	Yukon
	Tutchone	Yukon
	Wet'suwet'en	British Columbia
Eskimo-Aleut	Inuktitut	Labrador, Nunavut, Quebec, Yukon, N.W.T.
Haida (isolate)	Haida	British Columbia
Iroquoian	Cayuga	Ontario
	Mohawk	Ontario, Quebec
	Oneida	Ontario
	Onondaga	Ontario
	Seneca	Ontario
	Tuscarora	Ontario

(continued)

Box 4-1	*(continued)*

Language Family	Language	Location in Canada
Kutenai (isolate)	Kutenai (Ktunaxa)	British Columbia
Salishan	Bella Coola (Nuxalk)	British Columbia
	Comox	British Columbia
	Cowichan	British Columbia
	Halkomelem	British Columbia
	Lillooet (St'at'imc)	British Columbia
	Okanagan (Nsilx)	British Columbia
	Pentlatch (extinct 1940)	British Columbia
	Sechelt (Sishiatl)	British Columbia
	Semiahmo	British Columbia
	Songish	British Columbia
	Squamish	British Columbia
	Northern Straits (Saanich)	British Columbia
	Thompson (Nlakapmx)	British Columbia
Siouan	Dakota	Manitoba and Saskatchewan
	Nakota	Manitoba and Saskatchewan
Tlingit (isolate)	Tlingit	British Columbia
Tsimshian	Coast Tsimshian	British Columbia
	Gitksan	British Columbia
	Nisga.a	British Columbia
Southern Tsimshian	British Columbia	
Wakashan	Dididaht (Nitinat)	British Columbia
	Haisla	British Columbia
	Heiltsuk	British Columbia
	Kwakw'ala	British Columbia
	Nootka (Nuchaanulth)	British Columbia
	Oweekeno (Oowekyala)	British Columbia

Dialects

Not all the people who speak the same language can understand each other. Sometimes people speak dialects that are different enough to make comprehension difficult. A **dialect** is a variation of a language. Dialects might differ in pronunciation or might have different words for the same thing, or different meanings for the same word. Fred Wheatley, a respected teacher of Ojibwe, used to tell stories of how speakers of different dialects of Ojibwe would joke around with each other at logging camps by using dialect differences. People asking someone to pass "that which spreads," meaning butter, would have knives given to them instead, since the word for "butter" was the word for "knife" in another dialect.

Cree has several dialects, as it is spoken across Canada's north from Quebec to Alberta. One of the main distinguishing characteristics concerns a particular **phoneme**, or sound. Table 4-3 on page 28 illustrates this. The word compared is the verb form "it is windy."

TABLE 4-3 Key Feature in Distinguishing Cree Dialects					
Plains Cree	**Woods Cree**	**Swampy Cree**	**Moose Cree**	**Attikamek**	**East Cree**
-y-	th-	-n-	-l-	-r-	-y-
yotin	thotin	notin	lotin	rotin	yuutin

Misconception 2: There Are Only a Small Number of Words in Native Languages

A strong stereotype exists that states there are only a few words in Aboriginal languages. This stereotype stems originally from the fact that the early missionaries, explorers, and other early-contact Europeans who first provided written descriptions of Aboriginal languages often wrote about them in terms of what the languages didn't have. Many, for example, stated their first impression was that Native languages lacked "abstract terms." However, if they had lived with the people and learned the languages in any depth, they would have discovered that such was not the case.

Later writers often repeated information from these earlier works, unthinkingly passing on a misconception to modern readers. A classic case is of Father Francis X. Talbot, who, in his 1956 publication *Saint Among the Hurons: The Life of Jean de Brébeuf,* wrote that Brébeuf was "puzzled as to how he could express abstract and spiritual concepts. Their vocabulary was limited to specialized, concrete, material things that they knew through their senses" (Talbot 1956:74). This reflects Brébeuf's often-cited first impressions of the Huron language. Brébeuf later learned much of the sophistication and potential for abstraction of the language. Unfortunately, he never wrote about that. His negative first impressions are what have survived into modern times.

Clearly, what Talbot should have said was that terms for abstract ideas deeply rooted in French culture did not have ready equivalents in the language of a different culture that didn't have those same concepts. The Huron didn't have terms for "heaven" and "hell," for example, because in their belief system they felt that they ideally went to a community specific to them (e.g., the Huron went to their afterlife community while the Mohawk went to theirs). They also didn't have a term for the single soul of Christian belief because they believed that people have two souls (see Box 4-2). So the Huron who first learned French must have thought the French language was incomplete because it lacked terms for important concepts in their language. For example, they must have had difficulty initially speaking about corn in French (see Table 4-4 on page 30).

These misconceptions reflect the simple notion that many non-Natives find it difficult to imagine what concepts Aboriginal words apply to. It reflects their ignorance of the huge world of possible meanings and of the knowledge held by traditional elders.

For example, there are concepts not well expressed in English or French that are represented by single words in some Aboriginal languages. Specialized vocabularies show these concepts. For example, corn was a staple in the diets of the Huron and other Iroquoians. It should therefore not be surprising to discover that these languages had a number of terms

Box 4-2   An Abstract Concept in Huron: The Dualic

The **dualic**, usually represented by -t(e)-, expresses "twoness." We find it used with a verb root that specifies a number, for example, -i- "to be two."

> Tendi: They two are two (the Huron number "2").
> Teyiatontariye: It is where a large body of water is two (i.e., Quebec).

Verb roots that express an obvious twoness (e.g., "to join," "to cut"), and those actions requiring two legs or two eyes also employed the dualic. However, it was also used more abstractly. The prefix is used with verbs that speak of uncertainty and of disturbances of the balanced order of life. Take the following example:

> Tehatoxwach: He practises divination (i.e., possibly determining whether a disease is caused by a malevolent spirit or by a sorcerer).
> Teoskendendakwan: She is as pale as a ghost (i.e., from fear or disease).

The verb root **-ndawa-** means "to hunt." Adding the dualic prefix to the verb gives it a more sinister nature, as is expressed in the following:

> Tehatendawaha: He goes hunting for a long time without encountering other hunters or animals (e.g., is in a state of uncertainty).

There is often a sense of conflict that comes with the addition of the dualic to a verb, as can be seen by contrasting two forms of the same verb, one having the dualic:

> Haonywandiyonkenni: They surpass us in mind, are more intelligent than we are.

> Tehaonywandiyonkenni: They fool us, trick us, out-think us in a conflicting way.

The conflicting, uncertain nature of twoness can be related to three aspects of Huron society: souls, political structure, and culture heroes. First, the Huron believed that everyone had two souls: the mind and the heart. The former was associated with wisdom, peace, and the thoughtful words of elders speaking in council. The latter was associated with strong emotions, such as sadness, anger, bravery and the desire for revenge. It was said that sometimes the heart was so powerful that it drove the rational mind out of a person. When the person calmed down, the mind returned. The potential for conflict between the two souls was always there.

Second, the Huron divided political functions into those of war and those of peace, with separate leaders and meeting houses. The interests of each function could come into conflict with the other, the existence of both being a stage for potentially destructive political uncertainty.

A spiritual parallel exists in the twin culture heroes who transformed the earth into the state in which we find it today. They worked at cross-purposes from the moment of their births. The first-born would act to help the Huron who were to come, while the second- born would negatively alter what his older brother had done. Eventually, the older brother killed his younger brother, leaving just one, and a state of peace.

TABLE 4-4   Some Huron Words for "Corn"

oionkwendaa	small ear of corn
ondista	the stem of an ear of corn
oiontsenda	point of an ear of corn that is not covered with kernels
oia	a row of corn kernels
oiachia	the bran or inner part of the kernel
oechia	the skin of the kernel
onniona	germinated seed or kernel
awenienta	non-germinated seed or kernel

relating to corn that have no equivalents in English or French. See Table 4-4 for a sampling of Huron terms for "corn."

Another way to counteract the notion that Aboriginal languages contain a small vocabulary is to show their productive capacity. For example, verb roots are the central building blocks around which the vast majority of Huron words are constructed. The greater part of learning to speak, understand, read, or write Huron involves the morphology or structure of the verb. This is quite different from English or French, both of which are languages that have relatively short words with relatively few meaningful parts, or **morphemes** (see discussion below).

An eighteenth-century Huron dictionary recorded approximately 1000 verb roots. To estimate how many words might be generated from one verb **root**, or lexical unit, we can take one verb root, -**atey**- ("to burn"), and see how many words we can generate with it. The answer is a very conservative estimate of 7669 words. If all verb roots are approximately this productive, then there are theoretically more than 7.5 million words in Huron. See Table 4-5 for some examples of words generated from -**atey**-.

TABLE 4-5   Words Generated from the Huron Verb Root -atey- ("to burn")

Huron Word	English Translation
uteyen	there is burning, a fire
teutende	there is not going to be fires
sateyaht	you (sing.) make fire
oteyannon	many things are burning
tewayateyasennik	fires don't start for me
esakwateyas	your shoes will burn
onteyatakwa	one makes fire with it (i.e., flint)
atayateyatandiha	come make me a fire!
atayateyatakwendiha	come make me a fire out of such material!
hoteyataskon	he frequently makes fires

There were many more words for corn in Huron. However, we will never know all the terms, since the language is now extinct. Our only remaining sources of information are the dictionaries compiled by French Jesuit missionaries. They did not know much about corn, so they could not have entered into a knowledgeable discussion in Huron on the subject.

Typically, modern dictionaries of Aboriginal languages do not come close to showing all the possible numbers of words that there are or could be. The Delaware-English section of John O'Meara's *Delaware-English/English-Delaware Dictionary* (1996) contains more than 7000 entries, the vast majority of them verb forms from which other words can be created. O'Meara gives about four or five words for each entry as a small, representative sample of what the root can create. If you were to count all the Delaware words in that dictionary, you would get close to 30,000. To see the productivity of Delaware, look at the list of words in Table 4-6, all based on the same noun root.

TABLE 4-6   Delaware Word Productivity: The Noun Root -aandpee- ("head")

English	Delaware
bang s.o.'s head against something	paakaandpéexumeew
be bare headed	mihtáandpeew
be red headed	maxkáandpeew
bump one's head	paakaandpexiin
crack one's head	pwahkaandpéexiin
forehead, top of head	laawáandpe
get hit on the head with a maul, have a bump on the head	mookkulaandpéexiin
have a swollen head	makwáandpeew
give s.o. a swollen head, hit s.o.	makwaandpéeheew
hit s.o. and give them a lump on the head	makwaandpehtéeheew
have a big head	xwáandpeew
have a bloody head	mohkwáandpeew
have a cracked head, have a cut on one's head	pasaandpéew
fall and. . . .	pasaandpéexiin
have one's head swell up	paasáandpeew
have a dirty head	niiskáandpeew
have a flat head	pàkáandpeew
have a flat head (of blow adders), have one's head go flat (when blowing)	pàkaandpéhleew
have a good head on one's shoulders	wuláandpeew
have a long head	kwunáandpeew
have a lump or bump on one's head	wchihkwáandpeew
have scabs on one's head	mukuyáandpeew
have one's head out in the open	mihtaandpéexiin

(continued)

TABLE 4-6 *(continued)*	
English	**Delaware**
have one's head lying by the length of something (e.g., by a door)	sahkaandpéexiin
have one's head sticking out, lie with one's head sticking out	saakáandpeew
stick one's head out	saakaandpéexiin
have one's heads together (plural)	kchukaandpeexíinook
have s.t. tied around one's head	kulaandpeepíisuw
have s.t. wrapped around one's head	kpaandpeepíisuw
hit someone on the head	chàhwaandpéeheew
nod one's head	tàtamakohkwaandpéhleew
rub, pet someone on the head	siikwaandpéeneew
scratch one's head, have an itchy head	kshiipáandpeew
shake one's head	kwàkwtukohkwaandpéhleew

Misconception 3: Native Languages Can't Be Used to Express "Modern" Life

All languages have equal structural capabilities for developing new terms. We discussed earlier the many terms the Huron had for corn in the seventeenth century. Yet less than 2000 years earlier, they didn't even have corn. When they began to grow corn, their vocabulary must have adapted. Further, when they first came into contact with the French, they quickly developed a term for "gun" using a word meaning "hollow tube" and a word for "metal" based on a noun root that referred to the hard skin of flint corn and to fish scales.

Keep in mind here that the fact that English is the most prominent language internationally has nothing to do with the structure of English. It is not bigger because it is better. It is bigger because of the power and influence of the countries in which it is spoken. Its structural adaptability is no better than the structural adaptability of all Native languages. Think of how English speakers dealt with the definitive "modern" piece of technology, the computer, with terms for an animal (the "mouse"), old religious symbols ("icons"), and the product of a pre-Industrial Revolution manufacture ("web" from "weave"). In medicine, compare how the English language borrowed a Latin term for an animal (a crab) to refer to "cancer" with how the Cree used a term in their own language for another animal (the worm):

ê-mowikot manicôsa

"he/she has cancer"

[literally: "little worms eat him/her"]

manicôsa k'âyâwât omihkohk

"he/she has leukemia"

[literally: "he/she has little worms in his/her blood"].

(Wolfart and Ahenakew 1987:213)

The following "modern" terms in Ojibwe all stem from **-mzinaa-**, which refers to "making marks":

mzinaaksijgan = camera

mzinaakziged = to print, type, make out notices

mzinaatesing = to be a projected picture

mzinaatesjigan = movie projector

From a cognate term in Blackfoot, we get the following:

áísfinaakiohpi = television

iihtáísínaakio'p = camera

Before we complete this section, we need to discuss one of the structural differences between many Native languages and French and English: word length. Languages differ in the way they form sentences. Some build relatively long words, typically verbs, and so have only a few words in a sentence. Other languages have relatively short words, so they have more words in a sentence (and word order tends to be significant). Both types of sentences are roughly equal in length and equally complex or simple to learn. It is only the boundary mechanisms that are different. For those languages with relatively long words, the boundaries are primarily between morphemes or word parts. For those languages with relatively short words, most of the boundaries are between words. But the total number of boundaries is about the same. Imagine you are a speaker of Mandarin and hear (but do not see) the following two sentences:

1. Ahayateyatakwendiheskwa.
2. He often used to go make fire for me out of such material.

Remember that we do not typically pause between words when we speak. To the Mandarin speaker, both sentences sound to be about the same length, the second being perhaps a little longer. However, to English speakers, the first sentence looks more complicated when both sentences are written. There is a "visual prejudice" against it because the boundaries cannot be seen. Fewer visual clues are there. But say we break the longer word down into constituent parts (i.e., morphemes), as demonstrated in Table 4-7 below.

TABLE 4-7 Huron Morphemes and Their Meanings

Huron Morpheme	Type of Morpheme	Meaning
a-	translocative	motion away from the speaker
-hay-	pronominal prefix	"he" (as subject), "me" (as object)
-atey-	verb root	"to burn"
-at-	causative	causing something, "to make"
-akw-	instrumental	"out of such material"
-endi-	dative	"for"
-he-	dislocative	motion, intention, "go"
-s-	habitual	"often"
-kwa-	past	"used to"

The Huron sentence has nine morphemes, and English has fifteen (the word "used" has two morphemes, "use" and "d"). Thus, the Huron sentence is simpler.

Most Aboriginal languages have this structural option. One of the problems that those working on preserving Aboriginal languages have to deal with is the expectation (sometimes held by Native peoples themselves) that words should be shorter. They have to overcome the visual prejudice that a group of many shorter words is somehow "easier" to understand than fewer, longer words.

A QUESTION OF SURVIVAL

We have seen that the structure of Native languages allows it to adapt to modern life. The big question that remains is whether or not the languages will survive to do that adapting. In 1982, linguist Michael Foster stated his belief that only three Native languages would survive: Cree, Inuktitut, and Ojibwe. Rough estimates of those languages state that there are 80,000 native speakers of Inuktitut, 30,000 of Cree, and between 24,000 and 30,000 of Ojibwe. Other languages with a significant number of native speakers include Innu (Montagnais-Naskapi), with close to 10,000, Mi'kmaq, with over 7000, and Dakota, with over 4000. In contrast, the Summer Institute of Linguistics lists 14 Canadian Aboriginal languages as "nearly extinct."

However, the people are determined to preserve the languages. A solid core of Native language teachers is being developed across the country. Languages are being recorded and taught to the next generation in some fashion; you could not say that, 20 years ago. There are success stories of minority languages around the world (e.g., Maori in New Zealand and Welsh in the United Kingdom) that have not only survived, but have increased their population of speakers.

Innovative strategies are required. And it is very important that the next generation be involved. A disproportionate number of speakers of Native languages are old people. However, information technology will help preserve these languages. Northern communities, where the languages are strongest, can and have overcome isolation with computers. Some languages may become extinct anyway, but the extinction of all these languages is not inevitable. Box 4-3 investigates some of the challenges Native languages face.

NON-NATIVE EXPECTATIONS

Apart from specific misconceptions, non-Natives bring different expectations of languages to their study of Aboriginal languages. The Indo-European language family is a large one, including the vast majority of the languages spoken in Europe. Languages with which most Canadians are familiar (English, French, Spanish, and Italian) are closely related to each other and have many similar features not shared as a package by languages belonging to other families. This leaves most Canadians with expectations about what languages "should be like" that draw from a narrow perspective of a fundamental sameness that, from the perspective of a speaker of an Aboriginal language, reaches across the relatively superficial differences that exist between these languages.

Gender is a significant part of Indo-European languages in a number of different ways. In the Romance branch of this family, which includes French, Italian, Spanish, and Portuguese, among others, gender exists as an either/or category for nouns, affecting the articles

Box 4-3	The State of Native Languages: The Problems to Be Overcome

In 1995, a committee of elders and language-resource people studied seven southern Shuswap communities to assess the Shuswap or Secwepemctsin language and figure out what kind of programs the schools could offer to improve the state of the language. They identified fluent speakers who could carry on and understand a conversation in Secwepemctsin, with vocabulary, grammar, and pronunciation acceptable to the elders. One community had no fluent speakers. In other communities, they found that only about 3.5 percent of people were fluent speakers, virtually all these fluent speakers were in their fifties or older, and people who could speak the language—especially younger generations—often did not use it in the home. These language problems are typical of those that Native communities across Canada face. The Shuswap are confronting these problems with at least one immersion school, and with university courses from beginner to advanced levels offered through the Secwepemc Cultural Education Society in liaison with Simon Fraser University. Like other First Nations, they are considering introducing the language into daycare centres, with the help of the elders. Time will tell whether this will be enough.

and pronouns used with the nouns. English speakers in French classes are familiar with the difficulty of trying to remember the gender of a noun. Gender also appears in pronouns, such as "he" versus "she," and "*il*" versus "*elle*." Almost every Aboriginal language spoken in Canada does not make this distinction in their pronominal prefixes. For example, see Table 4-8 on p. 36.

In most Aboriginal languages, context determines what gender you are talking about. I remember a Cree from Waswanipi who, as a mature student and the mother of three children, told the story in class of returning as a child from residential school and listening to the grandmother tell a traditional story. The child interrupted the grandmother and asked: "Are you talking about a man or a woman?" The grandmother just replied: "You have been with the White people too long."

How this language feature reflects the ways of thinking of the Ojibwe and their fellow Algonquians is open to discussion. In this case, we believe that this linguistic feature, built into the structure of the language itself, sheds light on traditional male–female relations in many First Nations cultures, where women were considered relatively equal with men (Brizinski 1993; Medicine 1983; Ezzo 1988; Ross 1996). This does not imply that such relative equality did not exist among speakers of other language families, just that it finds expression in these cultures in this way.

NATIVE EXPECTATIONS

Hierarchy of Person

It is not enough to consider just what Aboriginal languages are not, or how they do not fulfill the linguistic expectations of a French or English speaker. We should also look at what they do have, what features speakers of Aboriginal languages might expect but find missing in English or French. Here are a few areas to show what those expectations might be. Let us examine pronouns in Ojibwe first. Ojibwe has what is referred to as **hierarchy of person**, which reflects the basic cultural value of *respect*. What this means is that the second person (i.e., "you"), always comes first in a word. In "**Niwaabamaa,**" meaning "I see him/her," **-ni-**, indicating the subject "I," goes first. In contrast, in the construction for "I see you," which is "**Giwaabaamin,**" the prefix is **-gi-**, which means "you." The suffix **-min-** indicates that it is "I" that is doing the seeing.

This hierarchy of person can also be seen in the distinction between first person plural (i.e., "we") forms. Algonquian languages distinguish between the "we" that includes the listener(s), called the first person inclusive, and the "we" that does not include the listener, called the first person exclusive. Take the example of the verb **-gindaas-**, "to read." Look at how the first and second person forms work in Table 4-8. You can see that the inclusive form begins with "you" (i.e., with **-gdoo-**) and ends with "we" (i.e., with **-mi-**), while the exclusive form begins and ends with "we" (i.e., with **-ndoo-** and **-mi-**).

This is not just a linguistic feature, but also one that seems to reflect a cultural preference for considering the "you," the other(s). Consider this reflection by linguist Roger Spielmann. He observed this cultural preference virtually every day in Pikogan, a language of the Algonquin First Nation, when people were making decisions. People he spoke with about decision making told him that they thought a lot about how what they were deciding would affect their families, extended families, their communities, and even their First Nation before making a major decision such as to go away to school or to take a job in another location—not the usual strategy of non-Natives. As Spielmann recounts:

> When making the decision to move away from the community to come to teach at the university . . . the decision was made by my wife and myself. We really didn't take into account at all our . . . (. . . parents, grandparents and relatives), nor did we share the same sense of "community" as shared by the people at Pikogan. And we certainly didn't consider (or care) how our decision might affect our nation or our "people"! As a corollary to that, the Elders would regularly comment on how difficult it must be for my wife to live so far away from her parents (who live in British Columbia). It was so rare for someone from Pikogan to actually "move away" from their support systems of the extended family and community. (Spielmann 1998:46)

TABLE 4-8 First and Second Forms of Pronouns in Ojibwe

Word	Translation	Pronoun	Person	
Ndoogindaas	I am reading	Ndoo	first	
Gdoogindaas	You (sing.) are reading	Gdoo-	second	
Ndoogindaasmi	We (excluding listeners) are reading	Ndoo- -mi	first	first (plural)
Gdoogiindaasmi	We (including listeners) are reading	Gdoo- -mi	second	first (plural)
Gdoogiindaasam	You (plural) are reading	Gdoo- -am	second	second (plural)

Animate and Inanimate in Algonquian Languages

Among speakers of Algonquian languages, an important expectation is the distinction of **animate** versus **inanimate**. It is just as all-encompassing as gender is in French and other Romance languages, affecting such key elements as noun plurals and the endings of verbs. In East Cree, for example, if the noun is animate, the plural ending is **-ak** (e.g., **awasisak**, "children"), while inanimate plural nouns end with **-a** (e.g., **maskisina**, "shoes"). Table 4-9 offers some examples of animate and inanimate nouns in East Cree.

As mentioned above, verb endings are affected as well. The following are examples of the distinction as reflected in intransitive verbs (i.e., those that do not take an object). Differences are underlined.

milwasisiw awasis S/he is good, child

milwasin maskisin It is good, shoe

chishiyaashuu S/he sails fast in the water

chishiyaashtin It sails fast in the water

The same applies with transitive verbs (i.e., those that do take an object):

niwapamaw awasis I see him/her, child

niwapahten maskisin I see it, shoe

piskuchiwepinew S/he tosses him/her up into the air

piskuchiwepinam S/he tosses it up into the air

It is not as easy as it might first seem to figure out what is animate and what is inanimate. There are things deemed animate (and thus a "she/he" or a "him/her") that someone outside the culture and the language might not think of as "alive." Note, for example, the following animate terms in East Cree:

kaasiihkweusuup hand soap

michihkun a bone flesher made with bear bone

chishtuhchikanahchaapi fiddle bow

TABLE 4-9   Animate and Inanimate Nouns in East Cree

Singular	Meaning	Plural	Meaning
Animate			
Es	sea shell (hinged)	esak	sea shells
Eskan	antle	reskanak	antlers
Inanimate			
Mishtikuut	wooden box	mishtikuuta	wooden boxes
Kaapaashtepaich	dryer	kaapaashtepaicha	dryers

Alternatively, some things an outsider might think of as "alive" might be deemed inanimate; for example, the following:

mihkwaapemikw red-osier dogwood

paastinaahkwaan club moss

wiihpaashkw cow parsnip (Heracleum mazimum)

Some words can be both animate and inanimate, depending on the usage. In East Cree, for example, "**ishkuteu**" is considered inanimate when it is referring to fire but animate when denoting a battery or a spark plug. And in some contexts and languages, a normally inanimate noun can be used with animate forms if it is considered alive (i.e., having a spirit) in the context of a story.

No two Algonquian languages have exactly the same set of animate and inanimate objects. Dialects of the same language sometimes differ. This should be expected; each people has a unique history. However, there is still a great deal of agreement in Algonquian languages as to what is usually animate and what is usually inanimate. Observe the following sample of shared distinctions with Blackfoot, Ojibwe, and Delaware, each belonging to a different branch of the Algonquian family (see Table 4-10).

SYLLABIC WRITING

The history of syllabic writing in Canada is a tale of success. According to Olive Dickason, "by the nineteenth century and the early part of the twentieth century, the Cree had one of

TABLE 4-10   Agreement in Animate and Inanimate in Blackfoot, Ojibwe, and Delaware

English	Blackfoot	Ojibwe	Delaware
knees	animate	animate	animate
fingernails	animate	animate	animate
skin	animate	animate	animate
horns	animate	animate	animate
feathers	animate	animate	animate
sun	animate	animate	animate
moon	animate	animate	animate
stars	animate	animate	animate
ice	animate	animate	animate
kettles/pots	animate	animate	animate
bark	animate	animate	animate
leaves	inanimate	inanimate	inanimate
strawberries	inanimate	inanimate	inanimate
hair	inanimate	inanimate	inanimate
foot	inanimate	inanimate	inanimate

the highest literacy rates in the world" (Dickason 1992:241). The person credited with first putting the syllabic system together was an Englishman, James Evans (1801–1846). He came to Canada as a young man and became both a teacher and a preacher among the Anishinabe (Ojibwa) of southern Ontario. In 1840, Evans went out west of Norway House, by Lake Winnipeg, north of Winnipeg, to work with the Cree people there. His work developing a writing system is a good example of the collaboration of two different peoples. Evans had seen the Anishinabe and later the Cree use many symbols both in their art and in their communication between travellers along pathways and portages. It is possible that he had heard or even seen examples of the then well-publicized syllabic system developed by the Cherokee educator Sequoyah (c. 1770–1843), which had produced amazing literacy gains and several printed works by the 1820s. From his European background, he took ideas from shorthand and Greek.

In June 1841, Evans printed a book of Cree Christian hymns written in syllabics, reputedly the first book published in western Canada. The Cree took over from there, with catechists, trappers, and traders spreading the use of the system—and literacy—across the West. By 1889, John Maclean could say with some accuracy of the Cree that:

> The Indians of this confederacy, with very few exceptions, read and write these characters; and many of them, with no other teachers but the Indians around the camp-fires, have so grasped these principles that they can read with fluency the books printed in the syllabic system. (Maclean 1970:256)

From about 1851 on, many Christian works were written in syllabics in the Moose Cree dialect, causing it to be a liturgical or religious language for speakers of Ojibwe and other dialects of Cree. In the 1980s, linguist Lisa Philips Valentine studied a Severn Ojibwe-speaking community in northwestern Ontario. She found that the standard religious texts (i.e., their Bible, prayer, and hymn books) of this very active Anglican parish were syllabic works written both in Moose and Plains Cree, something that contributed greatly to the high rate of syllabic literacy in the community.

Today, this syllabics system is used for every dialect of Cree and two dialects of Ojibwe (Severn, or Oji-Cree, and Saulteaux). Educational material for all grades covered by the Cree School Board of East James Bay in Quebec is produced in syllabics. Computer fonts containing syllabics are now readily available.

But this system is not confined just to Algonquian languages. At one time the Athapaskan languages—Chipewyan, Beaver, Slavey, and Carrier—used a version of this system. In 1879, Reverend Edmond J. Peck, an Anglican missionary, altered the system to suit the different sounds of the Eastern Arctic dialects of Inuktitut (e.g., -v-, -g-, -ng-, and -q-), thus initiating a boom in Inuktitut religious material and literacy similar to that which had begun earlier among Algonquian speakers. When Nunavut came into official existence in 1999, this syllabic writing took on official status.

The Benefits of Using Syllabics

Understanding syllabics is easier than a reader accustomed to the Roman alphabet might think. This is especially true for children, who early on perceive syllables and, without the biases of having learned an alphabet first, seem to learn this system as quickly as they would an alphabet. And they don't have to worry about some problems familiar to English spellers, such as a sound being represented by more than one symbol (e.g., the -f- sound being represented by -f-, -ph-, and -gh- in the English words "fine," "phone," and "enough"). Cree children taught literacy first in syllabics appear to be able to later transfer their literacy skills well into using an alphabet for learning English or French.

A syllabic system has the advantage of using fewer symbols in writing long words, cutting down somewhat on the visual prejudice of people accustomed to languages such as French and English that tend to have shorter words than do Cree, Ojibwe, and Inuktitut. Look at the following East Cree word written in syllabics and in Roman letters:

nanakwaanechishkuwew   = 20 letters
ᓇᓇ�b ᓲ ᒢᒃᑦ ᐁᐧ°   = 9 characters (plus three diacritics)
s/he wrinkled it by sitting on it

Further, the "identifiable Nativeness" of the syllabic system is a big plus. Native people were instrumental in its development and spread and it has formed a key part in Native literary traditions. Give students something that they can identify with, and their performance in school improves.

Reading the Symbols

Basically, the system involves a given symbol representing a given consonant plus a vowel. The vowel that is being indicated differs according to which of four positions the symbol has been rotated to face. The position of -i- (pronounced -ee-) is always in opposition to that of -e- (pronounced -eh-), with -a- and -o- or -u- (in the case of East Cree) likewise opposites. The following examples using the -p- symbol will illustrate how this works. Like all examples to follow, they are from East Cree:

pe:	∨	petaapin	∨ᒼᐱᑭᐊ	(it is daybreak)
pi:	∧	pisaaw	∧ᒋᐧ°	(it is a trench)
pa:	<	pataham	<ᒐ"ᐊᒫ	(s/he misses hitting it)
pu:	>	puwaatam	>·ᐊᒐᒫ	(s/he dreams of it)

A syllable final is a consonant that comes after a vowel and before another consonant or the end of a word. There are two different traditions as to how these are to be represented. The Eastern tradition involves smaller, raised versions of the consonant plus the -a- symbol, as can be seen in the following words:

| n: | ᓇ | eshkan | ᐁᑊᐸᓇ | (ice chisel) |
| na: | ᓇ | nanamichuu | ᓄᓇᒢᒎ | (s/he shivers with cold) |

In the Western tradition, special small symbols are employed. In the first word presented above, ᐞ would be used. In both traditions, " signifies a syllable final -h-. Both use a small raised circle (°) for a final -w-.

There are also diacritics, marks added to the basic symbols. One is a dot over the symbol, indicating that the vowel is long:

| taa: | ᒼ | petaapin | ∨ᒼᐱᐊ | (it is daybreak) |

When a dot appears before a vowel in the Eastern and Western Catholic tradition (after the vowel in the Western tradition), that signifies that the consonant and vowel have a -w- between them:

| kwaa: | ·ᑭ | mihkwaaw | ᒥ"·ᑭ° | (it is red) |

KEY TERMS

cognates
dialect
hierarchy of person
language family

language isolate
morpheme
root

CONTENT QUESTIONS

1. What are three misconceptions about Native languages?
2. How many Native language families and isolates exist in Canada today?
3. How are Inuktitut, Algonquian, and Athapaskan languages different from English and French in representing gender?
4. What is "hierarchy of person"?
5. What important distinction exists in Algonquian languages?

WEBLINKS

www.ethnologue.com/show_country.asp?name=CA
This Summer Institute of Linguistics website lists the Native languages of Canada, where they are spoken, and their numbers of speakers.

www.afn.ca/article.asp?id=122
The leading Canadian political body for Native bands, the Assembly of First Nations, includes discussions of the state of Aboriginal languages in Canada and of policies designed to improve that state.

FIGURE 4-1

Courtesy of DK Images.

chapter five

The Arctic

PALAEO-ESKIMO (3000 B.C. TO 500 B.C.)

It began at least 5000 years ago. People who were capable of making their home where no one else had lived, in the barren tundra and frozen coastlines of the North American Arctic, appeared in Alaska. Within about 200 years, they spread across the north, some even reaching Greenland, extending the Arctic human lifeline nearly 5000 kilometres east to west.

What did these first peoples have that enabled them to live in the Arctic? Their hunting arsenal was impressive: Asian-style, double-curved bows made out of several materials bound together, lances bristling with sharp-edged **microblades**, and perhaps spear-throwers to help them fling those weapons farther. Probably from their Native neighbours on the East Coast they learned to make and use harpoons that were armed with deadly detachable heads that stuck into marine mammals. Worked flint flakes, or microblades, were used for cutting meats and skins, and burins with edges for carving antler and bone. The latter enabled them to make the small bone needles they used to stitch together with sinew thread the airtight tailored clothing necessary for keeping the cold out.

Their homes were tents, usually single-family dwellings. For cooking, they had stone-lined hearths or fireboxes in which they burned scavenged driftwood, twigs of dwarf willow, and fat-smeared bones of animals. Had they learned yet how to use the more plentiful oil rendered from animal fat to heat themselves? We don't know. Some stone lamps existed, but not until relatively late, and in small numbers. Perhaps they used skin or some other archaeologically invisible substance. Did they have boats at this time? It's not known for sure. From 2500 to 1500 B.C., the Arctic climate warmed, creating more open water stretches to travel or hunt in than had existed before or that exist now. There is no direct evidence for their use of skin boats, but skin does not survive long to provide archaeological evidence. Still, one wonders how they could have crossed the Bering Strait without boats.

DORSET (1000 B.C. TO A.D. 1000)

From 2000 to 1000 B.C., the Arctic became colder. The Arctic people used technological innovation to meet the challenge in what is called the Dorset cultural tradition, named after Cape Dorset on Baffin Island, where the first Dorset sites were found. The Dorset people used more materials than before, including slate, which they ground into knives and projectile points. Robert McGhee estimated that the population within the core area of the northern parts of the Foxe Basin, Baffin Island, the islands in northern Hudson Bay, and both sides of the Hudson Strait, grew from an earlier population of somewhere between 1000 to 3000 to between 2000 to 5000 during this time. Dorset innovative adaptations to colder weather include the familiar **igloos**, but also homes that were partially sunk into the ground, with sod walls and roofs made of skin. Oil-burning stone lamps, necessary for keeping both kinds of houses warm, also started to appear in large numbers at this time. Dorset people were better equipped than their predecessors for winter travel. They had sleds, with "shoes" or ivory plates protecting the runners of the sleds from rough ice. For walking on smooth ice, they had **ice creepers**, pieces of ivory notched to form treads and attached to their footwear to act like the spikes used today to climb telephone poles and mountains.

THULE (A.D. 1000 TO PRESENT)

With a warming trend between A.D. 900 and 1200 that produced ice-free summers and milder winters, the Thule tradition developed. Its innovations increased the capacity to hunt sea mammals, particularly the massive bowhead whales. The Thule developed **kayaks**, **umiaks** (skinboats eight to ten metres long that typically held 12 men), and harpoons with sealskin floats. When a seal, walrus, or whale was struck by such a harpoon, the float would wear the animal out and keep it from sinking. Land travel improved with the first clearly proven use of sled dogs. As a result, we find more permanent and larger communities, particularly in those areas where whale hunting was prominent.

What was the relationship between the Thule, who are directly connected with today's Inuit, and their Dorset predecessors? The Inuit have long told stories of the **Tunnit** or **Tunrit**, a seal-hunting people with whom they initially coexisted in peace, until they eventually fought. There is no evidence that the Thule killed off the Tunnit, so it is likely that the prevailing scenario was intermarriage and teaching of new skills. During the early 1920s, Knud Rasmussen, who was of mixed Danish-Inuit parentage, led a scientific expedition across the Arctic from Greenland to Alaska. An Inuk told him: "We counted the Tunrit a foreign people, yet they spoke our language, lived with us, and had the same habits and customs as we had" (Wright 1995:444).

INUIT

Up until 1200 A.D., there was a great uniformity within the Thule culture, something reflected today in the linguistic uniformity of **Inuktitut**, the language of the Inuit. This language is fundamentally the same from Alaska across the Canadian Arctic to Greenland. Fitting it into its broader context, Inuktitut belongs to the **Eskimo-Aleut** family, which has member languages (e.g., Yup'ik and Aleut) spoken on both sides of the Bering Strait, which separates North America from Asia.

Area	Singular	Plural
TABLE 5-1		
Most of the Canadian Arctic	Inuk	Inuit
Mackenzie Delta	Inuvialuk	Inuvialuit
North Alaska	Inupiaq	Inupiat
South Alaska	Yupik	Yupik
Siberia and St. Lawrence Island	Yuk	Yuit

Estimates of Thule/Inuit pre-contact population in Canada range from about 22,000 to 35,000. The word "Inuit" means "men, people." Within the last 20 years, this word replaced the more familiar word **Eskimo**, which was based on an Algonquian root meaning "raw," said to relate to the Inuit practice of eating certain forms of meat and blubber raw. It is important to recognize that Inuit is a plural form. The word "Inuits" does not exist. There is a singular form as well: Inuk. But this is not the only name used by and for the people. Inuit is only really appropriate for those people who live in Canada, but even then it is not appropriate for all of those either (see Table 5-1 above). In the Mackenzie Delta, the word used is *Inuvialuk,* and the plural is *Inuvialuit*, meaning "real, genuine people." In Alaska, two terms tend to be used: *Inupiaq* (singular) and *Inupiat* (plural) in the north, and *Yup'ik* in the southwest (singular and plural). Greenland languages use *Katladlit* and *Kalaallisut*. In the far west, Siberia and St. Lawrence Island, the people use *Yuk* and *Yuit* ("people").

A European parallel may help clarify these various terms. People who speak German and live in Germany are called Germans. People who speak a German language in the Netherlands are called Dutch, and in Belgium are called Flemish. In Austria, they are called Austrians; in Switzerland they are called Swiss Germans. This is just as confusing to outsiders as the different names for the "Inuit".

Beginning from about 1200 A.D., and peaking between 1600 and 1850, the climate of the Arctic cooled, making up what is termed the Little Ice Age. During this period, the extent and duration of sea ice in the Arctic kept the bowhead whales in many areas from their summer feeding grounds. The Thule peoples were forced to move to different places and rely upon different animals, depending on local availability. This caused the previous cultural uniformity to break up.

In Canada, anthropologists have subdivided the Inuit into eight cultural groups, from west to east: the **Mackenzie Delta**, **Copper**, **Caribou**, **Netsilik** (Netsilingmiut), **Sadlermiut**, **Iglulik** (Iglulingmiut), **South Baffin Island**, and **Labrador and Quebec**. Note that for the most part, this does not reflect any "tribal" distinction in terms of a people's sense of who they are. It is more a distinction imposed by outsiders, based on geography and a few distinct traits. The Mackenzie Inuit took advantage of great numbers of beluga swimming up the Mackenzie River, herding them into shallow waters with their kayaks. One of their communities, Kittagazuit, a summer beluga camp, was occupied for centuries by up to 1000 people, what McGhee rightly terms "the largest Inuit community between Bering Strait and Greenland" (McGhee 1978:116). Today, the Mackenzie Delta Inuit consider themselves distinct from other Inuit and call themselves **Inuvialuit**, "the real people." The Copper Inuit were

Box 5-1	Pibloktuq

Distortions and mistakes have been perpetuated in literature about the Inuit. The following story, a subject recorded in the 1892 journal of Josephine, the wife of American Arctic explorer Robert Peary, is an example. There are historical rumours that Josephine accompanied her husband because she had heard stories (they were true) of his "Eskimo wife." Josephine was the first to describe the "crazy" acts of Inuit women who would suddenly scream, tear their clothes off, imitate the sound of a bird or animal, and go running around until they dropped. The name that emerged from the early White visitors to the Arctic who recorded this phenomenon was **pibloktuq**.

The term pibloktuq first entered the psychiatric medical record as a form of "Arctic hysteria." It still exists as a psychological disorder legitimated by a medical name, "authenticated" by case studies. It also became enshrined in anthropology as one of a number of culturally specific syndromes or psychoses. However, in a 1995 article in *Arctic Anthropology,* "Pibloktoq" (Arctic Hysteria): A Construction of European-Inuit Relations?", historian Lyle Dick challenged the existence of the phenomenon as a part of traditional Inuit culture. He rightfully suspects that it is more likely the creature of the White-Inuit power imbalance embodied in such contexts as the obsessively driven Robert Peary forcing the Inuit to take unwise risks in exploration that they would not normally take, and in sexual abuse by White men of Inuit women.

primarily distinctive because of their use of copper in tools. The Caribou Inuit relied more on caribou than on other food sources, especially during the nineteenth century. Netsilik ("people of the seal") relied upon a variety of animals, but have long been particularly skilled, as their name suggests, at the seal hunt. Similarly, the Iglulik were more involved with pursuing walrus than were other Inuit ethnic groups.

These Inuit groups differed too in social features. The Copper Inuit traditionally were "rugged individualists." They stressed the nuclear family over the extended family, which was the basis of other Inuit cultures. They were much more egalitarian than the Iglulingmiut, whose leaders' authority extended beyond the camp to include a whole band.

Box 5-1 describes the widely perpetuated misconception of Pibloktuq.

SOCIAL ORGANIZATION AND LEADERSHIP AMONG THE TRADITIONAL INUIT

For most Canadian Inuit groups, leadership existed in the form of an **isumataq** (or **ihumataq**), "one who thinks." He was usually an older man who held respected kinship status, such as father, older brother, cousin, uncle, father-in-law, and/or grandfather, with respect to those he led. But one did not gain that position purely on status. John Matthiasson, speaking about the Tununermiut of Baffin Island, describes the ideal attributes of an isumataq as follows:

> . . . a wise decision-maker, a good hunter, and an exemplar of Inuit values, and must have demonstrated all three qualities over time. He might be asked for advice on where men should hunt, or may decide when it was time for the band to separate. Although a skilled hunter, he would be sure to share his kills with members of his band and to loan his hunting equipment to other men when not using it himself . . . (Matthiasson 1992:91; see Burch 1995:128)

Matthiasson also pointed out that the band had the freedom to choose whether to ignore or to follow the isumataq's advice. They could even leave the band if they believed that the isumataq's advice was not sound. Outside of kinship, group identity existed at various levels, beginning with camps. While these were variable in size, the figures derived by anthropologist Marc Stevenson from a map drawn in 1839 by **Eenoolooapik**, a Baffin Island Inuk, are fairly typical (Stevenson 1997:62). The camps portrayed in that map ranged from about 33 to 51 in population. Winter hunting involved breathing-hole (**mauliqtuq**) sealing, done in winter. To be done effectively, many hunters were needed, since seals use many breathing holes, all of which needed to be watched. Traditionally, this might involve a camp of around 50. Combinations of camps made up bands, signified by names ending in **-miut**. Eenoolooapik's map shows three bands in the area: the **Talirpingmiut**, the **Kingnaimiut**, and the **Kinguamiut**, numbering roughly 375, 211–257, and 434. Terms ending with **-miut** could also be used to refer to collections of bands, as can be seen in the name **Netsilingmiut**. Box 5-2 explores some other words in Inuktitut.

Box 5-2   Words in Inuktitut

You will notice that many Inuktitut words end with -k- or -q-. That is because those letters represent a sound that is used for a third person singular pronominal suffix: she, he, and it. Also, different dialects are distinguished by such features as the -h- in one dialect being an -s- in another.

angajuqqaq: An Inuktitut term for leader that implies the capacity to give orders to another.

igloo: Inuktitut term for any type of house.

i(s/h)umataq: "One who thinks"; Inuktitut term for a leader who suggests but does not give orders.

kayak: One-person skin boat invented by the Thule people.

maqtaak: The blubber from a marine mammal.

mauliqtuq: Breathing hole of a seal.

-miut: a suffix used to denote a group of people.

tuktuk: Caribou.

Tun(n/r)it: A gentle, seal-hunting people in traditional Inuit stories, thought to be the Dorset people.

umiak: Large, seal-skin boat typically holding 12 people, which could be over nine metres in length.

ARCTIC RESOURCES AND THE INUIT

Most often remarked upon in anthropological literature are the many ways in which the Inuit adapted to life in a very difficult environment. This section examines some of the resources the Inuit used, both for commercial purposes and for subsistence.

Marine Mammals and Fish

The largest of the marine mammals the Inuit ate was the bowhead whale, which can reach a weight of more than 40,000 kilograms. A successful hunt yielded **maqtaak** (blubber) to eat, oil for lamps, and jaw and rib bones twice the height of a man to be used for sled runners, or as the frames for houses made of stone and sod. One whale could keep several families well supplied with food, dog food, fuel, and building supplies for a year. The commercial uses of these whales involved two parts of the whale. First was **baleen**, a flexible bone-like material growing in thin strips in the palates of certain species of whales, used by whales to trap tiny sea creatures for food. Nineteenth-century Euro-Americans used baleen for making the corsets that forced women's bodies into the thin-waisted hourglass shapes considered fashionable at the time. According to Keith Crowe (1974:104), the baleen from one whale could pay the cost of a year's voyage for a ship and its crew. Second, Euro-Americans also rendered whale blubber into oil that was burned as fuel and used as lubrication for machinery in the fast-growing factories of the Industrial Revolution.

The smaller beluga whale (500 to 1000 kilograms) was also an important source of meat, maqtaak, and oil. It was hunted commercially in great numbers by the Inuit during the twentieth century, up until 1963. The hide would be made into leather and the blubber rendered into the oil that would be used in cooking fats and for cosmetics.

Walrus were hunted for their skin, meat, bone, and oil and also for their tusks, which provided the ivory used in jewellery, sled shoes, ice creepers, fish spears, and a broad variety of tools generally. Their thick hide was useful for boots and for special outer winter pants that allowed the hunter to sit still on the ice while waiting to spear seals.

The most consistently hunted marine mammals for the Inuit were seals, namely, the larger bearded seal (250 to 350 kilograms), the harp seal, and the smaller ringed seal (up to 80 kilograms). Seals provided fat for oil and meat, and, very significantly, had waterproof skin, which was used for kayaks and umiaks, harpoon floats, summer coats and tents, and boots and beds. Initially, the commercial hunt for this animal was primarily for the oil, but during the twentieth century the seals were hunted more for the skins, particularly the "whitecoats" of the pups, once fashionable but no longer accepted by consumers.

Fishing, especially of arctic char, was important as well. Techniques included jigging, ice fishing, and constructing stone weirs that would direct the fish to where they could be speared. Scientists who wondered why the Inuit could eat so much animal fat and not die of heart attacks learned that the fish oils the Inuit consumed were important in lowering cholesterol. The traditional Inuit have thus given modern medicine assistance in the fight against heart disease.

Land Mammals

The most important land mammal was the barren ground caribou. Caribou hair is hollow and traps air, thus making it ideal for insulation, softness, and lightness, and for clothing, footwear,

Same sentence 2x

tents, bedding, blankets, and bags. It has been calculated that fifty caribou were required to meet the needs of each person for a single year, with eight to eleven skins per person for clothing and twenty to thirty skins for tent coverings (see Wright 1995:425). E.S. Burch provides a good description of the use of other parts of the caribou:

> Excellent thread can be made from their back sinew, and components of tools, weapons and utensils can be manufactured from their antlers and bones. People who consume all of the meat, viscera, stomach contents (rich in vitamin C), and fat of caribou are able to satisfy all of their nutritional requirements. If caribou are available in sufficient numbers at appropriate times of year, and if they are fully utilized, they can provide for the **total** subsistence requirements of a human population. (Burch 1995:129)

The degree of usefulness of caribou changes with the seasons. During the fall and early winter, they have plenty of fat and their skins are in prime condition. But during the spring and early summer, their meat is very lean and therefore of limited nutritional value. The skins are thinner and have holes in them, courtesy of warble flies.

Like other important aspects of Inuit culture, **tuktuk** (caribou) are the subject of thousands of songs. The following song comes from **Krilugok**, a songwriter and singer as well as a hunter (like many traditional Inuit):

> Tuktuk, tuktuk, caribou, caribou, come to me!
>
> I'll make boots with the skin of thy legs;
>
> Stay, stay with me, o creature of the land,
>
> Roamer of the valleys, wanderer of the mountains;
>
> Fear me not, and let me catch thee,
>
> Eyaya, eya, eya, eyaya, ya, ya. (de Coccola and King 1986:201)

Musk ox were also hunted, not just for meat but as a multi-faceted resource. Their up-sweeping horns were used as material for scrapers and for components in the composite bows. The fine underlying "wool" plus long-haired fur made their skins ideal for cold-resistant blankets, robes, and tents. But nineteenth-century hunting technology was deadly to these creatures, which were easy victims because they tend to stand and protect the herd rather than running away. Inuit armed with guns and desperately needing food because of the vagaries of the whaling industry, combined with a late nineteenth-century commercial hunt of musk ox for robes, drove the musk ox nearly to extinction.

The word "parka" entered the English language from Aleutian, a language related to that of the Inuit. This northern Native coat was carefully crafted with furs such as those of the wolverine, wolf, and dog that would not collect the moisture from human breath. The term **"husky"** comes from the word "Eskimo." These dogs, which might have accompanied people across the Bering Strait, were used both to hunt and to pull dogsleds, a uniquely Arctic mode of transportation that used two to more than fifteen dogs per sled (see Box 5-3 for more on the **qimmiq**, a dog native to the Canadian Arctic). Polar bear fur was highly valued because of its resistance to cold water and because it was difficult to obtain. Fox fur, traditionally used for a number of minor purposes, became quite valuable in commercial trapping.

INUIT PHYSICAL ADAPTATION

Inuit adaptation to the Arctic is physical as well as cultural. Longer torsos, shorter limbs and relatively few active sweat glands on their chests and backs have facilitated heat retention.

Box 5-3   The Qimmiq: Canada's Aboriginal Breed

Scholars who study the domestication and development of the domestic dogs suggest that there were close to 20 types of dog in the Americas before Europeans arrived. Of these, eight were found in what is now Canada. Regrettably, only one of the eight still exists.

The "Canadian Eskimo Dog" bears this name courtesy of the Canadian Kennel Club. His real name, given him by the Inuit, is *Qimmiq* (sometimes spelled Kimmiq, or Kingmiq). Recent evidence indicates that the dog has been resident in the Arctic for at least 4000 years. The Qimmiq is the dog of the coastal and archipelago area of Arctic Canada and is distinct from other, far more common Arctic draft dog breeds, such as the Alaskan Malamute and Siberian Husky.

The Qimmiq had three important roles in Inuit society: backpacking, hauling sleds, and hunting. Arguably their role as hunters was of equal if not greater importance than as a beast of burden. Depending upon the particular Inuit

nation, the dogs were used for hunting musk oxen, polar bears and, especially, seals. In the case of seal hunting, the dogs were used to detect the animals' breathing holes. Without dogs to locate these holes, hunting—and surviving—would have been much more difficult. After a successful hunt, the Qimmiq returned to his better-known role as a draft animal, hauling the seal home.

The Qimmiq breed was almost extinct 40 years ago. As a result of the influx of other breeds as well as the arrival of the snowmobile, the population had dropped from an estimated 20,000 dogs in 1920 to fewer than 200 in 1970. Its existence today is attributable to biologist William J. Carpenter, who made it his mission to save the breed. Today the Qimmiq is again threatened with extinction with fewer than 300 dogs left.

Source: Cummins, Bryan. 2002. *First Nations, First Dogs: Canadian Aboriginal Ethnocynology.* Calgary: Detselig Enterprises.

Inuit also have proportionally larger sinuses than non-Inuit, allowing for the greater warming of air before its passage into the more sensitive lungs. Another crucial physical adaptation concerns their Basal Metabolic Rate (BMR), the rate at which the body metabolizes food. The Inuit have a higher-than-average BMR. When they eat food, the rate at which their body metabolizes and activates it into energy is comparatively quick, making the Inuit better able to fight the cold.

Another adaptation is **Hunter's Response**, a phenomenon also shared by subarctic Native hunters. Imagine submerging your arm in near-freezing ice water for a while and then removing it from the water. For most people, it would take a long time for their arm's skin temperature to return to normal. Hunter's Response is a rapid readjustment to normal skin temperature as a greater-than-average amount of blood flows to the body's extremities.

POST-CONTACT HISTORY

The first contact between Inuit and Europeans probably took place when the Vikings briefly settled on the northern tip of Newfoundland about 1000 years ago. By the late 1400s, the Inuit first met European whalers. That contact reached a height during the nineteenth century. Between 1820 and 1840, whalers on more than 1300 British ships sailed by the north shore of Baffin Island, killing more than 13,000 whales. Commercial whaling peaked between 1868 and 1883, when American whalers were active between Alaska and Hudson Bay.

There were good and bad ramifications of whaling for the Inuit. The British in the east and Americans in the west needed the skilled help of the Inuit, so some Inuit became prominent figures in the industry, first as members of whaleboat crews and later as owners of boats, including some large schooners. Cultural go-betweens often became traders, some eventually running their own trading posts or working as managers for the big company posts. Prominent hunters became successful leaders of communities of increased size, particularly in whaling centres such as Baffin Island. Such figures were known as **angajuqqaq**, leaders with more authority than the more egalitarian **isumataq**.

But there was a downside to commercial whaling: starvation and disease. In the winter of 1847–48, 20 people of a population of 160 at the Baffin Island community of Naujateling died of hunger "of whom several, horrible to relate, had gnawed the flesh from their own arms" (Stevenson 1997:75). In 1853–54, the same population lost about a third of their population to cholera. By 1883, it was a community of 20. There are many such stories.

The twentieth century started out badly for the Inuit. In 1899, three sailors from the Scottish ship *Active* landed on Sadliq (Southampton Island). During the next three years, all but five of the Sadlermiut died of the diseases those men carried. The last survivor of that little-known group, which might have numbered around 200 at the time of contact, died in 1948. Similarly, in 1919, a supply ship arrived at the Labrador Inuit community of Okak, bringing with it Spanish flu with the usual supplies. Only a handful of people survived; and Okak, founded as a mission community in 1776, disbanded.

In addition, from 1915 to 1925, the caribou population west of Hudson Bay suffered a sharp decline. The Caribou Inuit themselves dwindled from 1500 to 500 during that same period. Their separate existence would end after 1948, when, in addition to the over-hunting of caribou by White southerners on northern projects, high levels of tuberculosis, influenza, and polio put their homeland under quarantine for almost two years. During the 1950s, the survivors moved to the coast to join newly formed combined villages. Individuals of Caribou Inuit descent would become prominent in Inuit activism, both in the formation of the Inuit Tapirisat and in the push for the Nunavut territory.

By the time the whaling industry collapsed early in the twentieth century, the commercial demand for whales had severely dropped. European women's garments no longer contained whalebone stays. Petroleum was replacing whale oil as a lubricant and fuel. In the 1920s, the commercial hunting of belugas and, more significantly, the trapping of Arctic fox, would take the place of large whale hunting. For a little over 10 years, fox hunting made some Inuit quite well off, particularly in the Mackenzie

Delta and on Banks Island. Catholic missionary Father Frank Raymond de Coccola stated that, in 1938:

> A white fox pelt would trade for about $40. To an Eskimo this represented three boxes of twenty rifle shells in each box, or ten yards of calico for his wife's sewing or twenty five pounds of flour and a pound of tea or tallow to boot. (de Coccola and King 1986: 72)

As such, a trapper could get from $30 to $70 for one fur, making at least $9000 during a good season, significantly more than the Canadian average annual income at that time.

But fox trapping was a risky business for the Inuit. Trapping fox took them away from where they could hunt their own food, making them dependent on expensive southern foods. In addition, fox numbers rose and fell in cycles. During the 1930s and 1940s, the industry crashed when fashion changed, prices fell, and the fox were overtrapped. Inuit starved as a result.

In 1939, when Canada wanted to assert its territorial claims to the Arctic, the federal government decided to take official responsibility for the Inuit. In 1953, the negative side of this relationship was made clear when the people of Inukjuak (Port Harrison) in Northern Quebec were forced to move some 3200 kilometres north to the uninhabited Ellesmere Island at Grise Fiord. Ottawa claimed that this was for the betterment of the people, as local natural resources were depleting and Ellesmere Island was untouched. A darker interpretation is that this forced move was made primarily to guarantee Canadian rights to that contested territory. Government officials did not seem to know or care that the resources available in the two areas were quite different, that Inuit who had adapted to life in one part of the Arctic weren't necessarily knowledgeable about surviving in another.

In the census of 1991, 30,085 people claimed Inuit as their sole ethnic origin. Another 19,165 listed it as one of their origins, for a total of 49,250. In the 1996 census, 26,840 people claimed Inuktitut as at least one of their mother tongues.

Timeline 5-1

3000 B.C. to 500 B.C.: Palaeo-Eskimo Period.

1000 B.C. to A.D. 1000: Dorset Period.

A.D. 1000 to date: Thule Period.

A.D. 1200 to 1850: Little Ice Age.

1820 to 1840: Whalers on British ships kill more than 13,000 whales.

1999: Birth of Nunavut territory (see Chapter 25).

KEY TERMS

angajuqqaq (Inuktitut)

Hunter's Response

ice creepers

i(s/h)umataq (Inuktitut)

microblades

Tun(n/r)it (Inuktitut)

umiak (Inuktitut)

CONTENT QUESTIONS

1. What innovations are associated with the Dorset Period?
2. What innovations are associated with the Thule Period?
3. What was the probable impact of the Little Ice Age?
4. How are **isumataq** and **angajuqqaq** different?
5. What, for the Inuit, were the good and bad aspects of nineteenth-century whaling and twentieth-century arctic fox trapping?

WEBLINKS

http://arcticcircle.uconn.edu
The Arctic Circle project provides extensive materials about northern Aboriginals.

chapter six

The Eastern Woodlands

OVERVIEW

The Eastern Woodlands in Canada encompasses two broad groups: Algonquians and Iroquoians. Most of the former speak languages that belong to the Eastern branch of the Algonquian family. In Canada, this includes Mi'kmaq, Maliseet, Western Abenaki, and Munsee (Delaware). Also in the area are the more southerly Central Algonquian peoples associated with the Ojibwa (e.g., the Mississauga, Potawatomi, Odawa, and Algonquin). The Iroquoians include the Huron and the Six Nations of the Iroquois.

Geographically, the Eastern Woodlands area is characterized by mixed deciduous and coniferous forests, providing a broad variety of wild plants and animals for the use of the people. The prominent presence of large bodies of water (i.e., the Atlantic, the St. Lawrence River, and the Great Lakes) made fishing a significant activity among all of these people. In the south, corn-based agriculture (sometimes supplemented by beans and squash) provided most of the food.

Within the Eastern Woodlands, we find complex social structures extending beyond the band or local group. This includes clans (except for the Mi'kmaq and Maliseet), "chiefs" (sometimes called "sagamores" for the Algonquians and "**sachems**" for the Iroquois—both sagamores and sachems derived from an Eastern Algonquian term that derived from "**saq-maw**" in the Mi'kmaq language), and federated tribes or confederacies, the most notable being the Iroquois Confederacy. Both clan organization and chief succession were **matrilineal** (i.e., by descent through the female line) among the Iroquoians and the Delaware, and **patrilineal** (i.e., by descent through the male line) for the other Eastern Algonquians.

THE ALGONQUIANS

The Mi'kmaq

The story of the Mi'kmaq is one of a fight for survival. They live along the East Coast but did not disappear, nor were forced west, as were almost all fellow coastal peoples of the United States. In what Olive Dickason termed the "longest of all Amerindian conflicts in North America" (Dickason 1992:149), the Mi'kmaq fought against the British in defence of their land, something few Canadian Native groups did.

The term "**Mi'kmaq**" (sometimes Mi'kmaw), preferred by the people today to the older "Micmac," is said to be derived from a term for "allies." A more traditional name is "**Ilnu**," which, like the cognate "Innu" (see Chapter 7, "The Eastern Subarctic"), means "people." Their country stretches over Nova Scotia, New Brunswick, Prince Edward Island, the Gaspé peninsula of Quebec, Anticosti Island, and parts of Newfoundland (See Box 6-1 for the Mi'kmaq origins of some of these place names). It is hard to determine Mi'kmaq numbers for the time of contact. When Father Pierre Biard estimated their population at just over 3000 in 1616, they had already suffered severe depopulation through roughly a century of European contact. They had probably lost at least 50 to 66 percent of their people to European diseases. In addition, because Biard was not aware of all of the Mi'kmaq communities, we can estimate a pre-contact figure that was probably more than 10,000.

In 1610, Marc Lescarbot writes of how the Mi'kmaq made good use of different local resources throughout the year. Lescarbot reports that in January of that year (*Jesuit Relations* [JR] 3:79–83), in small local groups of perhaps 30 to 40, the Mi'kmaq hunted seal, both for the meat and oil that they would keep in moose-bladder containers. In February and early March, they hunted a variety of animals, including beaver, otter, bear, moose, and **caribou** (a Mi'kmaq word meaning "one who scratches," because caribou scratch through the snow for food). It wasn't until the middle of March that great amounts of food were available as fish began to spawn, coming from the sea up the rivers and streams, at the mouths of which the Mi'kmaq set traps. First came the smelt, then the herring near the end of April into early May. Also available at that time were salmon and sturgeon. One Mi'kmaq name for April was "Egg-Laying," as migrating waterfowl laid eggs in great numbers, which the Mi'kmaq then gathered. May was called "Young Seals" or "Get Herring."

In the summer, food was available in even greater abundance. As a result, the Mi'kmaq formed larger groups, numbering perhaps 200 to 300. From the sea, they harvested oysters, clams, and lobsters. Using **weirs** (fish traps built of sticks) and spears or bone hooks and lines, they fished for cod, plaice, and striped bass, and speared porpoises and even small whales. As much as 90 percent of their food may have come from the sea (Miller 1995:349).

Box 6-1	Place Names in Mi'kmaq

Anticosti (Island): "forward land"   **Quebec:** "it narrows"

Gaspé: from *kaspe:k*, or "outer ends"

In the fall, they returned to smaller groups in order to pursue migrating birds, moose, and caribou. September was termed "Moose Calling," and October was called "Fat, Tame Animals." Especially sought were eels, which the Mi'kmaq boiled, roasted, or smoked for winter.

A key component of traditional Mi'kmaq social structure was the "**saqmaw**," a **patrilineal** position typically inherited by the eldest son. A seventeenth-century Jesuit missionary described the duties of the saqmaw (which he writes as "sagamore") as follows, overemphasizing somewhat the power of the position. He stated that the saqmaw provided hunting dogs, canoes, and provisions for travel to members of the group:

> The young people flatter him, hunt, and serve their apprenticeship under him, not being allowed to have anything before they are married, for then only can they have a dog and a bag; that is, have something of their own, and do for themselves. Nevertheless they continue to live under the authority of the sagamore, and very often in his company; as also do several others who have no relations, or those who of their own free will place themselves under his protection and guidance, being themselves weak and without a following. Now all that the young men capture belongs to the Sagamore; but the married ones give him only a part, and if these leave him, as they often do for the sake of the chase and supplies, returning afterwards, they pay their dues and homage in skins and like gifts. (JR3:87–91)

Saqmaw leadership existed at various levels, from the small fall and winter groups, to the larger summer groups, to the district level, and, finally, to the "kji'saqmaw" or "great chief." Mi'kmaq country was divided into seven districts. The responsibilities of the district saqmaw included assigning hunting territories according to changing family grouping size and local resource conditions, meeting to decide issues of war and peace, conferring with saqmaw of lesser standing, and making sure that everyone had enough food and resources. Generosity was a prized value among saqmaws, which meant that some district saqmaw gave away their best clothes and other possessions (Miller 1995:354).

The Mi'kmaq were involved with the fur trade and with Catholic missionaries early on, which drew them closer to the French than to the English. But the Mi'kmaq fought the English for their own reasons, coming into conflict several times during the seventeenth and eighteenth centuries. The first "war" began in 1722, which led to a treaty in 1725, in which the Mi'kmaq exchanged their promise of peace for hunting and fishing rights. It was an uneasy peace.

The 1740s hit the Mi'kmaq hard. In 1746, typhus spread from the French fleet to the Mi'kmaq, killing an estimated 4000, perhaps one third of their number in Nova Scotia. In July 1749, Colonel Edward Cornwallis led more than 2400 English settlers into the east coast region of Nova Scotia, landing where Halifax is today. The Mi'kmaq reacted by declaring war on the intruders on September 24. On October 2, Cornwallis responded by issuing a proclamation "to Annoy, distress or destroy the Savages commonly called Micmacks, wherever they are found" (Upton 1979:52). A bounty of first £10 and later £50 was put on their heads, dead or alive. The conflict between the two cultures lasted until November 1752, when the 1725 treaty was reaffirmed. However, this treaty was later broken by English sailors who, for bounty money, killed and scalped six friendly Mi'kmaq who had helped them after they had been shipwrecked. Peace had to be re-established in 1762, but the situation became tense when the Americans sought Mi'kmaq aid in the American Revolution. The bounty exists in legal limbo today. The Nova Scotia government sent a "Resolution on Bounty Proclamation" on March 28, 2000, asking the federal government to take action and remove the bounty from law. Taking the bounty out of Nova Scotia law was one of the prerequisites given by the Mi'kmaq for signing what is called the umbrella or general agreement of June 7, 2002, which officially began the process of treaty negotiations between Canada, Nova Scotia, and Mi'kmaq. But to date, no news release or official document has been issued that the bounty has been taken off the books.

The aftermath of the American Revolutionary War was deadly to the Mi'kmaq. After the fighting stopped in 1782, Loyalists from New York flooded Nova Scotia, tripling their population in one year to 42 000. This was particularly devastating to Mi'kmaq use of marine resources because the settlers established communities along the coasts. Powerful as well was their impact on land animals, which one statistic demonstrates. In the winter of 1789, gangs of English poachers killed off a reported 9000 moose and caribou in Cape Breton alone. During the next few years, there were reports of starvation among the Mi'kmaq.

During the nineteenth century, the rights of the Mi'kmaq were constantly trampled. English squatters moved onto officially declared Mi'kmaq land, sometimes even taking over Mi'kmaq farms when the owners were away. The Mi'kmaq fought back through legal channels. **Andrew Meuse**, sagamore of the Bear River band, tried to fight the alcoholism that was being inflicted on his people by unscrupulous traders. His 1828 petition called for an end to the sale of alcohol to his people. The result was a law that left final action to the discretion of local magistrates. None of them acted to stop the trade.

The most famous Mi'kmaq petition came from sagamore **Paussamigh Pemmeenauweet (Louis Benjamin Peminout)**, who sent these heartfelt words to Queen Victoria in 1840:

> I cannot cross the great lake to talk to you for my canoe is too small, and I am old and weak. I cannot look upon you for my eyes not see so far. You cannot hear my voice across the great waters. I therefore send this wampum and paper talk to tell the Queen I am in trouble. My people are in trouble. When I was young I had plenty: now I am old, poor and sickly too. My people are poor. No hunting grounds. No beaver. No otter. No nothing. Indians poor—poor for ever. No store. No chest. No clothes. All these woods once ours. Our fathers possessed them all. Now we cannot cut a tree to warm our wigwams in winter unless the white man please. (Upton 1979:89–90)

This petition initially made a great stir, but in the end little was done.

The Mi'kmaq are still fighting for their survival, the most recent struggle being over their rights to fish (see Chapter 13). Today, there are more than 20,000 registered Mi'kmaq in Canada, in 27 bands (13 of which are in Nova Scotia, nine of which are in New Brunswick). One Mi'kmaq community exists in Maine. The census of 1996 recorded that 6720 people speak Mi'kmaq.

The Maliseet

The Maliseet live in six communities in New Brunswick, with a combined registered population of 5583. Approximately 40 percent live off-reserve. About 600 live in Quebec, but although these people have two reserves, they have no collective community. Another 800 live in Maine. The name "**Maliseet**" (also spelled Malecite) is derived from a Mi'kmaq word, usually translated as "broken or lazy speakers," showing a Mi'kmaq bias concerning the slight differences between the two languages. The Maliseet prefer to name themselves after the river, **Wolastoqewi**, "of the good (i.e., beautiful, navigable, and/or bountiful) river." The French first termed them "Etchemin" for reasons that are not clear.

Because they lived closer to the English of the United States than did the Mi'kmaq, the Maliseet were less inclined to raid the English and were quicker to come to agreement with them. The Maliseet were the main signatories of the 1713 Treaty of Portsmouth, New Hampshire, the first British treaty involving Canadian Natives. As Dickason states, this treaty "broke new ground by adding that Amerindians were not to be molested in the territories where they lived, and they were to enjoy free liberty for Hunting, Fishing and Fowling, and all other their 'Lawful Liberties & Privileges'" (Dickason 1992:178).

A well-known Maliseet story tells us something about the poor treatment the Maliseet sometimes received in nineteenth-century New Brunswick. The story takes place around 1840. A young Maliseet man named **Pierre Lola** went to buy a ticket on the stagecoach from Fredericton to Woodstock, a distance of some 100 kilometres. He was refused because he was Native. Angry, he vowed to beat the stagecoach to its destination. They both started at eight o'clock in the morning. Lola led all the way through the rugged dirt roads, eventually winning the race by a narrow margin, a moral victory.

In 1612, Father Pierre Biard reckoned there were fewer than 1000 Etchemin. Today there are about 1200 speakers of the Maliseet language in Canada and maybe 300 more in the United States (Morrison and Wilson 1995:29).

The Western Abenaki

"**Abenaki**" is a general word of reference to different peoples living traditionally in what is now New England. It also refers to a confederacy that once linked the Mi'kmaq, Maliseet, Passamaquoddy, and Penobscot. The word is derived from **Aben-**, meaning "white or light," referring to morning and the east, and **-aki**, meaning "earth" or "land" (Hodge 1971:1). Canadian Abenaki are mostly descendants of people who came from the river valley area of the Connecticut River, which covers parts of New Hampshire, Massachusetts, and Connecticut. Particularly important in the development of the Canadian communities were the **Sokoki**, whose name (s. Ozokwaki, pl. Ozokwakiak), means "the ones who broke up, broke away" (Day 1978:159), perhaps referring to a historic event when one Abenaki group departed from the others.

The Sokoki and the French first came into contact in the 1640s through the conflict the Sokoki had with the Montagnais and Algonquin allies of the French. Gradually, the Sokoki began to ally themselves with the French against their common Iroquois and English enemies. As they did so, they moved closer to French territory, coming down the St. François River to its mouth, across the St. Lawrence from Trois-Rivières. A mission was established there in 1700. That community became known as Saint-François-de-Sales in French and Odanak in Abenaki. Members of the Odanak community would participate in virtually every French military move of the late seventeenth and eighteenth century, but would do so as allies with a sense of their own independence.

Abenaki opposition to English incursion on their land can be seen in the following statement from **Jérôme Atecouando** ("Deer spirit-power"), a leader at Odanak. In 1752, he challenged the authority of the British to survey Abenaki lands without their permission: "We forbid you very expressly to kill a single beaver or to take a single stick of wood on the lands we live on. If you want wood, we will sell it to you, but you shall not have it without our permission" (Dickason 1992:120).

Culturally, the Abenaki were similar to the Mi'kmaq and the Maliseet, but their more southerly residence resulted in some differences. They grew corn, beans, and squash and harvested the nuts of the butternut and chestnut trees. They were patrilineal, as were their northern cousins, but differed in having the more southerly traits of totemic clans (the turtle, bear, beaver, otter, and partridge clans existed at Odanak in 1736) and a clear distinction between peace and war leaders.

The pre-contact population of the Western Abenaki was at least 5000; the total Abenaki population was probably more than double that. In 2006, their population was about 2000, with about 90 percent affiliated with Odanak. In 1999, only one speaker of Abenaki remained in Canada, Cécile Wawanolet. Her work has contributed a great deal to the preservation and understanding of her language.

Box 6-2 introduces an Abenaki filmmaker whose films have examined events at Restigouche, Oka, and Kanehsatake.

The Delaware

At the time of first contact, the Delaware were located in the lands drained by the Delaware River, its tributaries, and the lower Hudson River. This put them in the area of what is now Pennsylvania, New Jersey, Delaware, and southeastern New York. At that time, there were about 40 Delaware village bands, with a total population of 8000 to 12,000. Linguistically, they formed three groups: the Munsee to the north and east, the northern Unami or Unalachtigo, and the southern Unami.

Box 6-2   Alanis Obomsawin

Alanis Obomsawin is a documentary filmmaker who has produced films through the National Film Board that have permitted Aboriginal views to be seen and Aboriginal voices to speak. She was born in Abenaki territory in New Hampshire, but was raised at Odanak until she was nine years old. During the 1980s, she made three powerful documentaries: *Incident at Restigouche* (1984), about a large scale Quebec police raid on a Mi'kmaq reserve to stop the people from fishing; *Richard Cardinal: Cry from a Diary of a Métis Child* (1986), which examined the suicide of an Aboriginal adolescent; and *No Address* (1988). In the 1990s she produced four films about the Oka Conflict: *Kanehsatake: 270 Years of Resistance* (1993), an overview of the conflict; *My Name Is Kahentiiosta* (1995) about a young Kahnawake Mohawk woman arrested during the standoff; *Spudwrench—Kahnawake Man* (1997), another biographical film; and *Rocks at Whiskey Trench* (2000), about a particularly nasty incident during the conflict. More recently, she has produced *Is the Crown at War with Us* (2002), about the clash over lobster fishing between the federal government and the Mi'kmaq community of Esgenoopetitj, or Burnt Church.

Delaware is not their name for themselves, but is a word derived from the name of a baron who was the governor of Virginia. They came to prefer the term **Lenape**, "real people," -**len**- meaning "ordinary, real, original" and -**ape**- meaning "man." Sometimes -**len**- is added again, giving the name **Lenni-Lenape**.

The Delaware were similar to the Iroquoians of the Eastern Woodlands. Corn was the staple food, with deer the most important game animal. As with the Iroquoians, the lineages seem to have been determined matrilineally. One lineage supplied the chiefs of the village, with a separation between war and peace chiefs, like the Iroquois. From at least 1750 on, there is evidence for a three-phratry (kinship) system similar to that of the Iroquoians, with three groupings of clans labelled as Turtle, Turkey, and Wolf.

The Delaware were forced to move west. By the mid-eighteenth century, they were in Ohio. Today, Delaware living in the United States have communities in Kansas, Wisconsin, and Oklahoma.

Some Munsee were influenced by Moravian missionaries to convert and form the Christian Delaware community of Gnadenhütten. Their leader was **Glickhican**, who had fought against the English but who became a Christian at about age 50 in 1769, baptized with the name Isaac in 1770. On April 13, 1773, he said:

> You appear to dread Glickhican, as formerly known to you. Yes, there was a time when I would have scorned to have been assailed in the manner you now meditate; but I am no more Glickhican, I am Isaac now, a believer in the true and living God, for whose sake I am willing to suffer anything—even death. (Curnoe 1996:36)

His statement was prophetic. On March 8, 1782, Isaac, his wife, 28 other men, 26 other women, and 34 children of the peaceful community of Gnadenhütten were murdered by Pennsylvania militia who falsely accused them of siding with the British.

Some of the survivors of this massacre went to live by the Thames River in what is now southwestern Ontario, founding the village of Moraviantown in 1792. This community would prosper until October 5, 1813, when it was burned and looted by the American army after the defeat, nearby, of the Native forces under the great Shawnee leader **Tecumseh** ("Across the Lake"). Tecumseh had been abandoned by the British forces under Major-General Henry Proctor.

Gradually, three Delaware communities developed in Ontario. These communities would be Moraviantown (or Moravian of the Thames), Munceytown (or Munceys of the Thames), and another group invited to live with the Six Nations by the Cayuga. The registered population of the first two communities in April 2006 was 1612. Their language today is severely under threat. In the introduction to his excellent dictionary of Munsee Delaware, John O'Meara writes:

> There may be no more than five or ten speakers of Ontario Delaware, as well as perhaps 10 or 15 individuals who understand Delaware to varying degrees. Most speakers known to me are in their seventies or eighties. (O'Meara 1996:vii)

THE IROQUOIANS

Iroquoian refers to a family of languages that at the time of contact were spoken along the eastern coast of the United States and into New York State. In Canada, speakers of these

Box 6-3	Iroquoian Placenames	
Word	**Language**	**Meaning**
Canada	St. Lawrence/Laurentian Iroquoians	village, community
Niagara	Neutral	neck
Ontario	Huron/Wendat	it is a large lake
Toronto	Mohawk	poles in water

languages lived along the St. Lawrence and in southern Ontario. All of those languages spoken in Canada are now dead. This includes what is called **St. Lawrence** or **Laurentian Iroquoians**, which was spoken by the people or peoples that Jacques Cartier encountered along the St. Lawrence in the 1530s. Ironically, these people gave us the word "**Canada**," meaning "village" or "community." The irony continues in that another one of those languages, Huron, gave us the name "**Ontario**," meaning "large lake," for the province that was their ancestral home but is more their symbolic home now. Box 6-3 shows other Iroquoian-derived placenames.

In addition to language, Iroquoians shared a corn-based agriculture, resulting in relatively permanent communities with populations up to 2500 in a matrilineal clan system typically comprised of eight clans (the Mohawk and Oneida have only three), and political mechanisms linking tribes in alliances or federations. The best-known example of such federations is the Iroquois Confederacy.

The Huron/Wendat

When the French Jesuit missionaries came to live with the **Wendat** people that they named **Huron** (see Box 6-4) during the 1630s, the Wendat was a five-member confederacy numbering between 20,000 and 30,000: the **Hatinniawenten** ("they are of bear country" or Bear); the **Hatingeennonniahak** ("they made or used to make fishing net cords" or Cord); the **Arendayeronnon** ("people at the rock" or Rock); the **Ataronchronnon** ("people in the clay or swamp" or Bog); and the **Atahontayenrat** ("one has two white ears" or Deer).

To the west of them were the **Etionnontateronnon**, "people at the mountain," a grouping of at least two tribes. The French called them **Petun** as they were vital intermediaries through whom the Huron obtained tobacco grown further south. The Petun might have numbered somewhere between 6200 to possibly as many as 10,000 during the 1620s. To the southwest of the Petun and Huron, from the western end of Lake Ontario to Niagara, lived a related people that the French referred to as the **Neutral**, because they appeared to be neutral in the conflict between the Huron and the Iroquois.

During the 1640s, the Huron lost most of their battles against the Iroquois, who were raiding them to seek revenge, to boost their numbers depleted by disease and war, and to gain a better position in the European trade. By the 1650s, the Huron, Petun, and Neutral had been driven out of their home territory.

After the Dispersal: The Wendat Tribes Follow Different Paths

The Wendat story does not end there, but follows three different plotlines. One led to joining the Iroquois. The Deer, along with the remnants of Neutral, joined the Seneca and formed a separate community in Seneca territory. During the 1650s, the Huron, who had moved close to the French settlements, were faced with some tough choices. The Mohawk and the Onondaga were competing with each other to get the Huron to join with them. Both had lost many people to European disease and to war. The Huron believed that the French were unable to protect them, particularly in 1656 when the Mohawk successfully attacked the Huron community at Isle d'Orleans, half way across the St. Lawrence from Quebec. The Wendat separated and moved into different regions. But their story continued, as Box 6-4 shows.

The Formation of the Wyandot

One group of Wendat people, primarily Petun, but including some Huron and possibly some Neutral, came together in the 1650s to form a people who came to be known as the **Wyandot**, from a mispronunciation of "Wendat." The Wyandot counterpart of the Huron title Tsawenhohi was **Sastaretsi**, the name of their leading chief from at least the 1650s until the nineteenth century. The post-dispersal history of the Wyandot has been one of periodic movement to far-flung places, moving in the seventeenth century throughout the Great Lakes, settling in around Windsor/Detroit in 1701, and gradually extending into Ohio. In the nineteenth century, they were forced to move west, first to Kansas and then to Oklahoma. Communities of Wyandot now live in these two states.

Box 6-4   The Homecoming

Late in August 1999, four groups of Wendat, coming from Quebec, Michigan, Kansas, and Oklahoma, returned home after 350 years. It was the first time the various groups had gotten together over that period of time. Their leaders had worked together to come up with a declaration of the reformation of the Wendat Confederacy.

According to tradition, their ancestors returned with them. In 1636, the Huron of the Bear tribe held a large Feast of the Dead. During this feast, more than 500 people who had died over the last 10 years or so were reburied together, in a powerful statement of the unity of the people: together as one in death as in life. In the mid-twentieth century, archaeologists interested in studying the Huron dug these individuals up. A good number of scientific publications came from that study. At the homecoming of the Wendat peoples, these remains of the ancestors were returned to the ground.

The Huron that remained with the French moved into their current home community of Lorette or Wendake ("at the Wendat") near Quebec City in 1697. From 1685 to 1844, their head chief would bear the name of **Tsawenhohi** ("Osprey"), with a brief hiatus in the mid-eighteenth century. A thriving community exists at Lorette today, contrary to the too commonly held belief that the Huron are "extinct." Their registered population in April 2006 was 3001.

THE IROQUOIS CONFEDERACY

In Chapter 1, we saw how the story of the formation of the people known usually as the Iroquois combines historical events and the principles by which an alliance was formed. The combination of the two is known as the Great Law of Peace (in Mohawk, **Gayanerengo:wa**, the Great Good). The resulting alliance or federation became known to the people by a name that means either "they build a house" or "they extend a house." Sometimes the people refer to themselves as **Ongwehon:we**, which, loosely translated, means "humans who are human."

As already discussed, the political system created involved 50 chiefs referred to in English as **sachems**. Each of the sachems was more or less hereditary, coming from the best qualified matrilineage in a particular clan. The holder of the position could lose his position if he were deemed to be acting for his own interests instead of those of his people. The woman who was the clan matron would divest him of the position, "de-horning" him, as the expression goes.

Not all leadership was held by the sachems, however. There were also **Pine Tree chiefs**, people of ability but not of a chiefly lineage, who rose to prominence because of what they had achieved.

The Mohawk

In the seventeenth century, the Mohawk had three principal communities of over 1000 people, plus at least several other villages. Mohawk is not their traditional name for themselves. Their own name is **Ganyen'geha:ga'**, meaning "people of Ganyen'ge," the latter usually translated as "At the Flint," a term for what once was their principal village. It is probable that each of the three clans of the Mohawk—the Bear, the Turtle, and the Wolf—dominated in each Mohawk community. Box 6-5 defines some key Native terms.

Box 6-5   Key Native Terms

Akwesasne: "Where the Partridge Drums," Mohawk community located at the connecting points of New York, Ontario, and Quebec.

Caughnawaga: "At the Rapids," a Mohawk community near Montreal.

Etionnontateronnon: "People at the mountain," the Petun or Tobacco nation.

Gaiwi:yoh: "It is a good, great, or beautiful matter," the name for the teachings that sprang from the visions of Handsome Lake.

Gayanerengo:wa: "It is a great good," the Great Law of Peace, the combination (Mohawk) history and set of teachings that brought the Iroquois together.

Kanehsatake: The name for the Mohawk community associated with Oka.

Oka: An Algonquin word meaning "walleye" or "pickerel."

Ongwehon:we: Loosely translated means "humans who are human," and refers to members of the Iroquois Confederacy.

Sokoki: From Ozokwaki (pl. Ozokwakiak), "the ones who broke up, broke away," the main group making up the Abenaki of Canada.

Wahta: "Maple," name for Mohawk community near Georgian Bay.

As the easternmost member of the confederacy, the Mohawk were first to fight the French. First blood went to the newcomers. In 1609, Samuel de Champlain decided to strengthen the French connection with their new allies, the Montagnais, Algonquin, and Huron, by joining in a raid on the Mohawk. Because these Native nations had helped the French, they then requested military assistance in return. In July, the combined forces attacked deep in Mohawk country and bolstered by the surprising effects of the French guns, they killed 50 Mohawk warriors and took 10 to 12 prisoners.

Thus began a smouldering antagonism that would flare up periodically through the seventeenth century, to be revived in nationalistic French history texts of the nineteenth and early twentieth centuries, and then again by ethnocentric elements in the Quebec media in the 1990s.

Some of the conflict occurred at mission sites. In the 1660s, French Jesuits founded **Caughnawaga** (Kahnawake, "At the Rapids"), a Native mission near Montreal. By 1673, there were possibly more Mohawks there than in the more independent villages in New York. From Caughnawaga came **Kateri Tekakwitha**, a Mohawk/Algonquin who died young but after her death became a heroine to Native and French Christians of New France through miraculous cures that were attributed to her spiritual intercession. She was beatified in 1980. In 2012, she was made the first Native saint. Today, her name is borne by a Native-Catholic movement.

Sometime around the mid-eighteenth century, along the border between Ontario, Quebec, and New York, the mission community of St. Regis or **Akwesasne** ("Where the Partridge Drums") was formed from part of the Caughnawaga community.

The Oka crisis of the 1990s had its roots in these missions. Early in the eighteenth century the Christian Mohawk community of **Oka** (Algonquin for "walleye" or "pickerel") or **Kanehsatake** (Mohawk, probably meaning "there is plenty of sand"), was founded by Sulpician missionaries, again in the Montreal area. The French king promised the land to the Mohawk. However, unknown to the Mohawk at the time, the powerful Sulpicians pulled some strings so that the land was given to them instead. For more than two centuries the Mohawk unsuccessfully appealed to French and British governments for basic rights to the land. They were even denied the right to cut firewood without Sulpician permission. Some Mohawk left for Ontario to form the **Wahta** ("Maple") community in 1881, in part because of the tension with the controlling Sulpicians, in part because the Ontario government made them an offer that would eventually prove better on paper than in reality. The Sulpicians left Oka early in the twentieth century, leaving the powder keg that would explode in Oka in 1990.

The Mohawks also experienced conflict during the American Revolution. During this time, a Mohawk named **Thayendanega** ("He sets two sticks," i.e., signifying bets, side by side), a Pine Tree Chief also known as **Joseph Brant,** rose to prominence. He also set side by side his loyalties to the British and to the Mohawk. While he respected the British and their religion, siding with them militarily and translating the gospel of St. Mark and the Book of Common Prayer into Mohawk, he also demanded that the British be true and faithful allies. At the end of the American Revolution, Thayendanega addressed British General Haldimand, requesting that the Native nations that had put their lives at risk in their ancestral homeland by their allegiance to the British not be abandoned. He said that he had been sent on behalf of all the Native allies of the King:

> . . . to know whether they are included in this treaty with the Americans as faithful allies should be, or not? and whether those lands which the great being above has pointed out for

our ancestors & their descendants, and placed them there from the beginning, and where the bones of our forefathers are laid is secured to them? or whether the blood of their grandchildren is to be mingled with their bones, thro' the means of our allies for whom we have often so freely bled? (Kelsay 1984:43)

In part as a response to these demands, land was purchased from the Mississauga in southwestern Ontario to be set aside for the Iroquois and those who wanted to come north with them. In 1785, that community had 464 Mohawk, 381 Cayuga, 245 Onondaga, 231 Delaware, 162 Oneida, 129 Tuscarora, 78 Seneca, 74 of the Siouan group, Tutelo, and the rest in smaller numbers of both Siouans and Algonquians. From some of the land later lost by the people, the city of Brantford in Ontario was formed, named after Joseph Brant.

At the same time, another group of Mohawks, following **John Deserontyon**, founded a community by the Bay of Quinte, at the eastern end of Lake Ontario. It is generally known today as Tyendinaga, after Joseph Brant's Mohawk name.

Today, there are reputedly 2000 Mohawk speakers in Canada, making it the strongest Iroquoian language in this country, with another 1000 in the United States. The Canadian Mohawk population is about 30,000.

The Oneida

Traditional western neighbours of the Mohawk, speaking a closely related language, are the Oneida. The name comes from **Onenyode'a:ga**, "people of the standing stone," referring both to the name of their principal historical village and to a particular rock said to be near its location. A stone returned to the Oneida community in New York in 1974 is said to have been the original standing stone.

The Oneida were smaller in number than the other Iroquois nations, with only one major community. This being the case, they had to replenish losses from war and disease from other peoples. The *Jesuit Relations* of the mid-1640s reported that Mohawk men had joined the Oneida to make up for warrior losses resulting from their fighting with the Huron and Algonquin (JR27:297 and JR28:281). Early in the eighteenth century, the Oneida generously gave the Tuscarora land on which to settle and invited various Eastern Algonquian groups to join them in the 1780s.

Originally neutral in the American Revolution, owing to the influence of Presbyterian minister Samuel Kirkland and the wishes of the young warriors, who opposed the sachems in this matter, most Oneida eventually joined the conflict and sided with the Americans. Some even participated in the 1779 American attacks against Onondaga, Cayuga, and Seneca communities. They would discover that loyalty to the Americans would not be rewarded. While the federal government made promises of land, New York worked to divest them of that land. Most of them were forced to leave the state that they had defended, the majority going west to Wisconsin. Some headed for Canada, as members of the Six Nations community. Four hundred and ten others purchased land near London, Ontario, and from 1840 to 1845 moved into a separate settlement.

Today, there are approximately 200 speakers of Oneida in Canada and fewer than 50 in the United States. The Oneida population, combining the people at Six Nations and of the Oneida Nation of the Thames, is around 6800.

The Onondaga

The name "Onondaga" comes from **Ononda'ge:ga**, "people of onon:da'ge," or "at the hill," their principal community, one of two reported during the seventeenth century. The Onondaga are also called the "Name Bearers" and "Fire-Keepers" in council, showing their significance in the confederacy. Today, between Six Nations in Canada and their community in New York, there are fewer than 100 speakers of Onondaga. The registered Onondaga population at Six Nations in April 2006 was 1198.

The Cayuga

The Cayuga had three principal villages during the seventeenth century, one of which gave them their name, **Gayohgho:non**, "people of Oiogouen." The meaning of the village name is unclear. Today, they have no community of their own. They live with the Seneca in New York and Oklahoma, with the Oneida in Wisconsin, and with the others of the Six Nations in Ontario. Currently, Cayuga is the second-strongest Iroquoian language in Canada, with 360 speakers here and 10 in the United States. The registered Cayuga population at Six Nations in April 2006 was 6179.

The Seneca

The Seneca were the largest Iroquois nation during the seventeenth century, with two main communities, one east, one west, each having several satellite villages. In 1665, the French were calculating the warrior strength of their Iroquois enemies. The Seneca were recorded as having 1200 warriors, the Mohawk between 300 and 400, the Cayuga and Onondaga 300, and the Oneida 140 (Tooker 1978a:421). Warriors of this period generally made up between 25 percent and 35 percent of the population. They enhanced their numbers through a community made up of the Deer tribe of the Huron, the Neutral, Susquehannock, and others who were Seneca by adoption.

The term "Seneca" is somewhat mysterious, used in different versions during the seventeenth century to refer to several Iroquois groups. No meaning is known. Their traditional term for themselves is **Onondowa'ga'**, "people of the large hill." Perhaps at some point that referred to a physical feature near a significant community. They are referred to as Doorkeepers in council, as they were the westernmost nation. There were 842 registered Seneca at Six Nations in April 2006.

Despite American attacks on villages in 1779, most of the Seneca decided to stay in New York. As a result, the Seneca have the fewest numbers of the confederacy in Six Nations. But New York became a hard place to live in the years following the revolution. The Seneca were hard hit by alcoholism and other nasty effects of social disruption. But with the problem also came an answer. On June 15, 1799, a Seneca bearing the sachem name of **Sganyadai:yo**, "Handsome or Beautiful Lake" (1735–1815) (but who had done little to that point to add distinction to that name) had a vision, the first of three that would follow over the next year. The visions provided the **Gaiwi:yoh**, or "good message," which combined condemnation of alcohol, witchcraft, love medicine, abortion, adultery, and other social ills, while promoting traditional songs, dances, prayers, and European methods of farming and formal education.

Handsome Lake spread his message across Iroquois country until his death in 1815. But the message did not die with him. Others codified what they had heard so that there developed a strong oral tradition of the words of Handsome Lake, known as the Longhouse Religion. That tradition is still strong today.

The Tuscarora

There is no agreement as to what the name "Tuscarora" actually means. What is known is that they took a hard road to Canada. At the time of first contact, there were several thousand Tuscarora living in Virginia and North Carolina. During the seventeenth and early eighteenth centuries, their land was taken from them. Legal agreements about their territory were violated by incoming settlers and their governments. For years, the Tuscarora protested peacefully, but unsuccessfully. Finally, in 1711, they reached their breaking point and attacked a settler community, beginning what is known as the Tuscarora War. For the next two years, battles raged, until late March 1713, when they were soundly defeated. Several hundred Tuscarora were killed and 400 more were sold into slavery. One hundred and twenty-nine ended up going to the Six Nations reserve. There were 1929 registered Tuscarora in Six Nations in April 2006.

The survivors looked north for a safe refuge. The Oneida invited them to live in their territory, sponsoring them in 1722–23 to join the confederacy as the sixth nation. By 1771, they numbered about 1000. During the American Revolution, some followed the Oneida in siding with the Americans, while others took the opposite position.

Tuscarora today is the most threatened of the languages of the Iroquois. In the 1980s, there were seven speakers in Canada and only forty in New York in the United States. There are fewer speakers today. The following two boxes note important dates and individuals for this area.

Native Individuals 6-1

Jérôme Atecouando ("Deer Spirit Power"): An eighteenth-century Abenaki leader at Odanak.

Atsena ("Dish"): The chief of the Hatinniawenten or Bear tribe of the Huron, who in 1657 led his people in joining the Mohawk.

John Deserontyon: An eighteenth-century Mohawk who led a group of his people to live in a community at the eastern end of Lake Ontario.

Glickhican: A Munsee leader killed at Gnadenhütten in 1782.

Pierre Lola: A nineteenth-century Maliseet known for a legendary race he won against a stagecoach.

Andrew Meuse: A nineteenth-century Mi'kmaq saqmaw of the Bear River band.

Alanis Obomsawin: An Abenaki documentary film producer.

Paussamigh Pemmeenauweet (Louis Benjamin Peminout): A Mi'kmaq saqmaw who sent a petition to Queen Victoria in 1840.

Sastaretsi: The name of the traditional chief of the Wyandot.

(continued)

Native Individuals 6-1   *(continued)*

Sganyadai:yo ("Handsome or Beautiful Lake"): A Seneca sachem whose visions led to the development of the Gaiwi:oh, or Good Message.

Kateri Tekakwitha ("She Moves Things"): A seventeenth-century Mohawk/Algonquin who is the first native saint.

Tecumseh ("Across the Lake"): A Shawnee leader who led Native troops from a number of nations on the British side during the War of 1812.

Thayendanega ("He sets two sticks side by side") or Joseph Brant: A Mohawk who, during the American Revolution, led his people in fighting on the side of the British and later in their forced migration to southwestern Ontario.

Tsawenhohi ("Osprey"): The name of the traditional chief of the Huron of Lorette for almost every year from 1685 to 1844.

Cécile Wawanolet: The last speaker of Abenaki at Odanak.

Timeline 6-1

2500 B.C.: First construction of the Mnjikaning fish weir.

1450s: Possible date for the formation of the Iroquois Confederacy.

1650s: The dispersal of the Wendat peoples (Huron and Petun).

1700: The establishment of the Abenaki mission at Odanak.

1713: The Maliseet sign a treaty with the English.

1722–3: The Tuscarora are asked to join the Iroquois Confederacy.

1725: First treaty between the Mi'kmaq and the English.

1746: Around 4000 Mi'kmaq die from typhus spread from the French fleet.

1752: Second treaty between the Mi'kmaq and the English.

1782: About 90 Delaware of Gnadenhütten are killed.

1785: The formation of the Six Nations community in southwestern Ontario.

1799: Seneca Handsome Lake's first vision.

1924: Six Nations forced to have elected rather than hereditary government.

1990: The conflict at Oka.

1999: The homecoming of the Wendat.

KEY TERMS

Gaiwi:yoh (Seneca)

matrilineal

patrilineal

Pine Tree chiefs

sachem

saqmaw (Mi'kmaq)

weir

CONTENT QUESTIONS

1. What two linguistic groups belong to the Eastern Woodlands culture area, and what nations does each include?
2. Where were the three different paths taken by the Wendat tribes?
3. How were the Delaware culturally similar to the Eastern Iroquoians?
4. What is the difference between "Iroquois" and "Iroquoian"?
5. What situation initially set the context for the Oka crisis?

WEBLINKS

www.aboriginalcanada.gc.ca

The statistics used for band and tribe figures for 2006 come from a very useful federal government website entitled "Aboriginal Canada Portal." Upon entering the English version of the website, go to "First Nations, Inuit, Métis Communities" at the lower left, select the political jurisdiction (province or territory), click "Go," and then click "All Aboriginal Communities" at the top left. That gives you a list of band names, with web pages for some of the bands, and access to band statistics in most bands. Please see the copyright page for more information.

www.tolatsga.org/aben.html

This site provides an introduction to Abenaki history.

www.delawaretribeofindians.nsn.us

This page provides an introduction to Delaware history and culture, and includes a talking dictionary for the Lenape language.

http://mrc.uccb.ns.ca

Sponsored by the University of Cape Breton, the Mi'kmaq Resource Centre contains a lot of useful information concerning the Mi'kmaq.

www.oneida-nation.net/

This site deals with Oneida history and the history of the Iroquois generally.

www.wyandot.org

Co-sponsored by the Wyandot of Kansas and the University of Kansas, this site presents useful information concerning the Huron and Wyandot.

chapter seven

The Eastern Subarctic

OVERVIEW

The Eastern Subarctic is physically dominated by the Canadian Shield. This means, first of all, that there is a lot of hard rock scraped bare by glaciers. Scattered throughout are glacially dumped sands, clays, and gravels, resulting in the type of northern swampland known as **muskeg** (originally a Cree word), as well as rivers and lakes. Combined with the long winters and short summers, the Subarctic might seem a harsh place to live, but it provides ideal habitat for a number of animal species that supplied a good living for the people. These include caribou in the north, **moose** ("muus" in East Cree) further south, beaver, muskrat, and hare. Birds are also in abundance, including grouse, migrating waterfowl such as Canada geese and snow geese, and a variety of ducks. Also plentiful are fish such as trout, whitefish, sturgeon, burbot, and pike.

A few features separate the Eastern Subarctic from its western counterpart. First, the area has had a shorter period of occupation. The first significant occupation in the Subarctic began in the west with the "Shield culture" archaeological complex about 8000 years ago, gradually moving east as the glaciers melted away (Wright 1995:261). Not until between about 5000 and 4000 years ago did Shield culture make its way to the Hudson Bay Lowlands of Ontario and Quebec and to Labrador.

Second, the languages spoken in the Eastern Subarctic are **Algonquian** (see Box 7-1), in contrast to the Athapaskan languages of the Western Subarctic. The languages and associated peoples typical of the Eastern Subarctic are **Cree**, **Montagnais**, **Naskapi**, **Ojibwa**, **Attikamek**, and **Beothuk** (who died off in Newfoundland by 1829). But this list suggests more diversity than actually exists. Montagnais, Naskapi, and Attikamek can be considered dialects of Cree, and Ojibwe is a near relative of Cree.

	Similarities Between Eastern Subarctic Algonquian Languages			
Box 7-1				

Montagnais	East Cree	Swampy Cree	Ojibwe	English
amishkw	amiskw	amisk	amikk	beaver
chiyaashkw	chiyaashkw	kiyaask	kayaashk	gull
chinosheew	chinushew	kinoseew	kinooshe	pike
ooteenaw	utenaaw	ooteenaw	ooteenaw	village
nameekwosh	namekush	nameekos	nameekoss	lake trout

Getting It Right 7-1   Algonquin vs. Algonquian

It is very confusing to have the almost identical terms "Algonquin" (or "Algonkin") and **Algonquian** (or "Algonkian"') refer to two different groups. Perhaps it is useful to remember that the smallest word ("Algonquin") has the smallest scope of reference (i.e., to a single people) while the largest word ("Algonquian") has the largest scope of reference (i.e., to a language family).

As well, the Algonquians of the Eastern Subarctic had a much longer period of contact with Europeans than did the Athapaskans of the Western Subarctic. The Montagnais, Naskapi, and Beothuk encountered whalers, fishermen, and explorers from at least the 1500s onwards. The Montagnais and the easternmost of the Ojibwa dealt with the French during the 1600s, while the Cree by the shores of Hudson Bay and James Bay connected with the Hudson's Bay Company and the fur trade from 1670.

THE CREE

The name "Cree" is not their own term for themselves. First written as "**Kiristinon**" in 1640 (JR18:229), the word "Cree" comes from a French version of part of an Ojibwe name for a Cree band living south of James Bay. English writers shortened that to a word they could more readily pronounce. Prior to contact, the home of the Cree centred on James Bay and the southern part of Hudson Bay, as well as the area of the rivers that flow into those bays. Their numbers at that time have been estimated as between 15,000 and 20 000. After contact, this homeland extended both north and west, largely on account of the fur trade. Today, the Cree are the largest and most widespread Canadian Native group, living from northern Quebec to northern Alberta. In the 1996 census, 76,475 people listed Cree as one of their mother tongues, the greatest number for any Native language.

One way of subdividing the groups of Cree is by dialect. Outside the Eastern Subarctic there are the **Plains Cree** of the three Prairie provinces. Within the Eastern Subarctic there are the **Swampy Cree** of the western James Bay and Hudson Bay drainage systems.

Along with the Plains Cree, they make up most of the Cree speakers. Then there are the **Woods Cree** of northern Manitoba and Saskatchewan, the **Moose Cree** (southern end of James Bay), the **Attikamek** (south-central Quebec), and the **East Cree** (east of James Bay and Hudson Bay).

Be wary of reading too much into dialect groups. These groups were not separate "tribes" with one leader or a linked council of leaders. Traditionally, the Cree were organized into smaller units, with informal leadership based on respect, wisdom, and suggestion.

Box 7-2 below gives the origin of five Cree words you already know, while Box 7-3 profiles three books by well-known Canadian Cree leaders.

Beyond the nuclear family, two other groups were important: the hunting group and the **macroband**. The hunting group, sometimes called the **microband**, was made up of several linked families, consisting of 10 to 20 people. Microbands would space themselves out according to the availability of local resources, often being from 15 to 80 kilometres away from their neighbouring group. Their kinship pattern is termed **bilateral**, meaning that both the mother's and the father's families were of equal importance. This made for greater flexibility in forming the hunting group than if only one side were important. The group would be together from late August until early June of the next year.

From late spring through the summer, a number of these hunting groups would get together to form macrobands of perhaps 75 to 150 people, possibly more in some instances. While the "food" reason for getting together was usually to fish at places where

---

Box 7-2   Five Cree Words You Know

Saskatoon: means "big, wood berry," referring to the Saskatoon or serviceberry, an important resource for Prairie people

Saskatchewan: means "it flows fast," referring to the Saskatchewan River

moose: means "moose"

muskeg: means "swamp"

Winnipeg: refers to salty, silty, or muddy water

Box 7-3   The Cree in Politics

Over the last 30 years, Cree leaders have had a strong impact on the Canadian political scene. Three of those leaders have had books written about their political lives:

Billy Diamond:
Chief: The Fearless Vision of Billy Diamond, by Roy MacGregor, Toronto: Penguin Books, 1989

Elijah Harper:
Elijah: No Ordinary Hero, by Pauline Comeau, Vancouver: Douglas & McIntyre, 1993

Ovide Mercredi:
In the Rapids: Navigating the Future of First Nations, by Ovide Mercredi and Mary Ellen Turpel, Toronto: Penguin Books, 1993

large numbers of fish could be found, this time together served social needs as well. It was a time to share information, to renew old acquaintances, and to pursue romance.

THE INNU: MONTAGNAIS AND NASKAPI

The population of the **Innu** (Montagnais and Naskapi) at the time of early contact is difficult to determine. The French encountered only some of their bands, and disease early struck the southernmost Innu quite hard. Estimates of their number vary from 4000 to 10,000, with the latter figure probably being closer to an accurate reckoning. Their registered population in April 2006 was 17,571.

Montagnais

The **Montagnais** ("people of the mountain") received that name in French first from Samuel de Champlain. The term refers to the hilly country in which some of the bands lived. Their own name for themselves comes from a word (**Ilnu** for the southern Montagnais, **Innu** for the eastern Montagnais) meaning "human being, person." They differ from the Naskapi in several ways. They speak a different dialect. They live further south, with almost all of their communities existing along or near the north shore of the Gulf of St. Lawrence to the southern portion of the Quebec–Labrador peninsula. This means that they have a greater variety of wildlife for hunting, instead of being dependent as the Naskapi are on one animal (i.e., herds of caribou). This also means that they have a longer history of contact with Euro-Canadians, involving a longer and more intense participation in the fur trade. This contact has been almost exclusively with the French, while the Naskapi have dealt more with the English; therefore, currently, the Montagnais are more likely to speak French while the Naskapi are more likely to speak English. See Box 7-4 for more information on some of the Montagnais's strengths.

Naskapi

Naskapi is a name that first appeared in the *Jesuit Relation* of 1643 as "Ouachkapiouek" (JR24:154). There is no definitive translation for this word. It seems, however, that

Box 7-4	The Endurance of the Montagnais

Jesuit Father Paul Le Jeune said little that was positive about Native culture. Still, he admired the way that the Montagnais would patiently endure hardship: "[they] surpass us to such an extent, in this respect, that we ought to be ashamed" (JR6:233). When he agreed to winter with the Montagnais in 1633–34, they let him know that he would have to be strong to endure the occasional hardships of their lives. They warned him that:

We shall be sometimes two days, sometimes three, without eating, for lack of food; take courage Chihiné, let thy soul be strong to endure suffering and hardship; keep thyself from being sad, otherwise thou wilt be sick; see how we do not cease to laugh, although we have little to eat. (JR6: 233)

negative connotations have become associated with the name (see Speck 1935/1977:241), most likely coming from missionaries and traders who thought them "less civilized" than the Montagnais. The Naskapi, supplied with most of their needs by the caribou, tended to keep themselves apart from the products and influence of these non-Natives. During the nineteenth century, frustrated fur traders pressed the reluctant Naskapi to bring in furs. One trader, Donald Henderson, refused ammunition to the Innu living near his post in the 1840s, with the intent of forcing them to bring in furs. Being then dependent on guns for their hunting, they starved, with more than 100 deaths reported (Wadden 1996:31).

Their term for themselves is **Mushuau-Innu**, "barren ground people," so used because of their association with the homeland of the barrens caribou upon which they live. The herd they hunt today is the world's largest wild caribou herd, numbering more than half a million animals. Because of their reliance on the caribou, the Mushuau Innu were tradition-ally quite nomadic, following the travelling of the caribou. Innu Elder **Maniaten**, a woman who had grown up when the caribou hunt was still relatively free from outsider influence, told Marie Wadden, author of the award-winning book *Nitassinan*, that in the fall her fam-ily used to go first from Uashat (Sept-Îles) to Schefferville, 490 kilometres, then sometimes to Kuujjuasq (Fort Chimo) by Ungava Bay, 370 kilometres, then to **Utshimassit** (Davis Inlet), 500 kilometres, then finally 300 kilometres to Michikamau Lake. Maniaten spoke of how hard those trips were:

> We carried our canoes, supplies, and even put the children on our backs. Many times the babies would cry and Mother would stop, unload what she was carrying and breastfeed the child. The older children walked behind because they were slow. Mother would keep encouraging the children; she would say, "Keep it up, we're getting closer to the next lake." When we got to a lake or river we'd pile everything back in the canoe and paddle off. (Wadden 1996:48–49)

Naskapi nomadism has been a strike against them politically. Missionaries and gov-ernment officials have negatively referred to such land use as "primitive." In the courts, it has typically been treated as "non-use" of the land. But, in some senses, we should consider how many of us are nomads, too. Imagine that you travel 20 kilometres to work each day, for a total of 200 kilometres a week. That means that in one year alone (with two weeks of holidays in which you might travel even farther), your "nomadism" takes you 10,000 kilometres, about six times the distance travelled by Maniaten's family. The serious point to be made here is that nomadism can be an effective, long-term use of the land and should not be dismissed as ineffective or outmoded. The Naskapi led a good life with their nomadism, the most efficient use for their country ever devised.

THE OJIBWA/ANISHINABE

The Ojibwa live in three of the seven culture areas: Eastern Subarctic; Eastern Wood-lands; and Prairies. As their origins are in the Eastern Subarctic, they are presented in this chapter. The name "**Ojibwa**" (sometimes spelled Ojibway in Canada, Chippewa in the United States, or Ojibwe when referring to the language) was originally recorded in 1667 as "Outchibouec," the name of a band living near what is now Sault Ste. Marie. The literature usually refers to this term as a reference to the "puckering up" of their moc-casins. The term that almost all groups of the Ojibwa use to refer to themselves is some form of **(A)nish(i)nabe** (plural ending, -k). Prior to contact with Europeans, this word was probably used primarily to refer to "human beings." After contact it came to refer to "Natives," particularly those of a shared linguistic and cultural heritage.

During the seventeenth century, a number of bands lived near the north shores of Georgian Bay and Lake Superior. These bands would have been similar in nature though perhaps larger in size than the Cree macrobands. Three of the band names survived: Mississauga, Saulteaux, and Ojibwa. Mississauga later came to refer to the mixture of Georgian Bay bands that fought their way south during the last two decades of the seventeenth century to settle into southern Ontario. "Saulteaux" (pronounced "so-toe") is now used to refer to the combined bands that moved out west into the Prairies with the fur trade and with the European push into Ojibwa country. They will be discussed in Chapter 9. More than half of the Ojibwa in Canada live in Ontario, where more than 75 bands have a collective population of over 70,000.

Some English words deriving from Ojibwe are shown in Box 7-5.

Two closely related people should be mentioned here, as they speak dialects of Ojibwe and are generally considered part of the Ojibwa. At the time of first contact, the **Odawa** or **Ottawa** lived on Manitoulin Island (where they still live today) and the Bruce Peninsula. Since that time, they have been associated with the history of Oklahoma and Michigan, an association reflected in the fact that General Motors in Detroit named a car after a great Odawa leader, **Pontiac**.

At the time of contact, the **Algonquin** (or **Algonkin**), whose name is said to be derived from the Maliseet word "elakomkwik," meaning "they are relatives or allies," lived along the Ottawa River and by the rivers that feed into it. Currently, they live in eastern Ontario and western Quebec.

One further group that should be mentioned is the **Potawatomi.** Their language is very close to that of the Ojibwa. During the 1830s, the American government issued the Indian Removal Act to push Aboriginal people west from the eastern states. Many deaths resulted, primarily among the Cherokee (estimates run to 4000), who were forced to march some 1200 miles to Indian Territory (later called Oklahoma). To avoid removal, some Potawatomi groups entered Ontario in the extreme southwest, where they joined the Ojibwa in communities such as Walpole Island, Stoney Point and Kettle Point. Others took a more northerly route, going to Manitoulin Island and to other Ojibwa communities by the shores of Georgian Bay. Some of these left when the situation cooled down in the U.S., but most stayed and intermarried with the local people.

Some key organizational differences exist between the Cree and the Ojibwa. Primary among these is that clans, which are important to the Ojibwa, were unknown to the Cree. The word "**totem**" itself comes from the Ojibwa word for clan. The following is a

Box 7-5	Four Ojibwe Words You Know

chipmunk: from an Ojibwe word referring to squirrels

Mississauga: from an Ojibwe word meaning "large river mouth"

totem: from an Ojibwe word referring to clan

pecan: from an Ojibwe word meaning "nut"

contemporary interpretation of the nature of this tradition coming from Edward Benton-Banai, a respected Elder within the Midewewin, an organization involved with the revival of Ojibwa traditions. After identifying the seven original clans, he stated that each clan had a specific function to play for the people:

Crane and Loon Clans = chieftainship, leadership

Fish Clan = settling disputes, meditation, philosophy

Bear Clan = protecting the community, medicinal plants

Marten Clan = warriors, war strategists

Deer Clan = poets

Bird Clan = spiritual leaders (Benton-Banai 1988:75–77)

THE ATTIKAMEK

The Attikamek (also spelled Atikamekw) are difficult to track historically. Most books about Natives in Canada fail to mention them or only refer to them as existing in the seventeenth century. Since that time, in part because they were forced to move several times, much of their story has only sketchily been told. They also have a name problem: too many names. Outsiders, including anthropologists, often call them Cree. The name **Attikamek** (literally "caribou fish," signifying the whitefish) first appeared in 1635, referring to a group numbering about 550. From 1692 until 1972, they were generally called "Têtes de Boule" ("Roundheads"), which also refers to whitefish. That year, the people declared that they preferred "Attikamek." Today they live in three communities in south-central Quebec, east of the Algonquin, south of the Cree, and west of the Montagnais, the people to whom they are most similar and most closely tied. The three bands had a registered population of 6086 in April 2006.

Box 7-6 profiles a notable Attikamek woman, Judith Kawiasiketcht.

Box 7-6	Judith Kawiasiketcht: Attikamek Medicine Woman

Judith Kawiasiketcht ("She dries meat") was born on May 10, 1916. She was married at 15 and bore 18 children. Over the many years of her life, she learned the traditional medicines of her people. Her knowledge of plants would impress any botanist. Her son is apprenticing with her to learn those ways—not an easy process, as the following words from his mother show:

The first time I sent him to look for a medicinal plant for a woman who was sick, he returned with the wrong plant . . . So I told him to go back to the bush and bring me a sample of all the species of pine he saw. That's what he did and I showed him the one I needed. Then, he went back and found the right one. Now he knows. When I ask him to go find a plant, he brings me exactly the one I want (Niquay 1995/1996:8–9).

Native Individuals 7-1

Edward Benton-Banai: An Ojibwa Midewewin Elder.

Judith Kawiasiketcht: An Attikamek Elder and medicine woman.

Maniaten: A woman who is a Sheshatshit Innu Elder.

Pontiac (c. 1720–1769): A Detroit area Odawa war chief who was a leading figure in a pan-Indian resistance during the period from 1762 to 1764.

Timeline 7-1

1500s: First European contact with the Montagnais, Naskapi, and Beothuk.

1635: First recording of the term "Attikamek."

1640: First recording of the word "Kiristinon" to refer to the Cree.

1643: First recording of the word "Naskapi."

1667: First recording of the word "Outchibouec" to refer to the Ojibwa.

1670: Establishment of the Hudson's Bay Company in Cree territory.

1762–1764: The pan-Indian resistance movement typically associated with Pontiac, the Odawa leader.

1950s: Development of the iron mines in Innu country.

1972: The Attikamek reclaim their traditional name.

KEY TERMS

Algon(qu/k)ian
(A)nishinabe (Ojibwe)
bilateral

macroband
microband
totem (Ojibwe)

CONTENT QUESTIONS

1. In what three ways is the Eastern Subarctic cultural area different from the Western Subarctic?
2. What peoples are typically associated with the Eastern Subarctic?
3. How many different dialects of Cree are spoken across Canada?
4. Distinguish between the hunting group (microband) and the macroband.
5. How is the traditional sociopolitical structure of the Ojibwa different from that of the Cree?

WEBLINKS

www.gardenriver.org
This is a comprehensive site concerning the Ojibwa of the Garden River First Nation.

www.nation.mistissini.qc.ca
This is a good website for learning about the Cree of Northern Quebec.

www.innu.ca
The Innu Nation home page provides a guide to Innu history and culture, rights, self-government, community issues, and other concerns.

chapter eight

The Western Subarctic

OVERVIEW

The Western Subarctic cultural area is a region of short summers and long winters. It is a bare, glacially swept land with streaks of rivers and depressions of lakes and swamps. In the north are treeless barrens and "small sticks" coniferous forests of black spruce, and in the south are slender deciduous gatherings of willow, birch, and poplar. Despite how harsh this sounds, the Western Subarctic is rich in animal life, primarily with vast herds of caribou and an abundance of fish such as pickerel, char, and whitefish.

With the exception of the northern Cree, who moved into the area over the last few centuries, Western Subarctic peoples speak Athapaskan languages. The speakers of this family of languages live in Alaska, the Yukon, the Northwest Territories, and the northern part of the Prairie provinces, and in the southwestern part of the United States (the Apache and the Navaho people once lived in Canada). The word "**Atha(b/p)aska(n)**" comes from a Woods Cree word translated as "there are reeds here and there'" (Smith 1981:269), referring to the lake of that name.

The Athapaskan-speaking peoples to be discussed in this chapter are the Chipewyan, Yellowknife, Dogrib, Hare, Slavey, Sahtú, Mountain, Gwich'in, Hän, Upper Tanana, Tutchone, Tahltan, Tagish, Kaska, Beaver, and Sekani. Box 8-1 introduces one term that all these languages share.

Chipewyan

At contact, the Chipewyan were and still are the largest and most widespread of the Western Subarctic First Nations. The Chipewyan's population at that time would have been at least 3500 to 4000. Now there are more than 5000. Their name (not to be

Box 8-1	Dene

One characteristic shared by all Athapaskan-speaking people (north and south) is the use of the term "**Dene**," meaning "man, person, or Indian." Four of the First Nations discussed in this chapter have a version of the word in their name. These include:

Thlingcha-dinneh, "Dog side people" = Dogrib

K'ashogotine, "Big willow people" = Hare

Dené Thá = Slavey

Dunne-za = Beaver

confused with Chippewa or Ojibwa, discussed in Chapter 7) was derived from a Cree word, "**Chipwayanewok**," meaning "Pointed Skins," as first recorded in 1776. This is generally said to refer to the way the fronts and backs of their traditional poncho-like robes dangled down in points. Today, they often refer to themselves and their language as Denesuline.

The Chipewyan are typically termed in the literature as being "edge of the forest" people, living primarily in the transitional area between the barrens and the boreal forest. In the woods was their main threat, the **Ena** ("Enemy"), known to English-speakers as the Cree. Their early eighteenth-century battles made such impact on them that 200 years later stories were still told of heroes. One story told of the woman **Thanadelthur** ("Marten Shakes") (see Chapter 1, "Oral Traditions"), who connected these conflicts with the fur trade and with a supply of guns, while other stories told of heroes such as **Dza-ghal-iaze** ("Lower Leg Trembles Little"), who led the Chipewyan to victories against the Cree. Today, Cree and Chipewyan live together in several First Nations communities without the prejudices of the past.

By the middle of the eighteenth century, the Chipewyan had established a relatively independent position in the fur trade. Much to the disappointment of the English traders, they traded almost exclusively for necessities and not for expensive frills. In the 1740s, James Isham characterized them as preferring "[d]ressing very plaine; using their former Custom's, Seldom trading [for] any finery for Such usses But what they traffick for is Chiefly necessary's for Life, such as powdr, shott Guns &c" (Abel 1993:61).

Chipewyan who became involved in the fur trade were more often middlemen than trappers, sometimes making profits that frustrated both their European and Native partners. In 1771, for example, they were recorded as charging their fellow Dene 60 marten skins for a brass kettle weighing about a kilogram, roughly 10 times what they had paid for it at the post at Churchill.

But contact with the trade also brought them into contact with European diseases, primarily smallpox. According to explorer/trader Samuel Hearne, smallpox killed up to about 90 percent of the Chipewyan in 1781. While he was probably speaking only about the eastern bands of the Chipewyan, the effects on the whole group would still have been devastating.

They recovered well, and today Chipewyan communities are thriving in the northern parts of all three Prairie provinces as well as in the Northwest Territories. In April 2006, their communities had a registered population of 13,602, with an undetermined number more in the two mixed Cree and Chipewyan communities in Alberta.

Yellowknife

The Yellowknife were named after the copper that they used for knives, awls, lance tips, axe heads, arrowheads, ice chisels, beads, bracelets, needles, necklaces, and even dishes. They tried to establish a middleman role in the fur trade similar to that of their culturally close but more powerful Chipewyan neighbours. Some minor battles ensued (see the next section on the Dogrib). Three settlements in the Northwest Territories today are part of the Yellowknife First Nation, which had a registered population of 1231 in April 2006. Their language, Weledeh, can be considered a dialect of Dogrib, with strong Chipewyan influences.

Box 8-2 profiles Akaitcho, a historical Yellowknife leader.

Dogrib

The name of this people was first written in 1678 as "Alim8spigoiak"—(Moose Cree for "dog side"). In 1829, Sir John Franklin recorded their name in their own language as **"Thlingcha-dinneh,"** "Dog side people." The name comes from a traditional Dene story. The Moose Cree term seems originally to have been preferred generally to the Dene, as was the English translation, but the Dene term gradually became permanently attached to the Dogrib (see Chapter 1, "Oral Traditions").

The traditional territory of the Dogrib is between the two largest bodies of water in the Northwest Territories: Great Slave Lake and Great Bear Lake. To the west, their neighbours are the Hare in the north and the Slavey in the south. Linguistically they are all very close. As late as the 1970s, Dogrib Elders could still understand those languages, but with

---

Box 8-2	Akaitcho

The best known figure in Yellowknife history is their nineteenth-century leader Akaitcho ("Big Foot"). His actions and views were frequently recorded in John Franklin's narrative of his polar exploration of 1819–22. Akaitcho accompanied Franklin on part of the journey. After Akaitcho left, the explorer and his men suffered from lack of food, forced to eat lichen for days at a time. On December 14, 1821, when Franklin and Akaitcho reunited, the Yellowknife leader provided Franklin and his men with much-needed food. Even though equally vital supplies that Franklin had promised Akaitcho had not arrived, Akaitcho made the following speech:

The world goes badly. . . all are poor; you are poor, the traders appear to be poor, I and my party are poor, likewise; and since the goods have not come in, we cannot have them. I do not regret having supplied you with provisions, for a Copper Indian can never permit white men to suffer from want of food on his lands, without flying to their aid. I trust, however, that we shall, as you say, receive what is due next autumn; and at all events," he added, in a tone of good-humour, "it is the first time that the white people have been indebted to the Copper Indians." (Franklin 2005:417) some difficulty. To the east were the Yellowknife, who entered into deadly conflict with the Dogrib. There had traditionally been some problems between the two people, but the disruption caused by the fur trade upped the stakes of their conflict.

The intensified battle between Dogrib and Yellowknife began during the 1780s but became particularly violent during the 1820s. Stories about the fighting differ, but it seems that the Yellowknife, with their earlier contact with the fur trade, were the primary aggressors, led by the indomitable Akaitcho. The kidnapping of women, a common element in traditional Dene stories, is prominent in the telling of the story of the struggle. A Dogrib leader, **Kanoobaw**, complained in 1824 that:

> We suffered our Wives, our Daughters and our Mothers to be taken from us, with their Children. Our Furs also, this we considered of little importance, they were only skins of Animals, but even our Nets upon which our existence depended, were likewise taken from us, and frequently our Axes, Guns or whatever was most useful or necessary to our Maintenance. (Abel 1993:91)

One reason given for the intensification of the fighting was that a Yellowknife man, **Tausigouai**, had allegedly kidnapped four Dogrib women, three of whom he then killed. The fourth woman slit his throat because she feared for her life.

Although there was killing on both sides, it seems that the Dogrib fared the worst until 1823. During that year, the Dogrib achieved their first significant victory, wiping out the encampment led by a Yellowknife named Longlegs. Thirty-four Yellowknife died.

Peace came about a few years later, largely through the oratorical force and spiritual strength of **Edzo**, who grew into a legendary figure in the history of the Dogrib. Stories differ as to how he brought about peace between his people and the Yellowknife. According to Kerry Abel, "there is agreement that Edzo's sister had married a man named Kaw-tay-whee who was living with Akaitcho's band, and through this connection a lasting peace was arranged" (Abel 1993:95). The peace that Edzo brought about was permanent, and his name lives on in Dogrib stories, and in the community name Rae-Edzo.

In the twentieth century, Dogrib leaders were prominent in the struggle for Native self-government. In 1969, **James Wah-Shee** became the first president of the influential Indian Brotherhood of the Northwest Territories. In 1971, the Dogrib became the first Dene to run their own school. They named it Chief Jimmy Bruneau Elementary School, after the man who led the fight in the mid-twentieth century to maintain traplines on Dogrib terms, not as dictated by the federal government. **George Erasmus** was president of the politically innovative Dene Nation from 1976 to 1983, eventually becoming the Chief of the Assembly of First Nations from 1985 to 1991. He received the Order of Canada in 1987.

The pre-contact population of the Dogrib was probably over 1200, but that number was later reduced, primarily by disease, to around 750 by the 1930s. During the last few generations, the number of Dogrib has slowly been growing, reaching 1700 by 1970 and extending beyond 1900 by 1986. In April 2006, there was a registered population of 3647.

Hare

The Hare live north and northwest of Great Bear Lake, along the Mackenzie River to the west. Half of their traditional territory is north of the Arctic Circle. At first contact, they probably numbered between 700 and 800. In April 2006, their registered population in their two communities of Fort Good Hope and Colville Lake or "Behdzi Ahda" First

Nation was 966. The Hare were first recorded as being the "Peaux de Lièvre" ("hare skins") by the French during the late eighteenth century. During the nineteenth century, they were typically referred to by some version of the Athapaskan term used by Sir John Franklin in 1824, **Kawchodinneh** (literally meaning "hare-big-people"), signifying "Arctic Hare people." Their main contemporary term for themselves is **K'ashogotine** (literally meaning "willow-big-people [of]"), signifying "Big willow people." It is so close to the other term that it is possible it started as a pun or a shaman's disguised term.

The name "Hare" stems from the people's practice of using hare skins cut in long spiralling strips, from which were woven capes, shirts, blankets, even tents, and from their general dependence on hares for food. This would have made for a precarious existence, since the population of the snowshoe hare, their main source of food, crashes every seven to ten years. In the more northerly barrens area, there were also moose, caribou, and musk ox in the willow, poplar, and birch-forested areas near the Mackenzie River and Great Bear Lake, and fish such as whitefish and trout in these bodies of water. However, there were still times during the nineteenth century (and as recently as 1920) that these resources could not compensate for the loss of the hares, and some people died of starvation.

An excerpt in Box 8-3 illustrates the oratorical skills of the Hare leader, Frank T'Seleie.

The Hare language is close to that of their southern neighbours, the Slavey and Dogrib. The Hare were unusual among the Dene in that they got along with their Inuit neighbours to the north.

Fort Good Hope, by the Mackenzie River, was a Northwest Company (later Hudson's Bay Company) post formed in 1806, which later became the largest Hare community. The fur trade would also have an occasionally lethal effect. In 1825–26, it brought fatal disease to the Hare. In 1835 and in 1841, some Hare also died fighting with Métis traders.

They had other bouts with disease during the twentieth century. In 1928, death came with cholera and influenza. In the 1930s, tuberculosis hit epidemic proportions. By the early 1960s, when the disease had been brought under control, more than half of the Hare adults had been hospitalized at some time.

Box 8-3   Frank T'Seleie's Speech

Oratorical skills have long been prized among the Hare. One good example comes from a speech made by **Frank T'Seleie**, chief at Fort Good Hope during the Mackenzie Valley Pipeline Inquiry.

On August 5, 1975, addressing the president of a gas company wanting to put a pipeline through the country of his people, he said:

. . . there is a life and death struggle going on between us, between you and me. Somehow in your carpeted board-rooms, in your panelled office, you are plotting to take away from me the very centre of my existence. You are stealing my soul. Deep in the glass and concrete of your world you are stealing my soul, my spirit. By scheming to torture my land you are torturing me. By plotting to invade my land you are invading me. If you ever dig a trench through my land, you are cutting through me. . . . (Watkins 1977:16)

Slave(y) or Dené Thá

The Slave(y) received that name because of a historic situation. The Cree who lived east and south of them had obtained weapons in the fur trade by the eighteenth century. This gave the Cree a weapons advantage over the Slavey, who were not so armed. The Slavey were driven further west towards the Mackenzie River from their traditional homes by Great Slave Lake, their namesake. The word "slave" is a somewhat misleading English translation of the Cree word "**Awokanak,**" which refers typically to a domesticated animal. While for a period of time Slavey were captured as prisoners by the Cree, and some were adopted into that people, it would be overstating the case to call them slaves. By the nineteenth century, the Slavey were part of the trade and were able to act independently, much to the chagrin of Chipewyan neighbours, who wished to control their access to trade goods. The name **Dené Thá** is now often used by the people to refer to themselves.

The Slavey lived by the Mackenzie River, and their diet accordingly consisted predominantly of fish, traditionally caught with nets or lines made of twisted willow bark, and with hooks made of bone, antler, wood, or birds' claws. As many as 200 people would gather together in a temporary community to catch fish. The Slavey also have long been involved in hunting, enticing moose with birchbark moose callers and by rubbing antlers on branches during mating season.

At the time of first contact, there were perhaps only about 1250 Slavey, but their numbers have grown since then, such that in 2006, their population in the Northwest Territories, northern Alberta, and northeastern British Columbia was over 4000.

Sahtú or Bear Lake Dene

A newly established but nonetheless important Dene group in the Western Subarctic is the **Sahtú** ("Bear Lake") **Dene**, a mixture of Slavey, Dogrib, and Hare who came together during the fur trade to form a distinct group. They are named after Great Bear Lake, where their home territory is located. Something of the toughness of traditional Sahtú Dene life can be seen in the words of George Blondin, describing a time in the 1940s when he was 19. He had just returned from trapping and taking his furs in with some friends. He was ready to go trapping again, but the others couldn't go. It was January, the coldest, darkest month of the year. What would he do?

> My own father, Edward, had an idea. "Go and get your traps," he said, "and trap for lynx at Turíli." Turíli was at the other end of Sahtú, about 320 kilometres from where I had last been trapping. I would have to travel 640 kilometres to pick up my traps.

> People thought I was too young to travel alone. But my father said, "I've taught him enough. He can look after himself. If something happens to him, it's his own fault." (Blondin 1996:256)

In 1994, along with the Métis, the Sahtú signed an agreement with the government that gave them title to 41437 square kilometres of land, $75 million in long-term compensation, and a share in resource royalties. Their exact population is difficult to determine, but including the Sahtu Métis could be about 2000.

Mountain

There exist unclear historical references to the "Mountain" Dene, which have them inhabiting the Mackenzie Mountains that straddle the Yukon and Northwest Territories border, territory associated today with the Hare and the Slavey. The modern survey literature of the area regularly makes reference to them and puts their name on maps, but does not say who they are or point out exactly where their communities might have been. There are people identifiable as Mountain Dene in Tulita First Nation, with a registered population in April 2006 of 588, but that community also includes Slavey people.

Gwich'in

The **Gwich'in** (sometimes written as "Kutchin") were early known in written history by an uncomplimentary name: "Loucheux," a word derived from the French word "louche," meaning "squint-eyed." Their own name for themselves, Gwich'in, means "people." With a designation of location, this word can be used to refer to any specific group. For example, members of the Old Crow band are known as Vuntut Gwich'in, "people of the lakes," referring to their annual muskrat hunt from April to June in an area where there are many small lakes.[1]

Traditional Gwich'in territory, which includes much of the interior of the Yukon, is divided by rivers, primarily the Yukon and Mackenzie rivers. The word "Yukon" itself is thought to be derived from a Gwich'in word referring to the Yukon River, with the probable meaning of "great river" or "white river." The main traditional source of food and supplies for the Gwich'in is caribou. At the time of first contact, they are believed to have numbered about 3000 people in nine or ten regional bands in the Yukon, the Northwest Territories, and Alaska. Their registered population in April 2006 was 3136.

The Gwich'in lived the furthest north of any Dene people, bordering on the land of the Inuit. Thus, it comes as no surprise that they shared aspects of Inuit material culture: fishing spears with strong double hooks; composite bows made from three pieces of wood joined together, reinforced by twisted sinew; and sleds with runners, rather than the toboggans of most northern Dene people.

Being situated in the western part of the region, they also came under the influence of people of the Northwest Coast. They had three ranked clans and a more hierarchical social structure than most of their Dene neighbours.

The Gwich'in language is most closely related to that of the Hän and of the Tutchone, so much so that a number of written works refer to the other peoples as speaking Gwich'in. They have a long, written tradition for the area, their language first having been written down in the 1860s with a script developed by Anglican missionary Robert McDonald. This script was used in the transcription of the Bible, the Book of Common Prayer, and hymns in Gwich'in, and is well known by many middle-aged and older Gwich'in today. Since the 1970s, in schools such as the Chief Zzeh Gittlit School at Old Crow, a more modern alphabet has been used to teach children the language of their ancestors. Charlie Peter Charlie is a major source of information on Gwich'in language and traditional culture. In 1988, at 69 years of age, he was awarded the Order of Canada for his work.

The Gwich'in have a distinct sense of being a people separate from other Dene nations. This might be one reason why, in 1991, they came to an agreement, separate from the others, with the federal government. The agreement reduced their land to 22,332 square kilometres (with subsurface rights to only 93 square kilometres) for a promised $75 million over 15 years. The Gwich'in showed the nature of their priorities when one of the first planned uses of that money was to set up the Tl'oondik Healing Camp.

Hän

The Hän speak a language close to that of the Gwich'in and of the Upper Tanana, which is not surprising, since they lived on what is now the Yukon and Alaska border, between these two cultures. Speakers of the language are called **"Hän Hwëch'in"** (the latter term cognate with Gwich'in), meaning "people of the river." The river referred to is the Yukon. Older people fluent in the language can read Robert McDonald's Christian literature in Gwich'in from the nineteenth century.

There were probably about a thousand Hän when gold was discovered in their territory in 1898. Within a year, there were about 25,000 newcomers in Dawson City, and the Hän were compelled to move to the Moosehide reserve, three kilometres away. By 1932, after being hit by newcomer-borne smallpox, influenza, typhus, and mumps, the community diminished to 56. The people survived and the community's population grew to the approximately 400 of today. Their language has had a tougher time of it, especially since 1957 when the federal government suspended services to Moosehide, forcing people to move to Dawson. Says **Archie Roberts**, Hän Elder and language teacher:

> Everyone spoke Hän in the village in them days. We used to have our own Indian constable and Indian court. But after we moved into Dawson all that stopped. You heard less and less of the language as the Elders died off. (Wright 1988)

That was over 10 years ago. Today there are about 20 speakers left, most of them living in the community of Eagle in Alaska, but the language is being taught to children and adults alike in Dawson. In April 2006, their registered population was 677.

Upper Tanana

The territory of the Upper Tanana is centred on the river of the same name, which flows into the Yukon River in Alaska. The people, who speak a language close to that of the Gwich'in and Hän, live in one Yukon community, Beaver Creek, and in three communities in Alaska, where they have been actively involved with Alaskan Native politics. They are sometimes referred to as Nabesna. The Beaver Creek community, known as White River First Nation, had a registered population of 134 in April 2006, combining people of Upper Tanana and Northern Tutchone heritage.

Tutchone

The Tutchone have long been associated with southern Yukon. Elders still tell stories of a volcanic eruption that occurred within their territory some 7000 years ago (See

Box 8-4 for a tale of an elder). The people's name, short for **Tutchun tah kutchin**, means "wooded country people." It is difficult to determine how many Tutchone there were at the time of first contact during the nineteenth century, but a fair estimate is around a thousand, similar to today's numbers.

The area traditionally provided a diverse life based on several different resources: wood bison (until their extinction a few hundred years ago), caribou, mountain sheep, mountain goat, moose, muskrat, beaver, and salmon. Copper was also an important resource that the Tutchone would heat, dip in cold water, and then hammer to make tools.

Prior to contact, the Tutchone were involved with a significant trade with the Chilkat Tlingit, exchanging the products of their hunting (hides, fur, and clothing) for products of the sea (walrus ivory, seal fat, the oil of the eulachon fish, dried clams, and shells), later expanding to include European trade goods in the 1790s. A trading post, Fort Selkirk, was established in their territory in 1848. This fort was overtaken in 1852 by the Tlingit, who asserted their rights to control local trade.

Linguists have only recently recognized that Tutchone is really two different but closely related languages: Northern Tutchone and Southern Tutchone. Of course, the people have known this for a long time. Northern Tutchone was first recorded in the 1890s by an Anglican missionary, but it wasn't until the 1970s that Southern Tutchone was written down systematically. This was achieved by **Daniel Tlen**, a Tutchone, who first began this life mission upon the death of his grandmother while he was living in Toronto:

> I realized then that no-one had done anything with Native languages. So I went to the faculty of linguistics at Victoria, and told them I was a Southern Tutchone speaker who wanted to work on my language. It took me about ten years to get my degree, studying part time and working in between. It was probably the hardest thing I've ever done (Wright 1988).

In April 2006, the three communities under the Northern Tutchone Tribal Council numbered 1534 in registered population, while the Southern Tutchone communities numbered 300.

Tahltan

The Tahltan live in the interior of British Columbia, close enough to the mountains that some writers have considered them Plateau peoples. The spiritual and material centre of their traditional world is the Stikine River, which traditionally supplied them with a trade route and an abundance of five different types of salmon. Situated as they are on the upper reaches of this river, which flows to the ocean, they have long been in close contact with Northwest Coast peoples, especially the Tlingit, their long-term trading partners. This connection shows in their sharing such cultural traits as social status, the potlatch, and the matrilineal moieties of Raven and Wolf. Their language was said to have between 100 and 1000 speakers in 1982. Their registered population in April 2006 was 1593.

Tagish

Box 8-4	Tagish: The Tale of an Elder

Like most people in her community in her time, Angela Sydney was both **Tagish** and **Tlingit** (see Chapter 11), having a name in both languages and a parent of each heritage (i.e., Tagish father and Tlingit mother). But her primary identity was Tagish. The name "Tagish" is an English transcription of a Tlingit mispronunciation of a Tagish community's self-designation: **ta:gizi**. It means "it [spring ice] is breaking up." Since the time of their first entry into written history during the last quarter of the nineteenth century, the Tagish have never numbered many more than a hundred.

During the nineteenth century, the Tlingit controlled the Tagish trade with the Pacific coast. At the same time, the two peoples intermarried to a great extent. The linguistic effect of the trade dominance and of the intermarriage was such that in 1887 a geologist named Dawson wrote of them as being Tlingit speakers with Dene culture.

The Tlingit trade control ended in 1896, with the discovery of gold by Skookum Jim, Angela Sydney's uncle. The resultant Yukon Gold Rush of 1896–98 swamped Tagish country with a sudden influx of between 30,000 and 40,000 prospectors and other outsiders.

Angela Sydney was born in 1902. What did it mean to be a Tagish woman then? It meant learning how to snare hare for food and how to trap, prepare, and sew the pelts of fox, mink, muskrat, and weasel. As Angela Sydney said:

> All women worked on skins, those days: women trapped around while men hunted. Then they made fur—when a woman fixes skin, then it belongs to her and she can trade it. (Cruikshank 1990:84)

At 14, Angela Sydney was married to a Tlingit man who was twice her age and was chosen by her parents. It was a common practice. Her mother had married the same way. The following year, she gave birth to the first of her seven children, four of whom were to die young of German measles.

She spoke Tlingit to her children because her husband didn't speak Tagish. She also would come to speak Tlingit to her grandchildren and great-grandchildren, but was recorded as saying, regretfully, "I wish they spoke Tagish, too, so they could understand me better."

The Tagish were matrilineal, reckoning descent along the female line of two matri-clans, each of which belonged to a separate **moiety**, or spiritual/ceremonial half of society. Angela Sydney was Beaver clan of the Crow moiety. Clan property was both material and non-material, possessing territories but also names, songs, stories, and curing knowledge. Both Angela Sydney's Tagish and Tlingit names were inherited from the stepmother of her mother. It was the usual practice for a child to inherit all of the names of an adult. Her Tagish name was **Ch'oonehte' Ma**, meaning "Mother of Deadfall." Deadfall was the name of a dog, and both Angela and her grandmother had a dog with that name. Angela's Tlingit name was **Stoow**.

Angela Sydney was fated to become a particularly important culture bearer. Her mother became blind when her daughter was very young, so Angela spent a great deal of time helping her with her work and listening to the stories

(continued)

| Box 8-4 | *(continued)* |

passed down through generations of mothers and daughters.

In 1912 and 1914, she had the good fortune to experience the last two potlatches in the area. The potlatch was the Pacific Coast's most important religious ceremony, made illegal by the federal government in 1884 (see Chapter 17), eight years before Angela was born. These potlatches made such a lasting impression on the teenage Angela that as an old woman, she was able to present and explain one of the sacred potlatch songs that told a story about how a woman raised a woodworm as her own child, until it got so big that her family felt they had to kill it because of how big it was getting (Cruikshank 1990:94–97). In 1984, she held a potlatch to mark the putting up of gravestones for her brothers and sisters who had died during the German measles epidemic in 1898.

In her early years, too, Angela Sydney heard and spoke the Tagish language:

Mom and Dad spoke Tagish lots of times, to each other, and my mother said when I was really small I used to talk like that too. But as soon as we [Angela and her sisters and brothers] got a little older—four or five years old—we started talking Tlingit. (Cruikshank 1990:69)

It is fortunate for the Tagish, and for the rest of us who can learn from the unique knowledge and vision of life contained in the Tagish language, that

Angela Sydney was so gifted with linguistic ability. We see this gift manifested in a number of ways. Not only was she able to retain a working knowledge of Tagish long after Tlingit and English became the tongues of her day-to-day speech, but also, when she was in her eighties, she could speak five of the seven Yukon Native languages: Tagish, Tlingit, Tahltan, Southern Tutchone, and Kaska.

It was estimated in 1982 that there were five speakers of Tagish left. This was probably an optimistic estimation. Angela Sydney seems to have been the only Native speaker working to preserve the language. For some 30 years she worked with linguists recording the language and other aspects of her cultural heritage as much as possible. In 1977, along with two other women, she put out a booklet of stories entitled *My Stories Are My Wealth*. Within a few years she had published the following: *Tagish Tlaagu/Tagish Stories*, *Haa Shagoon*, and *Placenames of the Tagish Region, Southern Yukon*.

In 1986 she received the Order of Canada, the first Yukon Native woman to do so. She died at 89. Her legacy is best summarized in her own words, "I have no money to leave to my grandchildren. . . My stories are my wealth" (Cruikshank 1990:36).

Today there is one Tagish band, the Carcross Tagish First Nation, with a population around 500.

Kaska

The Kaska people appear in the literature with two different names: Nahani and Kaska. We are using Kaska here, as it reflects the usage of the people themselves.

The western location of the Kaska people, in northern British Columbia and southern Yukon, gave them close contact with Tlingit traders. Not surprisingly, then, they shared a significant number of cultural traits with the Northwest Coast nations. These traits include matrilineally determined moieties (Wolf and Crow) and potlatching.

The Kaska language has several dialects, each influenced by whoever their neighbours were: Tagish, Tahltan, or Sekani. The Kaska's population has been small, perhaps 1500 at the time of first contact and a few hundred speakers today in a population of a little over 2100 (the legacy of repression of Kaska in residential schools). This combined with the lack of written materials in the language has made preservation of the language a difficult job, but one that the people feel is necessary. A good sense of this is captured in the words of Kaska Chief Hammond Dick in 1988:

> During our annual general assembly we translated everything to the Elders and to the public. It was tedious but people realized the importance. When you've been brought up to be ashamed of your own language, it helps to see it given respect that way. (Wright 1988)

In 1998, the Kaska of the Liard First Nation were the first Yukon people to sign a tripartite agreement on policing with the Yukon and federal governments. Because of this agreement, this community of a little over 1000 people would get four Aboriginal police officers stationed at the local RCMP detachment. As part of this agreement, the community formed a committee that would influence decisions on key restorative justice issues involving pre-charge diversion, bail, and sentencing. While this might not seem important to non-Natives with no understanding of the problems of First Nations' justice (see Chapter 24), the importance of this agreement was underlined by Chief Ann Bayne: " 'The Dena Keh Justice Program validates through empowerment that we are building a healthier community. It is an approach that can serve as a basis for administering justice under self-government'" (Justice Canada 1998).

Dunne-za or Beaver

In northwestern Alberta and northeastern British Columbia live the **Dunne-za** or Beaver. Their territory is varied, stretching between the Rocky Mountains to the west and Lake Athabaska to the east, and dominated by the Peace River. It consists of rich prairie lands, along with muskeg, forest, and mountainous terrain. That has enabled the people to draw upon a variety of resources, with one author claiming 46 different mammal species,[2] the most significant of which are moose, bison, and caribou. In order to take advantage of such diverse species, the Beaver historically had to move often from place to place, travelling as much as 400 kilometres during a year. Hunters were said to have the capacity to kill particular animals because they had sought out the animal spiritually and learned from its **muyine'** ("song"), a word used to refer to spiritual power or to a person's medicine bundle. Robin Ridington describes this spiritual relationship as follows:

> In order for a hunt to be successfully completed, the animal had to have previously given itself to the hunter in a dream. Both animal and hunter were supposed to have been known to one another before their physical meeting in the hunt itself. Animals were believed to be pleased by the hunter's respect for their bodies[3] and to notice his generosity in distributing the meat. Hunters sought to develop an ability to think like game animals in order to predict their behaviour. They were trained to interpret the environment from an animal's perspective. The hunter's

understanding of an animal's thought process was believed to be mirrored by the animal's understanding of how humans fulfilled obligations incurred in the hunt. (Ridington 1982:161)

The Beaver language is very close to that of the Sekani, the Kaska, and the Slavey, close enough to be at or near to mutual intelligibility. Although the Beaver used to be connected with the Sarcee before the latter linked their fate to the Blackfoot Confederacy, their time apart separated their languages.

The people refer to themselves as "Dunne-za," usually translated as "real people." The Beaver appellation seems to have come from the Chipewyan word for the Peace River, once written as **Tsa des**, meaning "beaver river." The northern Plains Cree called them **amiskiwiyiniw**, meaning "beaver person."

By about 1760, the Beaver had been driven out of the eastern part of their traditional territory by the Cree, who were armed with guns obtained through the fur trade. The Beaver allied with the Slavey to fend off the intruders. When the Cree and the Beaver agreed in the early 1780s to stop fighting, the peace they achieved was memorialized in the name now held by the main river in Beaver territory: the Peace River. Fighting resumed, however, from the 1790s into the 1820s.

At the time of first contact, the Beaver probably numbered around a thousand. As of April 2006, three communities in northern Alberta and four in northeastern British Columbia have a combined registered population of 2935.

Sekani

The word "**Sekani**" means "People of [on] the Rocks," in which "Rocks" refers to the Rocky Mountains. They seem to have been part of the Beaver First Nation who were driven west into the mountains, where they took on this new name. In 1968, the W.A.C Bennett Dam created Lake Williston, at the time the largest artificial reservoir in the world. It flooded Sekani land and forced the Sekani to relocate. Not surprisingly, the Sekani language is very close to Beaver, and, to a lesser extent, to Sarcee. It is difficult to know how many Sekani there were at the time of contact, but they probably numbered at least 500. The Tsay Key Dene Band numbered 362 at the end of 2005.

The Sekani territory, which included the river valleys of the Parsnip and Findlay Rivers and the plateau and mountain regions of northern British Columbia, while not particularly rich in resources, at least offered a diversity that could be accessed at different times of the year. This would traditionally include buffalo, moose, caribou, bear, porcupine, beaver, woodchuck, deer, mountain goat, and mountain sheep. Diamond Jenness, who studied the Sekani in 1924, referred to their feeling disdain for fishing as something to be done only when absolutely necessary (Jenness 1932:379).

The small numbers of the Sekani, probably only around a thousand during the nineteenth century, have historically and presently put them in the position of needing to establish good relationships with their Native neighbours. Today, one community, Fort Ware, is affiliated with the Kaska Tribal Council, and other Sekani are connected with the Carrier-Sekani Tribal Council.

Native Individuals 8-1

Akaitcho: Nineteenth-century Yellow-knife leader.

Dza-ghal-iaze ("Lower leg trembles little"): Legendary eighteenth-century Chipewyan leader.

Edzo: A Dogrib leader who brought peace between his people and the Yellowknife during the 1820s.

George Erasmus: Dogrib leader who was the Chief of the Assembly of First Nations, 1985–1991.

Angela Sydney: Last speaker of Tagish.

Thanadelthur: Eighteenth-century Chipewyan woman who was instrumental in connecting her people with the fur trade.

Daniel Tlen: A Southern Tutchone linguist.

James Wah-Shee: Dogrib leader, and the first president of the Indian Brotherhood of the Northwest Territories.

Timeline 8-1

1781: Smallpox kills a reputed 90 percent of the Chipewyan.

1780s: Peace is established between the Beaver and the Cree, giving Peace River its name.

1820s: Dogrib Edzo brings peace between his people and the Yellowknife.

1860s: Gwich'in language first written down.

1896–8: Gold rush in the Yukon.

1930s: Tuberculosis hits epidemic proportions among the Hare.

1968: Sekani land is flooded in the creation of Lake Williston.

1986: Tagish woman, Angela Sydney, receives Order of Canada.

1988: Gwich'in man, Charlie Peter Charlie, receives Order of Canada.

1985–1991: Dogrib George Erasmus chief of the Assembly of First Nations.

ENDNOTES

1. The English name "Old Crow" comes from the name of a nineteenth-century Gwich'in leader, Te Trhim Gevtik ("Walking Crow").

2. This includes moose, wood bison, beaver, muskrat, marten, red fox, black-footed ferret, raccoon, weasel, rabbit, deer, caribou, hare, black bear, grizzly bear, and porcupine, to name just a few.

3. As with other Native cultures, this included treating the bones with respect (e.g., not throwing them to the dogs or into the fire) and addressing the animal respectfully after death.

KEY TERMS

Atha(b/p)aska(n) (Cree)   moiety
Awokanak (Cree)   muyine' (Beaver)
Dene

CONTENT QUESTIONS

1. To what language family do all the languages of the peoples of the Western Subarctic belong?
2. Which of the people have a word for "people" as part of their name?
3. Why was one of these groups called "Slave(y)"?
4. Why are there no more speakers of Tagish?
5. How did Peace River get its name?

WEBLINKS

www.ctfn.ca
This is the website for the Carcross/Tagish First Nation, and it contains useful information concerning their history, culture, and contemporary views.

www.gwichin.nt.ca
This is a comprehensive website concerning the Gwich'in people.

www.ynlc.ca
This site discusses the Yukon Native Language Centre and the languages spoken in the Yukon.

chapter nine

The Plains

FOUNDATIONS OF PLAINS LIFE

Archaeologists have evidence that people lived in the Canadian Plains (i.e., most of Alberta and Saskatchewan and part of Manitoba) about 11,500 years ago. The grasslands and bison that we associate with the Plains came shortly afterwards, about 11,000 years ago.

The Buffalo

Buffalo (technically, bison) provided for almost all the needs of Plains life. The first need was food. The Blackfoot refer to buffalo meat as **nitapiksisako**, meaning "real meat." This included not only fresh meat but also **pemmican**, buffalo jerky made by pulverizing thin strips of dried, lean buffalo meat, adding to it crushed, dried **saskatoon** (service) berries, and hot fat produced by boiling the marrow of the bones. It supplied important food in the winter when fresh meat was not readily available. It would later become a major component involved with the fur trade, serving as "fuel" for canoeing travellers.

But the buffalo didn't just give the people food. Their summer-slain skins provided lodge covers and bags for holding household goods. Their winter hides provided overcoats, mittens, caps, and warm moccasins. The thick hide on the buffalo's neck was used for making shields, and strips of untanned rawhide were used for binding cords for knives, clubs, and other tools (Friesen 1997:97).

Plains society was constructed around its relationship to the buffalo. Bands of 25 to 100 reflected the number of people needed to drive buffalo. Warrior societies were developed primarily to police the hunt so that no one would spook the buffalo herd.

Plains people developed ingenious hunting methods. Earliest was the **buffalo cliff drive** or **jump**. At sites such as the 3000-year-old Head-Smashed-In-Buffalo-Jump in southern Alberta, buffalo were driven through carefully created lanes, then over a cliff.

The **buffalo pound** evolved around 250 A.D., once bows and arrows entered the Plains. Compared to spears, these weapons were safer and more efficient for the hunter in killing large numbers of buffalo. The work involved was complex. If a natural pound site, such as a canyon, was not available, a corral was constructed. This consisted of

> . . . a walled enclosure, generally circular in shape, ranging from 10 to 75 metres in diameter. Extending from the entrance in a "v" shape were two wings of spaced stations made of piles of rocks, wood, or dried buffalo chips. . . . These lines stretched out for several kilometres and the open mouth of the "v" was almost two kilometres in width. The pound itself was hidden from the view of the bison as they ran towards it, following the lines of the "v," which grew ever narrower, and then it was too late. (Friesen 1997:101)

During the nineteenth century, Euro-Americans slaughtered buffalo by the tens of thousands, often just for the hides, leaving the flesh to rot. In 1876, the Blackfoot leader **Crowfoot** said, "We all see that the day is coming when the buffalo will all be killed, and we shall have nothing more to live on . . . then you will come into our camp and see the poor Blackfoot starving" (Dempsey 1972:89). By the 1880s, the large buffalo herds were no more. Only a few hundred buffalo remained.

Spiritual Foundations of Plains Culture

One key aspect of the spiritual life of Plains culture is the **iniskim**, or "buffalo stone." The practice of using these stones, usually fossils bearing a spiral shell, goes back thousands of years. The story of the first iniskim tells of a woman trying to find food during a time of famine. An iniskim spoke to her, teaching her the prayers and ceremonies necessary to bring buffalo to the people. Blackfoot children wore iniskim in necklaces; warriors had iniskim woven into their hair; shamans carried iniskim in medicine bundles; the dead were buried with iniskim.

For thousands of years, **medicine wheels** have been part of spiritual life in the Canadian Plains. These stone structures are typically centred on a cairn or pile of stones on top of a prominent hill. Stone "spokes" radiate outwards. Individual medicine wheels often had long histories of use. The Majorville Medicine Wheel, constructed of about 40 tonnes of rock, dates to around 5000 B.P. and was still the focus of religious activity when Europeans first came to the Plains. At the centre is a cairn of fieldstones and soil 9 metres in diameter and 1.6 metres high. Surrounding it is an oval ring some 29 metres by 26 metres, connected with 26 to 28 boulder spokes.

The **Okan** (Blackfoot for "ceremonial pole"), or Sun Dance, was the main ceremony of the Plains people. It was initiated, sponsored, and presided over by a woman:

> The decision to hold a Sun Dance was made by a pure woman—i.e., a virgin or faithful wife—who had a male relative in danger of losing his life. A husband might be ill or a son may not have returned from a raid. The woman made a public vow that if the person's life was spared, she would sponsor a Sun Dance. Then, if her prayer was answered, she began preparations for the summer festival. (Dempsey 1995:392)

Sometimes, as a spiritual offering, young men inserted leather thongs through their chest or back muscles, attaching the other end either to a pole or to a buffalo skull. Then they would dance until the thongs ripped free. This was one reason given in 1895 when the federal government banned the Sun Dance. The following is a response by an anonymous Blackfoot:

> We know that there is nothing injurious to our people in the Sun-dance. . . . It has been our custom, during many years, to assemble once every summer for this festival . . . We fast and pray, that we may be able to lead good lives and to act more kindly towards each other.
>
> I do not understand why the white men desire to put an end to our religious ceremonials. What harm can they do our people? If they deprive us of our religion, we will have nothing left, for we know of no other that can take its place. (Nabokov 1991:225)

The ban was lifted in 1951 when the Indian Act was changed.

Innovations That Changed Plains Life

Several times in Plains history, innovations have swept across the grasslands, changing people's lives, sometimes bringing new people to the area. When Europeans came to the Canadian Plains, six First Nations lived there, of which only one had lived in the area from before the seventeenth century.

Prior to Contact

Around 8000 years ago, an invention that had developed in the southeastern United States arrived which transformed Plains culture. The atlatl, or spear-thrower, was a device held in the hand into which the blunt end of the spear was placed. This meant that the spear could be thrown with greater force and accuracy, rather like adding length to a person's arm.

Over the next few thousand years, other innovations enhanced Plains life. Dogs were domesticated and trained to transport loads by carrying bundles and pulling **travois**, devices made from poles. Plains people also learned how to render the marrow of bones into fat by boiling cracked bones in containers heated by placing hot rocks inside. This enabled them to make pemmican, a Plains staple.

The Horse: Changing the Human Face of the Canadian Plains

The horse had a huge impact on Plains culture. People could travel farther, more often, and carry more things with them. Homes and bands became larger. The horse changed the buffalo hunt through the development of the dramatic and potentially deadly "**surround**" of buffalo by racing riders. The horse also became a standard of wealth. Some individuals acquired more horses than they could possibly ever use, between 50 and 300. **Sackomaph**, a Peigan chief, is reported to have had between 4000 and 5000 horses, 150 of which were sacrificed at his death. Desire for horses also created strife between peoples. The fastest way of obtaining horses was to steal them, which became a test of young manhood. Finally, the horse changed the human map of the Plains, for those with horses had a huge military advantage over those who did not.

Horses were not indigenous to the Plains. Their trail began in New Mexico around the turn of the seventeenth century, when the Spanish established horse ranches, where they employed and exploited Apache workers. The Apache stole some of the horses and took off, quickly becoming some of the best riders in the world. Horses gradually moved north, sometimes ridden by peoples looking to expand their territory. In about 1700, the Shoshoni rode onto the southern edges of the Canadian Plains, threatening the Blackfoot. Over the next few decades, the Blackfoot, Sarcee, Assiniboine, and Cree joined together to fend them off, a difficult task, since the Shoshoni had greater access to horses. However, the tide of the conflict turned when the Blackfoot acquired both horses and guns.

CANADIAN PLAINS NATIONS IN THE NINETEENTH AND TWENTIETH CENTURIES

There are seven nations that live in the Canadian Plains today, who are speakers of languages of three different language families.

Blackfoot

The Blackfoot speak a Western Algonquian language. Connections with Central or Eastern Algonquian languages are shown in Box 9-1.

Nineteenth-century artist George Catlin referred to the Blackfoot as "the most powerful tribe of Indians on the continent." Three tribes make up the Blackfoot nation: **Siksika**, **Kainai**, and **Peigan**. In 1823, it was estimated that there were 4200 Siksika, 2800 Kainai, and 4200 Peigan. Current figures show that there are 15,000 Piegan (Peigan) in the United States, and 8000 Kainai, 5000 Siksika, and 2500 Peigan in Canada.

Historically, these three tribes shared language and customs, intermarried, and were military allies. Their collective name in their own language can be **Sakoyitapix** ("prairie people"), **Apikunipuyi** ("speakers of the same language"), or **Nitsitapix** ("real or true people"), a term the Blackfoot also use to refer to Natives generally (Frantz and Russell 1995:135).

The word "siksika" means "black foot." The name is derived from an individual in the origin story who walked over the ashes of a prairie fire, making his moccasins black in the process. The English collective name of the allied tribes, "Blackfoot" ("Blackfeet" in the United States), reflects the fact that White traders established first contact with Siksika and does not indicate any special status of that group over the other two.

"**Kainai**" means "many chiefs." In the origin story, when the black-footed traveller walked into the Kainai village, he asked who the chief was. Many claimed to be the chief.

BOX 9-1	Blackfoot Connections with Algonquian Languages			
Blackfoot	Ojibwe	Delaware	English	Word Form
k-	msko-	maxkii-	red	prefix
aapi	waab-	waapii	white	prefix
owaa	waawaan	wahwal	egg	inanimate noun
naamoo	aamoo	aamweew	bee	animate noun

This nation's English name, **Blood**, comes from a name given to them by the Cree, a reference to their practice of sometimes covering their clothes with red ochre.

Peigan ("Piegan" in the United States) is derived from the word **Apikuni**, variously translated as "scabby robes" or "poorly dressed robes." The black-footed traveller called them that in the origin story because their women had scraped the buffalo skins poorly, leaving pieces of meat and fur.

Traditional Blackfoot social organization began with a **tipi**, which would house a single household, including a husband, wife or wives, and children. The next level of social organization was the band, built usually on the extended family. This band could number from 25 to over 100. Its size related to such practical considerations as the number of people needed to hunt buffalo and the amount of grass available for the band's horses. Households might shift membership in the bands according to kinship alliances, friendships, agreement or disagreement with band leadership, and the band's hunting and raiding success. They would camp together during the winter, usually for defensive purposes, only a short distance from other bands. Like the buffalo they hunted, they would amalgamate into larger groupings of 100 to 200 households during the summer.

Bands had names based on incidents or distinctive features of individual band members, often with a humorous twist. The following are names taken from a recently published Blackfoot dictionary: Many Ghosts, Hairy Nose, Never Laughs, Padded Saddle, White Robe, Never Lonesome, and Gopher Eater. Names could also change with new incidents. For example, "the Followers of the Buffalo" became "Camps in a Bunch" once they had settled on a reserve.

Bands would have peace chiefs and war chiefs. There was no formal chief beyond that level. When bands got together, the most respected leader might be appointed as the head for that particular context. That went for both war and peace leaders. When the Kainai got together during the middle of the nineteenth century, **Mekaisto**, or **Red Crow**, would tend to be chosen to lead. If the collection of bands faced danger, **White Calf** would be put in charge.

Important to traditional Blackfoot life were age-graded Warrior or All Comrades societies. A boy would join such a society in his early teens. After about five years, those in his group would purchase the emblems and rights of the society one step older than they, in return selling the emblems and rights to those one step younger. Those in the age ranges of 20 to 25 and 25 to 30 were most often used to police a camp, especially during the buffalo hunt. Not all men moved up. Some stayed with younger men, a sign that they were not as effective or successful as their peers.

Women were and still are major players in Blackfoot society. The Blackfoot have a term, **ninauposkitzipxpe**, which means "manly hearted woman," referring to a type of woman well described in the following passage from anthropologist Oscar Lewis in 1941:

> About a third of elderly (sixty years or older) North Piegan women in 1939, and a few younger women, were considered manly hearted . . . Such women own property, were good managers and usually effective workers, were forthright and assertive in public, in their homes, and as sexual partners, and were active in religious rituals. They were called "manly-hearted" because boldness, aggressiveness, and a drive to amass property and social power are held to be ideal traits for men . . . [T]he manly-hearted woman is admired as well as feared by both men and women. (Lewis in Kehoe 1995:115)

The combined population of the three communities of the Blood, Piikani Nation and Siksika Nation in Canada was 19,381 in April 2006. The "Blackfeet" Nation in the United States is one of the 10 largest tribes, numbering more than four times the Blackfoot population in Canada.

Plains Cree

The Plains Cree are known in their own language as **Mamihkiyiniwak** ("Downstream People"). They were relatively new to the Plains, formerly living in parkland and woodland areas. They began to move into the Plains by at least the seventeenth century. As they became involved with the fur trade, they moved deeper into the grasslands.

Much has been written about the conflict between Plains Cree and Blackfoot during the nineteenth century. Less stressed is the equally long alliance and trade relationship that previously existed. According to **Saukamappee**, the linking up began because of a call for help. It was 1722. The Peigan, hard hit by Shoshoni incursions into their land, sent out messengers to ask for assistance. Two arrived at Saukamappee's camp and 20 Cree joined the fight. No one won the battle, but the connection was made.

In 1732, the Cree and Assiniboine again joined the Blackfoot against the Shoshoni. This time, the Cree and Assiniboine had with them 10 guns. According to Saukamappee's account, "Our shots caused consternation and dismay along their whole line. The battle had begun about Noon, and the sun was not yet half down, when we perceived some of them had crawled away from their shields, and were taking to flight" (Milloy 1988:8). The Cree then began to supply guns in trade with the Blackfoot.

This positive relationship ended, in part, because the Cree found horses hard to come by through trade. An easier way to obtain horses was raiding. A particular target for the Cree from at least the 1790s onwards was the **A'ani** ("White Clay People") of south Saskatchewan, better known by the insulting term Gros Ventre ("Big Belly"). The Cree raids put the Blackfoot in a difficult position. The Cree were their main gun connection, but the A'ani were their main link to the southern horse market. Once the Blackfoot could obtain guns directly from a source other than the Cree—the trading posts of Edmonton House and Rocky Mountain House—the choice became easier. In 1806, the Blackfoot chose sides, attacking the Cree. Battles were fought off and on from that time until their last major conflict in 1870. The A'ani were forced to retreat to the United States.

The Plains Cree flourished in the Plains, their numbers growing from an estimated 4900 in 1809 to around 12,500 by 1860. Their numbers and military reputation caused them to be feared by federal officials of a newly formed Canada expanding into the west. After the Riel Rebellion of 1885, fear led to blame. But the vast majority of the Plains Cree remained loyal to the Queen, in whose name their treaties had been signed. They put their trust in peaceful processes, despite the fact that the federal government was confining them to small reserves and starving the people by not delivering on oral and written promises made in the treaties. One person particularly prominent in both the peaceful process and in the falsely assigned blame was **Mistahimaskwa** ("Big Bear"). He risked his life trying to maintain peace but was put in prison for not being able to control young men frustrated with how the Plains Cree were being treated.

In the three Prairie provinces, there are currently more than 156,000 Cree.

Assiniboine

The word "**Assiniboine**" is derived from a Cree term meaning "they cook with stones," giving them their English name, "Stonies." This refers to the Assiniboine method of cooking in which a hole lined with rawhide was filled with water. Heated rocks were then placed inside to cook meat and vegetables in a stew or soup. The Assiniboine prefer to be called Nakota (also spelled Nakoda), which is cognate with the word "Dakota."

The Siouan-speaking Assiniboine were relative newcomers to the Plains. They moved onto the Plains during the latter half of the seventeenth and early eighteenth centuries, almost totally abandoning their woodland territories north of Lake Superior and the parklands of southern Manitoba and northern Minnesota.

The connection between Cree and Assiniboine was very close. Many in both societies could speak each other's unrelated language. They fought side by side against the Dakota and Blackfoot. The Blackfoot called the Assiniboine **Niitsisinaa**, "original Cree" (Frantz and Russell 1995:135). In Saskatchewan there are four main Nakota bands; two are shared with the Cree. Carry the Kettle, with an April 2006 registered population of 2252, and Pheasant's Rump, with 354, are Nakota, while Mosquito First Nation and White Bear are both Nakota/Cree. In Alberta, there is the Stoney Nakoda Nation, made up of three bands with an April 2006 population of 4383, and the Alexis Nakota Nation with 1519.

Dakota

Most of the literature on the Canadian Plains, and about Native people in Canada generally, ignores the presence of the Siouan-speaking Dakota in Manitoba and Saskatchewan. Yet today, Dakota speakers outnumber those of Assiniboine. They very quietly moved north into the area during the nineteenth century, becoming closely linked with the Saulteaux. There are seven bands in Canada, with a combined population of 4611 for six of them. The seventh band, Dakota Tipi, has disallowed Statistics Canada from counting their population, as they disagree with how they arrive at their figures. Box 9-2 explains why Dakota have objected to being called "Sioux."

Tsuu T'ina (Sarcee/Sarsi)

Also relative newcomers to the Plains are the **Tsuu T'ina** ("earth people" or "many people"), an Athapaskan-speaking people. Until recently they were usually known as **Sarcee**, a Blackfoot term with a number of different translations. During the eighteenth century,

---

BOX 9-2   Why Object to Being Called "Sioux"?

Imagine if you were called by the name used to refer to you by neighbours who don't like you. Sioux is an abbreviated English version of a French adaptation of the word "Nadouessioux," meaning "little snakes"—an insulting term that Ojibwe speakers used to refer to people who didn't speak an Algonquian language. Dakota has long been a term used by the people themselves. Sioux was a name imposed by English-speaking people.

they split from the **Tsatine** ("Beaver people") or **Dunne-za** ("real people") who live in the Northwest Territories, just south of Great Slave Lake. They are linked linguistically with peoples who had moved south through central British Columbia over a thousand years before, eventually ending up in the American Southwest. These travellers are the Apache and the Navajo. There were 1982 people in their community in 2001.

During the latter part of the eighteenth century, the Sarcee linked their military fate with the Blackfoot as part of the Blackfoot Confederacy. Even though their numbers were relatively small, estimated at 840 in 1809, they were not to be discounted as a fighting force and did help drive back the Shoshoni. Around 1800, Alexander Henry wrote:

> These people have a reputation of being the bravest tribe in all the plains, who dare to face ten times their own numbers, and of this I have convincing proof during my residence in the country. (Hungry Wolf and Hungry Wolf 1991 in Friesen 1997:127)

Disease hit the Tsuu T'ina hard during the nineteenth century, reducing the numbers of their single community to 160. Today, their numbers have risen to about 1200 but their language is severely threatened, with only about 10 speakers left.

Saulteaux

Also entering the Plains during the eighteenth century was the branch of the Anishinabe known usually as **Saulteaux**. They received this name because many of their ancestors came from the area of the "sault," or "rapids," of Sault Ste. Marie, where Lake Huron and Lake Superior meet. They often refer to themselves as **Bungee**, a term derived from an Ojibwe word meaning "few, little, a little."

As a Plains people, the Saulteaux usually allied themselves with the Plains Cree during the battles of the eighteenth and nineteenth centuries, fighting alongside the Plains Cree and the Assiniboine against the Sioux during the late eighteenth century and with the Cree against the Blackfoot in the 1860s.

The Saulteaux had the smallest number of any Plains people at that time, with their population being estimated as 336 in 1809. Today their communities are found in Manitoba, Saskatchewan, and British Columbia, and they number around 50,000.

Métis

The story of the Métis in Canada is one of a unique people. Genetically and culturally, their formation represents a mixture of European (primarily French) and Native (primarily Cree). Their language, **Michif**, is a clear example of that uniqueness, because it is partially French (mostly the nouns) and partially Cree (mostly the verbs).

The Métis came into being during the eighteenth century, when the fur trade was extending west into the Prairies. The French voyageurs who manned the big canoes made personal connections with Natives in the area—very personal, when it came to Plains Cree women. The marriages between the two (whether or not they were sanctified by the Catholic church) were practical for both cultures. Their children learned from each people.

From the Native culture they learned how to hunt buffalo and how to prepare pemmican, the staple food for the fur trade. European culture taught them how to farm and how to build and use the big ox-driven carts they utilized to carry large loads of pemmican from the hunt to their homes.

By the beginning of the nineteenth century, there were several thousand Métis, most of them around the area of present-day southern Manitoba.

The Métis developed a sense of nationhood not only from their distinct culture but from battles they won. One of the "enemies" that they fought was the Hudson's Bay Company (HBC). This organization had been given most of what is now Canada in 1670 by King Charles II, who had little idea of what he was giving away so freely: a monopoly of trade on the lands drained by the waters that flow into Hudson Bay.

In 1811, Lord Selkirk, a leading official in the HBC, arranged for settlers to be brought to what is now the Winnipeg area. The settlers got along with the Métis, whose land they were sharing, but the governor of this new colony made enemies with the Métis by declaring that they should not be providing pemmican for the trade, as the trade was an HBC monopoly. This conflict came to a head in 1816 when Governor Semple and about 25 of his men challenged the leader of the Métis, Cuthbert Grant (c. 1793–1854), and a slightly smaller group of his people. When the smoke cleared, the governor and his men were dead, as was only one of the Métis. A song was composed to celebrate this victory (unfortunately referred to as the Seven Oaks "massacre" in many history textbooks). The people started calling themselves the "New Nation," and the song became their national anthem.

For several generations, the Métis worked for the Northwest Company, a Montreal-based rival of the HBC. In 1821, the HBC absorbed its competitor, giving it a virtual "official" monopoly of the fur trade. But the Métis continued to challenge the company. This came to a head in 1849 when a Métis named **Pierre-Guillaume Sayer** was charged with fur trafficking. Although he was charged, he was let go once the trial was over. This perhaps reflected the fact that several armed Métis were waiting outside the courtroom.

The Métis inherited the political alliances and enemies of their Cree mothers, grand-mothers, and great-grandmothers. They fought alongside the Assiniboine and Saulteaux and fought against the Dakota and the Blackfoot. In 1851, a group of Métis met and defeated a much larger force of Dakota at the Battle of Grand Coteau, another victory for the New Nation.

This sense of self was severely threatened during the 1860s. In 1867, the year of Confederation, the new country began negotiating with the HBC for a massive land transfer. People moving out west at that time included "Canada Firsters," who arrogantly declared to the Métis that the future in the West belonged to them and not the "half breeds." The antagonism was exacerbated by the presence of outsiders surveying land held by the Métis for generations. In 1869, the Métis took action. A 25-year-old, college-educated man named **Louis Riel** emerged as their leader. They formed a provisional government and blocked the entry of the Canadian governor at the U.S.–Canada border. Their government had the support of most people but made the unfortunate mistake of imprisoning, and later executing, an especially obnoxious White Protestant Ontarian, Thomas Scott, an action that would have dire consequences for Louis Riel.

In 1870, most of the proposals put forward by the provisional Métis government were made legal by the Manitoba Act. The Métis had their rights to the land recognized through legal papers known as "scrip." Riel's status became an unusual one. He was officially exiled by the federal government, but time and again he was elected to parliament by the people of Manitoba, both Métis and non-Métis alike.

In Manitoba in 1871, there were 9800 Métis, 5270 of whom were French-speaking (the rest spoke English). In the same area there were only 1600 Whites, and a greater, undetermined number of Cree. That changed with the westward migration of settlers. With them came land speculators and government officials who were not above working out scams to cheat the Métis of their scrip. The laws relating to scrip changed 11 times over 12 years. Most Métis moved west into what is now Saskatchewan and Alberta.

Box 9-3 tells the story of Gabriel Dumont, another important Métis leader.

Box 9-3   Gabriel Dumont

The life of Gabriel Dumont (1837–1906) more epitomized the day-to-day living of the Métis than did the experiences of the more famous Louis Riel. While Riel received a college education and worked as a teacher, Dumont spent most of his years hunting buffalo, trapping, fishing, farming, and defending his people against their enemies. He may have spoken six of the languages of the area (Michif, French, Cree, Dakota, Blackfoot, and Crow). In 1851, at 14, he had his first taste of warfare, against the Dakota in the Battle of Grand Coteau. By the time he was 25, he was elected leader of the Métis buffalo hunt based in Saskatchewan. By the early 1870s, he would establish himself as farmer/store-owner/ferry-operator at a place that came to be called "Gabriel's Crossing."

We know about this important figure because of two published sources based on his own words. The first, published in 1889 as part of *La Verité sur la Question Métisse au Nord Ouest* [The Truth about the Question of the Métis of the Northwest], was something of a political document used, as was Dumont himself for a short time, to further the agenda of the Liberals in Quebec (who looked upon the Riel Rebellion more as a French vs. English issue than one of Natives vs. Newcomers). It was first published in English in 1949, and has been often quoted by historians. Less well known is a memoir dictated by Dumont in

1903 (Dumont 1903/1993). It would be 90 years before it would be published in English (as *Gabriel Dumont Speaks*). In what follows we will use several quotations from this work to hear his views on some of the key events of his life and times.

Petitions

One of the main political means that the Métis of Saskatchewan employed to fight for their rights were petitions sent to the government. One issue they fought for was the right to cut wood, a right for which many Natives throughout Canada had to fight:

> Around 1880 or 1881, the Métis of Batoche and St. Laurent got very tired of having to pay for wood they cut for planks and firewood . . . We called a meeting at Batoche . . . I [said to] them 'We left Manitoba because we were not free, and we came to this new wild country to be free. And now we have to pay to cut firewood? . . . We cannot let this happen. The government has made its first move against us and if we let them get away with it, there will be more laws coming.'" (Dumont 1903/1993:37-8)

Their petition was successful, unlike most of their petitions in those years.

Provocation for Battle

Lawrence Clarke was the chief factor of the nearest Hudson's Bay Company post, Fort Carlton. On several occasions

(continued)

Box 9-3 *(continued)*

he tried to stir things up so that the army would come into the area, and he wasn't above spreading false rumours to do so (see Dickason 2002:274). It has been speculated that he did this to benefit from the money that would be brought in with hundreds of soldiers (Siggins 1994:374). In this passage, Dumont accuses him of causing armed rebellion in 1884 with his misinformation:

> Without the news that Clarke had reported. . . no one ever dreamed that a military insurgence would come again. . . In any case, we tried all peaceful means to obtain our rights. It was Clarke who put fire to the powder by reporting the news. The news was false.

It was invented to scare off the organizers of the meetings.

(Dumont 1903/1993:48)

After the battle of Batoche, Dumont fled to the United States, where he signed on to perform as a rider and shooter in Buffalo Bill's Wild West Show. While he was away, in July 1886, he received a pardon from the Canadian government. After he quit the show, he engaged in public speaking in Quebec and eventually returned to Saskatchewan in 1890. He applied for the patent to the lands he had originally occupied by Gabriel's Crossing 20 years before, and he received them 10 years later in 1903, with governments obstructing him almost to the last.

In the 1880s, the Métis found themselves in a similar situation to that which they had faced earlier in Manitoba. They again called upon Louis Riel, then living in Montana, to lead them in what would become known as the Second Riel Rebellion. They would lose this time, due to the technology used against them (i.e., the new railroad, steamboats, and the precursor to machine guns) and to Riel's reluctance to fight. He was hanged in 1885, largely because of his authorization of the execution of Thomas Scott years earlier.

Throughout the twentieth century, the Métis remained in an uncertain political position. Some in Alberta live in "colonies" developed during the 1930s and fought for royalties for the oil and gas extracted from their land. Other Métis organizations suffer from the lack of definition of who is Métis and from a lack of federal recognition of their status. In the 1981 census, 98,255 Canadians identified themselves as Métis, while in 1991, 75,150 did so, with 137,500 others saying they were Métis and something else.

According to a recent court decision, the definition of Métis is someone who:

1. has some ancestral family connection (not necessarily genetic),
2. identifies himself or herself as Métis, and
3. is accepted by the Métis community or a locally organized community branch, chapter, or council of a Métis association or organization with which that person wishes to be associated. (Plainspeak 2000:4)

The Métis population in the Prairies is made up, in part, of communities of varying sizes (e.g., hamlets, villages, and towns). In 2001, there were four Alberta municipalities with 21,858 people; in Saskatchewan, 28 rural communities numbering from 27 to 4582 for a combined population of 15,805; and in Manitoba, 13 rural communities, totalling 11,617.

The early months of 2013 brought good news for the Métis. In early January, the Federal Court of Canada ruled that Métis and Non-Status Indians qualify as "Indians" under the 1867 Constitution Act. While the ruling was encouraging for the nearly one million Métis and Non-Status people, it is unlikely that it will go unchallenged by either Ottawa or those First Nations that come under the Indian Act. The Court's ruling essentially doubles the number of "recognized" Aboriginal people in Canada, thereby putting considerable economic and other strain on the federal government. Demands for health, education, and additional considerations by Métis and Non-Status peoples would likely result in Ottawa challenging the ruling or redefining its relationship with indigenous peoples.

In March, there was more good news. In a 144-page decision, the Supreme Court of Canada declared that the Crown had failed the Métis over 140 years ago. The Manitoba Act of 1870, by which the province entered Confederation, had promised the Métis 1.4 million acres of land. This land was never properly distributed because, in the words of the Court's ruling, "of repeated mistakes and inaction that persisted for more than a decade." The Manitoba Métis Federation had pursued the case for 30 years, not with the intention of claiming Winnipeg (which rests on some of the land allotted to the Métis) nor to reclaim land by way of compensation, but because they sought an acknowledgment of past injustices. The Crown's lawyers, on the other hand, had argued that the case should have been thrown out because it was more than a century old (Paradis, 2013).

In March, in the wake of the Supreme Court's ruling over the lost 1870 Métis lands, Alberta signed an $85 million agreement to help improve the province's eight Métis settlements. The agreement, signed with the Métis Settlements General Council, was for 10 years of funding to help the settlements become self-sustaining municipalities and to improve education, employment, and local government accountability, but most will likely go toward upgrading crumbling infrastructure. Randy Hardy, president of the Métis Settlements General Council, praised the deal, calling it "a significant milestone in [Métis] history" and lauded Alberta as the only province to have "stepped up to the plate and took the initiative and claimed responsibility for the Métis" (Walton and Wingrove, 2013). Alberta is the only province to have set aside land (which it did in 1938) for the Métis. As of 2013, there were about 4,800 people living in eight settlements in the province.

Native Individuals 9-1

Gabriel Dumont: Métis war leader, Wild West show performer, trader, and farmer.

Cuthbert Grant: Métis leader who won the Battle of Seven Oaks in 1816.

Mekaisto ("Red Crow"): Great nineteenth-century Blackfoot leader.

Mistahimaskwa ("Big Bear"): A nineteenth-century Plains Cree leader who fought for a good treaty for his people and who was wrongfully imprisoned for the actions of others during the Second Riel Rebellion.

Louis Riel: College-educated Métis who was chosen to lead his people in two rebellions against mistreatment by the federal government.

Sackomaph: A nineteenth-century Peigan chief reported to have had many horses.

Saukamappee: An eighteenth-century Plains Cree from whom we have learned much about his people and their relationship to the Blackfoot.

Timeline 9-1

9500 B.C.: First archaeologically documented arrival of people on the Plains.

9000 B.C.: Arrival of buffalo and grasslands on the Plains.

6000 B.C.: Introduction of the atlatl, or spear-thrower, to the Plains.

3000 B.C.: First construction of the Majorville Medicine Wheel.

1000 B.C.: Creation of Head-Smashed-In-Buffalo-Jump.

A.D. 250: Bows and arrows come to the Plains.

1700: Horses appear on the Canadian Plains.

1722: The Plains Cree and Blackfoot join forces against the Shoshoni.

1790s: The Gros Ventre are driven out of the Canadian Plains.

1816: The Métis defeat Governor Semple at the Battle of Seven Oaks.

1849: Métis trader Pierre Guillaume Sayer is released at the end of his trial.

1851: The Métis defeat the Sioux at the Battle of Grand Coteau.

1869–70: First Riel Rebellion.

1880s: Large buffalo herds are no more.

1885: Second Riel Rebellion.

1895: The Sun Dance is made illegal.

1951: Ban on Sun Dance is lifted.

KEY TERMS

atlatl (Nahuatl)

iniskim (Blackfoot)

medicine wheels

Michif

Ninauposkitzipxpe (Blackfoot)

Nitapiksisako (Blackfoot)

tipi

CONTENT QUESTIONS

1. What did buffalo provide for the Plains people?
2. What is the Sun Dance?
3. How did the horse change Plains life?
4. Identify the three language families spoken in the Canadian Plains.
5. What are Warrior Societies?

WEBLINKS

www.bloodtribe.org

This is a comprehensive website about the government, history, and community of the Kainai or Blood Nation people in southwestern Alberta.

www.carrythekettle.ca

This is the website of an Assiniboine people that tells an interesting story about the origin of their band and their name.

www.tsuutina.ca

This is a good, comprehensive website about the culture, lands, history, and administration of the Tsuu Tina or Sarcee people.

chapter ten

The Plateau

OVERVIEW

The Plateau (often earlier referred to as the Cordillera) is a diverse region—physically, linguistically, and culturally. The Plateau people live in areas of plateaus, mountains, and river valleys, which supply them with valued resources, such as salmon (particularly in the lower river regions), black-tailed deer, elk, beaver, marmot, mountain goat, and important roots, such as the **camas** (a lily-related edible bulb) and the **bitterroot** (a root that is sweet and edible in spring, but bitter in the summer). Linguistically, there are three different Plateau groups: Athapaskan, Salishan, and Kootenayan—the same amount of linguistic variation that you would find in the eastern six provinces of Canada.

THE ATHAPASKANS

Carrier

The name "Carrier" is derived from the Sekani term **"aghelhne,"** meaning "the ones who pack." This is a reference to a funeral ritual in which a widow gathered and carried the cremated remains of her spouse for three years. A more generally preferred name in most Carrier communities, for them and for their language, is Dakelh, from **"uda ukelha"** ("people who travel by water in the morning," which has a general meaning, that of "Natives"). Different names appear for distinct groups within the Carrier. The northern Carrier of Moricetown and Hagwilget refer to themselves as **Wet'suwet'en**. The people from the Babine Lake area are sometimes called **Ned'ut'en**. Similar to the peoples of the Northwest Coast, the Carrier (and their fellow Athapaskan-speaking Chilcotin) had matrilineal clans, and social divisions that have been termed "nobles," "commoners," and "slaves." It should be noted that these European terms exaggerate the social distance between the different divisions and don't allow for the social mobility that existed between these groups. While precise numbers are difficult to arrive at, there were more than 7500 Carrier in the spring of 2006.

The Carrier were the predominant Native group in the Plateau that the Northwest Company encountered when it established a network of inland posts in 1805. The Carrier established their own powerful trade networks, particularly through one leader, named **Kwah** (meaning "chief, leader"; c. 1755–1850). One famous incident happened that included Kwah and James Douglas, who would later become governor of the colony. In 1823, two Carrier killed two White men. One of these Carrier was quietly killed under mysterious circumstances, and the other evaded the Hudson's Bay Company (which had taken over the Northwest Company in 1821) until 1828, when he was killed either by Douglas or by someone connected with Douglas. This could have led to an escalated conflict between the Carrier and Whites, but the situation was defused. Two different versions of the events attempt to explain why trouble didn't happen. Non-Native writers have long claimed that Douglas's diplomacy and strength defused the situation. However, Carrier oral tradition suggests that Kwah refrained from retaliation for his own reasons, probably under the influence of his two grandsons, then young men.

In 1996, 1510 people reported themselves as speaking Carrier (both Southern and Northern dialects), making it the leading British Columbian Native language in terms of numbers. However, there will be an ongoing struggle to preserve this language. Fluent speakers in most Carrier communities are 40 years old or over. Younger adults raising small children do not or cannot speak Dakelh and, therefore, very few children are still being raised in the language. Turning this trend around will be a struggle.

Box 10-1 describes the Wet'suwet'en's actions to conserve salmon stocks.

Chilcotin

The name traditionally written as Chilcotin but often written now as Tsilhqot'in, means "young-man's river people." Estimates of their pre-contact numbers vary from 1500 to 2500, not far off their numbers today. In 1982, it was reported that there were 1200 speakers out of a population of 1800, but studies have pointed to a severe decline in the number of speakers of Tsilhqot'in since then. Today, Tsilhqot'in live on a few reserves on their own and in at least one in which they are mixed in with the Carrier. They are best known historically for an incident that was destructive to their people and that still lives on in the memories of the people's Elders. This incident is known by the somewhat exaggerated name of the Chilcotin War.

The Chilcotin War

Although a fur trade post had been established and ultimately abandoned in their country, the Chilcotin were fundamentally untouched by European society until 1862, when they were hit hard by both the Gold Rush and smallpox. They were then powerfully affected by two White men, with disastrous results. One of the men was Joseph Trutch. His deep-seated racial prejudice can be seen in the following quote from 1850: "I think they are ugliest & laziest creatures I ever saw, & we sho[ul]d as soon think of being afraid of our dogs as of them" (Fisher 1977:161). Trutch arrived in British Columbia in 1859 and worked for five years as a surveyor and engineer. In 1864, he was made the Chief Commissioner of Lands

BOX 10-1   Wet'suwet'en Salmon Conservation

At the time of first contact, the Wet'suwet'en enjoyed a rich salmon fishery on the Bulkley River, a tributary of the Skeena River. Their preferred method of fishing was through the use of weirs and other traps. These methods enabled them to practise sound conservation as they were selective; that is, they made it relatively easy for the people to select how many and what age fish they would catch and how many they should let go, thus ensuring that the fish population stayed at a healthy level. However, beginning in the early 1900s, federal fisheries officers claimed that the Wet'suwet'en were taking too many fish. Perhaps it would be more accurate to say that their perception was that such fishing took too many fish away from the more highly regarded non-Native enterprises that harvested many more salmon. The Wet'suwet'en fish weirs persisted until the mid-1930s, when fishways were installed. While these helped the salmon swim upstream, they also destroyed the weirs. The Wet'suwet'en had to use other fishing methods, such as gill netting, jigging, and gaffing, which weren't as selective as the weirs and the traps.

During the 1990s, conservation became very important as the stocks of salmon became depleted. Two conservation measures taken by the Wet'suwet'en show how they acted to preserve the salmon. One of these measures was banning jigging for salmon. This practice involved using a short pole with a heavy line and sinker and a large three-pronged hook. The idea was to snag the fish as they went past. This method had a high loss rate (17 percent, according to a Wet'suwet'en Watershed Authority study published in 1994), which included injuring but not immediately killing the fish that got away. The Wet'suwet'en Hereditary Chiefs banned the practice in 1994, and the ban was enforced by the Wet'suwet'en Rangers. They were successful. Had the ban been set and enforced by the Department of Fisheries and Oceans, it might not have had a high level of success.

and Works. His land policies continue to have a negative impact on Aboriginal land claims in British Columbia. Trutch could not "see why they should either retain these lands to the prejudice of the general [i.e., White] interest of the Colony, or be allowed to make a market of them either to the Government or to Individuals." Making "a market of them" was the legally prescribed act of making treaties, something that took place that century in every province west of Quebec. The Chilcotin rightly felt that the official policy in the young colony was to take their land with no recompense. This feeling was exacerbated when British entrepreneur Alfred Waddington began to construct a road through the heart of Chilcotin territory in 1863. The road crew hired Chilcotin to work for them. The Chilcotin were treated poorly, promissory notes were issued instead of pay, and the people had little food.

In the spring of 1864, a road crew foreman named Brewster accused half-starved Chilcotin workers of stealing flour. He took down their names and issued a prediction that they would die of smallpox. To the Chilcotin, that probably sounded like a threat, as if he would deliberately spread the disease. On April 29, three Chilcotin went to the man who operated a ferry on the Homathko River and asked him to share food with them. In Chilcotin culture, those who had food shared it with those who did not. The ferryman apparently refused to share. He was killed, and the food was taken.

The three Chilcotin went to the road crew that night, and talked with 16 Chilcotin who worked with 12 White men. The Chilcotin road crew members were fairly easily persuaded to attack the White men. Their food situation, and the Whites' move onto their land, were probably the main factors in their decision. The Chilcotin killed nine of the road crew; three Whites escaped. Further down the road was the hated Brewster and three other Whites. The Chilcotin soon killed them as well.

The Chilcotin met up with a respected older leader of their people, Telloot (sometimes Taloot or Tellot), and their number grew to about 30. They later killed a White settler who, like Brewster, had apparently threatened them with smallpox and had earlier driven them off of a traditional campsite, claiming it as his own.

When the newspapers in the capital of Victoria found out about these incidents, their reports were predictably one-sided and they called for vengeance. The editor of the *British Colonist* said that White colonists should not rest until "every member of that rascally murderous tribe is suspended to the trees of their own forests" ("Indian Murders" 1864). Governor Seymour organized two parties to go to Chilcotin country. A man called Cox led one group of about 50 men, mostly Americans, to bring back gold from the area. A Chilcotin leader referred to as Chief Alexis, who had not been involved with the action, was sent to Seymour to bring a message from the two leaders of the uprising, Telloot and Klatsassin. Those two men offered to cease hostilities and give themselves up. According to the Chilcotin, Cox said that he would guarantee the Chilcotin's safety if they came peacefully to a meeting arranged for August 11, 1864. Telloot, Klatsassin, and six others accompanied Chief Alexis in good faith. Cox apparently broke his word, surrounded them, and commanded them to lay down their weapons and surrender. Telloot is reputed to have smashed his rifle against a tree in response.

Two were freed with no charges laid and one escaped. Five were convicted: Telloot, Klatsassin, Klatsassin's 18-year-old son, and two others. The judge, Chief Justice Matthew Baillie Begbie, was not without sympathy for their cause, saying "[t]he treatment of the Indians, employed in packing, received at the hands of Brewster and his party was at once calculated to arouse their cupidity [desire for goods] and provoke their vengeance" ("Sir James Douglas and the Indians" 1864). However, in September they were hanged in front of an audience of about 200. All told, 20 White men had been killed, but the death toll for the Chilcotin was not recorded. If it had been, it might have included those Chilcotin who died of starvation in the winter of 1864–65, driven out of their homeland by the disruption of the time. The road they had fought to stop ended up stretching only 64 kilometres. A mountain was eventually named after the entrepreneur who planned the road, Alfred Waddington.

It is important to discuss this issue because, for the Chilcotin, the affair is still very much alive. In 1993, B.C. Attorney-General Colin Gabelmann apologized to the Chilcotin for the executions of the five men, calling the hangings a tragedy.

Box 10-2 explains the origin of some British Columbia placenames, including "Chilcotin."

	British Columbia Placenames from Plateau Peoples
BOX 10-2	

Name	Nation	Meaning
Chilcotin	Chilcotin	young man's river people
Kamloops	Shuswap	meeting of the waters
Okanagan	Okanagan	head of the river
Kootenay	Ktunaxa	people of the dense forest or brush

KOOTENAYAN
Ktunaxa or Kutenai

The Kootenayan people call themselves "Ktunaxa," which is sometimes translated as "people of the dense forest or brush." The English name "Kutenai" (also spelled "Kootenay") is said to have come from the Blackfoot pronunciation of their name.

While the people have been in the mountains for thousands of years, their territory used to extend east into the Prairies, about halfway across what is now Alberta. Their traditional culture incorporated such Plains features as a military/police group (e.g., the Crazy Dogs Society) and the Sun Dance. The more powerful Blackfoot drove the Ktunaxa out of the Prairies by the middle of the nineteenth century.

Their language is unique, related to no other. But with fewer than 200 speakers, and a writing system that came into existence only 25 years ago, it is under threat of extinction. However, the people are fighting for its survival. Elders present the language in the Ktunaxa daycare centres, and the people have developed learning modules in the language for at least Grades 4 and 6.

Traditionally, the people were divided into two separate bands, called the Upper Kutenai and Lower Kutenai in English (based on their position on the Columbia and Kutenai rivers). Now, under the Ktunaxa-Kinbasket Tribal Council, there are seven bands, or First Nations. Five are located in Canada—the St. Mary's or A'Qam, the Lower Kootenay or Yaqan nukiy ("the people where the rock is standing"), Tobacco Plains or ʔakin'kuntlasnuqtli? ("people of the place of the flying head"), Columbia Lake or Akisq'nuk ("two bodies of water"), and Shuswap (where Shuswap is spoken)—and two are located in northern Idaho and northwestern Montana. The Kutenai number fewer than 1000 in Canada today, probably slightly less than half their population at first contact.

INTERIOR SALISH

The Salish (meaning "people") live both in the Plateau region (where anthropologists have termed them "Interior Salish") and on the Northwest Coast (where they have been termed "Coast Salish"). Anthropologists typically group the Interior Salish into five different divisions, including the Shuswap, Okanagan, Lillooet, Thompson, and Lake, but the latter group has disappeared in Canada, moving to the United States.

Shuswap or Secwepemc

The Shuswap or Secwepemc (as they prefer to be called) are Salish speakers who live in south-central British Columbia. They were hit hard by the smallpox epidemic of 1862 but still numbered about 7200 late in the nineteenth century, a figure only a few hundred less than their population in 2006. There are fewer than 700 speakers of Secwepemc.

The Shuswap have long been prominently involved with Native politics on provincial, national, and international levels. Along with the Chilcotin, they formed the British Columbia Interior Confederacy in 1945 and were the main driving force behind the North American Indian Brotherhood. A leading figure in that involvement was **George Manuel**, who was first president of the largely British Columbia–centred North American Indian Brotherhood, then the National Indian Brotherhood (precursor to the Assembly of First Nations) from its beginning in 1970 to 1976, and finally the World Council of Indigenous People, an international organization launched at Port Alberni, B.C.

Okanagan

The name Okanagan comes from a word meaning "head of the river," referring to the highest point to which salmon could ascend. The people live both in northern Washington and in south-central British Columbia, with fewer than 500 fluent speakers of their language, Nsilxcin. Today the people are promoting their language in two main ways. In the Okanagan First Nation community, they have developed a daycare centre where an Elders' group, the Okanagan Language and Cultural Society, and a local theatre group are adapting children's games and stories incorporating the Okanagan language. They also have an educational institution, the E'nowkin Centre in Penticton, at which courses in speaking, reading, and writing Nsilxcin are taught. The registered population in May 2006 was 4218.

Lillooet

The Lillooet or Lil'wat ("Wild Onion") speak a language that has two dialects, Upper and Lower St'at'imc. In Mount Currie, their largest community (with a registered population of 1892 in May 2006), they were one of the first bands in Canada (beginning in 1975) to successfully run an in-community teacher training program, in connection with Simon Fraser University. Together, the university students and staff developed a program that not only successfully graduated fully qualified teachers but also brought their language into modern times with an accurate writing system, rigorous language curriculum, and a dictionary. Initially, the children they taught were somewhat resistant to the language lessons, thinking (like many non-Natives) that these languages were irrelevant to their future careers and lives. However, through extension of the language material into social studies and science classes, the students began to realize the interconnection of identity (through language and culture) and a career in the "modern" world. The education of the children in the language is necessary to its survival, as there are around 300 fluent speakers. Their registered population was over 4000 in May 2006.

Box 10-3 excerpts an important declaration by the Lillooet people in 1911.

BOX 10-3   The Declaration of the Lillooet Tribe

On May 10, 1911, at Seton Bridge, British Columbia, the 16 chiefs of the Lillooet signed a written declaration as a statement of their sovereignty and as a protest against the encroachment on their land by local settlers. This is a small part of the "Declaration of the Lillooet Tribe:"

> We claim that we are the rightful owners of our tribal territory . . . We have always lived in our country; at no time have we ever deserted it, or left it to others. We have retained it from the invasion of other tribes at the cost of our blood. Our

ancestors were in possession of our country centuries before the whites came . . . . We are aware the B.C. government claims our country . . . but we deny their right to it. We never gave it nor sold it to them. They certainly never got the title to the country from us, neither by agreement nor conquest . . . We have felt keenly the stealing of our lands by the B.C. government . . . We felt helpless and dejected; but lately we begin to hope. We think that perhaps after all we may get redress from the greater white chiefs away in the King's country, or in Ottawa (Lil' Wat Nation 1911).

Thompson/Nicola/Ntlakyapamuk

The people sometimes labelled as Thompson and Nicola (or just one of the two), or sometimes Ntlakyapamuk, are speakers of a language currently written as Nle7kepmxcin (as taught through the Nicola Institute of Technology).

One reason for this labelling confusion is that these people have had a long tradition of working together in common initiatives, crossing the ethnic borders placed upon them by outsiders. In 1879, a large number of these people and some of their neighbours gathered together at Lytton to come up with solutions to the problems of adapting to the newcomers. According to Robin Fisher, they

> . . . agreed on a set of regulations designed to foster the education of their children, to improve sanitary and medical facilities in the village, to subdivide arable land on an individual basis, to reduce the number of non-working days, to abolish the potlatch, and to levy fines for drunkenness and gambling. (Fisher 1977:179)

They elected a Nicola head chief and a council of 13 people to administer these important ordinances. The local Indian reserve commissioner, Gilbert Sproat, wrote to Ottawa saying that the Lytton meeting demonstrated "the laudable desire of the Indians to make efforts, at their own cost principally, to improve the physical condition and the minds of their children and to train themselves for citizenship" (Fisher 1977:179).

The settlers were horrified by any thought of a confederation of Natives (who still outnumbered the settlers). The editor of an influential newspaper, the *Victoria Daily Standard*, referred to the meeting and its developments as "in every way objectionable," and expressed his concern that the people might try to "obtain some privilege or concession antagonistic to white interests" (in Fisher 1977:179). His influence, plus settler letters to Ottawa, plus the opposition to Native political initiatives by the Indian superintendent in

Victoria and the department responsible for "Indian Affairs" in Ottawa quashed this move for self-government. Sproat was bullied out of his job the next year and was replaced by Peter O'Reilly, brother-in-law of the hated Joseph Trutch and a man with a track record of imposing reserves on the people that ignored such concerns as burial grounds and fields the people had been planting and grazing their cattle on for years. In May 2006, their registered population was more than 4400.

Native Individuals 10-1

Kwah ("leader, chief"; c. 1755–1850): An important historical Carrier chief.

George Manuel: A Shuswap politician who became the president of the National Indian Brotherhood.

Timeline 10-1

1828: Confrontation between Kwah and James Douglas.

1862: Gold rush in the interior of British Columbia.

1862: Epidemic of smallpox strikes the interior of British Columbia.

1864: Joseph Trutch made the Chief Commissioner of Lands and Works.

1864: Chilcotin War.

1880: Aboriginals constitute a majority of the recorded population of British Columbia of 49,459.

1891: Aboriginals considered to constitute less than one third of the population of 98,173.

KEY TERMS

bitterroot   camas

CONTENT QUESTIONS

1. What three language groups exist in the Plateau?
2. Identify two salmon conservation measures initiated by the Wet'suwet'en (Carrier).
3. Which of the Plateau languages has no known related languages?
4. Why did the Chilcotin War take place?
5. Why was the group that gathered at Lytton in 1879 unable to achieve its goals?

WEBLINKS

www.ktunaxa.org
This is the website of the Ktunaxa or Kootenay nation.

http://enowkin.tripod.com
This website deals with the En'owkin Centre, where the Okanagan people teach their language, Nsilxcin, and other aspects of their culture.

www.secwepemc.org
This is the website of the Secwepemc Cultural Education Society.

www.wetsuweten.com
This is the comprehensive website of the Wet'suwet'en people.

www.canadianmysteries.ca/sites/klatsassin/home/indexen.html
This site provides a fascinating archive of primary sources and a useful discussion of the Chilcotin war.

chapter eleven

The Northwest Coast

OVERVIEW

The Northwest Coast is unique. There are more superlatives that can be used for this cultural area than any other. One is that the people drew from the richest natural resources in Canada. The sea provided well for the people, with whales, several varieties of seals, porpoises, sea lions, sea otter, five main species of salmon (sockeye, coho, chinook, chum, and pink), halibut, herring, cod, **oolichan** or candlefish (so named because of all the oil they contain), clams, mussels, crabs, eggs from sea birds, and seaweed. And then there are the trees. The spectacular woods in British Columbia helped the Northwest Coast people become accomplished woodworkers, with tall totem poles, 42-metre-long houses made out of massive poles and planks, impressive cedar war canoes up to 20 metres long that could carry 60 people, and square boxes made out of one flat piece of wood steamed until it was pliable enough to bend. Not surprisingly, with these rich resources and with the people's careful management of the resources, the Northwest Coast had the densest population: at least 50,000 people along a fairly narrow 2000-kilometre stretch of coastline in British Columbia. Villages lasted longer than anywhere else, some showing continuous occupation for as many as 4000 years. Imagine a Canadian town being 4000 years old! The societies had the greatest degree of stratification. They had what anthropologists term "chiefs," powerful figures whose authority would have far exceeded that of the tribal leaders found elsewhere in traditional Aboriginal cultures in Canada. Other groups included the nobility, commoners, and even prisoners who constituted a servant/slave class (although with more rights and respect than was ever afforded to African slaves brought to the Americas).

The Northwest Coast also has the greatest variety of languages in Canada, more than the diversity of languages that exists in all of Europe. There are the language isolates of

Tlingit, Haida, and Tsimshian, and the language families of Salish and Wakashan—five of the eleven Aboriginal language varieties found in Canada.

A key feature of Northwest Coast cultures, one that has slowly come to affect decisions in their land claims, is that these cultures arguably have the clearest defined notion of property in Native Canada. Families or lineages had clearly demarcated ownership of rights to hunt, fish, pick berries, or harvest other materials from a geographically defined territory. In a number of ways these concepts are closer to European notions of "ownership of land" than those that existed in the rest of Native Canada. Northwest Coast cultures have had a long, hard fight, however, to demonstrate that to anthropologically ignorant judges.

One more traditional feature should be mentioned here. Kinship was determined matrilineally among the Tlingit, Haida, and Tsimshian to the north, with two major organizations (typically identified as the Raven and the Eagle or Wolf), known by anthropologists as moieties, being the main social divisions.

TLINGIT

The Tlingit ("people"), whose traditional homeland stretched over some 640 kilometres of coastline, are the northernmost of the Northwest Coast peoples and, at one time, might also have been the most numerous. It has been estimated that in the eighteenth century they numbered as many as 15,000. They were also a powerful people, successful as raiders to the south and as traders into the interior of Alaska, British Columbia, and the Yukon. As traders into the interior, they held a virtual monopoly on goods from the sea and on the cedar bark and wild mountain goat wool blend blankets that came to be named after one of the Tlingit groups, the Chilkat. The Tlingit's trade grew stronger with early European contact, as both Russians and British saw the practicality of having Tlingit middlemen. This contact also had an inevitable negative side, as smallpox diminished Tlingit numbers first in 1775 and then, more seriously, in the great epidemic of 1835–40, which, some writers claim, killed off half of the people. The Gold Rush in 1895, with the influx of so many outsiders, finally broke the back of the Tlingit trade.

While the Tlingit language has a similar grammar to neighbouring Athapaskan languages, the two do not share vocabulary to any significant extent. This is a good argument for the position that Tlingit is a language isolate. The close contact between Tlingit and Athapaskan peoples, including a significant amount of intermarriage, not only produced grammatical similarity but also made the cultures very similar, too.

The majority of Tlingit live along the Alaskan panhandle, the narrow southern coastline of that state. There are two groups in Canada that belong to the Daak Ka Tlingit Nation: the Taku River Tlingit, whose community straddles the British Columbia/Yukon border of Atlin, and the Carcross-Tagish First Nation, in the Yukon. The latter community involves Tagish who speak Tlingit and have some other Tlingit features. All three are descended from coastal Tlingit who moved up the Taku River and who married extensively with Athapaskans living in the interior. Despite the political difficulties of claiming land divided by the non-Tlingit borders of Alaska, British Columbia, and the Yukon, all three groups have been able to reach advanced stages of the treaty process. The Tlingit connection with the land to which they are asserting their rights was well expressed in 1915 by Chief Taku Jack to the Royal Commission for Indian Affairs for British Columbia:

Atlin means big lake, and that is the place where we used to stay. That is the reason I used to think that the whites were not going to give me any trouble because they call us after this lake. They call us Atlin Indians because they know I belong to this country. (Hudson 1989:3)

The registered population in May 2006 was 969 for the two communities.

HAIDA

The Haida, whose name (actually Xa'ida) means "people," are strongly connected with the islands known in English as the Queen Charlotte Islands, but in Haida as "Haida Gwaii." As is typical of Northwest Coast peoples, the sea and the forests provided well for them, with the sea providing them with fur seals, sea otters, and sea lions in particular.

The Haida numbered over 8000 at the time of first contact, near the end of the eighteenth century. But with smallpox and the other negative effects of dealing with the newcomers, their numbers diminished to about 500 by 1915. They once had 14 communities but were compelled to relocate into two: Massett and Skidegate. The villages they were forced to abandon now stand as sacred places, and efforts are being made to preserve the totem poles and buildings that still remain. Their language, called Xaadas, is generally considered to be a language isolate (although a few scholars have tried to connect it with the Dene languages). It has fewer than 100 speakers, most of them in Canada. Their registered population in May 2006 was 3976.

The Haida have long offered resistance to outsider control. This tradition featured such leaders as **Koyah** ("Raven," died circa 1791), who resisted English attempts at controlling the fur trade by attacking ships with his war canoes; **Reverend Peter Kelly** (1885–1966), who fought for Aboriginal rights in British Columbia through the Allied Tribes of British Columbia (formed in 1916); and **Bill Wilson**, who continued that fight in modern times. The tradition continues today with **Guujaaw** ("Drum"), president of the Haida Nation, who is suing the British Columbia Supreme Court for recognition of Haida rights to Haida Gwaii.

Box 11-1 introduces some of the names of Haida families, or social divisions. Box 11-2 introduces Bill Reid, a Haida artist whose work has created some controversy.

BOX 11-1   Families or Houses of the Haida

Traditional social divisions of the Haida begin with two moieties, Raven and Eagle, which break down into clans, which could be divided into houses or families. The following are names of some of these houses:

House	Meaning
Naalgus-haida	dark house people
Nakalas-hadai	clay house people
Nakalnas-hadai	empty house people
Nakedduts-hadai	people of the house that went away discouraged
Nayuuns-haidagai	great house people
Nasagas-haidagai	rotten house people

What do you think -**na**- means in these words?

BOX 11-2   Bill Reid (1920–1998)

Bill Reid is a controversial Haida artist who combined two worlds to draw attention to Haida art and land claims, in the process making himself rich and famous. His father was White and his mother was Haida. As with many Canadians with mixed Native heritage, his Native ancestry was hidden from him. He was raised in Victoria. It wasn't until he was a teenager that he learned of his Haida background. A powerful moment in Bill Reid's life came when he was 23, during his first trip to Haida Gwaii, where he met his grandfather, Charles Gladstone, a stone carver of argillite and an engraver in silver. Gladstone had inherited the tools and probably had been taught by his uncle, noted Haida sculptor Charles Edenshaw, whose work can be seen in museums and in books around the world. Both would be indirect mentors of Bill Reid.

Reid got a job working as a CBC radio announcer in Toronto in 1948. In Toronto he studied jewellery making part-time at what is now Ryerson University and apprenticed at the Platinum Art Company. He also spent hours studying a Haida totem pole that was kept at the Royal Ontario Museum. That totem pole gave him his first significant insights into the patterns of Haida art.

He returned to Vancouver in 1951 where, between hours working for the CBC, he worked on his art in a basement workshop. He began to study the works of his great-great-uncle Charles Edenshaw—the hundreds of pieces of gold and silver jewellery his ancestor had created.

Reid next became involved with the salvage and restoration of rotting Haida totem poles and houses, through the Department of Anthropology at the University of British Columbia. When he received his first big contract in 1958, he quit the CBC to dedicate himself to this project, now an outdoor exhibit at the University of British Columbia Museum of Anthropology. From the 1960s to the 1970s, he became well known for creating beautiful jewellery and small, wooden carvings using Haida designs.

His major fame, however, came about in a controversial way. He contracted Parkinson's disease, a neurological disorder that made it increasingly difficult for him to use the fine motor skills necessary for carving. But during the 1980s, his previous works and his ability to deal with non-Native media enabled him to acquire lucrative contracts that he could not refuse. In 1982, the Dogfish Transformation Pendant, a gold necklace based on a boxwood carving he had made earlier, sold for $100,000. Jim Hart, a young Haida artist did much of the work. Increasingly, through the 1980s and early 1990s, Haida artists such as Hart, Guujaaw, Sharon Hitchcock, Don Yeomans, Kwakiutl painter Ben Houstie, and local White artists, such as George Rammell, worked on Reid's art. Famous pieces were designed and supervised by Reid, with a great deal of the creative and manual input coming from the others. These include such works of art as "Lootas," a 15-metre war canoe displayed at Vancouver's world fair, Expo 86; "The Spirit of Haida Gwaii," a five-ton bronze sculpture based on a small, black argillite "spirit canoe" Reid studied at a museum, which was purchased for $1.5 million in 1991 for the Canadian Embassy in Washington; and a copy of the "spirit canoe," called "The Jade Canoe," purchased by the Vancouver

(continued)

airport for $3 million (the highest price ever paid for a Canadian work of art).

Reid's position among the Haida is complicated. He is respected for popularizing Haida art and for his public support of Haida land claims. However, he is criticized by some of the people for overstating his role in the preservation of traditional Haida art forms, for sometimes exploiting and not properly crediting the input of other Haida artists in "his" works, and for using non-Native artists in the making of "Native art."

TSIMSHIAN

The different Tsimshian peoples are named after the two rivers at the centre of their traditional territory: the Tsimshian ("people [inside] of the Skeena River") and Gitxsan (earlier spelt Gitksan, "Skeena River people") after the more southerly of the rivers, and the Nisga'a after the more northerly, the Nass River. The Gitxsan and the Nisga'a can be considered as speaking dialects of a language, while the Tsimshian speak a dialect different enough to be considered a related language. Most scholars consider Tsimshian to be a language isolate, while some consider it a distant branch of the Penutian family.

The Tsimshian had a population of between 6000 and 10,000 at the time of first contact and number more than 11,000 now. They are culturally similar to the Tlingit and the Haida but differ in having four main social divisions, or **phratries** (Eagle, Raven, Wolf, and Killer Whale), rather than the two moieties of the Haida.

WAKASHAN

The name Wakashan is said to be derived from a word, "waukash," meaning "good," that Captain James Cook heard and assumed was the name of a people living by Nootka Sound. Wakashan peoples were traditionally similar socially to their northern neighbours in that the structure of their society was **hierarchical**, with leaders that were heads of powerful houses owned by leading lineages. They were different from the northerners, however, in that their society was not divided into two moieties. There were at least 10,000 Wakashan-speaking people during the early nineteenth century.

The people are divided linguistically into two groups: Northern and Southern Wakashan. The Northern Wakashan include the **Haisla**, who live just south of the Tsimshian and are associated with the community of Kitimaat; the **Heiltsuk**, who are particularly associated

The names "Haida" and "Haisla" look quite similar. The authors have read several books in which the lesser-known Haisla should have been referred to (see, for example, Friesen 1997:177).

with the community of Bella Bella; and the **Kwakiutl** (a name that is properly applied to only one community) or, more correctly **Kwakwaka'wakw**, by far the most numerous, powerful, and most often academically discussed group. In May 2006, the Haisla had a registered population of 1566 and the Heiltsuk had 2172. The Kwakwaka'wakw probably had a population of somewhere over 5500 (see Box 11-3).

The Southern Wakashan include the single community people of the **Nitinat (or Ditidaht)**, and the more numerous **Nootka** or **Nuu'chah'nulth** ("All along the mountains"). The latter name is the name that the people use, while the word Nootka, assigned to them by English speakers, is said to come from the time in 1778 when the people met with Captain Cook. According to the story, he asked them what sound they were at (now called Nootka Sound), they interpreted him as asking directions concerning Vancouver Island,

BOX 11-3   Carla and Eden Robinson

Carla Robinson, the evening anchor for CBC Newsworld, is part Haisla and part Heiltsuk. She was born and spent most of her childhood in her father's Haisla community of Kitimat, but also lived for a while in her mother's Heiltsuk community of Bella Bella. She was first inspired to be a journalist when she was 14. She saw a Native television reporter and felt that she could also get such a job. At 16, she got a job as a reporter at the *Northern Sentinel Press* (circulation approximately 25,000), where she first achieved some prominence for writing front-page articles on the death and subsequent memorial feast for Nisga'a hereditary Chief James Gosnell.

Since then, she has worked her way up the journalistic ladder, by writing for Native print media such as *Aboriginal Voices* and *Dreamspeaker*, mainstream media such as CBC's "Midday" (B.C.), CBC's Native current affairs series, and CBC's "All My Relations" (which had about 350,000 listeners after the first show), before she landed an anchor position at CBC Newsworld.

Carla has commented on her career and the role of employment equity in her

success. When she was asked about being a "token Indian" at the CBC, she replied:

> Like others, perhaps because I am Native I have managed to get a few jobs. If it was not for employment equity, I would more than likely not be given half the chances I have had. However, some people have had similar appointments and have not taken advantage of the opportunities available . . . Unless we get a few Native people in there, we will continue to appear to exist on charity and tokenism. But employment equity is not charity nor is it tokenism, it is necessary and important to address the historic disadvantages we face as Native people. (Robinson 1999)

Carla's older sister is Eden Robinson, who was born in 1968 in Kitamaat, and is an award-winning novelist, with three books: *Traplines* (1996), *Monkey Beach* (2000), and *Blood Sports* (2006). Eden Robinson has an M.A. in English from the University of British Columbia. Her writing is based in her culture and beliefs, but adds a strong psycho-thriller component from her favourite author when she was growing up: Stephen King.

and they then responded with **notka**, meaning "circle around." The Nootka had a registered population of 6146 in May 2006, while the Nitinat had 690.

The Nuu'chah'nulth hunted whales, including humpbacks, which could reach 15 metres in length, and grey whales, which could reach nearly 14 metres. That was one reason why they had to build especially large canoes (i.e., boats approximating the size of the animals they hunted), which other peoples were eager to obtain through trade. Typical of this hierarchical people, only the chief had the right to hunt whales, and he would go through an elaborate eight-month ritual before the hunt. Beginning in November, he would walk into the cold Pacific Ocean and rub his skin with nettles until he bled. The ceremonial name of the great Nuu'chah'nulth leader, Maquina, was **Tsaxhw'sip**, meaning "harpooner" (see Box 11-4).

COAST SALISH

The Coast Salish are divided into a number of separate groups, most prominently the **Stó:lo** Nation (formerly often referred to as the Cowichan), which encompasses 19 bands: the Squamish, Sechelt, Songish (Lkungen), Nuxalk (Bella Coola), and Comox. It has been estimated that at the time of contact, the Coast Salish had as many as 32,000 people but

---

BOX 11-4 | **Maquina (c. 1786-1825): A Man of Extreme Numbers**

Maquina ("moon" or "possessor of pebbles") was a powerful Nuu'chah'nulth chief whom we know a lot about because of an Englishman named John Jewitt. In 1815, Jewitt published an account of his three years living as a captive with Maquina. Of course, this account shows the biases of an outsider, but it is a good source for numbers:

Number of wives:	9 (at one time)
Number of "slaves":	50
Number of people living in his house:	100
Size of his house (Dimensions):	45 metres long
	11 to 12 metres wide
	4.2 metres high
Ridge Pole:	30 metres long × 2.5 metres in circumference
Planks:	3 metres long × 1.2 to 1.5 metres wide
Size of his canoe:	14 metres (hollowed out pine)

Maquina is a good extreme example of Northwest Coast hierarchical society (in the same way that kings Louis XIV and Henry VIII are good extreme examples of European monarchies). Keep in mind, however, that Nuu'chah'nulth society, even in Maquina's day, did not have the poverty or starvation of European monarchical societies. Also keep in mind that one reason that Maquina's numbers were as high as they were is that he and his people were going through a "sudden riches" period due to the fur trade.

were reduced to as few as 4120 in 1915. In May 2006, there was a registered population of more than 25,300.

The word Stó:lo means "river [people]," the Fraser River of southern British Columbia, beside which many of the Stó:lo live. Estimates of their population prior to contact vary, with 10,000 being the minimum figure. Being so close to the growing settler centres (e.g., Vancouver and New Westminster), they were hard hit by the effects of European colonization. In 1782, for example, it has been estimated that about 62 percent died of smallpox.

The language of these people is Halq'eméylem (or Halkomelem), which has three dialects: Upriver, with such communities as Chehalis and Chilliwack; Downriver, with such communities as Musqueam and Coquitlam; and Island, the most populated, with communities with such well-known names as Cowichan and Nanaimo ("named people"). Among the most notable achievements of the Stó:lo today is the curriculum they have developed for both their own schools and the non-Native schools in the urban areas that are near to the people. Their educational website, put together by the Stó:lo Curriculum Consortium, is a model for other Native and non-Native peoples (see the recommended website at the end of the chapter). Innovative education initiatives of the Stó:lo also include Chemainus Native College and Malaspina University College.

Native Individuals 11-1

Maquin(n)a: A powerful Nootka leader of the late eighteenth and early nineteenth century.

Bill Reid: A prominent twentieth-century Haida artist.

Carla Robinson: A Haisla/Heiltsuk anchorwoman for CBC Newsworld.

Eden Robinson: A Haisla/Heiltsuk author.

KEY TERMS

hierarchical

notka

oolichan

phratries

CONTENT QUESTIONS

1. Why were the peoples of the Northwest Coast able to have stratified societies and long-term houses and communities?

2. What is the longest period of continuous occupation of a Northwest Coast community?

3. How many language isolates and families are found in the Northwest Coast?

4. What are the main social divisions of the Tlingit, Haida, and Tsimshian?

5. At the time of contact, which was the largest in number of the Northwest Coast peoples?

WEBLINKS

www.haidanation.ca
This is a very comprehensive site concerning the Haida Nation.

www.mala.bc.ca
This website describes Malaspina University College and its programs concerning the local Native groups.

www.stolonation.bc.ca
This is a good site concerning the Stó:lo Nation or Coast Salish.

www.danaxdaxw.com
This is a comprehensive site concerning the Da'naxda'xw/Awaetlals First Nation of the Kwakiutl people.

chapter twelve

The Royal Proclamation and the Indian Act

THE ROYAL PROCLAMATION OF 1763

After the Treaty of Paris, which concluded the Seven Years War with France, British King George III issued the Royal Proclamation of 1763. This proclamation dealt with several issues, including some pertaining to Natives in Canada. It stated that any lands within the territorial confines of the new governments (which included present-day Quebec, Florida, and Grenada) that had not been ceded by the Indians ". . . are reserved to them, or any of them as their Hunting Grounds."

The reason cited for this was:

> whereas it is just and reasonable, and essential to our Interest, and the Security of our Colonies, that the Several Nations or Tribes of Indians with whom We are connected, and who live under our Protection, should not be molested or disturbed . . . (Great Britain 1763/1824)

The proclamation also dealt with land *not* within the limits of the new government. It reserved ". . . for the use of said Indians, all Land Territories not included within the limits of our Said . . . governments, or within the Limits of the Territory granted to the Hudson's Bay Company" (Great Britain 1763/1824).

In 1670, the Hudson's Bay Company received its charter from the British Crown. The new king, Charles II, gave the company monopoly of trade in the lands drained by the waters that flow into Hudson Bay. He also gave the company the rights to the land as well, calling it Rupert's Land, after the prince who had helped set up the company. At the time, no one had any idea of the size of the land parcel being given to the company. In essence, that land amounted to most of Quebec, a large portion of Ontario, all of Manitoba and Saskatchewan, and a major part of Alberta.

To prevent fraud, the proclamation provided a way in which lands could be acquired for settlement. Indian lands "shall be purchased only for Us, in our Name, at some public Meeting of Assembly of the said Indians." This implied that all lands that had not been surrendered by the Indians to the Crown belonged to the Indians. It reserved all unsettled land for the use of the Indians as their hunting grounds. It provided that lands required for settlement had to be bought from the Indians and could only be bought by the Crown at a public meeting.

The Royal Proclamation, therefore, set the stage for land surrender treaties signed by the Indians and the Crown. The reason for this is that under the Canadian legal system, English laws became a part of the law of Canada on the dates when colonial governments were formed. Under colonial rule, the Royal Proclamation became a part of Canadian law. Without the passing of a specific law overruling such a law (which hasn't taken place), the Royal Proclamation is still valid.

However, this leaves several questions that have been and are still being disputed in the courts. Despite the apparent clarity of the proclamation, several questions arise. Did the proclamation provide the source of Native title to the land or did it merely recognize the pre-existing reality that the lands belonged to the Indians? Not surprisingly, Native activists and leaders, as well as anthropologists and other scholars, take the position that the land did in fact belong to Aboriginal people and George III's proclamation simply affirmed this recognition. Did the proclamation apply to all of what is now Canada (as Native people contend)? Or did it apply simply to lands that had been discovered by the British up to 1763? The province of British Columbia has long operated on the basis of the latter argument, maintaining that the proclamation does not, therefore, apply to them.

THE INDIAN ACT

Since 1876, the Indian Act has existed as a tool of a large government bureaucracy "to deal" with Indians. But this bureaucratic management of Natives predates Confederation by over a hundred years, going back to 1755. Initially, the administration of Natives was in the hands of the military, reflecting the role and importance of Native people in inter-European wars. After the American War of Independence (American Revolution) and the War of 1812, European settlers believed that Natives posed a potential threat to them. Hence Indian affairs continued as a military concern.

In Upper Canada (Ontario), Native concerns remained in the hands of the military until 1830, when they were turned over to the lieutenant governor of the colony and the reserve system was implemented to encourage Indians to become farmers. Agrarianization and Christianization were seen as the best means of "civilizing" Indians.

In Lower Canada (Quebec), the military remained in charge of Indians until Lower and Upper Canada were united as the Province of Canada in 1840. At this time, all Native matters were transferred to the governor general. However, there was no budget for Native affairs and no Indian Department.

It was not until 1860 that Britain assigned full control of Indian matters to the colonies. The transfer of full control marked a change in the nature of Native–White relations. Until that time, Natives had retained a fair amount of autonomy. As long as Indian matters had remained in the hands of the military and later the British Colonial Office (1840–1860), there had been little interference. The British Colonial Office was far away and could do little about colonial matters.

Then in 1867, the British North America Act explicitly made "Indians and lands reserved for Indians" a federal responsibility. From 1867 to 1873, Natives were under the jurisdiction of the secretary of state. In 1873, they were transferred to the Department of the Interior. In 1880, a separate Indian Affairs Department was set up under John A. Macdonald, who was both Minister of the Interior and prime minister at the time.

Moving the Indian Affairs Department to the Ministry of the Interior reflects a trend that persists to this day. The department or ministry that houses Indian Affairs invariably reflects the primary concerns of the government at the time. Thus, we find Indian Affairs a branch of the Department of Mines and Resources in 1936, of Citizenship and Immigration in 1949 (a move found by First Nations to be rather ironic), of Northern Affairs and National Resources in 1965, and, finally, of the Department of Indian Affairs and Northern Development in 1966. Today it is called Indian and Northern Affairs Canada (INAC).

It is important to realize that the Indian Act of 1876, the tool with which the government controls Native people, was not a new piece of legislation. Rather, it was a consolidation of various pieces of existing federal and colonial statutes. The essential thrust of the legislation was to centralize and codify all legislation and to solidify the position of Natives as wards of the state.

Bands

The term **band** can be used in several ways. Chapter 7 showed that from an anthropological perspective, bands (i.e., microbands and macrobands) can be defined as small groupings of Native peoples based on fishing, hunting, and gathering activities. That chapter discussed bands (sometimes historically based on microbands and macrobands) as sociopolitical organizations within the federal system. Around 600 bands exist today. Their political structure and sometimes their very existence is a creature of the federal government. Bands are usually, but not always, of one cultural tradition. Their creation denied the existence of larger socio-political units meaningful to Aboriginal peoples, most particularly the tribe. In a way, the creation of formal bands can be considered a form of divide-and-conquer: the smaller the political unit, the less ability it will have to oppose the federal government. Recently, **tribal councils** have been created as larger units, but these sometimes involve peoples of different cultural traditions and have as yet relatively little power, although this might be changing.

Historically band officials have had little power, limited to minor issues such as truancy from school, weed and animal control, the construction and maintenance of roads, bridges, ditches and public buildings, distribution of land on the reserves, timber cutting permits, and relief for the sick and the aged. Even in these areas the federal government has long had the right to disallow any acts of band governments. Moreover, the chief and council are put in power through federal government-mandated, European-style, winner-take-all majoritarian elections. In some cases, such as with the Mohawk of Akwesasne and the Iroquois of Six Nations, the police had to force traditional chiefs out of power in order to introduce this form of government. Therefore the legitimacy of elected versus traditional chiefs is an issue of contention in some communities.

It is a common complaint that the Natives are over-governed. Insofar as Natives and Native affairs are big business, there are 14 federal government departments, including Health and Welfare and the Secretary of State, which have Native programs. In addition, there are provincial agencies that run Native programs. Some provinces, like Ontario, have Native affairs secretariats that function as provincial Indian affairs departments. It is important to realize that non-Natives run these departments with Natives occupying only minor positions. However, a Mohawk from Kahnawâke has risen to the position of deputy minister in the Department of Indian Affairs. With this exception, most Natives never rise above middle management. Therefore, the paternalistic attitude that was created over a hundred years ago and that was initiated with the arrival of the first Europeans still prevails, with Natives having little say in their own government.

Limitations of the Indian Act

The Indian Act has a history of restricting the personal freedoms of Native people in the name of assimilation or control. As we will see in Chapter 17, the potlatch ceremony was banned in 1884, in large part because the giveaways involved were viewed as "communist," against the principle of private property that governments were trying to instill. During the course of the next few decades, the Sun Dance and other traditional dances and ceremonies were outlawed as well. The ban on these activities lasted until 1951, when a number of revisions were made to the Indian Act. Also ended that year were two other severe restrictions: the ban on raising money to fight land claims cases, and the ban on western Natives forbidding them to appear in their traditional dress off reserve without the permission of the **Indian agent**.

Indian agents were white and male (with one female exception during World War II) and required no formal qualifications—just government experience or approval. The government's idea of the role of the Indian agent with respect to the bands under their control is well described by Robin Brownlie:

> The ideal that hovered before the officials' eyes was a quiet, hard-working, co-operative set of clients who offered no opposition to the agent's or the Indian department's authority. Agents did not want to hear about unfulfilled treaty provisions, unresolved grievances about lands and unsurrendered islands, or the argument of some that an outsider was not required to run the reserve. They did not want to see band councils used as political instruments to empower First Nations communities—the councils were designed merely as convenient handmaidens of DIA policy. Whenever the elected leaders attempted to reach beyond their extremely limited jurisdiction to matters of political importance, they ran headlong into the department's restrictive regulations and the determined opposition of its agents. (Brownlie 2003:xiv)

Indian agents were given a great deal of discretionary power to control various aspects of people's lives. If Native people wanted to sell the crops they had grown and harvested and the animals they had raised on reserve land, they had to ask for the Indian agent's permission. Fear of Natives brought on by the second Riel Rebellion in the Prairie Provinces also gave power to the Indian agent in the form of the Pass System (see Chapter 22). Natives could not leave their reserves unless they had received a "pass" (like a visa) permitting them to do so.

The Indian agents also issued food vouchers. In the late nineteenth century, Natives out west were low on food, even starving. This starvation was the product of the near-extinction of the buffalo, the poor lands many bands were forced to live on, and the inadequate way the government delivered the assistance promised in the treaties—assistance that was supposed to enable Natives to become farmers. The Indian agent controlled who would receive these food vouchers and who would not. Offend the Indian agent, and you could jeopardize your chances of receiving the food your family needed.

The Indian Act also restricted many recreational rights that other Canadians took for granted. Natives were forbidden to gamble, and people were encouraged to "snitch" on others. A person informing on a friend or family member could receive half of the fine the offender would have to pay (usually around $10). Indian agents could prevent Natives from shooting pool in a pool hall. Not until 1951 could Status Indians drink in licensed bars.

Some restrictions lasted until 1960. Prior to that year, Status Indians could not vote federally without losing their status (they had obtained the right to vote provincially a number of years earlier, the dates varying for different provinces; Inuit received the federal vote in 1950). Further, they would lose their status if they became doctors, lawyers, or ministers, or even if they obtained university degrees. Indian agents existed until the 1960s.

Indian Status: Who Defines Who Is an "Indian"?

Not surprisingly, there have been few issues that have generated as much controversy as who gets to define who is and isn't "Indian." Native people contend, rightly enough, that they are the best determiners of who is Native and who is not. Conversely, because the federal government funds Indians, it feels that it has a right to determine who should get **status**. Being "Indian" in Canada, in the eyes of the federal government, has nothing to do with biology or culture. "Indian" in Canada is a legal/political classification, subject to the Indian Act. It is the Indian Act that defines who is and is not Indian.

Government definition of "Indian" goes back to early legislation (1850) in Lower Canada (Quebec), which defined Indian in sweeping terms, including all persons of Indian ancestry, all persons married to Indians, anyone adopted by Indians and living in his or her adopted community, and, finally, anybody living with the band and recognized as being Indian by the band. The definition has become severely narrowed by subsequent government legislation.

Discriminating Against Women

Shortly after the early legislation (1851), the legal definition of who was "Indian" was amended. In order for a person to be an Indian, that person was required to be of Indian blood or, alternatively, at least show that his or her father was Indian. The law was also changed to provide that marriage only conferred status on non-Status Indian women, not vice versa. This set a precedent. Section 12 (1)(b) of the Indian Act was to read as follows:

12 (1) The following persons are not entitled to be registered, namely,

(b) a woman who married a person who is not an Indian . . .

Her children would likewise not have status, unlike the children of White women who married Status Indian men. Similarly, upon marriage, a woman lost her band status and became a member of her husband's band. These provisions violated notions of equality of the sexes and ran counter to notions of matrilineality (you belong to the clan or lineage of your mother, rather than of your father) held by a good number of Canadian First Nations.

Legal discrimination against Native women took a number of other different forms as well. Until 1951, the Indian Act forbade women from voting for band council.

In 1970, Jeannette Corbière Lavell, a Status Indian from the Ojibwa reserve of Wik-wemikong, was going to marry a non-Aboriginal man. She contested the discriminatory sections of the Indian Act on the grounds that it violated the Canadian Bill of Rights. In 1971, the Ontario County Court dismissed the case, essentially on the grounds that she had equal rights with other married Canadian women. She made an appeal to the Federal Court of Appeals and won, but the federal government decided that it would bring this case before the Supreme Court of Canada. Along with her case was that of Yvonne Bedard. She was a woman from the Six Nations Reserve who had lost her status when she married a non-Aboriginal man. After their separation, she tried unsuccessfully to return to live in the house that had been willed to her by her parents.

The federal government's appeal reflected its concerns that the change could complicate and make more expensive its handling of Native matters. Plus it was receiving pressure from the male-controlled and aptly named National Indian Brotherhood (NIB). The NIB had two main concerns. It was worried that this case might set a precedent for federal government tinkering with the Indian Act, not an unreasonable fear after the threats of the infamous White Paper of 1969, in which the federal government had proposed scrapping the Indian Act, and with it Indian rights and status. Second, the NIB was worried that this would result in further crowding on reserves, with non-Native men and their families moving into their communities.

In 1973, the Supreme Court voted five to four against the women, saying that they did not feel that the Bill of Rights could overrule the Indian Act in this way. Not surprisingly, the Native Women's Association of Canada was born around that time, writing its constitution that same year.

The United Nations condemned Canada in 1981 after Sandra Lovelace of the Tobique Reserve in New Brunswick complained that she was denied the right to live on her reserve after her failed marriage to a non-Native. Finally, the discriminatory clause was removed with the passage of Bill C-31 in 1985. However, the debate was not a peaceful one, and indeed, there are still bitter feelings within the Native community. When the debate was being conducted, Native leaders (especially male Native leaders) took the position that if Native women had made the decision to marry non-Natives, they should be prepared to live with the consequences of that decision.

Perhaps the main cause of the anger had to do with the distribution of reserve and band resources as well as the limited benefits of being a Status Indian, such as funds for post-secondary education and a reserve home. Some Alberta reserves have oil royalties, which some leaders feared sharing with recently returned **Bill C-31**s (see also Box 12-1). But the 1985 changes to the Indian Act allow some Indian control over status. The federal government now decides whose names get on the Indian register; however, bands may vote to take control of band membership and establish their own rules for deciding who will be part of the band.

ENFRANCHISEMENT

Reference was made earlier to Aboriginal **enfranchisement**, that is, the loss of Indian status upon acquisition of the right to vote and full citizenship. This whole process goes back to 1857, when the United Canada passed a law entitled "An Act of the Gradual Civilization of the Indian Tribes in the Canadas" as a means of granting full citizenship to Native people.

BOX 12-1   The Division of Bill C-31

The following is taken from something written by one of the authors:

> I was teaching in a summer program for Natives wanting to work as education counsellors. I remember two men of the same nation who were staying in the same house, almost always seen together, sitting together in my class. Both were proud of their nation and its heritage. Both taught me significant aspects of their heritage. In one class, it came out that one of these men lived on the nation's reserve, and had always had membership in the band, while the other was Bill C-31, and therefore had to live in a nearby town, although his heart was with the community that had no space for him. The first man made reference to his having a greater connection with his people and their heritage because he had always lived in the community of his nation. The other, who, because his mother had lost her status through marriage, had not been raised on the reserve, was hurt by what the first had said. He felt he was just as much a member of the nation as the "Status Indian." Some harsh words were said, but owing largely to their ability to draw upon the spiritual and conciliatory traditions of their people, peace between the two of them was finally achieved. (Steckley 1997:148)

As a consequence of this act, local White authorities were obliged to report any Native ". . . of the male sex, not under 21 years of age, able to speak, read and write the English or French language readily and well, and is sufficiently advanced in the elementary branches of education and is of good moral character and is free of debt." Such people were to be reported to the governor who could then declare "that such Indian is enfranchised under this Act . . . and thereof" (Dickason 1997:225). If the Native met the criteria, he was put on probation for a year, granted 20 hectares of land, and given full citizenship after one year. These were tough criteria, and only one applicant, Elias Hill, was accepted. Few Whites could meet the standard. The government, not surprisingly, blamed the Natives—and it was partly right, for at least one band, Six Nations, was opposed to the whole scheme.

The government responded with another plan, the 1869 Act for the Gradual Enfranchisement of Indians. This imposed an elected municipal form of government on Indian bands. The chief and councillors were to be elected by all males over 21 years of age, despite the fact that most nations didn't have chiefs. Of course, the government retained the right to remove any elected official. This model has persisted to the present day.

In 1920 and 1922, laws were passed to allow enfranchisement with or without consent. The various reincarnations of the Indian Act had provisions whereby Indians could voluntarily give up status. From the 1920s to the 1940s, some Natives gave up status in order to receive the right to go to school, vote, or drink. It wasn't until 1960 that Natives got the federal vote, while in some provinces, they got the provincial vote even later. Many servicemen who fought in World War I and the Korean War were persuaded to give up status.

Canada gave up enfranchisement in 1985 with the passage of Bill C-31. The Indian Act was amended so that people who had given up status could regain it. The enfranchisement provisions of the act were removed, making it impossible to give up status.

NATIVE VETERANS: LEGAL DEFINITIONS GETTING IN THE WAY

World War I (1914–1918)

The federal government originally had a policy that no Aboriginal people could become involved with World War I. Historians believed this policy existed because the government thought Aboriginals would be considered "savage" by the enemy and would therefore be treated inhumanely if captured. This policy was not enforced and was eventually cancelled by 1915.

Unlike other Canadians, Natives were not conscripted because of their legal status. Yet they volunteered in high numbers. Over 4000 Status Indians volunteered, approximately 35 percent of all Status Indian males of an age eligible to enlist. This number does not include the Métis, Inuit, or non-Status Indians, as well as the Aboriginals that lived in Yukon, Northwest Territories, and Newfoundland. In 1920, Canada's deputy superintendent general remarked on this patriotic spirit of volunteerism in the following way:

> The fine record of the Indians in the great war appears in a peculiarly favourable light when it is remembered that their services were absolutely voluntary, as they were exempted from the operation of the Military Service Act, and that they were prepared to give their lives for their country without compulsion or even the fear of compulsion. ("Native Veterans" 1920/2000)

They also contributed in another way. Reserve land was taken away from them by lease and by appropriation for purposes of farming for the war effort. The local bands involved were not asked for permission. The amount of land taken in this way totalled 25,142 hectares. This set a precedent for World War II, which, as described in the section on Dudley George, would have deadly implications. Box 12-2 describes Corporal Pegahmagabow, a courageous veteran of World War I.

BOX 12-2   Francis Pegahmagabow

Corporal Francis Pegahmagabow (1891–1952), an Ojibwa from Parry Island, was the most decorated Aboriginal soldier in World War I. As a tribute to his courage, and his adaptation of traditional hunting skills to acting as a scout and sniper, he was awarded two bars, one at Passchendale. For his actions in France and Belgium, he was first awarded the prestigious Military Medal in 1916 and had added to that two bars for his bravery and fast thinking in two subsequent battles, in 1917 and 1918. His citation for the first bar stated that:

> Before and after the attack he kept in touch with the flanks, advising the units what he had seen, this information proving the success of the attack and saving valuable time in consolidating. He also guided relief to its proper place after it had become mixed up. (Veteran Affairs Canada 2005).

After the war, he returned to his community, where he became chief and band councillor at different times.

World War II (1939-1945)

For the first three years of World War II, Natives wanting to join the forces faced racist barriers. The air force required that recruits be of "pure European descent," and the Royal Canadian Navy stipulated that their recruits be "a British born subject, of a White Race." Mi'kmaq Max Basque encountered this form of discrimination when he went to enlist with the navy. In his words: "The Navy recruiting officer looked at me. He said, 'Are you an Indian?' I said, 'Yes, sir.' 'Sorry, we don't take Indians in the Navy.'" When he noticed that the young man in front of him was not a "full-blooded" Indian, the navy recruiter said that it would be possible for Max to enlist as a Basque (a person from a group that lives in the north of Spain). Max replied:

> No. On the books, I was born on the Indian reservation and I've always gone as an Indian all my life. What in the world? Disown my own race, just to get in the Navy? I said, "I'm a Canadian, even if I am an Indian. Same as you are . . . I was born here in Canada." ("Native Veterans" 1920/2000)

Max never joined the navy, but he did serve his country in the army. His experience of being asked to enlist under a "false" race was not uncommon. Many Status Indians were called French, Italian, or Caucasian in the official records since Indians were considered unsuitable to go overseas to fight.

Again, enlistment figures are hard to calculate accurately. Native volunteers (and conscripts, after 1943) came out in significant numbers. In 1945, the Department of Indian Affairs noted that 3090 Status Indians had enlisted, but this would again not include all Aboriginals who joined up. Some estimates reach as high as 6000.

During the war, the provisions of the Indian Act were used against Native people in ways that would disadvantage them after the war was over. The Veterans' Land Act rewarded non-Native veterans for their contribution to the war effort by providing them with a $6000 loan (a large sum of money in those days) toward buying land and/or a house. This was later adapted to apply to fishing. Of this loan, $2320 was an outright grant. The balance was payable over 25 years at the low interest rate of 3.5 percent per year. Once the money was paid off, the veteran's improved credit rating enabled him to more readily open commercial loans.

This was revised in 1942 so that the law would not act in the same way for Natives. Since reserve land, or Crown land, could not act as security for loans, the federal government decided that no loan could be awarded to Status Indians. It didn't have to be that way, however. The Department of Indian Affairs could have guaranteed the loan or arranged it so the local band could have done so. What was left to the Status Indian veterans? They could receive a direct grant of $2320 applicable to farming, fishing, forestry, or trapping. Still, there were strings attached. According to section 35A of the act, the money was not given to the Status Indian, as it would have been to the non-Native veteran. It was "to be paid to the Minister of Mines and Resources who shall have the control and management thereof on behalf of the Indian veteran" (Indian and Northern Affairs Canada 1996). That was not the only string. The veteran could not apply directly to the minister to get the money, but would have to go through the local Indian agent. The agent would submit, among other things, a certificate "that the applicant is qualified to engage in the occupation he proposes to follow." The process was a slow, complicated one, and one open to manipulation and even fraud by the Indian agent. And even if the Aboriginal veteran were able to cut through all these strings, the Department of Indian Affairs still held ownership of all materials purchased under the grant for a period of 10 years.

Some Indian agents openly advised Status Indians that if they wanted the grants, they should enfranchise (i.e., give up their status and their rights). There was a significant rise in the number of people who enfranchised (from 45 in 1942–43 to 447 in 1948–49), which might in part reflect the number of people who followed this advice. Things would not be easy for them. They would be separated from their reserve home, their extended family, and their community. Some were taken by force from their reserves.

Legal restrictions would harm Native veterans in other ways. They were not permitted to join the local Legion, as they were still prohibited from entering drinking establishments. These Legions were great places to find out about potential veterans' programs, as that was where such information was posted, and where veterans who had benefited from such programs would be around to pass on valuable tips about ways to take advantage of them. Natives' lack of access to Legions, among other factors, contributed to Status Indian veterans not fully benefiting from disability pensions, war service gratuities, dependents' allowances, re-establishment grants, and education and training provisions.

So Native veterans started to fight for their rights. The Parliamentary Hearings in 1946–47, and other official opportunities for the veterans to speak out, helped spark some of the 1951 changes to the Indian Act. The right to vote was not long in following.

Even with those changes, the Native veterans of the two world wars and the Korean War (1950–1953) were still treated as second-class veterans, still short-changed in terms of the benefits owed them and the official recognition of their role in the war, something that had long been downplayed, even ignored, in official ceremonies and in textbooks. This disparity was not really dealt with in any meaningful way until the 1990s.

In the 1990s, the Royal Commission on Aboriginal Peoples (RCAP) spent a good deal of time listening to the veterans. The final report, published in 1996, contained a thoughtful look at the situation and made the following recommendations.

First, the Royal Commission stated that there should be greater acknowledgement of the contribution of Aboriginal peoples to the world wars and the Korean War. This was to be done by giving Aboriginal veterans a higher profile at national Remembrance Day services (until 1992, they had not been permitted to place a wreath on the national cenotaph at the same ceremony with other veterans) and by funding Aboriginal veterans' organizations and the construction of war memorials on reserves.

Second, the Commission recommended that an ombudsman be hired to work with the appropriate federal departments to resolve the issues of veterans' benefits and "the legality and fairness of the sales, leases, and appropriations of Indian lands for purposes related to the war effort and for distribution to returning veterans of the two world wars." The commission also recommended that Aboriginal people be hired in the Department of Veterans' Affairs, people who had both the language skills and cultural understanding necessary for dealing with Elders in their communities.

Finally, the report recommended education and research in Aboriginal history as well as funding for Aboriginal students (Indian and Northern Affairs Canada 1996).

As a result of the Commission, on November 11, 1996, the federal government announced the establishment of the Aboriginal Veterans' Scholarship Trust, to be administered by the National Aboriginal Achievement Foundation. In 1998, that fund provided $254,831 in bursaries to Aboriginal students. As of 1997, November 8 was declared National Aboriginal Veterans Day. Monies were raised to create a national monument to the Aboriginal veterans, which was designed by Native artist Lloyd Pinay, and unveiled in Ottawa on June 21, 2001. Still, there is work to be done. In December 1998, the Federation of Saskatchewan Indian Nations and the Saskatchewan First Nations Veterans Association launched a lawsuit to obtain lost veterans' benefits for the 125 veterans who were still living (out of an original 800).

In 2005, The Year of the Veteran, an Aboriginal Spiritual Journey to Europe was undertaken, involving Aboriginal veterans, spiritual elders and youth, visiting sites where Aboriginal soldiers had died. It was initiated by Aboriginal veterans' groups and the Assembly of First Nations, and supported by Indian Affairs and by Veteran Affairs Canada.

Native Individuals 12-1

Yvonne Bedard: A Six Nations woman who fought her loss of status in the courts during the early 1970s.

Jeannette Corbiere-Lavell: A Wikwemikong woman who contested her loss of status; the case went to the Supreme Court.

Francis Pegahmagabow (1891–1952): A Parry Island Ojibwa who was the most-decorated aboriginal soldier in World War I.

KEY TERMS

band

Bill C-31

enfranchisement

Indian agent

tribal council

status

CONTENT QUESTIONS

1. What is the significance of the Royal Proclamation of 1763?
2. What is the Indian Act?
3. How did the Indian Act discriminate against women prior to Bill C-31?
4. In what ways did the Indian Act limit Native people prior to 1960?
5. How were Native veterans of the world wars discriminated against?

WEBLINKS

http://lois.justice.gc.ca/en/I.5

This site is useful for information on the Indian Act, past and present.

www.ainc-inac.gc.ca/ch/rcap/sg/sg48_e.html
The Veterans' Land Act is described in section 4.5 of the Royal Commission on Aboriginal Peoples, Final Report, vol. 1, *Looking Forward, Looking Back*. For material on Aboriginal participation in the Canadian military, see the writings of John Moses.

www.forces.gc.ca/hr/dhh/downloads/Official_Histories/sketch_e.pdf
This 88-page PDF file, "A Sketch Account of Aboriginal Peoples in the Canadian Military," recounts the history of Aboriginal participation in Canadian wars and expeditions.

chapter thirteen

The Treaties

OVERVIEW

What is a treaty? Generally, treaties are agreements by certain Aboriginal people to give up their rights to a piece of land that was traditionally theirs. In return, they would have a **reserve**, a much smaller area or areas reserved for their use. That is why the term "reserve" is used in Canada (as opposed to "reservation," which is used in the United States). Treaties 1 and 2 provided for 160 acres per family of five, and Treaties 3 through 11 provided for one square mile per family of five. The title remained with the government. No one plan determined the location of **reserves**. The Robinson Treaties specified where reserves would be located, however. Treaties 1, 2, 5, and 7 stipulated that reserves would be near specific lakes and rivers, while with treaties 3, 4, 6, and 8 reserve location was to be determined through consultation.

Often, the location of reserves has caused great concern and problems. The Little Red River Band had its reserve determined by a government agent who, upon flying over a prairie, determined that it would be a good site. The Natives in question were Woodland Cree, not Plains peoples. The site had no water and was an alien environment.

The Attawapiskat Cree had their reserve located 200 kilometres inland from the coast. The Hudson's Bay Company Post was on the mouth of the Attawapiskat River on James Bay where the people traded and hunted for geese. After 40 years during which the Cree did not use the inland reserve, the government built them another reserve—on the coast, but one-sixteenth the size of the original reserve.

Aboriginal people signing a treaty would also receive a certain amount of money. In that sense, treaties were somewhat like land sales. They were different, however, in that the Natives involved were not permitted to get their hands on the money. It was held for them "in trust" by the government. From 1818 onward, Natives signing treaties would

FIGURE 13-1   Indian Land Surrendered for Treaties, up to 1921

A - Robinson Superior, 1850
B - Robinson Huron, 1850
C - Williams Treaties, 1923
D - Treaties of 1781–1857
E - Douglas Treaties, 1850–54

No.11 1921

Adhesion No.5 1875

No.8 1899

No.10 1906

No.6 1876

No.5 1875

No.9 1905

E

A

No.7 1877

No.4 1874

No.2 1871

No.1 1871

No.3 1873

B

C

D

Source: Taken from *Native Peoples in Canada: Contemporary Conflicts*, 4th edition, by James S. Frideres.

also receive **annuities**, or annual payments, typically involving a small sum per person. Monies usually were in the order of $12 for every man, woman, and child upon signing and $5 each year thereafter. The "chief" typically received slightly more.

Treaties also often involved hunting and fishing rights, which can be problematic, as we will see with the Mi'kmaq treaties. An interesting example is the Peterborough Bullfrog Incident in 1977, in which two Aboriginal men were charged with hunting bullfrogs out of season. This charge occurred because an 1818 treaty made no written reference to hunting rights. However, the Natives contended that the right to hunt was given verbally to their ancestors at the time of signing. Subsequent research proved them to be correct. They were acquitted and the right to hunt and fish was recognized by the court.

There are legal limits on these rights. For example, the Migratory Birds Convention Act (which applies to geese and ducks) overrides any treaty rights. So does the federal Fisheries Act. A case in 1962, involving the shooting of a mallard, confirmed the supremacy of federal legislation over treaties.

THE MI'KMAQ TREATIES

The Mi'kmaq treaties are both the oldest in date and the newest in interpretation, yet they are still not completely resolved. The first Mi'kmaq treaty (although this was more of a Maliseet treaty) was the Treaty of Portsmouth, New Hampshire, in 1713. While it involved statements of "peace and friendship," as other treaties had before, it allowed the Native peoples "free

liberty for Hunting, Fishing, Fowling, and all other their Lawful Liberties and Privileges"
(Dickason 1997:151). Statements to this effect were also included in the two treaties of 1725
that more directly affected the Mi'kmaq: the Mascarene Treaty of 1725, named after Major
Paul Mascarene, the chief delegate from the colonial government of Nova Scotia to the treaty
negotiations, and the Treaty of Boston. For years, all that was known about the conditions
of those treaties was one side: the obligations of the Mi'kmaq and the Maliseet to keep the
peace. In 1984, however, the "other side" of the Mascarene agreement was discovered in the
public archives: it spelled out the obligations of the English to respect the hunting and fishing
rights of the people. This discovery would have a significant impact on how this treaty (and
the 1752 Treaty that followed it as a reaffirmation) would be interpreted legally. Prior to that
discovery, in the 1929 Nova Scotia County Court decision in *Rex v. Syliboy*, and in court
decisions in 1958 and 1969, the treaties were not seen as guaranteeing **Aboriginal rights**
(i.e., rights to self-determination and self-government).

The 1752 Treaty was signed between Governor Peregrine Thomas Hopson and

> Major Jean Baptiste Cope, chief Sachem of the Tribe of Mick Mack Indians inhabiting the
> Eastern Coast of the said Province, and Andrew Hadley Martin, Gabriel Martin & Francis
> Jeremiah, Members and Delegates of the said Tribe, for themselves and their said Tribe their
> Heirs, and the Heirs of their Heirs forever. . . . (Kulchyski 1994:195).

In *Simon v. The Queen* (1985), the Chief Justice recognized the supremacy of the 1752
Treaty over provincial hunting laws:

> In my opinion, both the Governor and the Micmac entered into the Treaty with the intention
> of creating mutually binding obligations that would be solemnly respected. The Treaty was
> an exchange of solemn promises between the Micmacs and the King's representative entered
> into to achieve and guarantee peace. It is an enforceable obligation between the Indians and
> the white man and, as such, falls within the meaning of the word "treaty" in s.88 of the Indian
> Act (Kulchyski 1994:192).

Then in 1988, a Nova Scotia Lands and Forests officer arrested 14 Mi'kmaq, charging
them for illegal hunting. The charges were dismissed after the Nova Scotia Court of Appeal
ruled in another case that the Mi'kmaq people did have the right to hunt and fish for food
and were exempt from provincial regulations when doing so. This still did not settle matters
of how those rights would be worked out regarding actual hunting and fishing. In 1989, the
Mi'kmaq were allowed a special limited hunting season but with no formal recognition of
their rights to do so. They were allowed to hunt moose from September 24–29 and again
from October 15–25, before and after the two-week season for non-Natives.

Several questions need to be asked here. Was this a reasonable resolution of the problem? How would non-Native hunters react to this? Does this make Natives active players
in interpreting their rights, or just recipients of a "gift" that could be taken away? How
would you resolve the issue?

The reaction to this treaty being upheld was small compared to the recognition of a treaty
in 1760, which involved the Mi'kmaq, the Maliseet in Nova Scotia and New Brunswick,
and the culturally related Passamaquoddy of Maine. In 1996, Donald Marshall, Jr., who had
earlier been wrongfully imprisoned for 11 years, was convicted of catching eels out of season. On September 17, 1999, this decision was overturned. The Supreme Court of Canada
declared that the treaty right

> . . . is not a right to trade generally for economic gain, but rather a right to trade for nec-
> essaries. Catch limits that could reasonably be expected to produce a moderate livelihood

for individual Micmac families at present day standards can be established by regulation. ("Fishing Rights," 1999)

The phrase "moderate livelihood" would appear in a good number of newspaper articles to follow.

As this was around the beginning of lobster season, the Mi'kmaq began to set up lobster traps. There was a strong negative reaction on the part of non-Native lobster fishers, as they had a sense that their "livelihood" was being threatened. They reacted first with harsh words, then with destructive action. Over 3500 Mi'kmaq traps were destroyed, processing plants thought to be handling Native-caught lobsters were vandalized, three Mi'kmaq were injured, and an arbour used for sacred ceremonies was burned. There was also retaliation, with the burning of a few trucks and of an Acadian flag.

Thirty-three of 35 affected Mi'kmaq communities eventually agreed to a 30-day moratorium. The two communities that did not agree were Burnt Church in New Brunswick, which was the scene of most of the confrontation (and the largest number of reporters) and Shubenacadie reserve near Indian Brook, Nova Scotia.

It is important to realize that the reaction was, to a certain extent, out of proportion to the numbers involved. Annually, about two million lobster traps are set in the Maritime provinces; after the Supreme Court decision, about 12,000 Native traps were put in the water. Burnt Church, with a population between 1200 and 1300, was allowed to use 600 traps; Shubenacadie, a slightly larger community, was allowed 800. Generally, commercial lobster fishermen are permitted 300 traps each.

To date, this issue is still not resolved. Questions need to be addressed. How could the federal government have handled the situation differently? How can this be resolved in a way that is fair to non-Native fishers but that respects the legal rights of the Mi'kmaq?

LAND SURRENDER TREATIES

While hundreds of small treaties exist, most of Canada was formed by **public purchase** through a series of large land transfers. In 1836, Upper Canada's Lieutenant-Governor Francis Bond Head initiated a treaty for Manitoulin Island in Georgian Bay. He planned for all Aboriginal people to possess all the land on the island forever. It would involve moving Aboriginal people from the surrounding area onto the island. Twenty-six years later, after only an approximate 1000 had moved to Manitoulin, the government, aware of the good farmland there and suspecting that there might be oil as well, attempted to get the people to surrender or cede their rights to the island. The Wikwemikong community, the largest on the island, resisted this move, and thus were not party to the Manitoulin Treaty of 1862. This is why even today this First Nation asserts that their territory is unceded.

Then came the Robinson Treaties of 1850, involving the land immediately to the north of Lake Superior and Lake Huron. Mineral deposits had been discovered north of Lake Superior, leading the colonial government of Upper Canada to authorize mining activities on Ojibwa land. In 1846, Shinguaconse ("Little Pine," c. 1773–1854), chief of the Ojibwa of Garden River (near Sault Ste. Marie), and other leaders made the long trip down to Toronto to ask for payment for the use of their land in this way. There was no official response. Three years later, they made the same trip and asked for a land settlement, and received none. Left with no apparent alternative, they closed a mine down by force. Troops were sent and the treaty process was hastened.

The Douglas Treaties and Numbered Treaties

The colony of Vancouver Island was created in 1849. Between 1850 and 1854, Governor James Douglas signed 14 treaties with Coast Salish First Nations on Vancouver Island. They surrendered land that amounted to about three percent of the island. Douglas paid the people in blankets and goods rather than cash, and he stopped signing treaties when he ran out of funding. With several small and separate parcels reserved to single bands, the reserves set a precedent in British Columbia, making it virtually impossible for most First Nations peoples to make good use of their land. Without the rights given by the large treaties, another 140 reserves were created elsewhere in British Columbia, prior to the colony joining Canada in 1871. At least 50 of these reserves were 100 acres or less (a little over 400 hectares), and slightly more than half were less than the 320 acres that the British Columbia government allotted to single-family homesteads for non-Natives at around the same time.

A few small victories have come from the Douglas treaties. The treaties stated that the Salish were "at liberty to hunt over the unoccupied lands and to carry on [their] fisheries as formerly" (Indian and Northern Affairs Canada 1996b). In the case of *Regina v. White and Bob*, their treaty right to hunt on unoccupied lands was affirmed in 1965 by the Supreme Court through the appeal of a conviction for hunting deer out of season.

The expansion of non-Native Canadian interests westward after the foundation of Canada and the purchase of Rupert's Land was the impetus for what are called the "numbered treaties," Treaties 1 to 11, signed between 1871 and 1921. These covered the territory from the eastern part of British Columbia and parts of Yukon Territory and the Northwest Territories in the west, across the Prairie Provinces to include most of northern Ontario. As was true of the Robinson treaties, there was a close connection between the federal government wanting something, and the pressure for treaties. The settling of the prairies by European farmers made the signing of Treaties 1 to 7 imperative. The discovery of gold in the Klondike in 1897 resulted in Treaty 8 in 1899. The building of roads and railroads to gain access to northern Ontario brought about Treaty 9. The provincial status of Alberta and Saskatchewan was followed by the signing of Treaty 10 in 1906, while the discovery of oil in Norman Wells was followed by Treaty 11 in 1921.

Box 13-1, which follows, tells the story of the land claims process for the Nisga'a.

WHEN TREATIES GO BAD: THE MISSISSAUGA TREATIES

To get a sense of the Aboriginal lack of trust that governments will keep their promises, it is useful to look in some detail at what happens "when treaties go bad."

Piece by large piece, the Mississauga of southern Ontario had their land "publicly purchased." Two of the early transfers provided a much welcomed home for the Mohawk and other Iroquois, who had been forced to abandon their ancestral territory after having fought on the losing side of the American Revolution. On October 9, 1783, land stretching back from the northeastern shores of Lake Ontario, from the Gananoque River in the east to the Trent River in the west, was "purchased" from the Mississauga. John Deserontyon and his band of Mohawks settled into the former Mississauga land that winter. On May 22, 1784, the Mississauga announced at a council meeting that they would permit a large tract

Box 13-1	A Brief History of Nisga'a Land Claims

The Tsimshian peoples are in the centre of Aboriginal rights issues in British Columbia. Along with the We'tsuwet'en Carrier, the Gitxsan are the Aboriginal parties involved in the Delgamuukw case. The Nisga'a are best known today by non-Natives in relation to the land claim settlement passed through Canada's Parliament in December 1999. It is important to understand that this is not a case that is "something new," nor part of a trend of "political correctness." For example, consider that the following statement from David McKay, chief of the Greenville Nisga'a, was made in 1888:

What we don't like about the government is their saying this: "We will give you this much land." How can they give it when it is our own? We cannot understand it. They have never bought it from us or our forefathers. They have never fought or conquered our people and taken the land in that way, and yet they say now that they will give us so much land—our own land. It would have been foolish, but it has been ours for a thousand years. (Dickason 1997:325)

The timeline for events related to the Nisga'a's land claims is described at the end of this chapter, in the Nisga'a Timeline 13-1 on page 147–48.

around the Grand River to be transferred to the Crown for the purposes of giving it to the Iroquois.

The Mississauga signatories of this **"public purchase"** included the "Sachems and War Chiefs and Principal Women of the Messissauga Indian Nation" (Hodge 1971b vol.1:5). It is noteworthy that Mississauga women had a say in political decisions, while other Canadian women would have to wait for more than a hundred years before they would receive the right to vote.

Next, in a series of poorly recorded deals in 1784, 1787, and 1788, the northern Lake Ontario shoreline from the Trent River west to what is now Scarborough changed hands. (How far inland the transfer went is the subject of historical rumours. Some sources claim it reached as far back as a man could walk, or go on foot in a day. Natives came to believe that it went the distance a gunshot could be heard. Another treaty had to be signed in 1923 to try to clear up the resultant legal mess.)

On September 23, 1787, the British and the Mississauga negotiated a provisional land surrender of some 620,000 hectares of land in what is now Toronto and surrounding townships. The deal, known as the Toronto Purchase, stayed in limbo until August 1, 1805, when eight Mississauga chiefs, headed by **Quinepenon** ("Golden Eagle"), met with government officials on the flatlands beside the Credit River. The Mississauga were beginning to distrust the treaty process. They already felt confined on the land left to them. This is noted by Quinepenon, as is the suspicion held by Mississauga women that the deal would further impoverish their nation:

> [I]t is hard to give away more land; the young men and women have found fault with so much having been sold before. It is true we are poor, and the women say we will be worse if we part with any more. . . . (Clarkson 1967:27)

Quinepenon had good reason to distrust both settlers and the government. He had initially believed that the earlier treaties had promised that "the Farmers would help us" and that his people could "encamp and fish where we pleased" (Smith 1979:467) and felt that these promises had been violated. In 1797, the government passed a "Proclamation to Protect the Fishing Places and Burying Grounds of the Mississauga," but neither type of valued location was protected effectively by this legislation.

The meeting of August 1, 1805, was not just to confirm the Toronto Purchase: the rest of Lake Ontario shoreline was coveted by the incoming, mostly American, immigrants, and by the government, which was eager to welcome them. On August 2, the Mississauga were persuaded to sign away land extending west from Etobicoke Creek to Burlington Bay. Fishing and corn-growing were vital to the survival of the Mississauga, so Quinepenon and other leaders fought hard to receive the concession of reserving

> . . . the sole right of the fisheries in the Twelve Mile [Bronte] Creek, the Sixteen Mile Creek, the Etobicoke River, together with the flats or low grounds on said creeks and river, which we have heretofore cultivated and where we have our camps. And also the sole right of fishery in the River Credit with one mile on each side of said river. (Hodge 1971b, vol.1:36)

Quinepenon's fears were realized. By the time the August 2 treaty was confirmed the next year, a settler had destroyed the chief's cornfield as well as the field of a Mississauga widow with four children. The same man, an illegal squatter on their land, built a fish weir on Bronte Creek that prevented the salmon from swimming upstream to spawn. According to Quinepenon, another White man had so polluted the Credit River "by washing with [soap] and other dirt, that the fish refuse coming into the River as usual, by which our families are in great distress for want of food" (Smith 1979:467).

Box 13-2 gives one Mississauga's account of how government promises were not kept.

Box 13-2	A Nineteenth-Century Mississauga View of Government Promises

The contrast between wartime promises and peacetime practices is summarized by Nahnebahwequay (Catherine Sutton) in her article published in the *Christian Guardian* of May 28, 1862:

> I cannot help thinking about those times, now past, when Governors and Generals used to meet our fathers in the Great Councils, and made great promises that were never, never to be broken while grass grew and waters ran. All our fathers who did not fall in the wars remained faithful to the British throne, and their children have followed their steps in loyalty. But the wars have passed away, . . . and advantage is taken of our weakness and ignorance, so that our fisheries, hunting-grounds, lands and homes are taken from us, whether we like it or not. They are first coveted, and then some plan is concocted to get them; and those pledges made to our grandsires by British noblemen have been and are still every day shamefully violated, so that the poor Indians have ceased to have any confidence in the Government. . . . Little did those bold Indian warriors think when they were listening to the fine promises made by British noblemen that the successors of those Crown officials would, in a few years, rob their children of their birthright. (Sutton 1862)

The next time the government came to ask for more Mississauga land was 1818. A lot had happened since 1806. Immigrants, mostly British, had swelled the ranks of White people in Upper Canada. By 1812, Natives made up barely more than 10 percent of that colony's population (Dickason 1992:224). The Credit River Mississauga continued to diminish in number. Their 330 had become 200. The toll on their chiefs was even heavier. Of the 10 leaders who had signed the last treaty, only two would be around to put their mark on paper in 1818. Among the dead was Quinepenon.

The land that the government wanted in 1818 was the "Mississauga Tract," a tract west of the Toronto Purchase and north of the land acquired during the other 1806 treaty. This 1818 treaty introduced the notion of annuities. In return for obtaining possession of some 1.6 million hectares, the king, through his representative William Claus, promised to pay the Mississauga, ". . . yearly and every year *for ever* the said sum of five hundred and twenty two pounds ten shillings currency in goods at the Montreal price. . . " (Hodge 1971b vol.1:48; emphasis is authors').

"For ever" lasted a short time. This promise was broken two years later, when William Claus, the deputy superintendent general of Indian affairs, came to speak with them again. The Mississauga were justifiably suspicious. What did he want now? So much had been taken. Claus wanted them to agree to give up their exclusive fishing rights and sell all of their remaining land:

> Saving and reserving, nevertheless, always to the said Acheton, Newoiquiquah, Woiqueshequome, Pausetawnouguetohe and Wabakagige and the people of the Mississauga Nation of Indians and their posterity for ever a certain parcel or tract of land containing two hundred acres (Hodge 1971b, vol.1:52).

According to Claus, the proceeds from the sale of the land would be used for

> . . . educating your Children & instructing yourselves in the principles of the Christian religion—and that a certain part of the said Tract never surrendered will be set apart for your accommodation & that of your families, on which Huts will be erected as soon as possible (Smith 1987:39–40).

Two things are generally true about such Native land agreements. One is that the two parties, Native and government, had a different understanding about what took place. The second is that the government rarely delivered all that it had promised. Concerning the first, Claus felt that with the 1820 treaty, the Mississauga had given up their rights to all the land but the 200 acres. The Credit River people thought differently. This can be seen in this quotation from a letter sent by two of their leaders to the lieutenant-governor in 1829. They believed that Claus had said:

> The white people are getting thick around you and we are afraid they, or the yankees, will cheat you out of your land, [so] you had better put it into the hands of your very Great father the king to keep for you till you want to settle, and he will appropriate it for your good and he will take good care of it; and will take you under his wing, and keep you under his arm, & give you schools, and build houses for you when you want to settle. (Smith 1987:40)

The land that was supposedly reserved for the Mississauga forever did not remain theirs for more than a few years. The Mississauga still haven't received the promised 200 acres, or compensation for its loss.

Further, there seem to have been two different timetables for the two sides of this transaction. The government got its hands on the land surrendered fairly quickly, but six years passed before the government began to fulfill even a part of its side of the bargain. Not until the fall of 1826 were 20 homes built for the Mississauga alongside the mouth of the Credit River.

Another part of the 1820 deal was that the Mississauga would receive annuities from the monies accrued from the sale of their lands. The monies were held for the Mississauga "in trust" by the government. But some of the government officials could not be trusted. Once the money was in their hands, they treated it as if it were their own.

In 1826, Mississauga leader Peter Jones confronted Colonel James Givins, their Indian agent, concerning the fact that they were being paid £50 less in annuities than was agreed upon in the treaty. Givins' reply smells of a cover-up. He claimed that he "was not at liberty to explain" (Smith 1987:79) why the Mississauga were not getting the sum of money owed to them.

The Mississauga of the Credit grew concerned about what their rights actually were to the land. They were hearing nasty rumours. Chief James Ajetance (spelled "Acheton" in previous quote), Peter Jones' adoptive father, said to Givins, "Having heard some bad birds crying that we did not own any lands on the Credit, we wish to know from our great father how much land we really possess" (Smith 1987:100). Givins flatly stated that in his opinion the Mississauga had surrendered all their rights away. Despite its questionable legality, his opinion carried weight.

The Mississauga felt increasingly hemmed in. They had established a trade of salmon in exchange for flour, cattle, and other goods, but this mutually beneficial commerce was being interfered with, as can be seen from the words of a petition signed by Peter Jones and 53 others on January 31, 1829, and sent to Sir John Colbourne, the Lieutenant-Governor of Upper Canada. They were upset by what some White men were doing:

> They burn and destroy our fences and boards in the night; they watch the salmon and take them as fast as they come up; they swear and get drunk and give a very bad example to our young people, and try to persuade them to be wicked like themselves. . . Others go to the mouth of the river and catch all the salmon; they put the offals of salmon in the mouth of the river to keep the fish from passing up, that they may take them with a seine near the mouth of the river in the lake; and often in the dark they set gill nets in the river and stop all the fish. (Mackenzie 1833/1960:47–48)

Over the next two decades, the Mississauga came to realize that they were going to lose their land. Their community appeared doomed. However, they received an offer that saved their community. In April 1847, the Six Nations Iroquois met in full council. They had heard of the desperate position of the Mississauga of the Credit. They remembered how the Mississauga had made land available to them when they had needed to flee from the resentful Americans after fighting on the British side during the American Revolution. Feeling "a great pleasure in returning the compliments to their descendants [i.e., those whose ancestors gave the land to the Iroquois]" (Smith 1987:212), they invited the Mississauga to take possession of some of their land, near what is now Hagersville, Ontario. That community today is known as the Mississauga of the New Credit.

URBAN RESERVES

A new type of reserve is being created in Saskatchewan: **urban reserves**. These are lands located in a municipality or Northern Administrative District. Their main function is to provide central urban locations for Aboriginal businesses. To enable the creation of these reserves, the Saskatchewan Treaty Land Entitlement Framework Agreement was signed in 1992. A fund of approximately $446 million was established so that the land could be purchased. Twenty-eight of the 70 Saskatchewan First Nations signed on, initiating the development of 28 urban reserves. Nine of them are located in cities. More than 1350 people work in the businesses developed there (Western Economic Diversification Canada 2005).

Urban reserves came about for several reasons. First of all, many treaty land entitlements in Saskatchewan were still outstanding. Land promised in the treaties had yet to be delivered to the people. Second, an increasingly high percentage of the Aboriginal population was moving (at least temporarily) from the rural reserves into cities. In the cities, however, Aboriginal people have been markedly less successful as a group than non-Aboriginal people. Third, the economic potential of rural reserves, on average, could not be as great as reserves located in cities. Fourth, for shared and different reasons, the federal government and First Nations wanted the latter to be more economically self-sufficient, that is, not as dependent on economic transfer payments from the federal government.

The first community to develop an urban reserve was the Muskeg Lake Cree Nation. It has about 1200 members, most of them living away from the main reserve (located 93 kilometres outside of Saskatoon). The leaders of this community first approached the federal government in 1984 and were granted 33 acres of land within Saskatoon. In 1993, they signed a services agreement with the city. This involved the band giving an annual payment for municipal services, such as snow and garbage removal, with electricity and water being billed directly to individual customers on the reserve. Businesses operating there are almost all Aboriginal-owned, with some 300 employees.

Nisga'a Timeline 13-1

1763: Royal Proclamation of 1763 in which King George III recognizes that aboriginal peoples legally possess traditional territories until these lands are "ceded to or purchased by" the government.

1778: Captain James Cook lands on the coast of British Columbia and claims the land for Britain.

1793: British sea captain George Vancouver makes first European contact with the Nisga'a.

1871: British Columbia becomes a province.

1881: Chief Mountain leads a Nisga'a protest delegation to Victoria.

1886: Nisga'a resist surveyors and begin organized pursuit of land claims, since no treaties have been signed with the Nisga'a (although they have been placed on reserves).

1887: Nisga'a (and Tsimshian) chiefs go to Victoria to discuss land claims and self-government with Premier William Smithe. Smithe responds with: "When the whites first came among you, you were little better than the wild beasts of the field" (Rose 2000:13) rejecting Nisga'a and Tsimshian claims to ownership.

1909: The Nisga'a Land Committee becomes part of the Native Tribes of British Columbia, who send a delegation

(continued)

Nisga'a Timeline 13-1   *(continued)*

to Britain to make a presentation on the land question.

1910: Prime Minister Wilfred Laurier promises to settle the Native land question in British Columbia.

1913: Nisga'a Land Committee submits petition to British Privy Council to resolve the land question. The petition is referred back to Canada.

1920: Bill 13, the British Columbia Indian Lands Settlement Act, is passed by the federal government. It allows reductions of reserves without consent of Aboriginal people, contrary to the Indian Act.

1924: Nisga'a have 76 square kilometres cut off their reserve without their consent.

1927: Parliament amends Indian Act to make it illegal for Aboriginal groups to raise money for the prosecution of land claims, so land claims activity has to go "underground" until 1951 when this amendment is repealed.

1955: Nisga'a Land Committee is re-established as the Nisga'a Tribal Council.

1967: Nisga'a leader Frank Calder takes the land question to court, seeking a declaration that they had held Aboriginal title in the land prior to colonization,

and that their title had never been extinguished. The Nisga'a lose the decision in the B.C. court, but appeal the decision, taking it to the Supreme Court of Canada.

1973: The appeal is lost on a split decision, but the Supreme Court judges agree that Aboriginal title had existed but disagree as to whether that title continues to exist.

1976: The federal government and the Nisga'a begin negotiation regarding land claims under the new "comprehensive land claims policy." The province of British Columbia does not join in the negotiations.

1990: The province of British Columbia joins in the land claims negotiations between the federal government and the Nisga'a.

1996: On March 22, the minister of Indian affairs, the B.C. Aboriginal affairs minister, and Nisga'a Tribal Council President, Joseph Gosnell, Sr., sign an agreement-in-principle for the first modern-day treaty in British Columbia.

1999: Parliament passes the bill for the Nisga'a treaty.

2000: The Senate passes the bill on April 13 and the treaty process is complete.

Nisga'a Treaty

The Nisga'a treaty involves "giving" the people title to 1930 square kilometres in the Nass valley and $487.1 million in benefits and in money (Rose 2000:26). It also gives them the right to make laws in several areas, including land use, employment, and cultural preservation. They will own the forest and mineral resources on their land (as a private owner would), but will manage them, like other owners, within British Columbia's laws and standards. In exchange, they give up future claims on what amounts to more than 80 percent of their traditional territory (less than 10 percent of their original claim) and they give up their tax exemptions. Although the non-Native media have often presented this as a step toward separation or the break-up of Canada, in actuality the move puts the Nisga'a in a position more like other Canadians in a number of ways, including their tax and ownership status.

Native Individuals 13-1

Jean Baptiste Cope: Leading Mi'kmaq saqmaw who signed the Treaty of 1752.

Kahkewaquonaby ("Sacred Feathers") or Peter Jones (1802–56): A nineteenth-century Mississauga writer, educator, and fundraiser.

Quinepenon ("Golden Eagle"): An important Mississauga leader of the eighteenth and nineteenth centuries.

KEY TERMS

Aboriginal rights

annuities

public purchase

reserves

urban reserves

CONTENT QUESTIONS

1. Which acts override treaty rights?
2. In the case of *Simon v. The Queen* (1985), which was ruled as having priority, the 1752 Treaty, or provincial hunting laws?
3. In the Supreme Court decision of 1999, what rights did the Mi'kmaq have that came from the Treaty of 1760?
4. What happened with the Mississauga treaties?
5. When did the Nisga'a begin their organized fight for land claims?

WEBLINKS

http://library.usask.ca/native/cnlch.html
This site provides a list of "Canadian-Indian Treaties."

http://scc.lexum.umontreal.ca/en/1985/1985rcs2-387/1985rcs2-387.pdf
This document is the legal case file for James Matthew Simon's case against the government regarding Mi'kmaq hunting rights.

www.inac.gc.ca/pr/trts/hti/site/maindex_e.html
The Historic Treaty Information Site gives an account of the treaties from 1701 to 1923, complete with maps.

http://mrc.uccb.ns.ca/treaties.html
This Mi'kmaq resource centre website presents comprehensive information on the Mi'kmaq treaties.

www.snuneymuxw.ca/treatydouglas.htm
This Snuneymuxw First Nation website presents a very thorough discussion of the Douglas treaties.

chapter fourteen

The Golden Lake Algonquin and Algonquin Park: Missed by Treaty

INTRODUCTION

As we have seen, groups with treaties face difficulties trying to make governments respect their rights. It is, of course, more difficult when a group has been missed by the treaty process. The land claim cases of the Lubicon Cree of Alberta and the Temagami Anishinabe are examples of the long-running problems that such groups can have. This section will discuss the land claim case of the Golden Lake Algonquin.

In the first half of the seventeenth century, several different bands referred to as "Algonquin" were living in the area of the Ottawa River and its tributaries. It is misleading that the river, the valley, and the city are called Ottawa, because the Ottawa, who are related to the Algonquin, spent only a few years during the 1680s in the area. Their home country was Manitoulin Island and the Bruce Peninsula to the west. The river should more accurately be called the Algonquin River, because those people lived in the area for at least hundreds of years. Perhaps it would have been better for their land claims if the river had been so named.

THE GOLDEN LAKE ALGONQUIN

The Golden Lake Algonquin live by the Bonnechere River, some 140 kilometres west of Ottawa. They have never surrendered their rights to the land and have never signed a treaty. But they did sign several petitions to ensure that their unsurrendered rights to their land were recognized, signing the first petition in 1772. Their message has changed little over the centuries, but government responses have changed from being initially positive to consistently negative. In 1774, Lord Dorchester, then governor, told them that "if you anciently held the rights to these lands, and if you have not been paid, the rights belong to you still" (Sarazin 1989:173). Later government officials would not respond in the same way.

Their situation deteriorated after the War of 1812. The Algonquin had fought on the British side but had not been rewarded for their efforts with any written guarantee of their rights. Instead, the government actively recruited veterans and others from Britain to live on Algonquin land. Passage was paid for, land given, and assistance promised to the newcomers. In 1820 alone, 2000 government-assisted Scots were brought to the Rideau district south of Ottawa. That same year, the Algonquin sent a petition to have their rights to their lands recognized. They were turned down. In 1822, the government claimed that the land had been signed away by a few Bay of Quinte Mississauga, people who had never lived on or used the land.

Throughout the 1820s, the immigrant onslaught continued. Non-Natives in charge of Indian affairs became quite concerned about the effects of this rapid settlement on the Algonquin. In 1828, General Darling said that "[t]heir situation is becoming alarming by . . . rapid settlement" (Sarazin 1989:177).

For a while, the government made paper promises to keep squatters off Algonquin land; but in 1836, the government turned about-face and responded to Algonquin petitions with the inaccurate statement that "the claims of the present petitioners were fully settled and adjusted at the respective times when the lands were surrendered by those tribes to the Government" (Sarazin 1989:178).

In an 1857 petition, five Algonquin heads of families asked for 80 hectares per family, the same amount of land many settler families had received. The local Crown Lands agent supported their petition, saying that "[t]hese men appear to be unusually intelligent and respectable; I have been informed that they are moral and industrious and well-deserving" (Sarazin 1989:186). But the commissioner of Crown Lands condemned them for being neither White men nor traditional Natives. He refused the land grant, calling them "half-bred, half-civilized Indians" (Sarazin 1989:186). Finally, in 1864, the Department of Indian Affairs used Indian funds to pay $156.10 (10 cents an acre) for 1561 acres (631 hectares) that they could live on. The Algonquin still had not signed their rights away, however.

Other families joined. By 1880, 83 Algonquin were living in the same area, 164 by 1924, and 475 by 1971. In 1986, there were 691 belonging to the band, with 285 living on the reserve and 406 off. In May 2006, the community that, since 1998, officially calls itself the Algonquins of Pikwakanagan had a reserve population of 410 and a total band population of 1919.

Box 14-1 gives Algonquin Chief Kaondinoketch's opinion of his land's treatment.

ALGONQUIN PARK

Algonquin Park was created in 1893 out of Crown land that had been withdrawn from sale for settlement, to a large extent so that the timber it contained could be "harvested" and sold by logging companies. At that time, there were at least three groups or bands of Algonquin living in what would later become the park. They sent several petitions to have land granted to them in the same fashion as the Golden Lake people had to them, offering to give up their rights to a larger piece for a written guarantee for less land. They received three types of responses: (1) petitions were ignored; (2) the Algonquin were allowed to hunt for a while at "the pleasure of the Crown," as long as they didn't cut any wood or bother those

| Box 14-1 | Chief Kaondinoketch's Petition of 1840 |

In 1840, Chief Kaondinoketch submitted a petition to the colonial government. After outlining in grim detail what had happened to the local resources, he made the following observation:

> Brothers, we are partly the cause of these our present misfortunes. We were too good and generous. We permitted strangers to come and settle in our grounds and cultivate the land, and traders to destroy our valuable timber, who have done us much injury, as by clearing our rich forest, they have annihilated our beaver and our peltries, and driven away our deer. Had our hunting grounds belonged to the whites, they would not have allowed this, but we had good hearts and took pity on our white brethren. (Sarazin 1989:182)

who did; or (3) the Algonquin were told to go live with the people of Golden Lake. One Ontario official even admitted that the government didn't want to create official Native settlements with such a reserve grant, as that would "render the localities in which they are situated less attractive for settlement than other localities in which there is no Indian population" (Sarazin 1989:188). However, the presence of an Indian population hadn't stopped settlers from crowding out the Algonquin of the Ottawa Valley earlier that century.

The Golden Lake Algonquin needed to hunt deer in Algonquin Park in order to survive. They knew how to hunt in a way that would not threaten the deer population. But these facts were not recognized by provincial game officials. In 1898, most of the Golden Lake men were summoned to court for hunting deer out of season. Most were convicted, given suspended sentences, and warned that they would be jailed if caught again. So the Algonquin learned how to hunt more carefully, like Canadian versions of Robin Hood, so they would not be caught. In the words of Chief **Greg Sarazin**:

> Our elders tell stories of hunting in Algonquin Park; of the man who used stilts to confuse the rangers who might try to track him, of the man who wore his snowshoes backwards, and of the family whose children were wrapped in "poached" furs under their snowsuits, which the rangers failed to search. At the portage store at Canoe Lake the Ontario Ministry of Natural Resources displays a birch-bark canoe blackened to avoid detection, seized from "an Indian poacher." (Sarazin 1989:190)

Petitions continued throughout the twentieth century. One in the 1980s yielded a surprising result. Provincial Court Judge Russell Meredew declared that the Algonquin still had Aboriginal rights to the areas, including Algonquin Park, that had never been surrendered, and further, that the Royal Proclamation of 1763 held the status of a treaty with the Algonquin. Predictably, the Supreme Court of Ontario overturned this decision.

On September 2, 1988, the Golden Lake Algonquin, along with their Native and non-Native supporters, staged a protest on the road that led to Algonquin Park. They put forward a claim of 34,000 square kilometres, including not only Algonquin Park but also the municipalities of Arnprior, Bancroft, Deep River, Mattawa, North Bay, Ottawa, Pembroke, and Renfrew. They did not want to take the land back, as some media pundits claimed. They consistently stressed that they were only negotiating to have unoccupied Crown land returned to the band. Private, corporate, and municipal lands would be untouched. The point of the exercise was to state dramatically that they had never signed that land away and that some recognition should be made of their rights. From their perspective, there were four issues involved: land, natural resources, self-government, and compensation for loss.

Nothing came of this until June 1991, when Ontario Minister of Natural Resources and Minister Responsible for Native Affairs Bud Wildman publicly acknowledged that the Golden Lake Algonquin had rights that needed to be dealt with. A Statement of Intent was signed, which outlined the intention to negotiate a land claim. It included an interim agreement allowing band members to hunt and fish in Algonquin Park. It was a first step toward resolution of the land claim and it was a form of recognition of Algonquin rights to hunt and fish for personal and community use. The hunt was to be regulated with sub-agreements specifying where hunting and fishing would be permitted, what limits would be placed on their "harvest," and what was needed to ensure public access and safety. Wildman assured concerned non-Native citizens and special interest groups, such as tour operators, that consultations with all parties would be a priority. It was a reversal of usual government policies across Canada, where an agreement would first be struck in favour of non-Natives, with Natives then assured that consultation would take place with them.

Public Relations

Native groups involved with land claim negotiations must engage in public relations. They have to engage in complicated communication with a number of different parties: the federal government, the party whose legal responsibility for and to Native peoples is the greatest; provincial governments, the party primarily responsible for natural resources; non-Native special interest groups; and the Canadian public in general. Often the most difficult to deal with is the last-named group, for while studies tend to show that on an abstract level, the Canadian public is sympathetic to "Native issues," those same studies also indicate that the public is fundamentally ignorant of the breadth, historical depth, and complexity of these issues. This ignorance has traditionally been used by governments and special interest groups to turn the public against the Natives, especially the case when the public comes to have perceptible self-interest in the outcome of the issue. Such was the case with the Algonquins and their negotiations concerning Algonquin Park.

Initial Negative Response

The initial response by local or special-interest non-Native print media was predictably negative. A case in point is an editorial in the *Ontario Fisherman* (August–September 1991) in which the writer claimed that being of mixed Austrian, English, Irish, Scottish, and Ukrainian descent made him immune to accusations of racism. The writer also suggested, like other non-Natives before him, that Natives should only be allowed to exercise their rights through fishing in a traditional way with no European technology. By that same logic, non-Native fishermen should not be permitted to use canoes, farmers should not be allowed to grow corn, potatoes, tomatoes, beans, squash, peppers, and tobacco, store owners should not be permitted to sell clothing made out of cotton, and White trappers should be banned from using snowshoes, since these were all Native inventions.

The same issue of that magazine carried an article dealing with alleged Native poaching in Ontario, but did not mention that most poaching is done by non-Natives.

More destructive to the Algonquin cause was how mainstream papers dealt with the issue. In *The Toronto Star*, on September 28, 1991, columnist Joey Slinger wrote an article with the leading headline of "Province Selling Off Our Algonquin Park Birthright" ("Our" presumably meaning non-Natives). Slinger made the following comments:

> That old devil liberal guilt has let the Indians pull a fast one on the Ontario government . . . But the government bought it and lent credence to a claim on the park's territory that is about as reasonable as my family's claim on Stonehenge. The only way there could ever be a truly just settlement for Canadian Indians is for all the rest of us to pack up and go back where we came from (Slinger 1991:A1).

Slinger might have had a case for his family's claim to Stonehenge if they had lived in that area for hundreds of years, maintained the grounds, buried their dead there, and then had it taken away illegally by foreign tourists or overseas businessmen. The Golden Lake Algonquin were just asking for "the rest of us" to keep our legal promises.

The Interim Agreement

The **Interim Agreement** regarding the Algonquin claim was unveiled early in October of 1991. It allowed members of the Golden Lake First Nation to hunt moose and deer between October 15, 1991, and January 15, 1992. Hunters were restricted to the eastern 40 percent of the park. The agreement restricted the use of all-terrain vehicles and snowmobiles for hunting within the park, placed limits on the use of cars, trucks, and motorboats, and limited the kill to 100 moose and 175 deer. This hunt limit would not have an adverse effect on the population of those animals. (For example, in 1992, there were an estimated 3800 moose in the park.) A further agreement would be hammered out regarding fishing rights.

Reaction was swift. Special interest groups such as the Wildlands League, the Huntsville/Lake of Bays Chamber of Commerce, the Federation of Ontario Naturalists, and the more anti-Native Ad Hoc Committee to Save Algonquin Park (hereafter called the Ad Hoc Committee) voiced alarm with predictable exaggeration. The Ontario government and the Golden Lake Algonquin held public meetings to try to soothe feelings of anxiety among non-Natives. On February 4, 1992, one such meeting was held in Pembroke. According to the local paper *The Eganville Leader* published the next day, this seemed to have done little more than give non-Natives an opportunity to vent their ignorance and prejudice. Accusations were made of anti-White discrimination and preferential treatment of Natives, and pleas for equality were also made.

One of the main complaints was that the government was moving too quickly in bringing about the Interim Agreement. As **Clifford Meness**, then chief of the Golden Lake First Nation, was to say, 200 years seemed to be a reasonable amount of time.

But the first real results of the Interim Agreement were favourable. *The Ottawa Citizen* of April 14, 1992, reported that the Golden Lake Algonquin took only 45 moose and 29 deer in the three-month season, considerably below the imposed limits. Of the roughly 300 people living on the reserve, Chief Meness estimated that only 20 to 30 were actually involved in the hunt. None of the fears of the opponents had come to pass, including the shooting of tourists mistaken for moose. However, this did not lessen the opposition. Scott Hayden, a resort owner and a highly vocal representative of the roughly 1000-member Ad Hoc Committee, suggested that the numbers indicated that the Golden Lake First Nation did not really need the hunt after all (*Ottawa Citizen* 1992).

The Algonquin were ready to speak to any media that would listen, but their voice was most often the quietest one in articles claiming to give a balanced approach. The summer issue of *Outdoor Canada* had an article that began with the unreasonable assertion that if the Algonquin claim were to be recognized, that would cause the park to be turned into their private grounds for fishing and hunting. Considerable space was then given to the Ad Hoc Committee's attack on the Algonquin claim. It was probably too little, too late, for Greg Sarazin's reassurance at the end of the article that cottagers were not going to be kicked out of their summer homes.

The Ad Hoc Committee continued to incite fear about the park's fate if the Algonquin assumed control. In July 1992, the committee issued a report stating that in order for the Golden Lake First Nation to maintain the park and guarantee financial stability, they would have to "introduce radically new revenue-generating activities—of which the most obvious would be massive real estate and rental development." In *Seasons*, the publication of the Federation of Ontario Naturalists, Scott Hayden expressed his alarmist view that the Algonquin were just beginning to act on a hidden agenda.

To counteract this flame of paranoia fanned by the Ad Hoc Committee and to allay the genuine concerns of people in the area, Golden Lake Algonquin representatives addressed the public whenever possible. In the fall they put together a newsletter and announced that they would have a full-time communications coordinator working on the reserve throughout the negotiation process.

Due to the success of the implementation of the first Interim Agreement, a second agreement was introduced in October 1992. This was done in spite of more protest, which included a 20-page "research" report from the Ad Hoc Committee disputing the claim.

The Ontario government again allowed the public one week to submit input on the agreement, which, with some modifications, closely resembled the first. Changes made reflected prior public input. The province would fund the Algonquin's cost for hiring and supporting an official to ensure that the rules of the agreement would be enforced. Additional enforcement would come from a tribunal set up by the Golden Lake band.

In December, the federal government entered the picture, with Minister of Indian Affairs Tom Siddon expressing the hope that the claim would be resolved within the next two years.

Federal participation increased the credibility of the Golden Lake claim, but their task still remained to gain public support and eradicate fears of the loss of private lands, the dismantling of the park, and overhunting. That would not be easy with the Ad Hoc Committee's political manoeuvring. In an apparent attempt to incite fear and anger, Scott Hayden stated in *The Huntsville Herald* (March 31, 1993) that dignitaries attending the opening ceremonies at the new visitor centre and logging museum at Algonquin Park might be confronted by a significant display of non-Native protest. He went on to say that he expected problems with crowd control and that he believed that a tent was being erected to keep politicians out of sight in case of any problems. But such problems existed only in his imagination. There was no Algonquin protest.

Howard Goldblatt, chief negotiator for the province, announced in April that there would be a series of open houses in the affected areas. They would enable people to speak their minds and meet with representatives of the Canadian, Ontario, and Golden Lake governments. In addition, a Native Affairs office was opened in Pembroke, in the middle of the claim territory, where people could go and ask questions about the claim and the process of negotiation.

The open houses seem to have worked well. They were well attended across the claim territory. One report, based on approximately one-third of 535 attendees at open houses who filled out evaluation forms, noted that 90 percent were satisfied with the quality and quantity of information given, as well as the format of the events.

To a large extent because of the open house process, local newspapers became more supportive of the Algonquin. Rather than playing upon the public's fears, as they had often done in the past, *Barry's Bay This Week* (May 11, 1993) and *The Eganville Leader* (May 12, 1993) provided the historical context and legal background of the issue. On May 14, *The Pembroke Observer* carried an article with the headline, "Land Claim Open House Allays Fears." And in an editorial celebrating the one-hundredth anniversary of Algonquin Park, *The Ottawa Citizen* came across as sympathetic to the Algonquin claim.

Rather than portraying the Algonquin as a depersonalized "they," as had often occurred in the past, newspapers were printing positive articles about individuals. On May 29, *The Pembroke Daily News* published a laudatory piece on the new chief of the Golden Lake band, **Robert Whiteduck**. In *The Bancroft Times* of June 8, Ernie Martelle, superintendent of Algonquin Park, stated his belief that **Dennis Sarazin**, the Golden Lake official in charge of enforcing the rules of the Interim Agreement, was highly regarded by everyone.

The second hunting season of the Interim Hunting Agreement found the Algonquin again shooting less than the allowed limit, with 89 moose (11 under the maximum allowed) and only 39 deer. This led Grant Hopkins, outdoors writer for *The Ottawa Citizen*, to conclude an article on the hunt by stating that he felt that the Algonquin laws were working. In November 1993, the agreement was renewed for the third year.

In December 1993, the situation looked positive for the Golden Lake Algonquin. The *Holmes Report*, a 2500-page independent study commissioned by the Ontario government, supported the Golden Lake claim.

Rather than settling the matter, this seemed to spur on increased criticism of the Golden Lake Algonquin and of the NDP Government. An editorial in *The Huntsville Forester* (January 5, 1994) claimed that the report demonstrated a politically biased NDP agenda. The Land O' Lakes Tourist Association, writing in *The North Frontenac News* (January 25, 1994), argued that no special rights of access, possession, or stewardship should be given to the Algonquin, as it felt that the First Nation's land claims were unrealistic.

Opposition was particularly vocal once it was reported that in Stringer Lake the Algonquin had caught their set quota of 50 fish. References were made in local newspapers to the "rape of Stringer Lake." Ed van Duuren, writing in *The Huntsville Forester* (May 25, 1994), stated his belief that many Natives believed they could operate outside of the laws of Canada.

On August 25, a "Framework for Negotiations" was signed by the Golden Lake Algonquin and the governments of Ontario and Canada. It set the scope, topics, and timetable for the actual negotiations. A companion document, "Shared Objectives," identified the areas that would guide the three parties in the negotiations. The second step, after the "Framework for Negotiations," would be an agreement in principle, followed by the third and last step, the final agreement. The framework documents stated optimistically that the whole process would take about two years.

Then the soon-to-be-premier of the province, Mike Harris, appeared on the scene. Showing the attitude that he would later bring to his government's dealing with all Native groups, in speaking to a meeting of tourism officials in Peterborough in October, he expressed his belief that White guilt and not justice was being served, and that Natives spent too much time in courts fighting for their rights (with the implication that they should be working instead).

Howard Bernard, Golden Lake communications officer, responded by pointing out that his community had held nine open houses and had met with organizations such as the Wildlands League, the Ontario Federation of Anglers and Hunters, the Renfrew County Economic Development Committee, Natural Resources Canada, the Ontario Ministry of Natural Resources, and the Ontario Ministry of the Environment.

The next summer, Harris asserted his wish to see Native land claim negotiations take place in public forums that required settlements to be approved through local referenda. Thus, any rightness of Native claims would be buried under the greater numbers of non-Natives. Justice would be sacrificed to popularity.

Harris also said that he wanted to put an end to interim policies such as the one in place at Golden Lake, despite the fact that it had worked efficiently each year.

The summer and fall of 1995 brought violent Native protests into the public eye (see Chapter 20 on Dudley George). Golden Lake Chief Robert Whiteduck assured non-Natives that they preferred talking to violent protest (*The Pembroke Observer*, September 12, 1995). He noted that through a quarter century of their talking with governments, the Golden Lake Algonquin had not instigated any confrontations, a policy they weren't about to change. Further, he stated that, "[i]f we can demonstrate in this process that there's a reasonable, constructive way to resolve the issues through negotiations, we can say we're doing it, and hopefully have an indirect impact on others. The only way I can see it being resolved is in a healthy fashion."

DIVIDING LINES

In recent years, problems of Algonquin unity have emerged to complicate the land claims issue. They represent the microcosm of problems faced by Aboriginal Canada. These problems include questions of status membership and eligibility for claim benefits and of representation. The Pikwakanagan (Golden Lake) council, which represents the registered Algonquin of their band, maintains that one should have 1/8 blood quantum (that is, the total of all Algonquin ancestors) in order to benefit from their land claims. But nine other Algonquin "communities" have started making claims to this land—Greater Golden Lake, Bancroft, Antoine, Whitney, Mattawa-North Bay, Bonnechere, Ardoch, Ottawa, and Sharbot Lake. These communities are for the most part made up of non-status Algonquin, each with their own representatives. These communities argue that eligibility for land claims should be based on being a descendant of an Algonquin ancestor, no matter how distant. But the Ardoch First Nation have their own land claim going back to 2000 acres promised them by Governor General Sir Charles Bagot in 1844. In 1992, they officially formed as a group to petition for part of the Golden Lake claim, but have not been recognized by the federal government.

This division can be seen in the hunting agreement of 2005–06, which includes two different hunts: one for Pikwakanagan (Golden Lake) and one for the Nine Communities.

Since the initial single-year Interim Agreements ended in 2001, moose hunting has been organized around a tag system similar to that which applies to non-Aboriginal hunters. A set number of tags are issued per year. For example, in Algonquin Park, the Nine Communities had tags for 24 bulls, 24 cows, and 25 calves. They could hunt from October 11, 2005 to January 15, 2006. The understated words of the 2005–06 Agreement between the Nine Algonquin Communities and The Ministry of Natural Resources demonstrate the delicate balancing act that the division requires.

As of February 2009, the Algonquin claim has still not been resolved. With the new divisions among the Algonquin, such a resolution, or one that will reflect well on Algonquin interests, is unlikely to happen soon.

Native Individuals 14-1

Greg Sarazin: Chief of the Golden Lake Algonquin throughout much of their negotiation in the 1980s and 1990s for their rights to Algonquin Park.

Timeline 14-1

1772: First Algonquin petition to have their rights to the area recognized.

1857: Five heads of families petition for land that would become the Golden Lake reserve.

1864: Land is purchased for them using funds from the sale of Native lands.

1893: Crown land is set aside for Algonquin Park.

1991: First Interim Agreement.

KEY TERM

Interim Agreement

CONTENT QUESTIONS

1. Did the Golden Lake Algonquin sign a treaty?
2. Through what means did the Golden Lake Algonquin receive their land?
3. What were the results of the Interim Agreements?
4. What happened to the Interim Agreements?
5. What public relations moves did the Algonquin make?

WEBLINK

www.msvu.ca/atlantis/vol/292pdf/292gehl.PDF
This website provides one Algonquin's view of the claim process.

chapter fifteen

Fighting for Recognition: The Sheshatshit Innu and the Megaprojects

OVERVIEW

The **Mushuau-Innu**, or "Barren Ground People," entered the twentieth century leading a traditional life, with their territory (which they called "Nitassinan") unceded to the government, still relatively untouched by outsiders. Several major projects would quickly alter that last fact but not the second one.

During the early years of this century, White trappers slowly encroached on the yet-to-be-signed-over territory around what is now **Sheshatshit** ("large inlet," pronounced sheh-shah-cheet), or Hamilton Inlet. Sheshatshit cuts deep into Labrador about halfway up the peninsula. This outsider incursion into centuries-old Naskapi hunting and trapping country increased greatly in 1942 with the building of the U.S. Armed Forces Base at Goose Bay. Newfoundland, then independent of Canada, had signed over the land for that purpose. However, no Innu was notified of this passing on of their land from foreign hand to foreign hand.

Newfoundland joined Canada in 1949, but the official status of Native people in the new province was not dealt with, even though Native rights to the land had not been extinguished. No treaties had been signed; no reserves had been created. So Newfoundland governments treated the Innu, Inuit, and Mi'kmaq of the province as if they had no Aboriginal rights.

This became particularly destructive to the Innu when the megaprojects arrived. To show the impact of these projects, we will refer throughout this chapter to statements from and about **Tshaukuesh (Elizabeth) Penashue**, a woman who is a key figure in the fight by the **Sheshashiwinnu** (Innu of Sheshatshit) for their well-being.

THE IRON MINES

In the early 1950s, the Quebec North Shore and Labrador Railway, which runs from Sept-Îles to Schefferville, cut through about 500 kilometres of Innu territory. The intention was to remove 10 million tonnes of ore a year from the huge iron deposits around Schefferville. A few Innu found jobs, many of them seasonal or temporary, but many more saw and felt the despoliation of their traditional lands. Furthermore, the original inhabitants were treated as second-class citizens by those who moved in to reap the wealth of their land.

For Euro-Canadians, the mines and spinoff industries were profitable, at least for a while. During that time, Sept-Îles was considered one of the richest cities in Canada, based on per-capita earnings. It is estimated that during the boom years (1975–1980) $257 million was made from mining (Wadden 1996:53). Predictably, the bottom fell out of the market during the 1980s; mines closed down, and Sept-Îles saw a third of its population, mostly White English-speakers ("**Akaneshau**" in Innu), leave town for greener pastures or more well-endowed motherlodes. The Innu, with a long-term investment in the area, had no such option.

It is ironic that an Innu hunter, **Mistanpeu (Mathieu Andre)**, had led geologists to the iron deposits in the late 1940s, receiving the Order of Canada for his efforts. He would later say that he had no idea the negative effects that subsequent activities would have on his people and on his land (Wadden 1996:52–53).

During the 1950s and 1960s, the Sheshatshit Innu were increasingly forced into sanitation-poor shacks, thought by outsider "experts" to be much better than the tents that had served them in good health for a long time. Tuberculosis and alcoholism were the predictable results. In words that could be echoed by the parents of the children that drew national attention years later at Davis Inlet, Tshaukuesh (Elizabeth) Penashue contrasts the effects on children of the new life in the outsider-imposed community and the traditional life in **nutshimit** (meaning "the bush," "inland," or "the country"):

> Life is important in the country because you don't have to worry about the children, you know they're close somewhere in the camp. But in the community I start worrying. I worry my children will drink, then they get involved in vandalism and have to go to court . . . My children, they're totally confused. Whereas in the country they're busy all the time. (Wadden 1996:87)

Box 15-1 gives one Innu's perspective on the iron mines.

Box 15-1   An Innu Reflects on the Iron Mines

In 1998, Kathleen Nuna spoke through a translator about the Innu's experiences of iron mines:

> When they talked about mining, the people were told, they were told you're not going to pay to train. So they [the mining companies] didn't pay. No more than ten years and then they started paying [for] training [to work in the mine]. 8 bucks. And first the Innu didn't understand because they were too excited at first. They bought it too early what has been said. Now here all the destruction is taking place in Schefferville. The only people that are there now is Innu and everywhere around them is like big holes and just like dump. They just—people just packed up and left. The only people there is Innu. (CEAA 1998)

Media horror stories of reserve life and stereotypes of downtown, outside-the-bar drunken Innu fail to give any indication that in "nutshimit," or its equivalent among other peoples, Native life is more complete, and the people are more whole, both having purpose. In part because of this holism, the number crunching of megaprojects' balance sheets insufficiently calculates the long-term value of "nutshimit" in providing the material necessities of life, as well as the nonphysical necessities of a supportive family, a community, a sense of purpose, and a spiritual balance.

CHURCHILL FALLS

The Churchill Falls Hydroelectric Project was built to fulfill the power demands of mining and other industries in Quebec and the northeastern United States. Constructed over the period from 1966 to 1974, this project involved damming the Churchill River near a spectacular waterfall. It was a megaproject with all the usual superlatives: the world's largest underground powerhouse, which created the Smallwood Reservoir; the third-largest artificial body of water in the world, at 6527 square kilometres; and the tenth-largest freshwater body in Canada.

The Innu were neither consulted nor notified, even though the land being flooded, some 1300 square kilometres of black spruce forest, had not been signed over. Like many other Innu, Tshaukuesh's parents were unaware that flooding was about to occur. One day in 1973, as usual, they left their canoes, traps, tents, and other belongings behind to go about their daily work. But their possessions and lands were soon covered with water. Later, no compensation was paid to them or to the others who had lost both supplies and hunting/trapping territory—their living—through this unannounced flood. With typical outsider blindness, the writer hired by the company to write its "official" glorifying history wrote: "The Churchill Falls project did not deprive a single person of his home or livelihood" (as quoted in Wadden 1996:45).

Billions of dollars would be generated by this project and related industries, but that money flowed freely out of the Innu country just as the waters of the Churchill River had once done, not staying to benefit the Innu. Box 15-2 gives Peter Penashue's opinion on the Churchill Falls project.

Box 15-2   An Innu Reflects on Churchill Falls

In 1998, in the environmental assessment for the Voisey's Bay project, some Innu commented negatively about how they felt about the Churchill Falls dam. Here are the words of Peter Penashue:

> Many people today . . . look at Churchill Falls and they say there was a great river there. You could hear it for miles. What is it that benefits the Innu today from Churchill Falls? We pay the monthly bills that come from Newfoundland Hydro which is, in my view, a great wrong committed to the people because the governments flood the river and take the land then they turn around and send a bill to the people that own the land. But I look at it and I say, well what did we accomplish? (CEAA 1998)

THE LOW-FLYING JETS

The Situation

In 1986, the Canadian government signed agreements with the governments of the United States, Britain, the Netherlands, and West Germany, permitting these NATO allies to train their air forces for 10 years over Innu land in Labrador. Again, there was no consultation or consideration of the Innu, who had still not signed away their land.

The pilot training consisted of low-level flying (30 metres above the ground) of 20-tonne jets streaking across the barrens at 900 kilometres an hour, achieving a noise level of between 110 to 140 decibels (Wadden 1996:36). To give some idea of the level of this noise, a jackhammer achieves 80 decibels, and 120 decibels causes physical pain to human ears. The number of flights in 1986 was 6000, rising to 7000 in 1988.

The effect of these flights on the environment has been a hotly debated subject, but it is hard to convincingly argue that there were no effects. Caribou tended to run without rest after being frightened by the jets. Thus, a typical caribou pace of 12 kilometres a day was extended to 55 or 60 kilometres a day without rest or food. Evidence of caribou starvation in increasing numbers has been found, and there is evidence of aborted births. Also, gas was dumped near the end of the flights, and the caribou would go out of their way to avoid the areas of this dumping. Migration paths and calving grounds have been altered in ways hazardous both to the caribou and to those who hunt them.

Judges, military leaders, and politicians have argued that not enough is "scientifically" known about the impact of the low-flying jets on caribou, that a people carrying the knowledge accumulated over thousands of years of hunting caribou cannot be considered "experts" because they don't have pieces of paper saying that they are experts. Yet farmers have received as much as $45,000 in compensation for incidents where domestic animals have been affected by jet-induced trauma: for example, goats and ranch fox which have aborted, turkeys which have had heart attacks, and hens which have stopped producing eggs (Wadden 1996:178). How much more might wild animals such as caribou be affected?

The Sheshatshiwinnu Fight Back

Innu resistance to outsider forces and their negative impact on their country has consistently followed a path of peaceful, nonviolent civil disobedience. Not surprisingly, the first act of resistance involved hunting. The Innu were increasingly becoming more and more restricted in this critical area of their lives by rule-makers who did not consult them, and by rules that often did not make any sense. One of the Sheshatshit band's foremost Elders, Tshaukuesh's father-in-law, had the proud name of **Kanatuakuet** ("Porcupine Hunter"), no doubt because he had often provided food for his family from that delicacy prized by the Innu. But Newfoundland provincial game laws prohibited the killing of porcupine, even though that species was in no way threatened. Kanatuakuet could no longer legally live up to his name.

For 15 years, the Sheshatshiwinnu were not permitted to hunt the Mealy Mountain caribou herd. In March 1987, the Innu saw signs that the herd had recovered from earlier low numbers. Having a great need for the meat, they staged an act of peaceful political protest. They hunted openly, not trying to hide from the provincial wildlife officers. **Peter Penashue**, Tshaukuesh's son, describes how they felt:

We were afraid, we'd never done anything like that before, actually provoking arrest. In the past, we would have hidden, but not any more, we're through hiding. It's time our rights are recognized on this land. So, when those Mounties finally caught up with us, you know, I felt they looked at us with some respect because they could see we were doing what we thought was right, and they could see we aren't afraid of them any more. (Wadden 1996:94)

They were arrested, convicted, and fined, but it was an important radicalizing first step. Their next step involved speaking out about the low-level flying that was so destructive to their lives. In the autumn of 1987 and of 1988, Tshaukuesh and others of like mind made camp on the bombing range, obliging the military to temporarily cancel the bombing runs.

In 1988, NATO officials were given a grand tour of the military installation by government representatives, in the hope that Goose Bay would be chosen as the site for the NATO-sponsored Tactical Fighter Weapons Training Centre. The visiting dignitaries were kept safely away from the Sheshatshiwinnu, who sought to speak with them in order to voice their legitimate concerns.

On September 15, 1988, one of the most dramatic moments in the history of the Innu unfolded. More than 75 Innu, including Tshaukuesh, marched onto the runway at Goose Bay and refused to leave until they spoke with the NATO officials. After being made to wait, they were eventually given their chance to speak. They told the people from NATO that the land proposed for the centre was unceded Innu land and that NATO would be complicit in an act of "ethnocide" by the Canadian government if it went ahead with its plans for the Strategic Fighter Weapons Training Centre.

The Innu occupied the runway seven times that fall, determined to change the deteriorating social conditions at Sheshatshit. That year, 21 teenagers from the community tried to commit suicide. Tshaukuesh was arrested on more than one occasion for her acts of protest. One suicide attempt hit particularly close to her. Her son, Peter, had taken an overdose of pills, but fortunately it was not enough to kill him. Box 15-3 gives one Innu's opinion of government promises about the low-flying jets, while Box 15-4 gives three perspectives on

---

Box 15-3   **An Innu Reflects on Government Promises Concerning Low-Flying Jets**

Through a translator, Innu Mary Ann Michel spoke in 1998 at the environmental assessment of Voisey's Bay about the promises made by the government concerning the Innu ceasing their protests of low-flying jets. Her interpretation of that situation led to her distrust of the Voisey's Bay Nickel Company (note authors' emphasis):

We fought low level flying . . . One year we were sitting—we got nothing and we were told . . . "Stop protesting. We will give you housing." [We're] going to

have nice housing, we were told. "We're going to give you . . . lots of cars . . . we're going to have houses near the base. There's going to be land there." . . . So we gave up the protest. On the 10th of December, we gave up protesting and when we gave up, one year, . . . and nothing happened. And today, still nothing. We didn't get anything and we were told we were going to get lots of money and lots of houses *and now, I hear you saying this. So we're told lies all the time like this. I hear them before . . .* (CEAA 1998)

Box 15-4 Framework Agreement

On March 29, 1996, the federal government, the Newfoundland government, and the Innu Nation that included a political association representing the approximately 1700 people of Sheshatshit and Davis Inlet, signed the Framework Agreement. This was the first step in the process of recognition of the Aboriginal rights of the Innu. The document appears to represent all three parties; but if you examine the perspectives of the three leaders, you find that there appear to be two different attitudes toward the agreement. What do you think?

1) Peter Penashue, president of the Innu Nation:

Today we have taken a small but significant step for all future generations of Innu people. Our land and resources are our way of life . . . In the many months of negotiations that lie ahead we trust that Canada and Newfoundland will recognize our rights. We hope to enter an honourable treaty in which our rights are honoured, the wrongdoings of the past are corrected, and we agree to share our land and resources with the newcomers to our homeland Nitassinan, where we have lived in harmony with

the land for thousands of years . . . (CEAA 1998)

2) Brian Tobin, premier of Newfoundland and Labrador:

Signing this Framework Agreement today represents a very important and positive step in treaty negotiations with the Innu Nation, paving the way for agreement of substantive issues . . . My government has identified treaty negotiations with Aboriginal peoples in Labrador as a top priority. We are fully committed to achieving settlement which will provide the Innu with means necessary to attain self-sufficiency and create a stable and certain environment for economic development in Labrador. (CEAA 1998)

3) Ronald Irwin, Minister of Indian Affairs and Northern Development:

The Innu Nation Framework Agreement forms the fundamental structure for building a new relationship with the Innu, based on partnership and mutual respect . . . Reaching a treaty with the Innu will be a major catalyst for improving the social and economic well-being of the Innu and achieving the certainty non-Aboriginal land and resource users need. (CEAA 1998)

the Framework Agreement between the federal government, Newfoundland, and the people of Sheshatshit and Davis Inlet.

In court in the spring of 1989, the 44-year-old Tshaukuesh spoke in her people's defence concerning the reasons for their acts of civil disobedience:

We will lose our culture if the land is destroyed . . . We will lose our identity as Innu people and will not survive in the country any more if the wildlife is demolished by development. For you people, European people, white people, you take your meals from the store. You can survive that, but our people have to depend on the land. (Wadden 1996:145)

The judge of the trial of Tshaukuesh and three other Innu was an Inuk by the name of **James Igloliorte**. He granted an injunction to prevent the military from low-level flying over Innu land. In pronouncing his judgment, Judge Igloliorte observed:

Each of these four persons based their belief of ownership on an honest belief on reasonable grounds . . . Through their knowledge of ancestry and kinship they have showed that none of their people ever gave away rights to the land of Canada, and this is an honest belief each person holds. The provincial and federal statutes do not include as third parties or signatories any Innu people. (Wadden 1996:150)

Predictably, the decision was overturned in a higher court. Tshaukuesh was arrested again on the runway. In 1990, the number of low-level jet flights increased to 9000. But the Innu continued to fight, beginning to reach a larger, even international, audience.

The news today is mixed. For the most part, the issue has been lost to the fickle consciousness of the Canadian public. On February 7, 1996, Canada signed a 10-year multilateral agreement following an environmental assessment. The low-level flying will continue, April to November, with a maximum of 18,000 sorties a season. You don't have to be an Innu hunter to know that the caribou herds will be affected.

VOISEY'S BAY

There are two new megaprojects on the Innu horizon. One is another dam on the Churchill River, this one on a slightly smaller scale, flooding only 1146 square kilometres of land. The other project, one that is moving ahead more quickly, is mining at Voisey's Bay, 335 kilometres northwest of Sheshatshit. In 1993, rich deposits of nickel, cobalt, and copper were discovered there. Voisey's Bay Nickel Company (owned by Inco Limited) is planning to develop an area it refers to as the Claims Block, an area measuring 18 kilometres by 29 kilometres.

Voisey's Bay Nickel Company has acted more responsibly and sympathetically to Innu concerns than its predecessors in the other megaprojects. During the environmental assessment hearing held in October 1998, the company made fair-sounding proposals concerning jobs and job training. But the Innu, justifiably, were suspicious. They had been led down that path before. The Innu presentations at the hearing spoke of how badly they had been treated before (see Box 15-1 on page 162, Box 15-2 on page 163, and Box 15-3 on page 165). In the following presentation (given in translation), **Francis Penashue** compared the Voisey's Bay Nickel Company representatives to the first priest that came to live with her people:

> I want to talk about 1950s towards today. I remember what this gentleman said, that he said it would be one year or two years that the work [project] will be working and that people would be able to get jobs, and I was just thinking about what he had just said. 1950s, the first one was, I guess the priest came to our communities, permanently, and those people like my grandmother and my grandfather were very committed to the church and very respect[ful] to the church much as if it was God, . . . and today I heard the gentleman here, and I was thinking about, he reminded me about the priest, 1950s . . . and so I was thinking, it was almost 50 years now, I guess and today just look at us now and see all the misery you see in the community of other people's culture coming into our communities and for us trying to adopt jobs and the way of life of others. (CEAA 1998)

In 2002, Tshaukuesh participated in a speaking tour across Canada to raise funds and awareness of the difficulties of her people. In October 2005, she received an honorary doctor of laws degree from Memorial University of Newfoundland. In 2002, her son, Peter Penashue, was named one of Canada's "top 40 under 40" by the *Globe and Mail*.

He has taken more of a compromising route to try to benefit his people. He moved out of politics to become more involved with Innu businesses that had benefited from his fight to have Innu workers and businesses involved with the nickel development in the area. In 2006, he was named to the Advisory Board of Crosshair Exploration and Mining Corporation.

In 2002, Inco signed a Statement of Principles with the government of Newfoundland and Labrador, as well as signing Impacts and Benefits Agreements with the Innu Nation.

Native Individuals 15-1

James Igloliorte: An Inuit judge who awarded a decision in favour of the protesting Sheshatshit Innu.

Mistanpeu: Mathieu Andre, an Innu who led geologists to the huge Schefferville iron deposits.

Peter Penashue: President of the Innu Nation during the signing of the Framework Agreement.

Tshaukuesh (Elizabeth) Penashue: A Sheshatshit Innu woman who has been at the forefront of the protest movement against low-flying jets.

Timeline 15-1

1949: American Armed Forces Base is built at Goose Bay.

Newfoundland joins Canada.

Early 1950s: The Quebec North Shore and Labrador Railway is cut through about 500 kilometres of Innu territory.

1973: The Churchill Falls dam floods Innu country.

1975–80: Boom period for the mines in Innu territory.

1986: The Canadian government signs an agreement with NATO countries permitting low-flying jets over Innu territory.

1987–89: Innu peacefully protest low-flying jets.

1993: Rich deposits are discovered at Voisey's Bay.

1996: The Framework Agreement is signed by the Innu Nation, the province of Newfoundland and Labrador, and the federal government.

2002: The Voisey Bay Nickel Company Ltd. Signs Impacts and Benefits Agreements with the Innu Nation.

KEY TERMS

Mushuau-Innu (Innu)

nutshimit (Innu)

CONTENT QUESTIONS

1. What unique situation has caused the Sheshatshit Innu to be treated, until recently, as if they had no Aboriginal rights?

2. In what sense would the Innu feel that they had already paid for their electricity from Churchill Falls?

3. What three megaprojects have had an impact on the Innu in the twentieth century?

4. Why are the Innu suspicious of the promises from the Voisey's Bay Nickel Company?

5. What do you think the Voisey's Bay Nickel Company representatives needed to learn from the Innu?

WEBLINKS

www.innu.ca/tshenish1.html
This website presents an article, "Hard to Say Goodbye to Emish," about Innu Elder Tshishenish, in which he talks about Voisey's Bay and his people's connections with the land there.

www.gov.nf.ca/voiseys/pdf/MemorandumAgreement.pdf
This presents the text of the 2002 Memorandum of Agreement established with the Innu, the government of Canada, and the government of Newfoundland and Labrador.

chapter sixteen

The James Bay and Northern Québec Agreement

OVERVIEW

The Cree have lived in the James Bay region for five to six thousand years. While we can never be sure of their population at the time of contact, it is estimated that they numbered at least 20,000 people. However, it was not until 1971 that the Cree who occupy present-day Quebec ever came together for a common cause. Until that time, they had been living in groups of less than a dozen villages in an essentially traditional way, hunting and trapping for food and income. They would spread out over the land for the winter months, exploiting territories that had been in families for generations. The care of the land was vested in an old man within the village.

When northern Quebec was handed over to the province by the federal government in 1898 and 1912, it was under the strict stipulation that the Cree, along with the Inuit and the Innu, would have their rights dealt with through treaties. But prior to 1971, not one Quebec provincial government had done anything to fulfill these requirements.

THE PROJECT OF THE CENTURY

In April 1971, Quebec Premier Robert Bourassa announced that the province was going to initiate a huge hydroelectric development project that would involve harnessing the rivers of the James Bay watershed. The government was totally oblivious to the fact that these rivers ran through the Cree hunting territories and were essential to the Cree way of life. The government's position was that the project would be constructed on provincial lands and would be beneficial to everybody, including First Nations people.

The Cree leaders met in Mistassini on June 29, 1971. During a three-day meeting, the Cree leaders decided that they would fight with all of their ability to protest and derail the government's plans. They would not tolerate the flooding of the area. They petitioned the Minister of Indian Affairs to intervene on their behalf.

The Native battle over the James Bay project would take nearly five years and would involve the province of Quebec, the federal government, the Cree, and the Inuit. The culmination would be the first major settlement of a Native land claim in recent years. The James Bay and Northern Quebec Agreement (1975) has generated dispute and debate since it was signed. Initially, it was believed that it would pave the way for all subsequent land claims settlements; but since its signing, it has come to be reassessed and reconsidered. The agreement was signed by the government of Quebec, three Quebec Crown corporations, the Grand Council of the Crees of Quebec, the Northern Quebec Inuit Association, and the Government of Canada. It involved 6650 Cree from eight communities and 4386 Inuit from fifteen communities.

A couple of facts about the historical context are important to the unfolding of events. First, the First Nations people who occupied the Quebec portion of James Bay had never signed any treaty or surrendered any land. Under Canadian law, based on the Royal Proclamation of 1763, the land was *ipso facto* Native land. Second, the Quebec government had had no prior consultations with the Cree or Inuit people before starting this project. This was very much consistent with previous actions on the part of the Quebec government in its dealings with Native people.

Perhaps the most remarkable aspect of the history of the project is the rapidity with which the Cree and Inuit responded to the threat by Quebec. The provincial government was totally unprepared for the response. Implicit in the government's total disregard for the concerns of the Natives was a belief that these were unsophisticated and politically naive peoples. The government was wrong. The Cree were led initially by a number of young people who had already had experience with the "outside world." The Cree decided at their initial meeting that the project would not benefit them in any way and would destroy land, animals, and their culture. Their strategy was to organize at a grassroots level, within their communities, and to solicit support not only from other Native groups but also from the public at large.

The Inuit reacted by forming themselves into a number of associations, which were then coordinated by the Inuit Tapirisat of Canada, a blanket organization for several Canadian groups representing the Inuit.

The Native groups affected decided to undertake talks with the government. But in January 1972, the government refused to discuss a claim for compensation that was put forward by the Indians of Quebec Association (IQA). However, a month later, a joint federal and provincial committee on environmental effects of the project stated that it would have a substantial impact on Native peoples of the region. The Cree did not want to convey the impression of being in total opposition to the project, and so adopted a position of moderation and accommodation. Above all, they wanted to discuss with the government alternative plans or modifications to the project so that the impact might be lessened. The government, for its part, refused to do anything but to agree to inform the First Nations of the plans as they developed. As a result, the Cree were obliged to assume a position of opposition.

Under the auspices of the IQA, the Cree met at Fort George in 1972. **Chief Billy Diamond** raised the possibility of a court case to stop the project, and the meeting extended a general mandate for this purpose to the IQA. At the same time, the Cree set up community liaison workers. The following month, the IQA formed a task force and called upon McGill University researchers to conduct environmental and social impact studies. The McGill University Department of Anthropology was a major contributor to these reports. During May 1972, the Cree and Inuit initiated action in the injunction.

In late October 1972, the government announced its policy of no modifications to its plans. That same week, the Cree, Inuit, and executives of the IQA met in Montreal to review the work of the task force. They subsequently met with Premier Bourassa, at a meeting that was essentially fruitless because of the government's no-modification policy. At this point, the Cree decided that they had no alternative but to pursue court action wholeheartedly. A week later, they filed papers for an injunction stopping the development. Justice Albert Malouf of the Quebec Superior Court granted a hearing on the petition by the Cree and Inuit. This would end up being the longest temporary injunction hearing in Canadian history. It lasted 71 days, from December 11, 1972, until May 24, 1973, and heard testimony from 167 witnesses, of whom nearly 100 were Cree and Inuit hunters. The First Nations had to prove that they had a *prima facie* (i.e., evidence adequate to establish a fact) claim to rights to the territory, and that the project would damage the exercising of these rights. Furthermore, they had to prove that these damages could not be reversed or remedied.

What caused this damage? The project to be undertaken by the government was enormous. Among other creations was a 700-kilometre road through traditional hunting territories, a new town to house the project's headquarters, several scattered construction camps, and airports and communications infrastructures. Additional long-term plans included mines and forestry operations.

The hydroelectric project itself involved diverting three major rivers into the La Grande River in order to increase its flow by 80 percent. What did this involve? It meant the construction of four main dams, 130 kilometres of dykes, and eight main reservoirs that would flood 8722 square kilometres (5 percent) of the land surface of Quebec. The reservoirs created by these dams would fill during the summer and release during the winter to produce electricity for more southerly cities and towns. This necessitated the construction of 960 kilometres of power lines through the bush, intersecting Cree hunting territories. All of these activities constituted only the first phase of the project.

The Cree argued their case based on the concept of Aboriginal rights, the essence of which is rights to the land based on traditional use and occupancy. They contended that flooding would destroy much of the wildlife, including beaver and other furbearers and game. The variability in water levels would be particularly dangerous, as animals would not be able to predict their levels. Fish levels would decline, vegetation would be lost, and the Cree's resources for subsistence would be destroyed. In sum, their livelihood would be lost.

The government's response was predictable. It argued that the Cree lived in settlements, made use of modern technology, and did not take much from the land. It stated that employment or government assistance provided much of their income. Furthermore, any damage would be temporary and reparable.

Justice Malouf agreed with the Cree and Inuit. In November 1973, he ruled that the government was trespassing, since the Cree and Inuit had title to the land. They had been occupying and using it to a full extent, hunting was of fundamental cultural and economic importance, and they had demonstrated their interest in pursuing their way of life. Any interference would compromise and interfere with their culture and way of life. He accorded the interlocutory injunction based on the evidence.

The Malouf Judgment was far more than anybody had expected. The government appealed, and a week later the Quebec Court of Appeal suspended the Malouf Judgment on the basis of the "balance of convenience," without specifically treating the issue of Native title to lands.

Between the date of the Malouf Judgment (November 15, 1973) and the Quebec suspension (November 22, 1973), the Bourassa Government had submitted an 11-page proposal for a settlement to the IQA executive and to the Cree and Inuit representatives. On December 10, the Cree chiefs met and agreed to enter negotiations and to extend a mandate to the IQA to seek funds and to undertake negotiations. The Cree also set the requirement that the IQA *must* consult with the villages prior to negotiations.

In the meantime, the Cree tried to appeal the suspension of the Malouf Judgment, but to no avail. The Cree chiefs met in Fort George (Chisasibi) and developed a counterproposal, which they titled *Our Land, Our Demand*. Billy Diamond held a press conference to say that the Cree rejected the province's 11-point proposal. At the same time, the Minister of Indian Affairs made threatening noises about cutting off funds to the Cree if they did not seriously consider the Bourassa proposal. He later backed down.

From February to July 1974, negotiations were undertaken with the Cree, who were represented by the IQA. The IQA created committees and subcommittees and put them into effect. Equally important, the IQA undertook consultations with all communities about offers and negotiations. However, early on during the negotiations, a rift developed between the Cree and the IQA. Some people have interpreted this as being a rift that was the product of Iroquois versus Cree interests, north versus south, urban versus rural. Regardless, as a result of dissatisfaction with the IQA, their mandate to represent the northern people was withdrawn at a meeting of the Cree chiefs in Fort George, and a three-man Cree negotiating team was created in its place. This committee drew up *Our Land, Our Demand #2 for Crees*. On August 16, 1974, the Grand Council of the Cree of Quebec (GCCQ) was created. It included a chief and another leader from each community on its board of directors and an executive group of four regional leaders. From then on, the council took over the negotiations. However, at all times, the Cree recognized that decisions had to be made at the grassroots level, and the Cree people remained the final decision makers.

On October 14–15, 1974, promises between the Cree and the province were exchanged. For the rest of the month, the Cree entered into consultations with their various communities. On November 15, an Agreement in Principle was signed, with the Cree leaders declaring it a victory for the Cree. The IQA, however, denounced the agreement in a press conference.

A week after the signing of the Agreement in Principle, the Quebec Court of Appeals overturned the Malouf Judgment. The justices declared that Native rights to the land were extinguished at the time of the Hudson's Bay Company Charter.

The entire year of 1975 was spent hammering out the final details of the James Bay and Northern Quebec Agreement. Negotiations for the final agreement were undertaken with subcommittees, working groups, and task forces. In August, the General Assembly of Crees decided to proceed with negotiations to reach an agreement, and the Grand Council of the Crees of Quebec was authorized to sign on behalf of the Cree Nation. In the final stages, beginning in September, the main committee moved into a Montreal hotel to review, edit, and negotiate final matters prepared by the subcommittees and working groups. For a month, from October 15 to November 11, 1975, all Cree band councils converged in Montreal for a close review of the agreement and signing of the agreement. Finally, on November 11, 1975, the James Bay and Northern Quebec Agreement was signed in Quebec. Between December 15–18, a 70-page text of this agreement was circulated and a ratification vote was held. Voter turnout was 24 percent, with 922 in favour and one opposed.

It is important to remember that while all of this was going on, the Cree had also turned to the public for support. There were massive demonstrations in Montreal, Quebec City, and Ottawa. Native peoples put on theatrical performances depicting both traditional and contemporary Cree life. In a move that fully demonstrated the Quebec government's ignorance of the people it was dealing with, the government sent a communiqué to the Cree written in the wrong dialect. The Cree capitalized on this gaffe by burning it in front of the print journalists and television cameras. While the mistake was hugely insulting (imagine if the Cree had communicated with the government in Acadian French), it provided the Cree with a wonderful opportunity to demonstrate the government's ignorance of them and their culture. At the same time, public support was being found at colleges, universities, environmental groups, and elsewhere. Books were being written, and films were being made.

TERMS OF THE AGREEMENT

The agreement includes not only all persons enrolled under the Indian Act, but also any person of Cree or Indian ancestry who is recognized by one of the Cree communities as having been on such date (November 15, 1974) a member thereof. Further, the natural and adopted descendants of persons so eligible would continue to enjoy benefits of the agreement. Thus, not only were the benefits of the agreement extended to non-Status Indians and Métis, but the provision giving the community the right to recognize particular people as beneficiaries also in effect leaves the definition of "beneficiaries" largely up to the local community.

So what did the Cree win in the case? The James Bay and Northern Quebec Agreement of 1975 has been described as the last of the old-time treaties, although it has at the same time been hailed for breaking new ground. It is both the last of the old and the first of the modern Aboriginal claims settlements in Canada, for it granted to the Cree and the Inuit communities of Quebec substantial control over economic, political, and social affairs (although final say in these issues rests with the government). In addition to a cash settlement greater than $230 million to be paid over 21 years, and special economic assistance, Natives maintained ownership of certain sections of land. These have been designated as Categories 1 (a and b), 2, and 3. **Category 1a** lands are those transferred to federal jurisdiction for the use of the Cree bands. They are reserves in the conventional sense. **Category 1b** are lands transferred to Cree Village Corporations, essentially "reserve" lands but under provincial jurisdiction. The principal distinction between Categories 1a and 1b relates to the role of the federal or provincial government. On Category 1b lands, the Cree are subject to provincial law, although they are regarded as full owners of the land. **Category 1** lands may not be bought or sold. The general public is restricted in its access and, if expropriated or subjected to public servitude, the lands taken in this way must be replaced by equivalent tracts. The province retains ownership of all subsurface rights but a prospective developer must obtain the consent of the Cree before undertaking exploitation of these resources.

Category 2 lands are those on which the Cree enjoy hunting, fishing, and trapping rights, as well as priority in certain development activities. They have the right to set conditions under which non-Cree sports users may have access. These lands are under provincial jurisdiction and may be readily appropriated for development activities. However, land taken for development must be replaced by equivalent lands or, if the Cree choose, monetary compensation.

The remainder of the territory is classified as **Category 3** lands, which are those governed by provincial legislation and regulations concerning public lands. The Cree have important protection for their harvesting activities without restriction but only within social and environmental protection guidelines.

In addition, three more provisions were include (1) for a minimum family income plan for those in wildlife harvesting; (2) for Native languages to be included as official languages of administration; and (3) for a James Bay Native Development Corporation to handle investments.

Financial compensation took a number of forms. The sums were payable to the Native population as a whole and then divided between the Cree and the Inuit on the basis of their respective populations. The split was roughly 60/40, with the Cree receiving the larger amount. The actual amount was $225 million, of which $150 million was basic compensation, and $75 million was considered compensation for future development.

The initial $150 million should best be perceived as compensation for the surrender of Aboriginal title. The payment was essentially broken down into two chunks of $75 million, the first for loss of title in the strict sense (for which the Government of Canada paid half), and the second being essentially a royalty payment in reference to installed hydroelectric generating capacity. The third $75 million was made to cover the cost of negotiations, and $4 million was paid in compensation to take into account the non-Status Native population in the region. The total compensation to the James Bay Cree then was $137.4 million. However, by 1983, unforeseen costs, particularly in the forms of new or unplanned medical, housing, and educational expenses, brought the total cost to over $500 million, or nearly $50,000 per Native person living in the region.

Native critics have not been kind to the agreement. They point to the cost involved, including the flooding of thousands of kilometres of prime habitat. Furthermore, the entire project involved a number of components eventually affecting an area the size of France. Critics suggested that the Cree sold out. Some media accused them of simply being money-hungry.

Critics also point out that Native rights fell far short of being entrenched in the agreement. Furthermore, time has shown that the government has not met its end of the bargain, and Natives contend that the government has not allowed them to have any say in the developments.

Fighting the Second Phase

The second phase of this project, known as the Great Whale Phase, was also strongly protested by the Cree, beginning in 1989. The Cree had decided that there was no fairness in the dealings by either Hydro Quebec or the government. In 1981, eight children in Cree villages died of diarrhea. The cause was determined to be open sewers that had been left by construction camps when money was cut off for completion of the construction. From a Cree perspective, as soon as the work on delivering power was completed, everybody ran to the south.

Mercury poisoning was also a problem. In 1984, tests on Chisasibi residents found high levels of mercury in 64 percent of the population. The land had not been cleared before flooding, and bacteria from the drowned, decomposing vegetation had transformed the insoluble mercury in the rocks into methylmercury. The methylmercury had then evaporated and returned to the waterways as rain, poisoning the food system. Elders in Chisasibi exhibited the symptoms of poisoning, including numbness, shakiness, and loss of peripheral vision. No one could eat river fish. Hydro Quebec initially said it would take six years for the methylmercury to dissipate, but now says it will take 30 years. More recent studies suggest that it will take 100 years.

Mercury poisoning is known as **nimass aksiwin**, "fish disease" in Cree. According to Cree fisherman George Lameboy:

> Nimass aksiwin strikes at the very heart of our society. It's like being told that Armageddon has started, and people are scared as hell. The scientists come in here and tell us we're getting better [by eating less fish], but hey, you can't measure the effects of nimass aksiwin by taking hair samples. How can you measure a man's fear? How can you measure your way of life coming to an end? (Richardson 1991:xi)

The protests to stop Great Whale have been far-reaching and dramatic. The most dramatic was a specially made canoe, named *Odeyak*, which sailed down the Ottawa and Hudson rivers to New York City, capturing the attention of the international media. The Cree have questioned the environmental, ethical, economic, and social benefits of Great Whale. People seem to be listening; as a result, the Second Phase was blocked.

The Cree's fight continues. Not long prior to the Referendum in Quebec in the fall of 1995, the Cree issued a declaration that if Quebec separated from Canada, they would separate from Quebec. The main legal argument they put forth in their massive document was that Quebec had failed to live up to its part of the bargain concerning the James Bay and Northern Quebec Agreement of 1975. More recently, the Cree have been trying to stop the sale of environmentally sensitive forests in Northern Quebec to forest-product companies.

It is important that we put the James Bay Agreement in a larger context. The late 1960s and early 1970s were a time of rapid social and political change epitomized by such events as the civil rights movement in the US, the women's movement, the Paris riots of 1968, the global hippie movement, gay rights demonstrations (such as the Stonewall riots in New York in 1969), anti-Vietnam protests in the US, and the separatist movement—culminating in the October 1970 crisis—in Québec. Across North America there was a "pan-Indian" movement in which indigenous peoples sought to reclaim their rights as well as their heritage and cultures.

In Canada, the Trudeau government's 1969 White Paper galvanized Native politics. The White Paper espoused equality and integration but it was thinly veiled assimilation. It advocated removal of the Indian Act, phasing out of Indian Affairs, and the eradication of "the constitutional and legislative bases of discrimination." The provinces and not the federal government would assume responsibilities for Native people. Reaction was swift: The late Sally Weaver, who conducted extensive research about Native issues in Canada, said it resulted in "a resounding nationalism unparalleled in Canadian history." It was in this social and political climate, but most especially in the wake of the 1969 White Paper, that Bourassa believed he could ram through the James Bay project without consultation with the rightful owners of the land. It is mere speculation to suggest that the Cree would not have been as motivated and determined to fight the project as they were had it been proposed in an earlier era, but undoubtedly the social and political climate in 1971 was ripe for resistance. The significance of the James Bay Agreement—the first Canadian treaty since the Williams Treaties of 1923—is suggested by the number of academic papers and books—including Salisbury's *A Homeland for the Cree* (1986) and Richardson's *Strangers Devour the Land* (1975)—that have been written about it.

Out of the struggles over the James Bay hydro-electric project came a new generation of Cree leaders who attained recognition on the national and international stages. Billy Diamond was perhaps the first to gain national attention when he signed the James Bay and Northern Québec Agreement on behalf of the Cree on November 11, 1975. Prior to that momentous occasion, in 1970 he was elected chief of Waskaganish (formerly known as Fort Rupert) and from 1974 to 1984, i.e., through the political struggles over the James Bay project and the creation of the new Cree homeland, he was grand chief of the Grand Council of the Crees. Billy Diamond has been praised for creating Air Creebec (the regional airline), Cree Construction Company Limited, and Cree Yamaha Motors from the monies derived from the James Bay and Northern Québec Agreement, thereby laying a financial foundation for Cree nation. He was the subject of Roy MacGregor's biography *Chief: The Fearless Vision of Billy Diamond* and the recipient of an honorary doctorate from Carleton University. He died in 2010.

Matthew Coon-Come was born near Mistassini, survived residential school, and went on to study political science at Trent University and law at McGill University. He was particularly active in the battle over the James Bay project. He served as chief of the Mistassini First Nation and was elected grand chief of the Grand Council of the Crees in 1987 and served four terms in that office. He was also grand chief of the Assembly of First Nations from 2000 to 2003. He has served on numerous boards, many to do with environmental issues, in James Bay, nationally, and internationally. Coon-Come is the recipient of honorary doctorates from Trent University (1998) and the University of Toronto (2000) as well being honoured with the National Aboriginal Achievement Award in 1995.

KEY TERMS

Category 1

Category 2

Category 3

nimass aksiwin (Cree)

CONTENT QUESTIONS

1. Under what conditions was the province of Quebec given its northern territories?
2. What had been done to resolve Cree aboriginal rights prior to the announcement of the James Bay project in 1971?
3. What was the Malouf Judgment?
4. How did the Quebec provincial government counteract the Malouf Judgment?
5. What has been the main environmental problem affecting the health of the Cree?

WEBLINKS

www.gcc.ca
This is the website of the Grand Council of the Crees.

www.gcc.ca/pdf/LEG000000006.pdf
This document is the complete 454-page version of the James Bay and Northern Quebec Agreement.

chapter seventeen

Religious Colonialism

OVERVIEW

In this section, you will read about the negative influence of European or Euro-Canadian colonialist forces (sometimes referred to as "settlers") on Natives in Canada. It is good to keep in mind when reading this chapter that there are numerous examples of Natives successfully resisting outsider influence.

RELIGIOUS COLONIALISM: THE SUPPRESSION OF THE POTLATCH

There are no Western cultural events that can directly compare with the **potlatch** ceremony of the peoples of the Northwest Coast. The potlatch is both a sacred ceremony and a social and recreational celebration. It is like a combination of a Christmas Mass, a christening, a confirmation, and the Bible; a country's constitution and a legal contract; a movie based on a true story and live theatre; a drug- and drink-free rave, the ballet and an art exhibition; and an old-style storyteller and a course in local history. It is unique.

Potlatches are traditionally centred on hereditary names. Potlatches are religious ceremonies, often brought about by births, coming-of-age events, marriages, and deaths. They demonstrate that the individuals and groups hosting the potlatch are socially, economically, and spiritually worthy of such an important inheritance. Names are connected with specific stories, songs, dances, carved and painted images, and the rights to fish, hunt, or harvest plants in a particular territory. Along with these rights come the responsibilities of passing down and performing well those art forms, conserving the life-forms in their territory, and maintaining the strength and social unity of the group. The potlatch reinforced the values of those sacred duties. James Sewid, a Kwakiutl of high rank, received the following names during the ceremony that followed his birth in 1913 (Note that the Kwiksutainuk and Mamalilikulla are Kwakwaka'wakw peoples):

> I received my father's father's name from the Kwiksutainuk people, Owadzidi, which means "people will do anything for him because he is so respected." My mother's father Jim Bell, was from the Mamalilikulla people and I received the name Poogleedee from him, which means "guests never leave his feasts hungry." I received the name Waltkeena, which was from Chief Goatlas of the Mamalilikulla and means "something very precious has been given to us." I received the name Sewid after my father and his father, which means "paddling towards the chief that is giving a potlatch." (Spradley 1969:16)

What happens at a potlatch? Stories are told: stories that go deep in time, often relating back to the first people who held the names being validated. These stories are not just told; they are also acted, sung, and danced. Sacred masks are often used to depict the characters involved. Sometimes strings are pulled that change the face of the mask to indicate some change that happened to the person portrayed by the mask.

A key component in the potlatch is giveaway. The word "potlatch" means "to give" in the Chinook trade language. While giveaway is a major component of Native ceremonies across North America, the amount of giveaway involved in a potlatch was on a scale unequalled elsewhere. One of the most lavish potlatches ever recorded by non-Native writers was, not surprisingly, given by Maquina of the Nuu'chah'nulth (see Box 11-4 on page 123). In his potlatch of 1803, he was reported to have given away 200 muskets, 200 yards of European-manufactured cloth, 100 shirts, 100 looking-glasses, and seven barrels of gunpowder. How much he gave away in Native goods such as wooden carvings, Chilkat blankets, and salmon was not written down, possibly reflecting the bias of the non-Native writer as to what was important.

Some misleading assumptions should be cleared up. No individual owned the large amount of gifts that were given away. The person hosting the potlatch traditionally drew upon his connections of family, secret society, clan, or moiety to get those gifts together. Building this collection could take a long time, as more and more people were included in the giving circle. Traditionally, two kinds of people attended a potlatch: hosts, who were involved with the bringing together of the gifts, and guests, who received the gifts.

Second, no one did without anything important for survival in order to give something away. The gifts tended to be more luxury items than necessities. Blankets, either Native-made or obtained through trade with the Hudson's Bay Company, were important potlatch gifts. And the gifts circulated around. At one potlatch you might be of the hosting party, and at the next potlatch, you might be a guest.

The Competitive Element

The fact that the Northwest Coast peoples were hierarchical contributed to an element of competition in the potlatch. One proof that a high-ranking man was worthy of his position was how much he could give away at a potlatch, particularly to other people of high rank, who would be given the largest number of gifts.

The greatest gifts were **coppers**. These treasured items are sheets of copper shaped like shields and covered with designs painted on with black lead. They traditionally came from copper that was mined in Alaska. Coppers have names, just as people do, putting them in the class of non-human persons, an important element in Northwest Coast as in all

Native spirituality. One particular copper is famous to anthropologists and to students of anthropology because a part of its story was recorded by the famous anthropologist Franz Boas during his stay with the Kwakiutl in the winter of 1894–95. The name of the copper was **Maxtsolem**, meaning "One of whom all [other coppers] are ashamed [to look at; i.e., because they are not Maxtsolem's equal]" (Kehoe 1992). At a potlatch held that winter, a high-ranking man named **Owaxalagilis** attempted to buy Maxtsolem. He began by placing 1200 blankets in front of the chief who was hosting the potlatch. Walas Nemogwis of the Wewamasquem clan of the Mamalilikulla nation then owned Maxtsolem. The speaker in the following quote is Yaqalenlis, a high-ranking man who had once purchased Maxtsolem and who wanted to encourage Owaxalagilis to really prove his worthiness by purchasing the copper with more gifts than anyone else had ever done before. He began his speech by announcing his name and telling of its history:

> The name began at the time when the world was made. I am a descendant of the chiefs about whom we hear in the earliest legends. The Hoxhoq came down to Xoxopa, and took off his bird mask and became a man. Then he took the name Yaqalenlis. That was my ancestor, the first of . . . [the Kwiksutainuk]. He married Laqoagilayuqoa, the daughter of Walas Nemogwis, the first chief of the great clan Wewamasquem of the . . . [Mamalilikulla]. . . . (Kehoe 1992:439)

He then challenged Owaxalagilis by bragging about what he paid for the copper:

> I know how to buy great coppers. I bought this copper Maxtsolem for 4000 blankets . . . What is it, Owaxalagilis? Come, did you not give any thought to my copper here? You always say that you are rich, Chief. Now give more, that it may be as great as I am. Give only ten times 100 blankets more, Chief Owaxalagilis. It will not be much, give 1000 more for my sake . . . (Kehoe 1992:439)

Owaxalagilis ended up paying 4200 blankets for the copper.

The level of competition involved in the giveaway part of the potlatch rose with European contact. This is partially because more goods became available with Native success in the fur trade, as the people obtained more and more European luxury goods. But there was another, more negative cause. European diseases hit the people hard. The Kwakwaka'wakw, for example, dropped in population from 8000 in 1835 to around 2000 in 1885. This disturbed the usually straightforward process of the inheritance of names, typically a choice between brothers, with the eldest having the best options. However, when diseases wiped out whole lineages, more distant relatives could sometimes vie for prestigious names. Competition for names could now be socially divisive and destructive. Heightened competition could also result when formerly separate peoples within nations moved into the same area, as happened at Fort Rupert with the Kwakwaka'wakw. While the ranking of names within any one of these peoples was clearly established, there were no traditional rules to follow when several peoples all participated in the same potlatch.

One point should be made here. There were incidents in the nineteenth century in which property was destroyed to show wealth and in which competition took a violent turn. But such incidents were rare. Unfortunately, they were overreported in local mainstream papers and by anthropologists. Both kinds of reporting made outsiders overlook the overall good that came from the potlatch (see Steckley 2003). Condemning the potlatch for these incidents is like using the conflict between Irish Catholics and Protestants as a reason for banning Christianity.

The Banning of the Potlatch

Missionaries who came to the Northwest Coast tended to see the potlatch as "the enemy," or at least the competition. In 1875, William Duncan, who worked with the Tsimshian, wrote that the potlatch was "by far the most formidable of all obstacles in the way of Indians becoming Christians, or even civilized" (Duncan in Fisher 1977:207) During the 1870s, government officials involved with Natives were made nervous by reading newspaper articles about Native uprisings in the American West. It was the decade during which the Apache leaders Cochise and Geronimo and the Nez Perce Chief Joseph successfully eluded the American army. As well, in June of 1876, Lakota Sioux leaders Sitting Bull and Crazy Horse triumphed at the Battle of the Little Bighorn. In Canada, the First Riel Rebellion of 1869–70 was fresh in people's memory, and government officials heard rumours and read reports of discontent among the Métis that would eventually lead to a second conflict in 1885. So the missionaries and officials pushed for the banning of the potlatch and successfully achieved their goal in 1884. The law read as follows:

> Every Indian or other person who engages in or assists in celebrating the Indian festival known as the "Potlatch" or in the Indian dance known as "Tamanawas" [the Spirit Dance of the Salish] is guilty of a misdemeanour, and shall be liable to imprisonment for a term of not more than six nor less than two months in any gaol or other place of confinement, and any Indian or other person who encourages, either directly of indirectly, an Indian or Indians to get up such a festival or dance, or to celebrate the same, or who shall assist in the celebration of same, is guilty of a like offense, and shall be liable to the same punishment. (An Act to Further Amend the Indian Act 1880)

The U.S. government was slower to act against the potlatch, waiting until the early twentieth century to do so. In Canada, the ban was extended to the Sun Dance of the Prairies in 1895. By 1914, Natives could not wear traditional clothing or perform dances even at fairs or stampedes without the written permission of the Indian agent.

Native people resisted, however. When Franz Boas came to study the Kwakiutl in 1886, he was told that if he was there to oppose the potlatch, he should leave. Their often-quoted declaration to him includes the following words:

> We will dance when our laws command us to dance, we will feast when our hearts desire to feast. Do we ask the white man, "Do as the Indian does"? No, we do not. Why then do you ask us, "Do as the white man does"?

> It is a strict law that bids us dance. It is a strict law that bids us distribute our property among our friends and neighbors. It is a good law. Let the white man observe his law, we shall observe ours. (Nabokov 1991:227)

In 1896, three Nisga'a Elders sent the following petition, which was published in the *Victoria Daily Colonist*:

> If we wish to perform an act moral in its nature, with no injury or damage, and pay for it, no law in equity can divest us of such a right. We see the Salvation Army parade through the streets of your town with music and drum, enchanting the town . . . We are puzzled to know whether in the estimation of civilization we are human or fish in the tributaries of the Na'as River, that the felicities of our ancestors should be denied us. (Dickason 1997:261)

Most resistance was covert. The potlatch went underground. For that and other reasons, the potlatch law was difficult to enforce. In 1889, Kwakwaka'wakw Chief Hamasak was convicted of holding a potlatch and sentenced to six months. But the judge discharged him on a technicality, noting that the law was imprecise.

James Sewid records the following almost comic situation concerning the potlatch that inducted him at 16 into the very important Hamatsa Society. Someone had reported a potlatch, and an RCMP officer had been sent from Ottawa to investigate. He asked the people to show him what they did. According to Sewid:

> He demanded to see it that night, so we put on a good show for him. The dances we did were all mixed together and not in the right way we had been doing them. I was dancing with a fool's mask on along with a group of [people wearing] masks. The mounted police was standing on one side of the house while the big dance was going on and one of our people was interpreting to him what it was all about . . . (Spradley 1969:92–93)

At the conclusion of the ceremony, the RCMP officer declared:

> "I'd like to see the young man that went through this thing. I'd like to see him dance for me tonight because I was sent here to investigate this young man. I want him to dance with everything he had on, all his masks and everything. I want him to do it just like the way he did it last week" (Spradley 1969:93).

James Sewid then heard from the village leaders that had to dance for the officer:

> So I got all my stuff on and the others who were dancing my dances and came out [and] started dancing. After I came out my masks [i.e., the people wearing the masks] came out and danced. At the end he got up and thanked the people and said, "It was a wonderful dance. I really enjoyed it. I can't see anything wrong with it" (Spradley 1969:93).

After that, the officer left for Ottawa.

But not all cases ended so positively. In 1921, 45 of the highest-ranking Kwakiutl were arrested. Twenty-two people were sentenced to prison terms of two to three months. The tragedy was twofold. First, the leaders of a community were taken from their people. You might compare it with locking up the CEOs of the most successful businesses, the mayor and councillors, priests and ministers, police chief, fire chief, and teachers of a small town. Second, the community's sacred items were also taken. The condition upon which the others were let go was that the coppers, masks, and other objects integral to the ceremony had to be surrendered. You might compare that with taking the company ledgers, the local law books, the Bibles and altars, and the textbooks and lesson plans. The comparison isn't completely fair, however, as the potlatch items were one-of-a-kind. The items thus taken were dispersed as personal possessions of the minister of Indian affairs, art collectors, and museums.

In 1951, the potlatch ban was repealed (some 17 years after the Americans repealed it). Shortly afterwards, famed Kwakiutl carver **Mungo Martin** (1879–1962) held the first public potlatch in the Royal British Columbia Museum's Thunderbird Park. In 1969, the people started negotiating for the return of their sacred things. In 1975, the National Museum of Man declared that it would return the items on the condition that they would be kept in museums. One, the Kwakwaka'wakw Museum of Cape Mudge, opened in 1979, and the other, the U'mista Cultural Centre (**u'mista** means "a special return"), opened in the 1980s. In 1988, the Royal Ontario Museum returned the items it had, and the National Museum of the American Indian in New York repatriated some objects in 1993. Some items have still not been recovered. For more information about potlatches, see Box 17–1 on page 186.

Selling the Sacred Objects of the Tsimshian

The fight for respect for the potlatch still goes on. Consider the following case. In the 1860s, Reverend Robert Dundas, a young Anglican missionary from Britain, obtained some Native goods. He is believed to have received them from Tsimshian Chief **Paul Legaic** of Fort Simpson by the Nass River in northern British Columbia, then the richest and most powerful of the Tsimshian leaders. The goods included beautifully crafted wooden masks, rattles, dolls, and instruments. Dundas was able to obtain these goods because Legaic had become a Christian. The missionaries forced Tsimshian people who became Christian to give away sacred objects related to the potlatch ceremony. It was the price to pay to become a Christian. The benefits included gaining advantages in trade with non-Natives, and Legaic wanted to maintain his strong position in the trade. So he sacrificed his people's traditions. Still, it would not be fair to judge him harshly. We don't know how much freedom of choice he really had.

Dundas took these items back to Britain, where he sold some and gave others away to museums, but kept the better part of his collection, displaying them in his home. After his death, they were kept in a box. When his daughter died in 1948, they were saved from being discarded by Dundas's great-grandson Simon Carey. He kept them at his home and his children played with them.

Carey, a retired professor of psychology, has been trying to sell the collection in one piece. He has entertained Canadian offers from the Museum of Civilization, the Royal Ontario Museum, and Canada Heritage, but they could not pay the price he was asking.

In 1999, he put the collection in the hands of the prestigious auction house of Sotheby's, which published a catalogue and mounted an exhibit, giving Native scholars and anthropologists an opportunity to study the pieces. Carey says that he was willing to provide Native carvers and scholars access to the collection so they could make copies. However, Sotheby's made a point of having the collection travel only to London, Paris, and New York, with no Canadian destinations, fearing the Canadian government would seize the collection. The director of Sotheby's American Indian art department said they wouldn't want to put the collection at risk.

Who owns the collection? What should be done with the pieces? These questions can only be answered once other questions are asked. Did Legaic have the right to give away the pieces? According to Art Sterrit, former president of the Tsimshian Tribal Council, they did not really belong to Legaic, but to the clan to which he belonged. He only had the rights to use them in ceremony. Is that not similar to a priest and the sacred objects that belong to his church? Were the objects coerced from him through "undue duress"? Can we say that they were "stolen" by the missionaries? Morally, we can say that they were. How should the Canadian courts interpret this?

In October 2006, the Tsimshian sacred collection sold for roughly $7 million, U.S. Thirty-six pieces were purchased by Canadian institutions and individuals. One piece, a painted wooden mask, sold for $1.8 million.

Native Individuals 17-1

Paul Legaic: A rich and powerful Tsimshian chief of the nineteenth century.

Mungo Martin: Kwakiutl carver who performed the first legal potlatch after the ban was lifted.

Timeline 17-1

1860s: Tsimshian leader Paul Legaic is pressured into giving up sacred potlatch goods as a condition of becoming a Christian.

1884: The potlatch is banned in Canada.

1889: Kwakiutl Chief Hamasak is convicted and sentenced to the maximum sentence of six months, but is discharged on a technicality.

1895: The Sun Dance is banned in Canada.

1914: Natives are prohibited from wearing traditional clothing or performing dances publicly without the written permission of the Indian agent.

1921: Forty-five of the highest-ranking Kwakiutl are arrested. Twenty-two are sentenced to prison terms of two to three months.

1951: The ban of the potlatch is repealed.

1975: The National Museum of Man declares it will return sacred items on the condition that they are kept in museums.

1979: The Kwakiutl Museum of Cape Mudge is built and receives sacred potlatch items.

1980: The U'mista Cultural Centre is built and receives sacred potlatch items.

1988: The Royal Ontario Museum returns sacred potlatch items.

1993: The National Museum of the American Indian in New York returns sacred potlatch items.

1999: A descendant of the missionary who received sacred potlatch items from Legaic puts together a travelling show of the collection with the aim of selling the items at auction through Sotheby's.

2006: Collection of sacred Tsimshian potlatch goods sold by auction in the United States.

Box 17-1	Books: Aboriginal Writers Talk About Their Potlatches

Assu, Harry. 1989. *Assu of Cape Mudge: Recollections of a Coastal Indian Chief*

Clutesi, George. 1969. *Potlatch*

Nowell, Charles James. 1941 and 1968. *Smoke from Their Fires: The Life of a Kwakiutl*

Sewid, James, 1969. *Guests Never Leave Hungry: The Autobiography of James Sewid, a Kwakiutl Indian*

KEY TERMS

copper

potlatch (Chinook)

u'mista (Kwakiutl)

CONTENT QUESTIONS

1. What is the potlatch?
2. Who worked to have the potlatch banned?
3. For how long was the potlatch banned in Canada?
4. What else was banned?
5. What happened to the sacred potlatch items that Legaic was forced to give away?

WEBLINKS

www.schoolnet.ca/aboriginal/umista2/index-e.html
This site is a description of the U'mista Cultural Centre's collection of sacred potlatch items.

chapter eighteen

Native Health Issues

COLONIALISM AND HEALTH

The Smallpox Story

No European disease had a larger impact on peoples in the Americas than smallpox. From the first case in Mexico in 1520 until 1618, smallpox reduced the population in Mexico and Central America from about 20 million to about 1.6 million. At various times and places, it had a similar impact in Native Canada.

Why was the impact so high? The disease was a European one, an offshoot of cowpox. Since Europeans and Asians had cows and Natives did not, the disease first struck people in Europe and Asia. The descendants of people who had survived the great smallpox infestations in European and Asian countries had inherited some immunities that enabled them to survive. No such immunities existed for Natives—they were completely vulnerable.

One of the nastiest stories concerning smallpox that can be found in the historical literature relates to Jeffrey Amherst, the commander-in-chief of the British forces in America during the so-called "Pontiac Uprising" (named after an Odawa leader). This uprising consisted of a series of battles by several First Nations of the Great Lakes, who were using the struggle between the French and British as an opportunity to assert their own independence. Amherst, who had a very poor understanding of Aboriginal peoples and the lack of sympathy that so often goes along with such a state of ignorance, distrusting and alienating his own Native allies, suggested in June of 1763 that blankets infected with smallpox be distributed to Natives as presents. While smallpox did hit several groups at that time, to the best of our knowledge, the British did not undertake this deliberate policy of germ warfare through infected blankets at that time. Still, the very idea that such a practice was being considered says a lot.

TABLE 18-1	Smallpox Chart	
Date	People	Estimated Decline
1640s	Mohawk	75%
1781	Chipewyan	90%
1782	Stó:lo	62%
1837	Blackfoot	50%
1835–40	Tlingit	50%

Accurate figures concerning the death toll of smallpox are hard to determine. Non-Native writers recording the numbers at the time often lacked contact with all the bands or groups of a particular First Nation and thus were unable to arrive at a reliable figure. The oft-repeated one-third death toll in the interior of British Columbia in 1862 has been challenged by some historians (Fisher 1977:21–22). Still, it can be stated that the effect was uniformly devastating wherever it hit. The following numbers in Table 18-1 are figures commonly found across the country at different times. Even if they only represent part of a people or seem somewhat high, they still document a series of tragedies.

The Inuit and Tuberculosis

While tuberculosis has hit all Native groups hard, it has been particularly devastating for the Inuit. In 1952, their mortality rate from tuberculosis peaked at 569 per 100,000 (then the highest in the world), which translates to 54 deaths of the roughly 10,000 Canadian Inuit population. That was about 20 times the rate for the rest of Canada.

The negative effects of tuberculosis were not just physical. The loss of family, language, and culture were also results. Treatment for tuberculosis involved six months to two years in a hospital or sanatorium. Sanatoriums were not built in the Arctic, so the Inuit with tuberculosis were taken south; however, "stolen" or "kidnapped" would be more accurate words than simply "taken." A ship would arrive at an Inuit village, and health professionals would X-ray the Inuit. What happened next is eloquently described by Pat Grygier in her book *A Long Way from Home: The Tuberculosis Epidemic Among the Inuit*. After the doctors had decided who would be taken:

> . . . the evacuees were sent down to the Inuit quarters in the prow of the ship and the rest were sent ashore. The evacuees were not allowed to go ashore to collect belongings, to say good-bye, or to make arrangements for their families or goods. If a mother was judged sick but her children were not infected, the children (sometimes including unweaned babies) were given to an Inuk woman going ashore. Fathers had no chance to arrange for someone to hunt for food for their families or to look after their dogs and equipment. Mothers had no chance to arrange for someone to care for their children or to sew and process the skins needed to keep the family warm. . . . Those needing hospital treatment were kept on board, the rest sent ashore, and on sailed the ship to the next settlement. (Gryier 1994:96)

One in five Inuit were said to have been afflicted in 1950. One in seven were flown south for treatment. Most returned, but some disappeared. Children were adopted into

White families even though their Inuit parents were not dead. Some families never discovered what happened to those who died. In 1989, a program was initiated to attempt to uncover the records of those Inuit who had died of tuberculosis at the Mountain Sanatorium in Hamilton, Ontario, and had vanished from the view of their relations. Seventy bodies have been tracked down through that program. In 1995, **Joanasie Salomonie** travelled to Hamilton to attend the dedication of a monument erected as a memorial to 39 Inuit buried anonymously in the poor person's section of a cemetery there. One of the graves belonged to his father. In Salomonie's words:

> I buried something there . . . I buried all my negative feelings and thoughts. I felt a lot of anger for a lot of years. But I'm OK now; it cured me of the negative things. I'm satisfied. (Bergman 1996:67)

Alcohol

Wilfred Pelletier, Ojibwa writer, educator, and activist of the 1960s and 1970s, wrote the following in 1973 about White hunters and their attitudes about giving alcohol to him, their Native guide:

> Most of them wouldn't offer me any drink at all because I'm Indian—like I go wild when I drink! So they wouldn't offer me the drink. But then sometimes a guy would. He'd ask me, though; he'd say, "This stuff won't get to you, will it chief?" And I'd say, "Well, I don't know. Don't you ever get drunk?" and he'd say, "Oh yeah." "Well, I get drunk sometimes," I'd say. (Pelletier and Poole 1973:91)

One of the most damaging stereotypes of all concerning Natives is the stereotype of the drunken Indian. A trip to downtown Toronto, Winnipeg, Regina, or Vancouver confirms it with a few examples. Conversely, non-Natives who walk by Natives who don't fit the stereotype simply don't "see" them.

The myth that Aboriginals generally are "biologically helpless" to resist alcohol is believed by many people, including, unfortunately, many Natives. However, it has never been clearly established that Natives as a group metabolize alcohol significantly differently from other groups. Box 18-1 discusses how old laws contributed to this stereotype.

As the quote above illustrates, one of the more destructive aspects of this stereotype is the **myth of biological helplessness** in the face of alcohol: a belief that Natives have no control when they drink. This myth is well developed in literature. Examine the following words from Diamond Jenness, whose *Indians of Canada* was probably the single-most influential book about Natives in Canada in the twentieth century. Although first published in 1932, reprints continue to be made and can be found in bookstores even now. According to Jenness:

> The Indians . . . had no alcoholic beverages in prehistoric times, and from the earliest days of settlement they abandoned every restraint in their frenzy for the white man's firewater. (Jenness 1932:253)

Federal policy was influenced by this misconception. Parts of the Indian Act strictly restricted Native contact with alcohol. Section 94 of the Indian Act reads as follows:

94. An Indian who

a) has intoxicants in his possession,

Box 18-1   Trapped by the Law

Sometimes drinking patterns affected by the old laws helped to contribute to the stereotype of the drunken Indian. Consider the following scenario described by Wilfred Pelletier in 1973:

> There are still some reserves where drinking is against the law, so Indians go into town and buy a bottle or maybe two. They can't take it home and drink it, and it's against the law to drink in a public place. So what do they do? They go in a back alley or maybe in a men's can and they knock the whole bottle off real quick. So then there are some drunken Indians staggering around the town, because drinking that fast will knock anybody on his ass (Pelletier and Poole 1973:90).

b) is intoxicated, or

c) makes or manufactures intoxicants off a reserve,

is guilty of an offence and is liable on summary conviction to a fine of not less than ten dollars and not more than fifty dollars or to imprisonment for term not exceeding three months to both fine and imprisonment. (as quoted in Kulchyski 1994:51)

The Flow of Profits: Alcohol in the Fur Trade

The myth of biological helplessness developed within a specific historical context: the fur trade. There was a brutally profitable economy to including alcohol in the trade. One keg of brandy could fetch as many furs as an entire canoe-load of useful goods. From at least the 1660s on, when English traders literally poured alcohol into their trade with the Mohawk, an overwhelming amount of alcohol was part of the fur trade. This was especially true when there was competition between the Hudson's Bay Company and the Northwest Company. The amounts of alcohol traded were staggering. At the Hudson's Bay Company trading post of York Factory, on the west side of Hudson Bay, the amount of rum traded per year rose to a peak of 864 gallons by 1753. Between 1720 and 1774, 21,634 gallons of rum were traded from that post alone. It was only in 1822, after the merger of the Hudson's Bay Company and the Northwest Company, that the Hudson's Bay Company seriously attempted to restrict the amount of alcohol involved in its business.

The destructive influence of alcohol was very real, of course, as can be seen in this sad story told by **Pahtahsegua** (Reverend Peter Jacobs), a Mississauga teacher, preacher, and writer, in a letter published in the *New York Christian Advocate* of June 17, 1836. After speaking generally of the devastating effect alcohol had on the Mississauga, he spoke in more personal terms:

> [M]y father and mother died when I was very young, in drinking the fire water to excess . . . My sister and brother-in-law then took me to bring me up. But in a short time they died also in drinking the fire water to excess. My sister was frozen to death on a drinking spree, on new year's day . . . And in about one year from this time one of my sisters, in a drunken spree, was struck with a club on her head by her husband, which caused her death. And in the same year my brother was tomahawked in a drinking spree. . . . (Schmalz 1991:133)

Although Pahtahsegua later published a small volume describing his travels and preached to the Saulteaux out west, he eventually "became constantly bedevilled by heavy drinking and sank into poverty and oblivion" (ibid.).

The hypocrisy of loading up the trade with alcohol and then blaming the results on Natives' nature was seen quite clearly by nineteenth-century Ojibwa writer George Copway, in a best-seller for its time, *The Traditional History and Characteristic Sketches of the Ojibway Nation* (originally published in 1850):

> The ministry of this country, and the sluggards in the cause of humanity, say now: **There is a fate or certain doom on the Indians, therefore we need do nothing for them.** How blasphemous! First you give us rum by the thousand barrels, and, before the presence of God and this enlightened world, point to God, and charge him as the murderer of the unfortunate Indians. (Copway 1972:264–65; our emphasis)

Perhaps one factor in the perpetuation of the myth of Native biological helplessness with respect to alcohol lies with its connections to some of the romantic heroism of part of Canadian history. As Daniel Francis, in *The Imaginary Indian: The Image of the Indian in Canadian Culture* (1992), points out, some early historians of the RCMP colourfully exaggerated Native helplessness in the face of American whisky traders in Alberta in order to enhance the heroic image of the beginnings of the force. The Northwest Mounted Police, precursor of the RCMP, did shut down the infamous Fort Whoop Up in a display of praiseworthy courage. However, distorting that fact with allusions to Native inferiority does not do justice to that brave tale.

The Brutal Statistics

The statistics concerning Natives and the negative impact of alcohol are brutal. Alcohol's relationship to high rates of kidney problems, injury, crime, accidental death, murder, and suicide cannot be ignored. Rather than dragging out the numbers at length, one statistic will be used here: alcohol involvement in homicides. The numbers used here are from Ontario between 1980 and 1990:

Alcohol and Homicide

	Natives on Reserves	Natives off Reserves	Non-Natives
Drinking involved	67%	65%	20%
Suspect drinking	64%	57%	15%
Victim drinking	57%	59%	15%
Both drinking	54%	52%	11%

Source: Whitehead and Hayes 1998:45

Two points need to be made here. One is that there are striking differences between individual Aboriginal communities. Some communities have fewer problems with drinking than most non-Native communities. So these statistics are not a reflection on every Native community. Further, statistics such as arrest records related to alcohol, particularly off-reserve, also reflect discriminatory practices within law enforcement. These high statistics are partially caused by the practices of non-Natives. Consider David Stymeist's classic portrayal of "Crow Lake," a railway town in northwestern Ontario in the 1970s:

Ontario Provincial Police cars park outside the entrance to the Crow Lake Hotel, the town's largest central pub, for an hour or so before and after the pub closes. The waiters will ask a drunk white man, who is perhaps a relative, friend or steady customer, if he wants to call a cab. The cab will arrive at the back door of the hotel and the man in question will leave unseen. Many Indians, however, are arrested as they leave the pub, and some have been arrested for public drunkenness as they were climbing the stairs to their rooms in the hotel. (Stymeist 1977:79)

Natives brought into the police station for drinking offences are also more likely to be charged and brought to court. A study by University of Regina Professor James Harding, published in 1980 (*Unemployment, Racial Discrimination and Public Drunkenness in Regina*), revealed that 30 percent of the Aboriginals arrested for drunkenness were charged and sent to court, while the figure was only 11 percent for non-Natives (as reported in York 1990:148). Box 18-2 describes the power of stereotypes to affect the hockey star Ted Nolan.

THE STORY OF MINNIE SUTHERLAND: DEATH BY STEREOTYPE?

On New Year's Day in 1989, Minnie Sutherland, a 40-year-old Cree woman, was struck by a car in downtown Hull, Quebec. It was about 3:30 a.m. Minnie, Minnie's cousin, whom we will call "Jean," and a few hundred others were milling around the street. The car's driver and passenger were nurses. They got out of their car when they heard the bump and saw Minnie fall. They checked her over but only discerned that she had severe eye trouble (she wore thick glasses) and that she had been drinking. Three male university students saw the accident and moved toward the scene to see if Minnie was okay. Two young male police officers noticed the sudden stoppage of traffic and got out of their van to see what had happened. One of the students told him that a car had hit the woman. One of the officers asked Jean what had happened. Minnie's cousin wasn't sure (she hadn't actually seen the accident). She mentioned that they had been drinking.

The officers then attempted to lift Minnie up to a sitting position. One of the students was upset by this, knowing that accident victims should not be moved until medical help

Box 18-2	Ted Nolan: The Power of a Stereotype

Ted Nolan is an Ojibwa who has both played and coached in the National Hockey League (NHL). He won the Jack Adams Trophy for the NHL coach of the year in 1997 and was fired that same year. From that time until June 2006, when he was hired by the New York Islanders he was not able to get another NHL coaching job, even though several positions opened up every year. He feels this has racist connotations.

Nolan had spent about 15 years visiting reserves and advising Native children, particularly teenagers, against the abuse of drugs and alcohol. When he was still coaching in Buffalo, he missed a couple of practices. The rumour began that he had been drunk for three days. The rumour was false.

arrives, and shouted at the officers. One officer told the student to leave and said that he would be arrested if he didn't keep quiet.

The officers asked the nurse who had been driving whether the car stopped was hers and requested that she move it. The nurse didn't want to leave until she knew for sure that Minnie was okay and wondered at the casual attitude of the officer concerning an accident victim. According to John Nihmey, who had access to the transcripts of the hearing that would follow, the attitude of the officers was as follows:

> They were perplexed by what seemed to be an overreaction to a drunk woman who had either slipped on an ice patch and fallen, or walked into a car that couldn't have been going very fast given all the traffic. (Nihmey 1998:82–83)

The officers picked Minnie up and deposited her at the side of the road, then asked Jean whether she wanted them to call a taxi. Jean said that she did. One of the students suggested an ambulance. That sounded like a better offer so Jean changed her mind and told the police. The officer called into Hull police headquarters and said, "Cancel the taxi now. The squaw decided otherwise" (Nihmey 1998:84). The police then left.

The students and the two Cree women went into a restaurant. The students, feeling that Minnie was looking a little better (although she was barely conscious), left. Two men then picked up the two women and drove them to Ottawa. But seeing the state that Minnie was in, they called 911 and dropped the women off beside a restaurant.

A female police officer responded to the call. She tried to rouse Minnie to consciousness but failed. An ambulance pulled up and a paramedic checked Minnie over. He stated that she was drunk and suggested that the officer take her to a detoxification centre. The ambulance then left.

The officer took Minnie to the detox centre but staff wouldn't admit her because of a policy of not taking non-ambulatory people. It was now about 5:00 a.m. The officer then drove Minnie to her station and conferred with her sergeant. He checked Minnie over and recommended that the officer drive Minnie to a nearby hospital.

Minnie arrived at the hospital at 5:45 a.m. She stayed there until she died on January 11 of a cardiac arrest, the result of a blood clot in the back of her brain caused by her accident. The doctors at the hospital had been unaware of the blood clot and hadn't felt her case was serious enough to warrant an MRI (magnetic resonance imaging) scan. This was new technology at that hospital and had a long waiting list there. On January 17, a doctor from the hospital sent the following letter to the Hull police:

> There is no doubt that the lack of information about the traumatic event was of great significance in making the initial diagnosis of the abnormality and in following this up to a logical conclusion which may have been able to prevent her demise. It is also unfortunate that Mrs. Sutherland received powerful antibiotics for her condition which would not have been necessary had this history been available. The antibiotics do have their own particular risks.
>
> In particular, if the allegations of the conduct of the Hull police are correct, then a serious error of judgment has been made by the officers concerned and this should be investigated. (Nihmey 1998:163)

An investigation was held. A coroner's jury ruled in March that Hull police should offer compulsory courses to sensitize officers to the needs of visible minorities, but four out of the five jurors felt that racism was not a factor in the case. The Quebec police commission cleared its officers of racism charges in 1990.

THE THRIFTY GENE AND DIABETES TYPE II: A TWIST OF EVOLUTIONARY FATE

Diabetes type II, or non-insulin-dependent diabetes, is the most common form of diabetes, accounting for 90 to 95 percent of all diabetics. In type II, the pancreatic cells are unable to use the insulin produced by the body. It is usually considered a disease of the middle-aged and elderly, most often developing in adults over 40.

During the 1980s and 1990s, several studies demonstrated that there was an abnormally high rate of diabetes type II among the Cree and Ojibwa of northwestern Ontario and Manitoba, and among the Algonquin of western Quebec. The Oji-Cree or Severn Ojibwa of Sandy Lake have a particularly high rate, often referred to as the third highest in the world. And the average age of onset in these communities is lower than usual. This contrasts not only with the non-Aboriginal population, but also with the Athabaskans and Inuit of the north, and the Aboriginal peoples of British Columbia.

Current theories place the blame primarily on a form of micro-evolution that resulted in what has been called the **thrifty gene** (i.e., one that enables the body to hold onto or "save" blood sugars longer). The ability to hold onto blood sugars gave people of certain families in the Eastern Subarctic an advantage in being able to deal with periodic famine. The thrifty gene slowed down the starvation process. However, once people began eating non-traditional foods, with high sugar content, and began living a more sedentary life, this gene became deadly to the people. Communities such as Sandy Lake are working with health professionals to initiate programs that monitor the food and activities of their children and of those diagnosed with diabetes. They are trying to return to some of the traditional ways as a preventative measure.

Two areas of concern in Aboriginal health are tuberculosis and HIV/AIDS. In both cases, Aboriginal people are overrepresented. What is particularly of concern is that the rates for HIV/AIDS are increasing among First Nations and Inuit while diminishing in the overall Canadian population. First Nations and Inuit are particularly vulnerable to increased risk for HIV infections for a number of reasons including social, economic, and behavioural factors, e.g., poverty, substance use (including injection drug use), and sexually transmitted diseases. As well, limited access to health services have increased their vulnerability. In 2002 (the most recent year for which we have data), Aboriginal peoples represented 3.3% of the population but 5–8% of prevalent infections, i.e., those currently living with HIV infection, and 6–12% of new HIV infections. Moreover, Aboriginal people are being infected with HIV at a younger age than non-Aboriginal Canadians and Aboriginal women are disproportionately affected by the HIV/AIDS epidemic (http://www.hc-sc.gc.ca/fniah-spnia/diseases-maladies/aids-sida/index-eng.php; http://www.phac-aspc.gc.ca/aids-sida/publication/ps-pd/aboriginal-autochtones/index-eng.php).

It is difficult to believe that tuberculosis (TB) is a problem in 21st century Canada, but it is a special concern in Aboriginal communities. Tuberculosis rates in Canada are among the lowest in the world and, while they have been decreasing somewhat among Aboriginal peoples in the last three decades, the rates are still high. More worrisome is that there is a connection between HIV/AIDS, diabetes (another disproportionately high disease in Aboriginal communities), and TB. The first two weaken the immune system. If a person with a weakened immune system has inactive TB bacteria in their body, they are at increased risk of developing active TB disease. Other factors, again, have to do with socioeconomic conditions. Overcrowded housing—as is the case on far too many reserves—leads to increased spread of the disease. Limited access to health care is another major factor (http://www.hc-sc.gc.ca/fniah-spnia/diseases-maladies/tuberculos/index-eng.php).

A CONCLUDING CAUTIONARY NOTE

Several false impressions can be created by the general literature about the Aboriginal people and health. And this includes this chapter. One false idea is that Aboriginal people had no diseases and health problems prior to contact. Aboriginal people did suffer from disorders such as arthritis, and eye problems caused by too much smoke in enclosed spaces, for example. It is just that the big-killer communicable diseases were not a problem. Second, there is what can be called the **myth of Native cultural helplessness**. This portrays Aboriginal people as victims of disease and ill-health. Yet Aboriginal medicine is still practised today. Strong Aboriginal traditions helped Aboriginal people deal with health problems prior to contact, and these traditions still function despite their oppression by the Western biomedicine tradition. For example, alcoholism is being combated with considerable success by Aboriginal communities and organizations that are typically tradition-based, but with a view to dealing with problems as they exist now (see Chapter 25).

KEY TERMS

diabetes type II

myth of Native biological helplessness

myth of Native cultural helplessness

thrifty gene

CONTENT QUESTIONS

1. Why did smallpox have such a devastating effect on Native peoples?
2. How did the treatment of tuberculosis hurt Inuit families?
3. Is there any physical reason why so many Native people have problems with alcohol?
4. In Stymeist's account, why is it that more Natives than non-Natives were arrested for drinking in the Crow Lake Hotel?
5. How did the stereotype of the "drunken Indian" contribute to Minnie Sutherland's death?

WEBLINKS

www.health-sciences.ubc.ca/iah
The Institute for Aboriginal Health is part of the University of British Columbia. It works on Aboriginal health issues at both the policy and the practical levels. This site contains a very good list of other health-related sites under the heading "Links."

www.hc-sc.gc.ca/jfy-spv/fni-pa_e.html
Health Canada's First Nations and Inuit health website, entitled *Just for You*, includes a discussion of Aboriginal health issues.

chapter nineteen

Colonialism, Native Education, and "Child Welfare"

INTRODUCTION

A good introduction to this section comes from the words of Ojibwa writer George Copway, or Kahgegagahbowh ("He who stands forever," 1818–69), from his 1850 best-seller *The Traditional History and Characteristic Sketches of the Ojibway Nation*:

> Much has been lost to the world, through a neglect of educating the red men who lived and died in the midst of educational privileges, but [who] have not been allowed to enjoy them. They hold a key that will unlock a library of information, the like of which is not. It is for the present generation to say, whether the last remnants of a powerful people shall perish through neglect, and as they depart bear with them that key.

> Give the Indian the means of education and he will avail himself of them. Keep them from him, and let me tell you he is not the only loser. (Copway 1850/1972:viii)

Note how similar the sentiments of that last sentence are to those articulated by Reverend Edward Ahenakew, a Cree graduate of the University of Saskatchewan, in an article published in the *Saskatchewan Daily Star* on June 1, 1918. In arguing for the government to put more money into Native education, he said:

> Surely the government is not thinking of being hampered by a race of ignorant and non-self-supporting people for all time to come. . . . Conditions as they are are neither fair to the Indians nor to the white people who have to live in the same country with them. (Ahenakew in Barman, Hébert, and McCaskill 1986:12)

A SEVENTEENTH-CENTURY STORY

Since the early 1600s in New France, Europeans coming to Canada have felt that they needed to take Native children away from their homes, their parents, their families, friends, and community in order to better educate them. Since that early beginning, Aboriginal education programs run by non-Aboriginal people have been overwhelming failures, but the Europeans never seemed to learn that important lesson. These schools would have devastating impacts on Native families and cultures in the twentieth century.

By 1668, Mother Marie de L'Incarnation of the Ursuline order had around 30 years of experience trying to educate Native children by boarding them apart from their people. While couched in prejudicial terms of "civilized" and "savage," the following quotation shows her awareness of the vital principle that separating Native children from their families for education purposes is wrong, a message that should have been listened to 300 years later:

> [W]e have remarked that out of a hundred that have passed through our hands scarcely have we civilized one. We find docility and intelligence in them, but when we are least expecting it they climb over our enclosure and go to run the woods with their relatives, where they find more pleasure than in all the amenities of our French houses . . . [T]hey cannot be constrained, and if they are they become melancholy . . . [T]he Savages love their children extraordinarily and when they know that they are sad they will do everything to get them back . . . (de L'Incarnation in Jaenen 1986:58)

Unlike their colleagues in the twentieth century, the Ursulines gave the children back in such situations.

ONTARIO SCHOOLS FOR OJIBWA IN THE FIRST HALF OF THE NINETEENTH CENTURY

During the first half of the nineteenth century in what is now Ontario, several schools for the Mississauga were opened, largely through the efforts of the Methodist church. These schools were arguably as good as any in the country at the time, but they still generally tended to promote Christianity and Western culture at the expense of Native culture. In 1830, there were 11 such schools, none better than the school that was located in the middle of the community of the Mississauga of the Credit. The following description of this school comes from William Lyon Mackenzie in a *Colonial Advocate* article of December 30, 1830. It well illustrates the culture of the school. He describes the one-room school building as being large:

> with tiers of raised benches in the rear; on one division of which sit the girls, and the boys on the other. There are also desks and slates for ciphering and copy books and copper-plate lines for those who write. The Bibles and Testaments are chiefly those of the London Society for Promoting Christian Knowledge . . . Among the school-furniture, are a handsome map of the world . . . attractive alphabets on pasteboard; regular figures illustrative of geometry . . . a clock. . . . The walls of the school are adorned with good moral maxims . . . [including] *"No blankets to be worn in school."* (Mackenzie 1960:46; authors' emphasis)

A number of well-educated people would graduate from those schools (including the best-selling writer George Copway quoted at the beginning of this chapter); but they would often have a hard time fitting in. In effect, they became people "between two worlds." A good example of this is Kahkewaquonaby ("Sacred Feathers"), also known as Peter Jones (1802–56). He went to the United States and Britain and successfully raised funds for

Native education. An accomplished writer, he translated hymns and parts of the Bible, and wrote the popular *History of the Ojebway Indians*. Yet there was a low-cloud ceiling to his flights of accomplishment: he was denied a mission of his own, even though he was more than qualified for the position. Likewise, the Indian Affairs department didn't give him a job he very much wanted, despite the support of the influential Egerton Ryerson, his good friend. Instead, the job was given to an ex-military man, scarcely experienced with Natives, and not knowledgeable in Native matters. Such a clipping of his eagle wings was a source of frustration for Sacred Feathers in his later years.

Furthermore, he seemed to have something of an ambivalent attitude toward the culture of his people. The following idea about how Native schools should be run sounds very similar to one of the main goals set by later residential schools: "Let all the children be placed entirely under the charge and management of the teachers & missionaries, so that their parents shall have no control over them" (memorandum: "Thoughts on Indian Schools" (1835) as quoted in Miller 1996:80). Box 19-1 tells the story of Oronhyateka (Burning Sky).

INDUSTRIAL AND BOARDING SCHOOLS

Gradually, a system of "industrial schools" was developed during the nineteenth century. In many ways, these schools combined academic studies with more practical matters, such as what you might find in a technical high school or at a community college. From 1879 on, they were modelled after the Carlisle Indian School in Pennsylvania, established in 1878 by Lt. Richard Henry Pratt. What could be called the mission statement of this influential school was Pratt's motto of what the school should do for the Native student: "Kill the Indian in him and save the man." The most effective weapon for "killing the Indian" in the students was taking the children away from their homes and often their home communities, thus separating them from their supports.

The federal government funded these schools, and religious denominations ran them. Students weren't forced to go to school. In 1900, of the roughly 20,000 Status Indians between the ages of 6 and 15 at that time, only 3285 were in the 22 industrial schools and 39 boarding schools. Another 6349 went to 226 day schools.

Literally, the most deadly aspect of these schools was the death rate. The schools, which were paid according to the number of students attending, recruited even sick children. The tough economics of these schools meant that dormitories were poorly heated and overcrowded, and these were ideal conditions for tuberculosis, which was the leading killer. The same economy meant that the food was less than nutritionally adequate.

In 1904, Doctor P.H. Bryce was appointed medical inspector for Indian Affairs and the Department of the Interior. He was conscientious about his job; so, in response to his superior's request in 1907 that he inspect health conditions in the industrial and boarding schools, he performed a thorough job. His alarming report found its way to the national media: the *Montreal Star* and *Saturday Night* in particular. In the latter magazine, one editorial read: "Even war seldom shows as large a percentage of fatalities as does the educational system we have imposed upon our Indian wards" (as quoted in Fournier and Crey 1997:49).

The figures in question included a 24 percent death rate of Aboriginal children in 15 prairie schools. At File Hills industrial school in Saskatchewan, 69 percent died of tuberculosis during one decade (Fournier and Crey 1997:58).

Box 19-1	Oronhyateka ("Burning Sky"): How Peter Martin Became a Doctor

Oronhyateka (Burning Sky) or Doctor Peter Martin (1841–1907) was a Mohawk whose success story is one of determination and courage. He became the head of the Independent Order of Foresters (IOF) in 1881 at a time when it had a debt of $4000 and a Canadian membership of 369. At his death, the IOF had accumulated funds of $11 million and a membership of more than 250,000. His early ambition was to be a doctor, but many obstacles stood in his way. This is the story of how he got his education:

> Attending a local school until he graduated at 14, on his own youthful initiative he took himself far afield to the Wesleyan Academy in Wilbraham, Massachusetts. With little money, he earned much of his board and tuition by cutting wood and performing similar chores [he would jokingly say that it kept him in bread, no butter]. After two years he graduated first in his class.
>
> A year's teaching at a newly-opened school on his home reserve [of Six Nations] was just a momentary break for money and family. Soon he was off to Kenyon College in Gambier, Ohio, from which he graduated in three years. Always possessing a showman's flair, he earned money running a "Wild West" show in which he dressed up white men as Natives.

Oronhyateka's greatest ambition was to become a doctor. But no Native had ever received a university degree from a Canadian university. Lack of money and opportunity, and no lack of prejudice, had proven formidable obstacles. In 1860 Oronhyateka had just managed a year at the University of Toronto, straining his always meagre financial resources. Opportunity and his own ability were soon to bring him the chance of a lifetime.

He had been chosen by the Six Nations leaders to address the visiting Prince of Wales, later Edward VII. As the most educated person in the community, he was probably picked because of his facility with formal, educated English. But that was not what the Prince was to hear. Proud of his heritage, Oronhyateka addressed the Prince in Mohawk, translated by an interpreter.

The Prince of Wales was so impressed by this, and by the story of the young man's determined fight for education, that he invited Oronhyateka to study at Oxford, under the supervision of Sir Henry Acland, Regius Professor of medicine and the Prince's personal physician.

After three years at Oxford and a final year at the University of Toronto, Oronhyateka became a doctor (Steckley 1987).

Hearing horror story after horror story, Indian Affairs seems to have developed a callous attitude in its approach to the problem, as is indicated in the following often quoted remark from a deputy superintendent general of Indian Affairs:

> It is quite within the mark to say that fifty per cent of the children who passed through these schools did not live to benefit from the education which they had received therein. (Miller 1996:133)

Nothing significant was done to improve the situation. Although the death rate would decline, death would become part of the residential school tradition.

Sifton's Two Faces

Sir Clifford Sifton became a federal minister upon the election of Wilfred Laurier's government in 1896. He opposed the relatively "good" (relative to the residential schools) education that Natives were receiving in the industrial schools. Two reasons he gave for this opposition were contradictory, leaving the reader to suspect deep anti-Native prejudice on his part. On the one hand, speaking to the House of Commons in 1897, he clearly displayed a "there is only so much room in the lifeboat" mentality when he stated that "we are educating these Indians to compete industrially with our own peoples, which seems to me a very undesirable use of public money" (as quoted in Barman, Hébert, and McCaskill 1986:7–8). On the other hand, in a speech to the House of Commons in 1904, he spoke of the inherent "racial" inability of Native people to become educated and prosper (perhaps he did not know about Burning Sky and others like him). He felt as follows:

> . . . the attempt to give a highly civilized education to the Indian child . . . was practically a failure. I have no hesitation in saying—we may as well be frank—that the Indian cannot go out from school, making his own way and compete with the white man . . . [The Indian] has not the physical, mental or moral get-up to enable him to compete. He cannot do it. (House of Commons, *Debates 1904*, 6948, 6956; in Miller 1996:134–35)

The failure of Native students of industrial schools to get jobs had a lot more to do with the "we–they" attitude of people like Sifton, who were much more willing to hire "our people" than they were to hire Natives.

DUMBING DOWN THE NATIVE SCHOOLS

In 1910, the federal government decided that it needed to change its schools. It decided to put most of its Native education "eggs" into the "basket" of the residential school system. The government would provide the money, while religious groups, such as the Catholic, Anglican, United, and Presbyterian churches, would deliver the education. The government generally provided funding that was insufficient, so these schools had to run themselves like self-sufficient businesses. "Student workers" were removed from classes so they could do the laundry, heat the buildings, and perform the farm work in order to cut down on expenses. These schools had an even greater impact on Natives in Canada once attendance was made compulsory in 1920.

The curriculum suffered in this new regime. Following the notions of Sifton and others like him, the academic goals of residential schools were "dumbed down" from those of their predecessors. The official statement of the residential schools was that they would be educating the Native student "to fit the Indian for civilized life in his own environment." What did this mean? It meant that the government felt that although the students should learn mainstream Canadian culture, they should be prepared for life on reserves only, apart from the bad influences in Canadian towns and cities. The protective aspect was particularly aimed at Native women. Minister of Indian Affairs Duncan Campbell Scott felt that they should be kept on the reserves away from White men of the "lowest type" (Barman 1986:120).

What did this mean for the curriculum? In Scott's words:

> To this end the curriculum in residential schools has been simplified and the practical instruction given is such as may be immediately of use to the pupil when he returns to the reserve after leaving school. (Barman 1986:120)

They didn't want students who would be "made too smart for the Indian villages" (Barman 1986:120), as Scott had stated about the girls.

This ran counter to what was going on elsewhere in Canada, where, throughout the twentieth century, it was increasingly felt that students required more education, not less, to succeed.

ABUSE

The worst aspect of the residential schools, and why they might readily qualify as the single worst thing that Europeans have done to Natives in Canada, was the abuse: emotional, physical, and sexual. J.R. Miller, in his classic study of residential schools, identifies enforced loneliness as the form of abuse "that probably did the most harm because it was the most pervasive and enduring done to students" (Miller 1996:337). The residential schools were designed to keep children from the "bad" influence of their parents. Children were taken from their parents and extended families for periods of time that often lasted the whole school year, even when the residential schools were located in the students' own communities. Parental visits, when they were permitted, were typically closely monitored in a special "visiting room." Brothers and sisters were often kept apart in strict sexual separation, sometimes meaning that the children could only communicate with each other by waving from one building to another or through secretly arranged meetings. Box 19-2 tells the story of Isabelle Knockwood, who witnessed a girl punished for speaking her native language.

Miller tells the story of a Cree woman who went to File Hills residential school. Her community was only 19 kilometres away but it might as well have been on the other side of the world. A fence surrounded the school property and the students. For hours on end,

Box 19-2	Punishment for Speaking Mi'kmaq

Isabelle Knockwood attended the Shubenacadie residential school in Nova Scotia. Her book, *Out of the Depths*, is an eloquent and tragic portrayal of life in a residential school. During her first year at Shubenacadie, she witnessed the following violent punishment of a little girl who had spoken Mi'kmaq:

> The nun came up from behind her and swung her around and began beating her up . . . then the Sister pinched her cheeks and her lips were drawn taut across her teeth and her eyes were wide with terror . . . Then the nun picked the little girl clean off the floor by the ears or hair and the girl stood on her tiptoes with her feet dangling in the air . . . The nun was yelling, "You bad, bad girl." Then she let go with one hand and continued slapping her in the mouth until her nose bled. (Knockwood 1992:97)

she and her friends would stand at the corner of the fence that was closest to their reserve. According to Miller:

> She would put her hand through the fence, because that meant she was closer to her home and family by the length of her arm and hand. Other times, she would observe the place where the road emerged from the trees and watch for her parents. She would say to herself, "the next black horse that comes along" will be drawing her parents' wagon on a visit. Disappointment only led to repetitions of the childlike incantation, a wish and a prayer that never seemed to come true. (Miller 1996:338–39)

The chain of abuse that began with the residential school continued into community life. At school, girls and boys alike were sexually assaulted by priests, nuns, doctors, teachers, and principals who worked for residential schools. All studies show that a very high percentage of physical and sexual abusers were abused once themselves. Sexual abuse has now been identified as the number one social problem in a good number of Native communities. Studies conducted at Hollow Water in Manitoba and Canim Lake have reported that at least 75 percent of their members experienced unwanted sexual contact as a child.

Short of funds and often desperate for staff, particularly after 1945, the residential schools were often careless when hiring. As J.R. Miller cleverly words it, the schools often ended up employing the "devoted and the deviant" (Miller 1996:321). These could range from the merely incompetent to the sexually predatory and the outright sadistic. Punishment was not merely strict: it could be brutal, cruel, life-threatening, and life-ending. Children had pins stuck in their tongues for speaking their Native language; they were punched in the face and scarred by studded belts. Punishment could be humiliating, as when bed-wetters had to walk around the school with their damp sheets on their heads, and sadistic, as when a boy was forced to eat porridge onto which he had poured salt. He threw it up and was forced to eat that twice until he fainted. Punishment could also be sexualized, as when girls were caught stealing food and were forced to stand in a line in front of the whole school with their skirts up and their genitals in full view.

It is small wonder why many former residential school students have been diagnosed as suffering from Post-Traumatic Stress Disorder, like war veterans or police officers. They exhibit symptoms such as panic attacks, insomnia, uncontrollable/unexplainable anger, alcohol and drug abuse, sexual inadequacy or addiction, the inability to form intimate relationships, and eating disorders.

When the students left the schools, they often had little experience of the caring parenting traditional to the people. Instead, they had been "parented" by outsiders, a few of them "nice," some of them "nasty," many more of them strict and impersonal. Three generations of parents would be influenced by these models when they became parents. Cinderina Williams, chief of the Spallumcheen First Nation, in her submission to the Royal Commission on Aboriginal Peoples, spoke of the returning children as "aliens." She explained this as follows:

> They did not speak their own language, so they could not communicate with anyone other than their own counterparts. Some looked down on their families because of their lack of English, their lifestyle, and some were just plain hostile. They had formed no bonds with their families, and some couldn't survive without the regimentation they had become so accustomed to . . . Perhaps the greatest tragedy of this background was the unemotional upbringing they had. Not being brought up in a loving, caring, sharing, nurturing environment, they did not have these skills as they are not inbred but learned through observation, participation, and interaction. Consequently, when these children became parents, and most did at an early age, they had no

parenting skills. They did not have the capability to show affection. They sired and bred children, but were unable to relate to them on any level." (Indian and Northern Affairs Canada 1996c)

Legal charges began in the late 1980s, a few years after the last residential school closed. One of the more spectacular cases involved a Catholic bishop, the former principal of St. Joseph's residential school in British Columbia. After four years of prosecution, he was finally convicted of raping one girl (now a chief) and sexually assaulting another, resulting in a sentence of two-and-a-half years. In 1995, a male supervisor at Port Alberni school was imprisoned for 11 years after pleading guilty to sexually assaulting 18 boys between the ages of 6 and 13 between 1948 and 1968. Over the next eight years, the churches that ran the schools all issued formal apologies, beginning with the United Church in 1986, and followed by the Anglican Church, the Canadian Conference of Catholic Bishops, and the Presbyterian Church. Agreements concerning compensation came from two branches of the Catholic Church in Canada (both in 2004), as well as from the Anglican and the Presbyterian Church, both in 2003.

On May 10, 2006, the federal government announced approval of a final Indian Residential Schools Settlement Agreement and the launch of an Advance Payment program (the latter for people 65 years and older as of May 30, 2005). According to the document issued by the government, the Settlement Agreement proposes

> . . . a Common Experience Payment for all eligible former students of Indian Residential Schools, an Independent Assessment Process for claims of sexual or serious physical abuse, as well as measures to support healing, commemorative activities, and in the establishment of a Truth and Reconciliation Commission. (IRSRC 2006a)

As with all such documents, it is difficult to know what it really means. Elders wanting to receive the Advance Payment must fill out an application to receive $8000. It remains to be seen how difficult or easy that process will be.

The government reckoned that as of June 12, 2006 there were about 80,000 people alive who had attended a residential school. At the same time, there were 13,406 claimants for litigation, with 2763 resolved, with a total value of compensation of $106.5 million (IRSRC 2006b).

The impact of the residential schools is immeasurable and the effects are still being felt. It is impossible to imagine the sheer terror young children must have experienced as they were wrenched from the loving arms of their parents and taken far away to be left in the care of complete strangers. These are just the immediate agonies endured by children as they embarked on their "education." Untold thousands of children died in the care of the church-run schools while even more endured emotional, physical, sexual, and psychological abuse. Decades after the schools closed, the effects, however, persist. As discussed above, many survivors suffer—quite understandably—from post-traumatic stress disorder. Equally tragic, generations of children never learned the parenting skills they would eventually need because they lacked parents for 10 months—and sometimes 12 months—a year. How tragic that is for the First Nations of Canada—indeed, for Canada as a whole.

"Ethnocide" is conventionally defined as the deliberate and systematic destruction of a culture—or, in this case, cultures (as opposed to "genocide," which is the killing of the people, not the culture). There is little doubt, as suggested by the discussion above—and the words (below) from those directly responsible for the implementation and running of the residential schools—that what happened in those schools was ethnocide. While the intentions of the government and churches might have been good (although that is surely debatable) we must question the ultimate results. Yes, children did learn to read and write and perhaps gained some useful skills, but at what cost? To no surprise in this enlightened era, and to the credit of the federal government and the churches, apologies—official acknowledgments—of the horrors committed in the residential schools were made. There was one notable exception, however. In a statement, the Canadian Conference of Catholic Bishops issued the following:

> The Catholic community in Canada has a decentralized structure. Each Diocesan Bishop is autonomous in his diocese and, although relating to the Canadian Conference of Catholic Bishops, is not responsible to it.

> Approximately 16 out of 70 Catholic dioceses in Canada were associated with the former Indian Residential Schools, in addition to about three dozen religious communities. Each diocese and religious community is legally responsible for its own actions. The Catholic Church as a whole was not associated with the Residential Schools, nor was the Canadian Conference of Catholic Bishops.

> These are the reasons why an apology on Residential Schools has not been made by the Canadian Conference of Catholic Bishops or in the name of the Catholic Church in Canada. (http://www.cccb.ca/site/eng/media-room/files/2630-apology-on-residential-schools-by-the-catholic-church)

One can only wonder what the victims of Catholic residential school abuse think of this non-apology.

For the apologies from the other players in this tragic saga see the following boxes.

Box 19-3   **Statement of Apology—To Former Students of Indian Residential Schools**

The treatment of children in Indian Residential Schools is a sad chapter in our history.

For more than a century, Indian Residential Schools separated over 150,000 Aboriginal children from their families and communities. In the 1870's, the federal government, partly in order to meet its obligation to educate Aboriginal children, began to play a role in the development and administration of these schools. Two primary objectives of the Residential Schools system were to remove and isolate children from the influence of their homes, families, traditions and cultures, and to assimilate them into the dominant culture. These objectives were based on the assumption Aboriginal cultures and spiritual beliefs were inferior and unequal. Indeed, some sought, as it was infamously said, "to kill the Indian in the child." Today, we recognize that this policy of assimilation was wrong, has caused great harm, and has no place in our country.

One hundred and thirty-two federally-supported schools were located in every province and territory, except Newfoundland, New Brunswick and Prince Edward Island. Most schools were operated as "joint ventures" with Anglican, Catholic, Presbyterian or United Churches. The Government of Canada built an educational system in which

(continued)

Box 19-3   (continued)

very young children were often forcibly removed from their homes, often taken far from their communities. Many were inadequately fed, clothed and housed. All were deprived of the care and nurturing of their parents, grandparents and communities. First Nations, Inuit and Métis languages and cultural practices were prohibited in these schools. Tragically, some of these children died while attending residential schools and others never returned home.

The government now recognizes that the consequences of the Indian Residential Schools policy were profoundly negative and that this policy has had a lasting and damaging impact on Aboriginal culture, heritage and language. While some former students have spoken positively about their experiences at residential schools, these stories are far overshadowed by tragic accounts of the emotional, physical and sexual abuse and neglect of helpless children, and their separation from powerless families and communities.

The legacy of Indian Residential Schools has contributed to social problems that continue to exist in many communities today.

It has taken extraordinary courage for the thousands of survivors that have come forward to speak publicly about the abuse they suffered. It is a testament to their resilience as individuals and to the strength of their cultures. Regrettably, many former students are not with us today and died never having received a full apology from the Government of Canada.

The government recognizes that the absence of an apology has been an impediment to healing and reconciliation. Therefore, on behalf of the Government of Canada and all Canadians, I stand before you, in this Chamber so central to our life as a country, to apologize to Aboriginal peoples for Canada's role in the Indian Residential Schools system.

To the approximately 80,000 living former students, and all family members and communities, the Government of Canada now recognizes that it was wrong to forcibly remove children from their homes and we apologize for having done this. We now recognize that it was wrong to separate children from rich and vibrant cultures and traditions, that it created a void in many lives and communities, and we apologize for having done this. We now recognize that, in separating children from their families, we undermined the ability of many to adequately parent their own children and sowed the seeds for generations to follow, and we apologize for having done this. We now recognize that, far too often, these institutions gave rise to abuse or neglect and were inadequately controlled, and we apologize for failing to protect you. Not only did you suffer these abuses as children, but as you became parents, you were powerless to protect your own children from suffering the same experience, and for this we are sorry.

The burden of this experience has been on your shoulders for far too long. The burden is properly ours as a Government, and as a country. There is no place

(continued)

Box 19-3   (continued)

in Canada for the attitudes that inspired the Indian Residential Schools system to ever prevail again. You have been working on recovering from this experience for a long time and in a very real sense, we are now joining you on this journey. The Government of Canada sincerely apologizes and asks the forgiveness of the Aboriginal peoples of this country for failing them so profoundly.

> Nous le regrettons
> We are sorry
> Nimitataynan
> Niminchinowesamin
> Mamiattugut

In moving towards healing, reconciliation and resolution of the sad legacy of Indian Residential Schools, implementation of the Indian Residential Schools Settlement Agreement began on September 19, 2007. Years of work by survivors, communities, and Aboriginal organizations culminated in an agreement that gives us a new beginning and an opportunity to move forward together in partnership.

A cornerstone of the Settlement Agreement is the Indian Residential Schools Truth and Reconciliation Commission. This Commission presents a unique opportunity to educate all Canadians on the Indian Residential Schools system. It will be a positive step in forging a new relationship between Aboriginal peoples and other Canadians, a relationship based on the knowledge of our shared history, a respect for each other and a desire to move forward together with a renewed understanding that strong families, strong communities and vibrant cultures and traditions will contribute to a stronger Canada for all of us.

On behalf of the Government of Canada The Right Honourable Stephen Harper,

Prime Minister of Canada

(http://www.aadnc-aandc.gc.ca/eng/1100100 015644/1100100015649)

Box 19-4	The Anglican Church of Canada's Apology for Residential Schools Anglican Church of Canada

Apology to Native People

A message from the Primate, Archbishop Michael Peers, to the National Native Convocation, Minaki, Ontario, Friday, August 6, 1993

My Brothers and Sisters:

Together here with you I have listened as you have told your stories of the residential schools.

I have heard the voices that have spoken of pain and hurt experienced in the schools, and of the scars which endure to this day.

I have felt shame and humiliation as I have heard of suffering inflicted by my people, and as I think of the part our church played in that suffering.

I am deeply conscious of the sacredness of the stories that you have told and I hold in the highest honour those who have told them.

I have heard with admiration the stories of people and communities who have worked at healing, and I am aware of how much healing is needed.

I also know that I am in need of healing, and my own people are in need of healing, and our church is in need of healing. Without that healing, we will continue the same attitudes that have done such damage in the past.

I also know that healing takes a long time, both for people and for communities.

I also know that it is God who heals, and that God can begin to heal when we open ourselves, our wounds, our failures and our shame to God. I want to take one step along that path here and now.

I accept and I confess before God and you, our failures in the residential schools. We failed you. We failed ourselves. We failed God.

I am sorry, more than I can say, that we were part of a system which took you and your children from home and family.

I am sorry, more than I can say, that we tried to remake you in our image, taking from you your language and the signs of your identity.

I am sorry, more than I can say, that in our schools so many were abused physically, sexually, culturally and emotionally.

On behalf of the Anglican Church of Canada, I present our apology.

I do this at the desire of those in the Church like the National Executive Council, who know some of your stories and have asked me to apologize.

I do this in the name of many who do not know these stories.

And I do this even though there are those in the church who cannot accept the fact that these things were done in our name.

As soon as I am home, I shall tell all the bishops what I have said, and ask them to co-operate with me and with the National Executive Council in helping this healing at the local level. Some bishops have already begun this work.

I know how often you have heard words which have been empty because they have not been accompanied by actions. I pledge to you my best efforts,

(continued)

Box 19-4   *(continued)*

and the efforts of our church at the national level, to walk with you along the path of God's healing.

The work of the Residential Schools Working Group, the video, the commitment and the effort of the Special Assistants to the Primate for this work, the grants available for healing conferences, are some signs of that pledge, and we shall work for others.

This is Friday, the day of Jesus' suffering and death. It is the anniversary of the first atomic bomb at Hiroshima, one of the most terrible injuries ever inflicted by one people on another.

But even atomic bombs and Good Friday are not the last word. God raised Jesus from the dead as a sign that life and wholeness are the everlasting and unquenchable purpose of God.

Thank you for listening to me.

(http://www.anglican.ca/relationships/files/2011/06/Apology-English.pdf)

Box 19-5   United Church Social Policy Positions

Apology to Former Students of United Church Indian Residential Schools, and to Their Families and Communities (1998)

From the deepest reaches of your memories, you have shared with us your stories of suffering from our church's involvement in the operation of Indian Residential Schools. You have shared the personal and historic pain that you still bear, and you have been vulnerable yet again. You have also shared with us your strength and wisdom born of the life-giving dignity of your communities and traditions and your stories of survival.

In response to our church's commitment to repentance, I spoke these words of apology on behalf of the General Council Executive on Tuesday, October 27, 1998:

"As Moderator of The United Church of Canada, I wish to speak the words that many people have wanted to hear for a very long time. On behalf of The United Church of Canada, I apologize for the pain and suffering that our church's involvement in the Indian Residential School system has caused. We are aware of some of the damage that this cruel and ill-conceived system of assimilation has perpetrated on Canada's First Nations peoples. For this we are truly and most humbly sorry.

"To those individuals who were physically, sexually, and mentally abused as students of the Indian Residential Schools in which The United Church of Canada was involved, I offer you our most sincere apology. You did nothing wrong. You were and are the victims of evil acts that cannot under any circumstances be justified or excused.

"We know that many within our church will still not understand why each of us must bear the scar, the blame for this horrendous period in Canadian history. But the truth is, we are the bearers

(continued)

Box 19-5	*(continued)*

of many blessings from our ancestors, and therefore, we must also bear their burdens."

Our burdens include dishonouring the depths of the struggles of First Nations peoples and the richness of your gifts. We seek God's forgiveness and healing grace as we take steps toward building respectful, compassionate, and loving relationships with First Nations peoples.

We are in the midst of a long and painful journey as we reflect on the cries that we did not or would not hear, and how we have behaved as a church. As we travel this difficult road of repentance, reconciliation, and healing, we commit ourselves to work toward ensuring that we will never again use our power as a church to hurt others with attitudes of racial and spiritual superiority.

"We pray that you will hear the sincerity of our words today and that you will witness the living out of our apology in our actions in the future."

The Right Rev. Bill Phipps
Moderator of The United Church of Canada

(http://www.united-church.ca/beliefs/policies/1998/a623)

Box 19-6	**Presbyterian Church in Canada's Residential Schools Apology**

Event Date: Sunday, June 5, 1994

The following confession was adopted by the Presbyterian General Assembly meeting in Toronto held June 5–10, 1994.

Our Confession

The Holy Spirit, speaking in and through Scripture, calls The Presbyterian Church in Canada to confession. This confession is our response to the word of God. We understand our mission and ministry in new ways, in part because of the testimony of Aboriginal peoples.

1. We, the 120th General Assembly of The Presbyterian Church in Canada, seeking the guidance of the Spirit of God, and aware of our own sin and shortcomings, are called to speak to the Church we love. We do this, out of new understandings of our past, not out of any sense of being superior to those who have gone before us, nor out of any sense that we would have done things differently in the same context. It is with deep humility and in great sorrow that we come before God and our Aboriginal brothers and sisters with our confession.

2. We acknowledge that the stated policy of the Government of Canada was to assimilate Aboriginal peoples to the dominant culture, and that The Presbyterian Church in

(continued)

Box 19-6   *(continued)*

Canada co-operated in this policy. We acknowledge that the roots of the harm we have done are found in the attitudes and values of western European colonialism, and the assumption that what was not yet moulded in our image was to be discovered and exploited. As part of that policy we, with other churches, encouraged the Government to ban some important spiritual practices through which Aboriginal peoples experienced the presence of the creator God. For the Church's complicity in this policy we ask forgiveness.

3. We recognize that there were many members of The Presbyterian Church in Canada who, in good faith, gave unstintingly of themselves in love and compassion for their aboriginal brothers and sisters. We acknowledge their devotion and commend them for their work. We recognize that there were some who, with prophetic insight, were aware of the damage that was being done and protested, but their efforts were thwarted. We acknowledge their insight. For the times we did not support them adequately nor hear their cries for justice, we ask forgiveness.

4. We confess that The Presbyterian Church in Canada presumed to know better than Aboriginal peoples what was needed for life. The Church said of our Aboriginal brothers and sisters, "If they could be like us, if they could think like us, talk like us, worship like us, sing like us, work like us, they would know God as

we know God and therefore would have life abundant." In our cultural arrogance we have been blind to the ways in which our own understanding of the Gospel has been culturally conditioned, and because of our insensitivity to aboriginal cultures, we have demanded more of Aboriginal peoples than the gospel requires, and have thus misrepresented Jesus Christ who loves all peoples with compassionate, suffering love that all may come to God through him. For the Church's presumption we ask forgiveness.

5. We confess that, with the encouragement and assistance of the Government of Canada, The Presbyterian Church in Canada agreed to take the children of Aboriginal peoples from their own homes and place them in Residential Schools. In these schools, children were deprived of their traditional ways, which were replaced with Euro-Canadian customs that were helpful in the process of assimilation. To carry out this process, The Presbyterian Church in Canada used disciplinary practices which were foreign to Aboriginal peoples, and open to exploitation in physical and psychological punishment beyond any Christian maxim of care and discipline. In a setting of obedience and acquiescence there was opportunity for sexual abuse, and some were so abused. The effect of all this, for Aboriginal peoples, was the loss of cultural identity and the loss of a secure sense of self. For

(continued)

Box 19-6 *(continued)*

the Church's insensitivity we ask forgiveness.

6. We regret that there are those whose lives have been deeply scarred by the effects of the mission and ministry of The Presbyterian Church in Canada. For our Church we ask forgiveness of God. It is our prayer that God, who is merciful, will guide us in compassionate ways towards helping them to heal.

We ask, also, for forgiveness from Aboriginal peoples. What we have heard we acknowledge. It is our hope that those whom we have wronged with a hurt too deep for telling will accept what we have to say. With God's guidance our Church will seek opportunities to walk with Aboriginal peoples to find healing and wholeness together as God's people.

(https://www.itk.ca/historical-event/presbyterian-church-canadas-residential-schools-apology)

STEALING THE CHILDREN: THE SIXTIES SCOOP

The harm we do children always becomes known in the end, even though we believe it to be well-hidden.

—Huron-Wendat writer Georges Sioui, summing up one of the
main moral messages of the traditional stories of his people (Sioui 1999:37)

In 1951, the Indian Act was changed so that provincial authorities would be responsible for the welfare of Indian children. Initially, this change had little effect. British Columbia's statistics for 1955 show that 29 of the 3433 children placed in protective care in the province were Native, or less than 1 percent of all provincial children. However, starting in the 1960s, policies of taking Native children from their families, from communities, and from the Native world became more aggressive. In 1964, the province of British Columbia took 1446 Native children out of a total of 4228 children, or 34.2 percent of the Native child population. In his book *Native Children and the Child Welfare System,* writer Patrick Johnston coined the term "Sixties Scoop" to refer to the forced migration of Aboriginal children.

The situation was worst in Manitoba. Between 1971 and 1981, over 3400 Native children were taken from their homes and removed from their province. More than a thousand of these children were sent to the United States, where there was a demand for children to adopt. American agencies could get $4000 for every child placed. Native children in the United States had been adopted in a similar way until 1978, when the Indian Child Welfare Act was passed, protecting the children from being taken from their people (see Box 19-7).

About 300 of the Canadian Native children went to Pennsylvania alone. A study of 100 of those children showed that they suffered more problems than any other children "of colour," including African-Americans, Vietnamese, and Koreans. By 1995, five had died, about one half had experienced "difficulties involving identity issues," only about one third had completed high school, and about the same percentage had lost all touch with their adoptive parents.

Box 19-7   Indian Child Welfare Act (U.S.)

The Indian Child Welfare Act (ICWA) was passed in 1978 by the government of the United States. It applies to any unmarried person under 18 who belongs or is eligible to belong to an "Indian tribe" in the United States. The declared purpose of the ICWA is "to protect the best interests of Indian children and to promote the stability and security of Indian tribes and families." An information sheet put out by the Wabanaki of Maine gives this answer to the question: "What does the law do?"

The ICWA requires that placement cases involving Indian children be heard in tribal courts if possible [some of the First Nations in the United States have their own courts], and permits a child's tribe to be involved in state court proceedings. It requires testimony from expert witnesses who are familiar with Indian culture before a child can be removed from his/her home. If a child is removed, either for foster care or adoption, the law requires that Indian children be placed with extended family members, other tribal members, or other Indian families. (Pine Tree Legal Assistance 2002)

There is no similar law in Canada.

In 1982, the Manitoba government finally agreed to impose a moratorium on the export of children outside of the province. It was the last province to do so. There was an investigation into the practice, however. Justice Edwin C. Kimelman wrote a report in 1985 entitled No Quiet Place, primarily studying the 93 children that were "exported" in 1981. He did not mince his words in his conclusions, saying:

> cultural genocide has been taking place in a systematic routine manner. One gets an image of children stacked in foster homes as used cars are stacked on corner lots, just waiting for the right "buyer" to stroll by. (Kimelman in Fournier and Crey 1997:88)

Two Manitoba Stories

Cameron Kerley

Two well-reported biographies of Manitoba Native children born in 1964 tell the stories for the others. **Cameron Kerley** was removed from his family when he was eight years old. His father had been killed in a fight and his mother was drinking heavily, creating a physical condition that would kill her two years later. Cameron and his three sisters were placed in non-Native foster homes. In 1975, at the age of 11, he was sent for adoption to a single man in Kansas. While he lived there, the man beat and sexually abused him. The authorities should have been aware of the signs of trouble. He was skipping school and running away from home for days on end. This happened before the adoption was made legal in 1977; the agency could have taken him away. School counsellors and social workers attempted to help him, but he couldn't speak of what was happening. In Cameron's words:

I didn't trust them . . . I wasn't able to tell them. I felt helpless. At that point there was nobody I could turn to for help. I was a kid, taken away from home . . . and put into a situation I didn't ask to be in. (York 1990:211)

He soon had run-ins with the police. In 1978, at 13, he ran away only to be picked up by the police. At 17, he dropped out of school and was soon arrested for burglary. At 19, he moved away from his abusive adoptive father. His initial plans were to find his way back to the Manitoba reserve in which he was born. But he got drunk one night, returned "home," and killed his adoptive father with a baseball bat. He was sentenced to 18 years; but after two years, he was transferred to Stony Mountain Penitentiary, north of Winnipeg. At least there he would be with others who would know from their own experiences what he had been through.

Carla Williams

Carla Williams was a Saulteaux from southern Manitoba. Her parents were alcoholics who had their four children taken from them in 1968. Her father hanged himself a few years later, and her mother also committed suicide at a later date. In 1972, Carla was placed in "permanent" adoption with a Dutch couple who were in Canada but were returning to the Netherlands. The adoption looked good on paper for the child welfare agency, for the man was a prominent physician. But the adoption broke down after six months, and Carla was fostered out. Unfortunately, her adoptive father received visitation rights. He got her pregnant twice, the first time when she was 14, the second time when she was 15. Both children were taken away from her. She was placed in a series of Dutch orphanages and mental institutions, worked as a prostitute for a while, and tried unsuccessfully to commit suicide.

Her luck changed somewhat when she met a group of Natives from Manitoba at a conference. They put her in touch with a Native-run agency that enabled her to obtain a passport and the funds necessary to return to Canada. In 1989, at Winnipeg International Airport, she saw her brothers and sisters for the first time in over 20 years.

Stó:lo Stories

Ernie Crey is a Stó:lo who co-authored the powerful book *Stolen from Our Embrace: The Abduction of First Nations Children and the Restoration of Aboriginal Communities* (Fournier and Crey 1997). It is a book of incredible tragedy as well as of hope, an amazing combination. In Chapter 1, "The Perpetual Stranger: Four Generations in My Stó:lo Family," Crey courageously tells his own story. His father died in 1961 when Crey was 12. Without the strong support of her husband, and without any job skills, his mother fell into depression and alcoholism. All but one of her children were taken away from her within a few months of the death of her husband. They would never be reunited again as a family. Crey was driven away in an RCMP cruiser to spend his first week away from home in a prison cell. He had been skipping school and had shoplifted (so did John Steckley, one of the authors of this book, at the same age). The judge sentenced him to Brannan Lake Industrial School, which was rife with physical and sexual abuse.

Crey would not see his mother or any other member of his family for four years. They grew up within a few miles of each other but didn't know where the others were. Crey would go through several foster homes and a group home run by a pedophile who was later convicted for his crimes. His brothers and sisters lived in foster homes, where one sibling was sexually abused, and where their punishment for "misbehaving" included being locked in a closet, having their heads stuck in a toilet bowl while the toilet was being flushed, and being forced to shovel chicken excrement throughout the night.

One of the most moving elements of this story involves Crey's mother's letters. She wrote letters to each of her children and gave them to the social workers, hoping they would be passed on. They weren't. Crey was shown those letters as an adult by a sympathetic social worker. According to Crey, in those letters:

> . . . my mother poured out her fears and concerns for me and tried to reassure me that she still loved me, that I should never think she did not. She told me how much she missed me and thought of me. And in one letter, she had an ingenious plan. The social workers would not tell her exactly where I was, but she proposed that I meet her one Saturday at a tiny park in Abbotsford . . . I couldn't help but wonder how many times she had driven by that park, looking for me. (Fournier and Crey 1997:35)

WHY TAKE THE CHILDREN AWAY?

Why did they take these children from their homes and from their people? There are a number of reasons. One reason is cultural. Non-Native social workers and agencies have set ideas about what a "family" and a "good home" are. A family has two parents and their children—the nuclear family. However, the traditional idea of family in Native cultures is usually much larger than this (see Box 19-8). This is well expressed in the words of **Wilfred Pelletier**, an Odawa from Wikwemikong on Manitoulin Island, who wrote in 1973 (when he was 45) of what family was like when he was growing up. The same story could be told in many places across Native Canada.

> If a man was having a hard time financially, it was quite common for someone in better circumstances to offer to take one of that man's kids and raise it as one of his own. So the child would have two sets of parents, and usually he'd end up with the name of his adopted parents just through usage. Of course, the child was free to stay where he chose, and often he would live with one set of parents for a while and then go home to the others. Either way, he went home. (Pelletier and Poole 1973:124–25)

Social workers envisioned a "good home" in terms of physical resources. For non-Native Canadians, this would include a separate bedroom for each child, a sewage or a septic tank, and running water. Most Native houses, often structures designed by Indian Affairs, could not meet those "standards." In 1981, 33 percent of all on-reserve dwellings had more than one person per room, as compared with 3 percent of such dwellings in all of Canada (Frideres 1998:171). In 1963, less than 10 percent of all on-reserve houses had access to sewers or septic tanks, a figure that rose to around 55 percent by 1980 (Frideres 1998:174). Similarly, around 12 percent of those houses had running water in 1963, rising to about 70 percent by 1981 (Frideres 1998:174).

Sometimes children were taken away from their families "for health reasons." This could mean that newborn infants needing to be in or near an urban hospital for treatment would be fostered to a non-Native family who lived nearby, and the child would never be given back to their Native parents—despite the fact that those parents had done nothing to harm the children. In Manitoba, 79 Sixties Scoop children were removed in this way.

Box 19-8   My Mothers

Traditional Aboriginal notions of family were different from modern North American notions. For example, there are differing notions of what "my mother" means. The Huron in the seventeenth century used the term "annen-en" to address or refer to the woman who gave birth to them. But she wasn't the only one a child would refer to that way. Annen-en was also used to refer to one's mother's sisters as well. They would reciprocate with a term meaning "my child." Often, female relatives would live with you in the traditional longhouse, which could house 40 or more people. If you needed a mother, there was bound to be one around.

The notion of having a mother term used for mother's sisters is not unique to the Huron, nor restricted to the past. In contemporary Blackfoot, the noun "iksísst" refers both to one's mother and her sisters, and the term "miksísstsiksi" means "my mothers" and refers collectively to one's mother and her sisters (Frantz and Russell 1995:51).

Terms for fathers and brothers can likewise be linked in some languages and cultures. Likewise, the children of the mother's sisters and father's brothers ("cousins" in English terminology) would be considered "brothers" and "sisters." Take, for example, the word "ndawemaa." In Ojibwe, it was traditionally used in the following ways:

> Female's use: brother, mother's sister's son, father's brother's son
>
> Male's use: sister, mother's sister's daughter, father's brother's daughter

It had the meaning of "sibling of the opposite sex." There was a similar term for "sibling of the same sex." The key thing to remember is that it meant including people that English speakers would call "cousins" into the circle of brothers and sisters.

There were, of course, many cases where children were physically, emotionally, and sexually abused and should have been removed from their parents and other potentially dangerous members of their family. But that did not mean that the children would be better off away from their extended families, their reserves, and their people.

DIFFICULTIES FOR RECOVERY IN MANITOBA

Manitoba Natives, who had borne the major brunt of the Sixties Scoop, would also have the hardest time in overcoming its effects. On July 1, 1981, Dakota Ojibway Child and Family Services (DOCFS), a child welfare program run by the Dakota people, received a legal mandate to reclaim their lost children. They took over the care of 49 Native children who had been apprehended by Manitoba's Children's Aid societies. The road ahead of them would be difficult. Within three years, the number of children in their care rose to 115. Between 1983 and 1987, the five Native child welfare agencies that had come into being had to face an increase in the number of registered Indian children in care, from 863 to 1563.

The Native children's agencies were swamped with incidents of child abuse that were beyond their meagre resources to cope with adequately. The lack of formal training of many of their workers diminished their effectiveness. When the agencies were first formed, it was believed that "Native-run" would be a panacea that would soon solve everything, so they were not prepared for the increasing numbers of children needing care.

Many of the negative effects of what was happening in Manitoba became public through the inquest following the death of **Lester Desjarlais**. Lester Desjarlais was Saulteaux, born in Sandy Bay, Manitoba, on June 7, 1974. He had an older brother and three younger sisters, so he was the "baby" of the family. He had a hard life, particularly when he was 12 and 13. Before you read the following list of what happened to him during that period of his life, picture the kind of life you had and what happened to you at 12 and 13.

During this period of his life, Lester

- weighed about 45 kilos and was a little over five feet tall.
- often got drunk and high by sniffing solvents, such as gas, cleaning fluid, and plastic cement.
- was raped by a large man from his community and was sexually molested by a male teacher.
- got into many fights and was beaten up several times at drinking parties at his mother's house.
- was placed in several foster homes in his own community as well as one in Brandon.
- was placed three times in the Seven Oaks Centre for Youth in Winnipeg.
- was put in a group home in Sioux Valley, which he escaped from, stole a bicycle, and rode 200 kilometres toward home.
- was twice admitted to the Brandon Mental Health Centre.
- had his much-loved mother call the police on him.
- committed suicide by hanging.

The inquest into his death, which began in April 1992, told a story of how the system had failed him, as it was continuing to fail other Native children. A few courageous women faced the opposition of influential people in their communities to reveal painful truths about life on reserves. The inquest showed the dark side of band and provincial politics. The band council was engaged in a power struggle with the DOCFS. Abusers were protected, and child abuse continued because of the political power of certain male band councillors in the community. The DOCFS did not want to go to non-Native agencies or professionals because many within the DOCFS felt this would be a step backwards. For historical reasons, it did not want to rely on outsiders; distrust was high. Since the DOCFS was the first Native-run child welfare organization of its kind, it had attracted a lot of attention from the media, academics, politicians, and Native leaders. Moreover, outside agencies and the provincial ministry did not want to be seen as racists, for stepping in and trying to resolve problems that were being reported. As well, the provincial government did not want to have the opposition of Native leaders during an election year. Thus, the children's welfare and happiness were sacrificed for politics.

Native Individuals 19-1

Ernie Crey: A Stó:lo man and co-author of *Stolen from Our Embrace* (Fournier and Crey 1997).

Lester Desjarlais: A Saulteaux boy whose tragic story was told in *Flowers on My Grave* (Teichroeb 1998).

Kahgegagahbowh ("He who stands forever," 1818–69): George Copway, a best-selling Ojibwa writer.

Cameron Kerley: One of the Manitoba Native children involved with the Sixties Scoop, he was convicted of killing his abusive adoptive father.

Isabelle Knockwood: A Mi'kmaq writer/educator who wrote *Out of the Depths* (Knockwood 1992), a moving book about the residential school experience.

Oronhyateka ("Burning Sky," 1841–1907): Doctor Peter Martin, a Mohawk whose hard work made him a doctor and the successful head of the Independent Order of Foresters.

Carla Williams: A Saulteaux woman whose failed adoption through the Sixties Scoop led her to the Netherlands and caused a life of hardship.

KEY TERMS

annen-en (Huron)

miks isstsiksi (Blackfoot)

residential schools

Sixties Scoop

CONTENT QUESTIONS

1. What two contradictory reasons did Clifford Sifton give for changing industrial schools?
2. What happened to the curriculum in residential schools in 1910?
3. To what does the term "Sixties Scoop" refer?
4. How many Native children were taken out of Manitoba between 1971 and 1981?
5. What is the Indian Child Welfare Act?

WEBLINKS

www.ncf.carleton.ca/~de723/bevbio.html
On this website, Beverley Mckiver, a Sixties Scoop survivor, tells her story.

www.afn.ca/residentialschools/index.html
The Assembly of First Nations website on the residential schools issue has useful news room and resource sections.

chapter twenty

Social Issues: The Dudley George Story

THE NINETEENTH CENTURY

The story of Dudley George actually begins in the 1820s. Anishinabe originally from northern Ontario had moved south around a century and a half before 1820 and had become known in the south as Chippewa or Mississauga. Mixing with them a short time later were the Potawatomi, a closely related people forced out of the United States.

In the 1820s, the relationship between the Anishinabe people and the British government was changing. From the American Revolution to the War of 1812, the British had considered the Anishinabe as valued allies against the Americans. After the war, however, the land they lived on was considered more valuable than any future services they could render to the Crown.

The "Chiefs and Principle Men of the Chippewa" signed a Provisional Agreement in 1825, which became the Treaty of Amherstburg in 1827. But the Elders who signed this treaty had been born in a time when their people far outnumbered the newcomers. By 1825, their people made up less than 10 percent of the population of Upper Canada (the heart of what is now Ontario). This treaty created four bands and four reserves: Sarnia, Walpole Island, Kettle Point, and Stoney Point. The latter reserve was "two miles square at the River aux Sable which empties into Lake Huron" (Gordon 1996).

THE APPROPRIATION OF LAND

Slightly more than 100 years after the Treaty of Amherstburg, the people of Stoney Point Band #43, whose name in Ojibwe is Aazhoodenaang Enjibaajig, were pressed by the federal and provincial governments to sell 377 acres in 1928 to "private interests." They really didn't have much say in the matter, as the federal government, through the

Department of Indian Affairs, held primary responsibility for the reserve. Natives couldn't even vote in federal elections at that time. In 1936, without the permission of the Stoney Point band, 108 of those acres were purchased to make Ipperwash Park. The Stoney Point people were not too happy about this situation, particularly because a cemetery had been dug into and violated during the making of the park in 1937.

Then came World War II. Natives volunteered to fight in numbers proportionally higher than any other group. In 1942, the federal government asked the Natives of the Stoney Point to make another sacrifice for their country, one not asked of others. Invoking the **War Measures Act**, the Department of National Defence appropriated the remaining land of the Stoney Point band, even though 85 percent of the members of the band were opposed to the appropriation. They would receive $50,000 in compensation for about 2211 acres of land (about $23 an acre), plus the promise that "if, at the termination of the war, no further use of the area is required by the Department of National Defence, negotiations will be entered into with the Department of Indian Affairs to transfer the lands back to the Indians at a reasonable price determined by mutual agreement" (Koehler 1996). The Stoney Point people were forced to live in the less-than-prime territory of their Kettle Point neighbours and were not given the same number or quality of houses as those they had been compelled to give up. Box 20-1 tells the reaction of a World War II veteran on returning home to find his home uprooted.

After the war, on May 31, 1946, the "Advanced Infantry Training Centre" in Ipperwash was closed, but negotiations did not follow. The Canadian Armed Forces continued to make peacetime use of the land that had been appropriated for war. From 1960 on, it was used as a six-week cadet training camp and recreation facility.

TRYING TO REGAIN LOST LAND

While the Stoney Point people never stopped trying to regain their land and their community, it wasn't until 1981 that they achieved a measure of success. The federal government agreed to pay $2.4 million in compensation for the nearly 40 years of use they had had of the land. But the return of the land was delayed pending an environmental assessment and cleanup, which was necessary since the land had been used for shooting practice of a number of different weapons. This would put plans on long-term hold.

In 1985, a small step was made in that the members of the Kettle and Stoney Point band were once again permitted to hunt and fish on the land during provincially approved seasons. The Department of National Defence agreed to review the need for the camp for

BOX 20-1   A Soldier Returns Home

In 1993, the following was written by a reporter covering a speech given at Trent University by Native Elder Clifford George:

> He told the crowd about when he returned home after fighting overseas in World War II. Upon his return, he found his people and his home uprooted and (mis)placed elsewhere. He said he'd been promised a forty-acre plot of land when he returned from the war, and his father had also written to him overseas telling him not to worry as their land would be returned to them after the war. (Koehler 1996)

military purposes every four years. This wasn't much of a concession, as it would not voluntarily give up the land.

No changes were made in the situation until 1992. In March of that year, the Standing Committee on Aboriginal People tabled its report recommending that the federal government return the land to its former Aboriginal inhabitants and their descendants, saying that the government's reasons for continuing to occupy the land were "spurious and without substance" (Gordon 1996). The Department of National Defence initially held its ground, literally. It replied to the Standing Committee in August, claiming that there was a continuing need for it to retain the Camp Ipperwash lands for military purposes. Eventually, the cadet camp was closed, but the department continued to assert possession of the land, agreeing merely to "consult" with the Kettle and Stoney Point First Nation, a word that Native people have learned to distrust.

In 1993, the Stoney Pointers took more radical steps to regain their land. On May 6, they moved onto the old firing range, living in makeshift dwellings such as small trailers and tents. They would be opposed on two fronts: by Native people themselves as well as Armed Forces. Tom Bressette, Chief of the Kettle and Stoney Point First Nation, showed his opposition to the move by asking the premier of the province to demand that it stop issuing general welfare to the Stoney Point people occupying Camp Ipperwash.

Why would Bressette take such a position? Consider the following. Media attention could cast his band in a bad light, as it had done with the earlier confrontations at Oka and Gustafsen Lake (see Box 20-2). He knew that it was often not a good thing for a Native community to draw federal government attention to itself, and for local non-Natives to see a First Nation as having a militant element. Finally, any action to split the band in two would diminish his budget, his power, and his general capacity to get things done in his community.

Chief Bressette and most of his council appear to have resented what they construed as "outsider" influence from the broader Native community. Gord Peters, Regional Chief of the Chiefs of Ontario, publicly advocated for resolution to the conflict. The council wrote to him, asking him to "refrain from your involvement with matters directly related to our First Nation" (Gordon 1996).

On September 12, the Stoney Pointers occupying the base walked from Stoney Point, by the shores of Lake Huron, across the breadth of Southern Ontario to Ottawa, to press the federal government to recognize their rights. The trip took two and a half weeks. Along the way, they stopped at Peterborough, where the Trent University Native Studies department had organized a rally for them. Media coverage was light.

The relationship between the Armed Forces personnel and the Stoney Pointers deteriorated. Time, escalating incidents of aggressiveness, and uncertainties concerning turnover combined to raise the tension at Camp Ipperwash. On June 27, 1995, Glenn Morris George, then 34, angered by the fact that the army had placed iron "tire slashers" on the roadway leading to a burial ground, started to remove these tire slashers. Captain Allan Howse saw this and got into a verbal fight with him. Following a series of events that took place between George, Howse, and at least one other Armed Forces personnel, George was charged with two counts of assault, one of mischief, and one of uttering a death threat. Howse alleged that George had driven a tractor that bumped an army truck, causing $900 damage. (Glenn Morris George was no relation to Dudley George: see Box 20-3 for a discussion of surnames in the Stoney Point area.)

| BOX 20-2 | The Tensions of the Times: Gustafsen Lake |

The summer of 1995 saw another Native hot spot develop in British Columbia. For six years, Natives of several different First Nations had held a Sun Dance at a ranch at Gustafsen Lake owned by an American, Lyle James. To that time there had been no problems. But in 1995, there was tension. Ranch hands were harassing Natives and, on June 13, a forestry worker was shot at. Following the eight-day ceremony, some people refused to leave the site, claiming that it was sacred ground. James had them served with trespass notices.

It was a complicated issue, with a number of divisive elements separating Native people. The Sun Dance was not traditional to the local First Nation, the Shuswap. Some of the dancers were not from the area. Not all dancers supported the occupiers. Some Shuswap Elders stated that the site was not a sacred one, but the occupiers claimed that three people had had visions there.

A division between Native officials and militants seemed to be forming. The occupiers issued a press release under the name of Shuswap Traditionalists, stating that the land had never been officially ceded or surrendered. The elected officials of the local band and tribal council failed to negotiate peace with the occupiers. Ovide Mercredi, Chief of the Assembly of First Nations, tried too, and likewise failed.

On September 11, four days after Dudley George died, 400 RCMP officers with helicopters and armed personnel carriers closed in. Shots were exchanged. It was the costliest police operation in British Columbia and in RCMP history. Six days later, the occupiers surrendered. Of the 18 arrested, 14 were Native and 4 were non-Natives (13 men and 5 women). Sixty charges were laid. They went to court on July 18, 1996, and the trial lasted 10 months. There were 39 acquittals and 21 convictions.

| BOX 20-3 | Why Is Everyone Called "George"? |

Why does everyone in this community seem to have the last name "George"? Do they all belong to just one family? The answer is that there is a limited number of surnames in a Native community. In the same area, the surname "Simon" and "Jacobs" also developed. Surnames were imposed on the people by missionaries and officials during the last two centuries, because of administrative

demands and an ethnocentric sense that Natives should be like "everybody else." (Surnames for Europeans themselves are only a few centuries old. Think of the Bible, where no one has a last name.)

Traditional Anishinabe naming traditions involve a person having one name, which could reflect a vision that the individual had, or which could be something passed down through the generations.

On July 29, in a mutually confrontational atmosphere, the military (numbering from 15 to 20 people) moved out, and about 100 Stoney Pointers moved into the barracks. Later, Cleve Jackson was charged with reckless driving when it was alleged that he drove a bus through the drill hall that day. Stoney Pointers claimed that he had not been the driver of the bus. They believed that the only reason Jackson was charged was because the Military Police saw his picture on the cover of the *London Free Press* and then decided that he was the culprit. Judge Louise Eddy dismissed the charges the following year.

The summer came to an end, unfortunately, with a passing written shot that would have repercussions later on. Kettle and Stoney Point Band Councillor Gerald George printed a letter in the local *Forest Standard*, which contained the following inflammatory remarks: "I am glad that these Army Camp Indians call themselves separate from my First Nation because I would not want any of my fellow band members to act like animals" (Gordon 1996).

THE OCCUPATION OF IPPERWASH PARK

On September 4, 1995, at least 24 Stoney Pointers occupied Ipperwash Park, which was closed because the summer tourist season was over. The Natives posed no physical threat to anyone. They expressed their concern about a sacred burial ground that was located in the park. This burial ground had been well documented in archaeological site reports on file at Queen's Park in Toronto and in Ottawa, but both the provincial and federal governments denied knowledge of these reports until after the issue came to a head and the damage was done.

On September 5, the newly elected Progressive Conservative government of Mike Harris held a closed, secret session to set out how it would handle the occupation of Ipperwash Park. Members of the new government had talked tough during the election campaign, and the next few months would show that they were anxious to demonstrate that their actions followed their words. Members of the cabinet, representatives of the Ministry of Natural Resources (who ran the park), the Ontario Native affairs secretariat, the attorney general, and the Ontario Provincial Police all attended. While exactly what was said during that meeting has not yet been revealed, pending a long-delayed and much-demanded inquiry, subsequent evidence suggests the provincial police received a clear message: "Get those Indians out of the park" (Gordon 1996). No mandate was given to negotiate or to respect the claims of the Stoney Pointers.

On September 6, Chief Tom Bressette was notified that an order had been given to get the protesters out of the park. He did not inform the Stoney Pointers of this order, not that they would have obeyed it had he done so.

"Escalating Violence Against Police"

Prior to the confrontation in Ipperwash Park, the Ontario Provincial Police (OPP) had gone through a very thorough preparation for battle, requesting from the army 50 gas masks, 50 pairs of night vision goggles, equipment for intercepting cellular telephone calls, 100 bullet-proof vests, two Huey helicopters, and two Bison personnel carriers. Two hundred and fifty officers were mobilized from across Ontario to face about 30 people with no firearms.

The Ipperwash Park situation was like a dry forest after a hot, dry summer—only a dropped match was needed for conflict to rage like a forest fire. At 7:55 p.m. on September 6, 1995, that match was lit. Stoney Pointer Stewart George got into an argument with Gerald George, the man who had referred in the paper to Stewart's group as "animals." Stewart took his anger at Gerald out on Gerald's car. At 8:19 p.m., Gerald George lodged a complaint with the OPP. (The next day, the OPP issued a news release stating that "A private citizen's vehicle was damaged by a number of First Nations people armed with baseball bats. As a result of this, the OPP Crowd Management Team was deployed . . ." ["National Defence Documents" 1995]. Stewart George later pled guilty to one count of mischief—another charge was dismissed—and was fined $300.)

At about 10:45 p.m., a team of 32 officers of the Crowd Management Unit, in riot gear that included shields, batons, and sidearms, advanced on about 30 unarmed Native men, women, and children. The officers were protected by a more heavily armed eight-man Tactics and Rescue Unit (a SWAT team).

Cecil Bernard George, a Kettle and Stoney Point band councillor, walked into the middle of the oncoming confrontation in an attempt to defuse the potential human explosion, but he was too late. The OPP beat him with clubs and kicked him. He later filed a civil action suit, in which a doctor's report revealed that he had injuries to 28 different places on his body.

The assault on Cecil George would cause Warren George, 22, to drive slowly onto the scene, trying to put his car between his people and the police. An officer pointed a gun directly at Warren, who then swerved and braked, making contact with five officers, one of whom suffered a sprained ankle. In February 1998, Warren was found guilty of criminal negligence causing bodily harm and assault with a weapon (his car). A charge of dangerous driving was stayed. Warren George was sentenced to six months and was banned from driving for two years. Strangely, although he was unarmed during the incident, he was also prohibited from possessing firearms for 10 years. Judge Greg Pockele, in pronouncing sentence, said that Warren lacked "remorse" for what he had done and had become part of the "escalating violence against police" in the situation (Hamilton 1998).

At about the same time, a youth made a similar attempt to block the advance of the police. This time the vehicle was a bus. Seven officers drew their weapons and fired, and a bullet struck the young man in his lower right back. The youth was acquitted of charges, with Judge Graham stating, "It is reasonable for [the youth] to assume that a breach of the peace was occurring and that Bernard George was being assaulted" (Anti-Racist Action 1997).

The Killing of Dudley George

Anthony O'Brien (Dudley) George was born in Sarnia on March 17, 1957. He was involved with every aspect of Stoney Point resistance, including the occupation of Camp Ipperwash and the march, and was a face familiar to all, including the police. He looked the part of the "militant Indian": long hair, short beard, and sunglasses. His familiarity and his "militant look" would make him an easy target for police anxiety. It is alleged that before the police advanced, the OPP had said to him, "Dudley, you are going to be first."[1]

Acting Sergeant Kenneth Deane was second in command of the Tactics and Rescue Unit. He later testified that he saw muzzle flashes coming from the bushes and that moments later Dudley stepped onto the road and scanned the police, pointing a rifle. Deane alleged that Dudley threw the rifle away after being hit in the collarbone by Deane's shot. This was proven untrue in court. The Natives fired no shots, although the police are rumoured to have fired 1000 shots (perhaps Deane mistook one of those for unfriendly fire), and Dudley had not been carrying a gun.

Deane shot Dudley, but the Stoney Pointer did not die right away. The police did not call any ambulances, however. Marcia Simon, a Stoney Pointer, tried to call an ambulance, but she was grabbed and arrested while trying to do so. Dudley's brother, Pierre, his sister, Carolyn, and a youth proceeded to drive him to the nearest hospital, some 50 kilometres away. A tire went flat but still they lumbered on.

When they got to the hospital, the OPP, who had been following the car, took Pierre and Carolyn into custody, claiming that they would be charged with attempted murder (although they had possessed no weapons and hadn't tried to harm anyone). They were held overnight and then let go. Dudley died at 12:45 a.m. on September 7, 1995.

The Investigation

The Ontario Special Investigations Unit arrived within hours of the shooting but was prevented by the OPP from entering the park until two weeks later. Although the OPP are required to file a report within 90 days of a shooting incident, their report wasn't released until July 23, 1996, more than 10 months later.

Kenneth Deane was charged the next day with criminal negligence causing death, for which the maximum penalty is life imprisonment. The trial began on April 1, 1997. On April 29, 1997, he was found guilty. Judge Hugh Fraser stated that Deane had "concocted a story . . . in an ill-fated attempt to disguise the fact that an unarmed man was shot."[2] The judge told Deane: "You were not honest in your statements to police investigators, to the S.I.U., and to this court." Brian Adkin, president of the OPP Association, said outside the court that he felt that government inaction on the land claim had created a "tragedy on both sides, a tragedy for the George family and a tragedy for Sgt. Deane."

On July 4, sentence was passed down. Deane was given a conditional sentence of two years less a day to be served in the community, and he was told to perform 180 hours of community work. Deane appealed the decision and lost the appeal on February 18, 2000. By then, he had served his sentence, with no penitentiary time.

For their activities of the summer and of September, the Stoney Pointers faced 62 charges. Most of those charges were dropped. For example, 20 charges of forcible entry were dropped because the police were unable to establish how the people got into the park. More significantly, 23 charges of forcible detainer were dropped because "The accused have raised the defence of colour of right on the basis that there is a Chippewa burial ground within Ipperwash Provincial Park and that therefore *they were justified in being in the Park during the time set out in the charges*" (authors' emphasis).[3]

On June 18, 1998, after roughly two years of negotiations, Minister of Indian Affairs and Northern Development Jane Stewart and Chief Norm Shawnoo of the Kettle and Stoney Point First Nation signed an Agreement-in-Principle on the return of the former Camp Ipperwash lands. It was anticipated that a Final Agreement would follow, as would an environmental assessment and cleanup, as stated in the government news release "because of the likelihood of contaminants and unexploded ordnances which accumulated during the time the site was used as a military training base."[4]

In August 2000, after almost five years of trying to obtain government documents, the George family lawyers were handed nine boxes or nearly 35,000 pages of records from government officials, in what appears to have been an attempt to bury them with too much information. Part two of that flood of information came in March 2001 when they received another 100,000 pages. In August that same year the George family was finally given the go-ahead by the Ontario Supreme Court to proceed with a lawsuit against Premier Harris, former Solicitor-General Bob Runciman, and former Attorney General Mike Harnick. They had been blocked before by the government's excuse that the official investigation had to be completed before any lawsuits could develop. Two months later, Harris resigned from his premiership, citing "personal reasons."

In October 2003, after receiving assurance by the Liberals that they would call for an official inquiry if elected, the George family dropped their lawsuit. The Liberals kept that promise the next month.

The Ipperwash Inquiry began its investigation in April 2004. The Inquiry had two parts: part one was to look at the events that surrounded the death of Dudley George; part two was expand to broad policy issues, with recommendations being made to try to avoid a similar tragedy in the future. In May 2004, the federal government agreed to pay $15,000 to each of the 105 people deemed affected by the 1942 land takeover at Camp Ipperwash. An Investigation Agreement was signed involving a joint process of determining where there might be unexploded ordnance and environmental contamination, stemming from the army's activities over the period of their possession of the land.

Ipperwash returned to the public stage in the fall of 2005 when high-profile government figures appeared to testify. Harnick had the testimony that was most damning of Harris, saying, among other things, that he had heard Harris issue the much-rumoured get "the fucking Indians out of the park" statement at a meeting held to develop strategies as to how to respond to the protest. Other officials alluded to Harris' "forceful personality" and his strong desire for quick action ("Harris denies" 2006).

The issue resurfaced in February 2006 with the showing on CTV of the made-for-television-movie *One Dead Indian*, based on the book of the same name published by *Toronto Star* reporter Peter Edwards in 2001. In the same month, the OPP made public the documents from an internal investigation that told their side of the story. Then, Harris made his long-awaited testimony. If it could be proven that he had exercised "undue influence" as a politician on the OPP (an organization which is supposed to be independent of government), it could lead to charges. Harris appeared to successfully stonewall the inquiry with his denials, accepting no responsibility for police action, and accusing the OPP of acting on its own. To add to the drama of the time, Kenneth Deane, who had been forced to retire from

BOX 20-4 **Non-Offensive to Whom?**

One of the contentious issues surrounding Ipperwash was the production of 150 mugs and an equal number of t-shirts commemorating the Ipperwash police operation. These both bore the OPP crest along with a white eagle feather, and were available at a local novelty shop.

Aboriginal complaints centred on the sacred nature of the eagle feather and that the feather could be seen as symbolizing a fallen warrior. In the OPP's internal investigation report it was felt that the officers acted in a proper manner and that the products were non-offensive.

the OPP in 2002, was killed in a car accident in February. He was the third officer involved at Ipperwash to die that way.

The news in 2007 was mixed. In May, while the judge criticized Harris' handling of the situation, he ruled that the premier did not interfere or give inappropriate directions to the police at Ipperwash. In December, the provincial government turned Ipperwash Park over to the people of Sydney Point. In February 2009, the Camp Ipperwash issue was still being negotiated.

Native Individuals 20-1

Dudley George (1957–1995): A Stoney Point Ojibwa whose occupation of Ipperwash Park in Ontario led to his being shot to death by the Ontario Provincial Police.

Timeline 20-1

1680: Mississauga and related peoples move south from Northern Ontario.

1827: Mississauga sign Treaty of Amherstburg.

1928: Stoney Point people forced to sell 377 acres of their reserve.

1936: 108 of those acres purchased to form Ipperwash Park.

1937: Mississauga cemetery violated during the making of Ipperwash Park.

1942: Federal government uses War Measures Act to expropriate the Stoney Point band's land for military training purposes, forcing them to live with the Kettle Point band.

1946: Advanced Infantry Training Centre closed, but military possession is maintained.

1993: Stoney Point people begin to occupy Camp Ipperwash.

1995:

July: The army moves out of Camp Ipperwash.

September 4: Ipperwash Park occupied by 24 Stoney Point people.

September 5: The provincial government holds closed meeting to deal with the occupation.

September 7: Dudley George dies.

1997: OPP officer Kenneth Deane found guilty of criminal negligence causing death and is given a suspended sentence with 180 hours of community work.

1998: Agreement-in-Principle signed for return of the Camp Ipperwash lands to the Stoney Point people.

ENDNOTES

1. See website www.turtleisland.org/discussion/viewtopic.php?t=2701

2. See website http://sisis.native.web.org/ipperwash/tnov97oil.html

3. See website http://sisis.nativeweb.org/ipperwash/toct22.htm

4. See website www.jmss.org/1999article4-INAC.html

KEY TERM

War Measures Act

CONTENT QUESTIONS

1. How did the Ipperwash Park land get transferred away from the Stoney Point band?

2. How did the Stoney Point people get the Camp Ipperwash land taken away from them?

3. How long did it take for the Stoney Point people to get their land back from the Department of National Defence?

4. Why did the Stoney Point people occupy Ipperwash Park?

5. What was the court's decision on the people's right to be in Ipperwash Park?

WEBLINKS

www.ipperwashinquiry.ca
This is the website for the Ipperwash Inquiry.

chapter twenty-one

Fighting for the Sacred Waters: The Peigan and the Oldman River Dam

OLDMAN RIVER, SACRED RIVER

According to the traditions of the Peigan, their nation first came to life in the waters and surrounding plains of the Oldman River. To them, the river, which winds through Peigan land in southwestern Alberta, is as sacred as the Jordan is to Christians or as the Ganges is to Hindus. They even named it **Na'pi**, meaning "Old Man,"[1] their name for the hero who was said to have created the first Peigan. The Peigan came to the Na'pi River to pray, to drink its water, and to take the plants and animals it nourished for medicine and food. In the Na'pi River, religion, history, and the necessities of life came together.

The traditional Peigan had a special relationship with bodies of water. They did not use canoes, nor did they eat fish. Yet, in the words of American Blackfoot writer Darrell Robes Kipp, the **Suyitapis** played a central cultural role:

> . . . [R]ivers and lakes hold a special power because they are inhabited by the Suyitapis, the Underwater People. Painted lodge covers, medicine bundles, and other sacred items were transferred to the tribe from the Suyitapis. In turn their power and domain are respected by the tribe. Today, the reservation waterways and lakes are touted as premier fishing spots. Yet most tribal members maintain the traditional ban on fishing. (Kipp 1996:76)

Peigan Elders can recount stories of **Ni'taiitsskaaiks** (literally "lone-fight," plural) or Lonefighters Society that trace it back at least to the 1700s, when horses first came to Peigan culture. According to **James Bad Eagle**, a descendant of the Lonefighters, the name came from a time when one lone warrior fought against impossibly heavy odds and did not give up. Today, the Elders can point to a one-kilometre stretch of the Oldman River as the original home of the society. By the banks of the river, this society buried its

Box 21-1	Blackfoot Names

There are a number of long-standing jokes about Native names. This is largely because the meanings of these names are so apparent, the result of their recently being translated from the language of their origin. Sometimes Native people feel pressured into changing their names because they believe they are targets because of this aspect of their names. A student of one of the authors had the last name Bigwin. It wasn't until the end of the semester when he discovered her Native ancestry, and she learned that a member of her family had changed the name so they would not be harassed for having the name "Big Wind," traditionally a name that gave the bearer pride.

Non-Natives should realize that at one point virtually all names held meaning of some kind. It is just that many English names (and, to a lesser extent, French names) have lost their cultural meaning and significance for English speakers.

dead, performed the sacred Sun Dance, held meetings, and prepared for war against threatening peoples. The Lonefighters were expected to protect their land and their people to the last warrior's last breath. This earned them the respect of other Plains nations.

The Peigan were hit hard during the nineteenth century. The buffalo were killed off. Strangers took their land and made them sign a treaty and put them on reserves. Their most sacred ceremony, the Sun Dance, was made illegal. The Lonefighters struggled to maintain Peigan ways. But they would disappear into the dust of the Peigan reserves.

James Bad Eagle's name is a translation, like many Native names. See Box 21-1 for more information about this practice.

FIGHTING FOR THE RIVER

The fight for the river began essentially in 1976, almost a century after the Peigan had signed the treaty surrendering most of their land but keeping rights that they believed include the Oldman River. In that year, the Alberta government declared its intention to dam the Oldman River, claiming that the project would create about 500 temporary construction jobs, increase the province's hydroelectric power potential, guarantee that Alberta could meets its water commitments to neighbouring Saskatchewan, and create irrigation that would benefit farms.[2] The Peigan were not considered in the plan, even though the dam would be a mere four kilometres upstream from their reserve and the flooding created by the project would mean the loss of sacred tribal burial grounds, 5000-year-old tipi rings, vision quest sites, and more than 200 archaeological sites.

The first battle between the provincial government and the Peigan over the river took place in 1978. That struggle involved a 23-day blockade initiated by Chief **Nelson Small Legs** over a diversion weir and canal, on what the Peigan believed to be their land. Following a series of confrontations, Alberta agreed in 1981 to pay the band a cash settlement of $4 million over an extended period of time, and an annual user fee of $300,000 for the water rights. The band, in return, would allow the province to use about 300,000 acres of land. Think of that as a payment of $13.33 per acre, plus a $1-a-year user fee, and it looks like a good deal for the government—especially as government monies promised sometimes get paid in services and in goods, the value of which can be inflated and sometimes don't get delivered.

There were environmental concerns that needed to be addressed, such as the impact of the dam on the local mule deer population (estimated at 500), the trout fishery, and six rare and threatened species of animals, not to mention the possibilities of pollution that had resulted from other such projects (see Chapter 16 on James Bay). These concerns were articulated by the Friends of the Oldman River (FOR), a protest group that included environmentalists, ranchers, and First Nations people.

The Environmental Council of Alberta, a semi-autonomous government body, heard over 250 briefs and technical submissions pertaining to the project. In 1979, it issued a report condemning the project. The provincial government ignored the report, refused to conduct an environmental assessment, and in 1984 announced its decision to go ahead with construction. In 1988, work was underway, the cost of which was estimated to be over $350 million.

Opponents of the project continued to mount protests. The largest of these occurred in June 1989, when FOR held a very successful "This Oldman" benefit concert on the banks of the river, attracting a crowd of between 15,000 and 18,000. Journalist David Suzuki and Peigan Elders addressed the crowd.

Treaty rights were also involved. The Peigan band insisted that Treaty #7, validated in the Constitution Act of 1982, granted them Aboriginal rights to the water. In 1989, the band sued the provincial government for illegally taking away those rights. There was legal precedent for them to do so, although only in court cases tried and won by American First Nations. No Canadian First Nation had ever filed such a case.

In 1990, the Lonefighter tradition re-emerged. **Milton Born With a Tooth** was the person who decided to resurrect the Lonefighter society, inspired, no doubt, by the Mohawk Warriors who had launched their own battle for land at Oka. There would be about 30 to 40 Lonefighters involved in the protest, ranging in age from 20 to about 45. Prominent among these would be **Devalon Small Legs**, the spiritual leader, and **Glenn North Peigan**, who frequently acted as spokesperson.

On August 2, with the dam mostly completed, the Lonefighters Society took action. Armed with a bulldozer and allegedly financed with $5000 by FOR, the Lonefighters started diverting the river in an attempt to sabotage the project. The plan was to cut a diversion ditch on Peigan reserve land, reconnecting the river to its natural creek bed, which had been blocked in the early 1920s. This would divert water away from the waterworks system managed by the provincial government, rendering the highly sophisticated and expensive dam useless.

The provincial government responded by obtaining a court injunction the next day, declaring the diversion illegal. Born With a Tooth countered that it was not illegal, because the work did not affect the weir and canal of the 1981 deal. He believed that the RCMP were not bothering them because they were aware that no laws were being broken. His view was the government was breaking the law by not conducting a proper environmental assessment study.

The 2300 Peigan of the local reserve were split concerning the tactics of opposition. **Chief Leonard Bastien** told reporters that the Lonefighters Society did not have the backing of the chief and council, that what they were doing was violating the 1981 agreement with respect to the supplying of water to 900 farm families in the Lethbridge Northern Irrigation District. The chief said that he and the council intended to meet with federal and provincial negotiators to try to bring about a peaceful resolution to the situation. Nonetheless, Bastien made it very clear that he understood the reasons for the protest. "Personally, I am against the Oldman River Dam because of the cultural genocide on our people," he told reporter Jackie Red Crow from *Windspeaker* (August 17, 1990).

The crisis at the Oldman River climaxed in violence on September 7 and 8, 1990. There are two versions of what happened, each represented in Native and in non-Native press, each with their own "we" and "they." An article in *Windspeaker* reported that a Lonefighter runner spotted what he claimed were 16 RCMP cruisers and vans, along with Lethbridge Northern Irrigation District officials. They had with them heavy equipment and were going toward the weir. The runner sounded the alarm to the rest of the Lonefighters' camp. The Lonefighters then assumed predetermined defensive positions and built bunkers. The RCMP added to the tension by flying their helicopters over the camp.

As the RCMP began to close the distance between the two groups, the Lonefighters began to yell at them, warning them off Peigan land. After some time, a number of the Lonefighters began to throw rocks at the advancing police. Then, Milton Born With a Tooth fired at least two warning shots.

Kenneth Whyte, writing for the conservative *Alberta Report* (September 17, 1990), gave a differing account, predictable in how it painted the picture:

> By last Friday, the RCMP were comfortable enough with the situation to accompany a small army of provincial environmental workers and several pieces of heavy equipment to the reserve to repair damage done by Indian bulldozers. They were greeted with gunfire . . . As RCMP and environment workers moved in . . . two or three shots were fired at them from across the river, one just missing a policeman . . . Milton Born With a Tooth, who was until very recently serving time for criminal negligent homicide, admitted in front of television cameras to sending the bullets. Soon after, some 40 riot-equipped police officers arrived on the Lonefighters' encampment in more than a dozen vehicles . . . A standoff was underway. (Whyte 1990)

Following the initial outburst of gunfire, the Lonefighters claimed a number of small victories. The RCMP removed the heavy equipment. They also complied with two Lonefighter demands. Some of the Lonefighters felt that Ray Gauthier, an officer from the Pinscher Creek detachment, was unduly biased against them. When they asked that he be taken away from the front lines, this was done. They also asked that the helicopter not fly over them. The RCMP again complied.

At the same time, the Peigan closed ranks. While initially, according to Chief Bastien, about 76 percent of his community was opposed to the diversion, the majority swung around to the Lonefighters' position. The band council passed a resolution that day, stating that the RCMP was trespassing. The resolution was read to the officers by Chief Bastien. Three days later, chief and council voted 9–1 to pass another resolution supporting the diversion. The Lonefighters said they were proud of the band and council, knowing that the council had been offered a great deal of money to decide otherwise.

All day during September 7, the RCMP sealed off the area and dug in for a siege, setting up a roadblock and constructing an observation tower. The Lonefighters heard that the Mounties were moving a tactical squad, riot police, and an ambulance into position. Police squad leaders were seen poring over a map, and a helicopter was again flying overhead. It didn't look as if they were interested in a peaceful resolution of the matter.

There was a lighter side to the conflict as well. Traditional Prairie Native practice was to "count coup" (coup is pronounced "coo") on enemies by sneaking into their camp unarmed and touching them with a "coup stick." During the night, one Lonefighter touched the sleeve of an officer. Some of the Lonefighters praised some of the RCMP, whom they saw as unwitting federal tools of a provincial government. Raymond Crow Shoe, who had been involved in a shoving match with some officers, had good words to say for RCMP. Superintendent Owen Maguire ordered his men to back away. Lonefighter spokesman Glenn North Peigan would say in front of a group of officers that there were many good police.

However, the situation worsened on September 8. Overnight, the RCMP tightened their position around the Lonefighters' camp. A warrant was issued for Born With a Tooth, but the Lonefighters refused to surrender their leader. Harsh words were exchanged when Glenn North Peigan encountered officer Ray Gauthier, who had supposedly been withdrawn from the action the day before.

THE TRIALS OF MILTON BORN WITH A TOOTH

After a tense 33-hour standoff, Milton Born With a Tooth was arrested. He was denied bail on the basis of the "public interest" and spent over three months in jail, some of it in solitary confinement. The Alberta government attempted to charge him with civil contempt for violating their August 29 court injunction preventing attempts at diverting the Oldman River. Judge Roy Dewell threw out the application, saying that it lacked detail and was deficient. Born With a Tooth was released on bail on December 18, only to have weapons charges laid against him. He was ordered to return to his home on the Peigan reserve.

He was found guilty on seven charges ranging from pointing a firearm to obstructing police officers and was sentenced to 18 months in jail. But there was evidence that racism affected this decision. When the verdict was appealed, the Alberta Court of Appeal quashed the seven convictions and ordered a new trial. In the opinion of that court, the presiding judge in the original case, Justice Laurie MacLean, had cut too short the cross-examination designed to raise doubt about police intentions and had unjustly deemed much of Peigan culture and traditions irrelevant to the case.

Justice MacLean was eventually reproached by the Canadian Judicial Council in 1993. The council's judicial conduct committee concluded that the record of the case was "filled with examples of how a judge should not conduct himself during the course of a high profile trial involving sensitive and cultural issues." The matter had been brought to the attention of the council by the Canadian Alliance in Solidarity with Native People, which accused the judge of having "displayed an insensitivity to cultural and religious differences" during the trial (*Western Report* 1995). The alliance claimed that Justice MacLean had said that "Native spirituality is as irrelevant as Satanism" (*Western Report* 1995) and that he used the word "fantasy" in reference to Native spiritual beliefs.

The new trial had difficulties from the beginning that also appeared to have a racial taint to them. The defence tried unsuccessfully to have the trial moved out of Fort McLeod, alleging that there was significant prejudice against First Nations' people there and that the community had vested interests in the dam. Chief Justice Kenneth Moore of Alberta's Court of Queen's Bench had instructed that half the jurors at the retrial be Native. However, the trial judge, Willis O'Leary, dismissed that order, claiming that it was incompatible with Canadian judicial practice and that no provision exists for composing juries based on race. He did, however, let Born With a Tooth take a traditional Blackfoot oath, involving the burning of sweetgrass and the touching of a sacred pipe, allowing that it was just like taking a biblical oath.

On March 14, 1994, after deliberating for four hours, the jury found him guilty of seven weapons charges. When the judge polled the jurors to see whether they had concurred, a Native woman broke down, sobbing. The judge ordered jury members back to chambers. They returned an hour-and-a-half later with the woman accepting the verdict. The defence attorney, Karen Gainer, suggested that the woman might have been pressured into compliance.

Before the sentence was imposed, Born With a Tooth addressed the government with the following statement:

> Why do I have to go to jail when Ralph Klein is the real criminal? Who administers the policies like the ones that govern the Oldman River dam? The government of Alberta still has a one-sided agenda and that's not just me saying that, that's society. I wasn't in it to win or lose. I've taken the responsibility and I have to take what comes with it ... I've been used as a scapegoat. Who are they going to use after I've gone? (Born With a Tooth 1994)

He also suggested that the police were responsible for much of what happened, saying "They should have sent a couple [of] RCMP officers down to the camp that day; instead they sent an army" (Born With a Tooth 1994). He received a 16-month sentence.

REPERCUSSIONS

Today, the Oldman dam is operational. However, some victories have been won. In December 1991, the Supreme Court of Canada made a ruling that could affect similar projects in the future. In response to a series of lawsuits submitted by the Friends of the Oldman River, the court concluded that the federal government had the constitutional power to review the environmental repercussions of any provincial project affecting territory such as reserves over which the federal government has regulatory powers. The Oldman River Dam affected federal jurisdiction over inland fisheries, Native lands, and navigable waters, and thus was an issue for Ottawa. The ruling also stated that all reviews of such matters should consider the physical, economic, and social environment.

The decision was received with mixed emotions by the Native community. It was hailed for its broad definition of the environment, though it was criticized by Born With a Tooth. Nor did it support Ottawa's fiduciary responsibility to First Nations people for environmental damage, according to Doris Ronnenberg, head of the Alberta branch of the Native Council of Canada. Nonetheless, she felt that the decision might prove useful in future. In the five years leading up to the ruling, Alberta spent $1 million fending off legal challenges from First Nations, environmentalists, and economists who questioned the wisdom of constructing the dam. It would not be so easy in the future with similar issues.

In September 2002, the Piikani Nation (Peigan) signed a settlement involving $64.3 million, about 10 percent of which was paid out the following year. The settlement also stated that they also are to have a role in environmental impact and safety related to the dam.

Native Individuals 21-1

James Bad Eagle: A Peigan Elder, descendant of the Lonefighters.

Milton Born With a Tooth: Peigan leader of the Lonefighters in their confrontation with the RCMP in opposition to the dam being built on the Oldman River.

Nelson Small Legs: Peigan chief who led a 23-day blockade in 1978.

Timeline 21-1

1700s: Origin of the Lonefighters Society with the coming of the horse.

1976: Alberta government declares that it will build a dam on the Oldman River.

1978: Peigan initiate a 23-day blockade over a diversion weir and dam.

1981: Agreement is signed between the Peigan and the Alberta government.

1988: Work begins on the dam on the Oldman River.

1989: June: Friends of the Oldman River hold a rally to oppose the dam. The Peigan sue the Alberta government for taking away rights to the water guaranteed in Treaty #7.

1990:

August 2: Lonefighters Society diverts the river with a bulldozer.

September 7–8: Confrontation between the Lonefighters and the RCMP.

1994: Milton Born With a Tooth found guilty of weapons charges.

KEY TERMS

Na'pi (Peigan)
Ni'taiitsskaaiks (Blackfoot)

Suyitapis (Peigan)

ENDNOTES

1. This is cognate with the -nabe- of Ojibwe and the -ape of Delaware. It is found in words depicting the male of a species, such as in the term (in Blackfoot) naapim ("male animal") and naapissko ("male gopher") (Frantz and Russell 1995:132).

2. Estimates vary from 150 to an optimistic 300 as to how many farmers would allegedly benefit from the irrigation produced by the dam.

CONTENT QUESTIONS

1. What is the significance of the river's name, "Oldman"?
2. What is the Lonefighters Society?
3. What was the result of the first conflict in 1978?
4. What action did the Lonefighters Society take in 1990?
5. What were the end results of the confrontation?

WEBLINKS

www.nisto.com/cree/Lubicon/1991/19910404b.html
This site provides a copy of a 1991 Globe and Mail article by Tony Hall, who teaches at the University of Lethbridge.

www.sisis.nativeweb.org/sov/milton.html
This 1995 statement by Milton Born With a Tooth connects events at the Oldman dam with the situations at Oka, Mount Currie, Ipperwash, and Gustafsen Lake.

chapter twenty-two

Native Policing

THE RCMP

The Image of the Mountie and the Indian in Canadian Culture

One of the few relatively distinct images of Western Canada's past is that of the "Mountie and the Indian." It is an image flattering to the Mountie but not complimentary to the Indian. As Daniel Francis describes the image in the chapter entitled "Red Coats and Redskins" in his excellent work *The Imaginary Indian: The Images of the Indian in Canadian Culture* (Francis 1992), there is the image of the Mountie being the saviour of the drunken Indian victimized by the unscrupulous American whisky trader at places such as Fort Whoop-Up, near present-day Calgary. While there is some truth to the fact that the North West Mounted Police (NWMP), formed in 1873, did act bravely in taking on the often well-armed traders, the image of the drunken and helpless Indian is an exaggeration and contributes to a negative stereotype.

Also negative is the image of **the confrontation**, with the Mountie facing down the "wild savage." It is part of the Mountie "always gets his man" mystique of the NWMP and later their descendant group, the Royal Canadian Mounted Police (RCMP). Again, it contributes only to negative stereotyping of Aboriginals. Further, it can be an exaggeration, even outright fiction. Such is the case with one story about Piapot.

Piapot (c. 1816–1908) was a Plains Cree leader who rose to prominence in the last half of the nineteenth century. In 1874, he signed Treaty #4. In that treaty, the leaders were promised they could choose their reserve lands. In 1879, he was one of a group of leaders who requested reserves side by side near the American border, which would allow them to continue to hunt the remaining buffalo in southern Saskatchewan. The federal Indian commissioner didn't want them there for three reasons: because the people would be harder to control, because they might cross the paper border into the United States, and because the railroad was planned through that area. Rather than negotiate with Piapot and the others, he reneged on the treaty promise of choice of reserve and declared that Piapot and his people had to move north, near Regina. He enforced his policy by withholding the rations of food that the people needed in the transition time between buffalo hunting and learning another way to provide food. Piapot resisted, in part because some of his people had died from the diet of fatty, salty bacon that could not replace the more nutritious buffalo meat, and in part because he knew that what he was being forced to do was not in the agreement. Eventually he was forced to give in, but not by military might or Mountie bravery. Because he believed in keeping his word, he did not join the Riel Rebellion of 1885.

Piapot's leadership, honesty, and loyalty were not well recorded in the history books produced in most of the next century. Instead, a fictitious story was composed by journalist William Fraser, first printed in 1899, and reproduced in well-read histories of the RCMP. It became part of the "Mountie mystique." Fraser's story was about a confrontation between a brave Mountie and a Native leader, the fictional stuff of the Wild West.

In Fraser's story, Piapot and his people were camped by the Canadian Pacific Railroad (CPR) lines, refusing to leave. Two Mounties were sent to defuse the situation, one named William Wilde. Daniel Francis summarizes Fraser's version of the story:

> When Piapot refuses to move . . . Wilde pulls out his watch and tells the Indians they have fifteen minutes to clear out. As the minutes slowly pass, Indian braves try to intimidate the Mounties by bumping their horses and firing guns into the air. Finally, when the time is up, Wilde calmly gets down from his horse, walks over to Piapot's tent and kicks down the lodge pole, collapsing the tent in a heap. He proceeds to knock over another tipi, and then another, until Piapot gets the message and shamefacedly orders his braves away. (Francis 1992:66–67)

It is important to mention the image of the "Mountie and the Indian" because both the RCMP and Natives are aware of this image. It has contributed to an atmosphere of confrontation that has existed between them. Trust is hard won between the two.

The Pass System

Image alone did not create the atmosphere of mistrust between Natives and the RCMP: memories did as well. Some of the most bitter memories that Natives in the West have concerning the RCMP include the removal of children from homes to go to residential schools and, in the Sixties Scoop, the removal of a later generation of children. Another bitter memory, not yet discussed, is that of RCMP enforcement of the pass system that existed in the West.

General Frederick Middleton introduced the **pass system** in 1885 during the second Riel resistance. Under the system, Natives could not leave their reserves without first obtaining a pass permitting them to do so. The goal was to control Natives, particularly the Plains Cree and the Blackfoot, so they would not join the Métis in their fight. In 1886, books of passes were issued. In order for Natives to obtain a pass, they would have to get permission from their farming instructor. The police enforced this rule, even though in 1892 government lawyers made it known that the system was illegal. Neither the Indian Act nor any other legislation allowed the Department of Indian Affairs to institute such a system. The North-West Mounted Police (NWMP) temporarily stopped trying to enforce it, but there were howls of public protest and statements of outrage from non-Natives. During the period of non-enforcement, the restriction of food rations was the sole means of forcing people to stay on the reserves.

The NWMP then returned to applying the rule, even though they, as well as some Natives, were aware of its illegality. As Natives were not permitted at that time to become lawyers, they could not fight it in the courts. The pass system continued until the 1930s, when many of today's Elders were children.

Other memories are more recent. In 1974, about 200 Aboriginal people travelled to Ottawa from British Columbia on the "Native Peoples' Caravan," a peaceful protest against poor living conditions. An RCMP riot squad was summoned, and a clash ensued. Conflict also ensued between the RCMP and the Peigan over the Oldman Dam in 1990 (see Chapter 21) and between Mounties and the Shuswap at Gustafsen Lake in 1995.

Box 22-1 examines some terms in Blackfoot and Ojibwe which suggest the historical role of the police in the lives of these peoples.

Joining the Force

One significant part of Native demands for self-government has been the right to police themselves, a right enjoyed by many non-Native cities and towns, but not by Native bands. It was a long time coming, and it came in small steps.

The concept of policing is not new to Canada's First Nations. Whether it was through the warrior societies that policed (among other things) the buffalo hunt in the Plains, or the more subtle influence of the Elders in council, the functions of policing were well handled prior to contact with Europeans.

In 1971, the Department of Indian Affairs and Northern Development issued Circular 55, which gave band councils the authority to create "special constables" who could enforce band by-laws, a far cry from the authority of a police officer. They were not permitted to carry firearms. Very little money was available for them, so they had very low salaries, were expected to provide their own vehicles, and sometimes did not even have uniforms (York 1990:147). From the mid-1970s to 1990, through the RCMP (see below), the Ontario Provincial Police (OPP), and the Sûreté du Québec (SQ), Special Constable programs were developed, but they

Box 22-1   To Serve and Protect?

The meanings of terms for groups of people have implications for how we see those people. For example, we have fairly recently replaced the word "policeman" in English with "police officer" because the former term conveys the idea that only men can work as police officers. Terms for a police officer in Native languages communicate some interesting perceptions. The word in Blackfoot is **iyinnakiikoan**. It is derived from the

verb stem **yinnaki**, which means "to grab, seize, hold, capture something living" (Frantz and Russell 1995:266). An almost identical term is found in Ojibwe, where the word **dkonwewnini** is used (Rhodes 1985:115). It, too, stems from a verb (**dkonaad**) meaning "to grab, seize, capture something living" and means "a man who captures, grabs, seizes something living." (Rhodes 1985:115) still had limited authority, less than that of a regular officer. According to Geoffrey York, the regular officers would often use the Special Constables "merely as translators and intermediaries in their dealings with the Indian communities" (York 1990:148).

The Winnipeg Police Service has since changed. In the 2001 census, there were 52 420 people of "Aboriginal Identity" in the city (you could probably add a few thousand to that figure to be accurate), slightly less than 9 percent of the population.[1] By 2005, of the 1240 police officers in the Winnipeg Police Service, 134 (roughly 11 percent) were Aboriginal.[2] If you calculate the total for the Metropolitan Winnipeg Area, the percentage doubles to about 18 percent.

Box 22-2 tells the story of J.J. Harper's death.

Changing the Relationship with the RCMP

Following a 1973 federal task force report recommending that changes be made to on-reserve policing, the RCMP came up with the "3(b) Option," which was implemented

---

Box 22-2 The J.J. Harper Story

In 1988, between 40,000 and 50,000 Aboriginals lived in the city of Winnipeg (Frideres 1998:241). The 1140-member police force had nine Native constables at that time.

At roughly 2:30 in the morning on March 9, 1988, John Joseph Harper was walking home in downtown Winnipeg after having a few coffee-and-whiskies at a local tavern. He was 36, the father of three, a leader in the Indian Lake Tribal Council, and a well-respected man in Native circles.

Meanwhile, elsewhere, a 22-year-old Native man had stolen a car and had been apprehended. The police were still in the area.

A police officer walked toward J.J. Harper. He ignored the officer, as he had committed no crime. The constable asked him to show identification, and Harper refused. The constable asked him again and Harper just walked away. The officer grabbed him by the arm and turned him around. Harper was dead within a few minutes, shot to death by the officer's gun.

The investigation was minimal. The scene of the death was hosed down before morning light, possibly washing clean clues that could have revealed what happened. In court, the officer claimed that Harper, whom the officer felt matched the auto thief's description more closely than the suspect did, had pushed him down and tried to grab his gun. In the ensuing struggle, according to this story, the officer's finger found its way to the trigger and the gun accidentally went off. Yet the gun had not been dusted for fingerprints to corroborate the story.

Within 36 hours of Harper's death, the police chief said his officer was innocent of any wrongdoing, and the mayor of Winnipeg agreed with him.

Reframe this picture with a Native constable and with a Native unit in the Winnipeg police force. How might it have proceeded differently?

For a more comprehensive version of this story, see Cummins and Steckley (2003:78–83).

in all provinces except for Ontario (where authority over on-reserve policing was being transferred to the OPP), Quebec (where the Sûreté du Québec had authority), and New Brunswick. The 3(b) Option created the position of Special Constable, a position with limited authority but still more authority than had existed in earlier constable positions. This program was terminated in 1990, as it was found to have several flaws. In an inquiry into the deaths of five Blood, or Kainai, a former Special Constable testified that he had had to put up with a constant barrage of racist remarks and anti-Native jokes from his fellow RCMP officers (York 1990:170).

Shortly after the Solicitor General initiated its comprehensive policy to change policing services to Native communities (see the discussion of the First Nations Policing Policy in the next section), the RCMP developed its own policy: the Royal Canadian Mounted Police First Nations Community Policing Service (RCMP–FNCPS). It "incorporates the principles and objectives of the First Nations Policing Policy (FNPP), including service levels equivalent to those of non-First Nations communities; compatibility and sensitivity to First Nations culture and beliefs; flexibility to accommodate local variations in policing needs; and a framework which allows for transition to an independent First Nations-administered police service where this is desired by the community."[3] The elements of the RCMP–FNCPS correspond very closely with those of the FNPP. Prior to this, the RCMP policed Native communities pursuant to provincial policing agreements. Later, this was enhanced by the Indian Special Constable Program, which was phased out during the 1980s.

The RCMP also offers several initiatives through its Aboriginal Policing Branch. Its Aboriginal Cadet Development Program funding is provided by Human Resources Development Canada. Under this program, Natives interested in a career with the RCMP who don't meet basic entrance requirements but who are otherwise suitable candidates can upgrade their qualifications. Following a three-week assessment, candidates are sent to their home areas with a program designed to bring them up to the appropriate qualification level. They are granted two years to meet the standards, and once they have met the standards they proceed to Regina to undergo basic cadet training.

The Aboriginal Youth Training Program provides Native young people with 17 weeks of summer employment, including three weeks of training in Regina. Once stationed at a detachment near their home, they are under the supervision of a regular member of the RCMP for the remaining 14 weeks. Major funding for the program comes from the Department of Indian Affairs and Northern Development.

Changing Policy

In 1991, the First Nations Policing Policy (FNPP) was initiated through the federal solicitor general. It represented a culmination of proposals from First Nations leaders and groups and the recommendations from commissions on justice and policing in Native communities. This policy was initiated "to provide First Nations across Canada with access to police services that are professional, effective, culturally appropriate, and accountable to the communities they serve."[4] It has been administered by the Department of the Solicitor General since April 1992, and operates on a principle of partnership involving First Nations, the federal government, and the provincial governments. These three parties enter into tripartite agreements to supply police services that meet the needs of the particular Aboriginal communities. The policy applies to all Native reserves, to certain other First Nations communities on Crown land, and to Inuit communities. By the end of 1999, there were 52 such agreements across the country.

Funding for the agreements is roughly evenly split: 52 percent comes from the federal government with the remaining 48 percent coming from the provincial or territorial government. The First Nations will, wherever possible, pay the cost of maintaining their police services, particularly for enhanced services. Several criteria determine whether an agreement qualifies for funding. First, all police officers in Native–administered policing services must be Native, except where the First Nation agrees to and participates in the staffing of a non-Native person. An example of this exists in the Nishnawbe-Aski Police Service (NAPS) in Northern Ontario. In 1998, NAPS appointed as the Commander of their "B" Division a non-Native man who had come to the NAPS after serving 25 years with the RCMP in Winnipeg, Brandon, Kenora, and Yukon, areas where there was a distinct Aboriginal presence.

Second, the First Nations police service must meet the standards of its home province or territory. In Ontario, for example, all Native constables must attend the Ontario Police College in Aylmer and take the same courses as the non-Native students. The Anishinabek Police Service in that province requires that all its potential applicants, like applicants for non-Native police services, successfully complete the Constable Selection System (involving a pre-interview, interview stages, and a background reference check) and possess the newly instituted Ontario Association of Chiefs of Police Certificate of Results.

Third, Native police officers must be properly appointed as peace officers and be empowered to enforce all applicable laws. And, finally, the police service must consult with and be accountable to the community it serves through a police board commission or advisory board.

There are several models for agreements that are eligible for federal funding. These include First Nations Administered Police Services organized on a band, "tribal," regional, or provincial basis, including arrangements providing for one First Nation to contract for the policing services of another. In Ontario, police services following this model include the Nishnawbe-Aski Police Services in the northwest, which covers 46 communities, and the Anishinabek Police Service, which administers 20 communities in north, central, and southwestern Ontario. In 1996, in a very important breakthrough, the troubled community of Kanehsatake (or Oka), which had major conflict with the Sûreté du Québec (and with the Canadian army) in 1990, was able to achieve a tripartite agreement with the governments of Quebec and Canada.

Another model provides for a special contingent of First Nations officers within an existing police service. This may include Native officers employed within a provincial or municipal police service with dedicated responsibilities to serve a Native community, or a group of Native police officers employed through a contractual arrangement to provide a policing service to a First Nations community. A third model is the Developmental Policing Arrangement, which is designed to smooth the transition from one type of policing arrangement to another.

THE ANISHINABEK POLICE SERVICE: A CASE STUDY

On March 30, 1992, the Anishinabek Nation, along with several other Ontario Native regional groups, signed a five-year tripartite agreement to form its own police force.

By 1994, the Ojibwa communities of Garden River, Curve Lake, Sagamok, and Saugeen First Nations withdrew from using the Ontario Provincial Police and formed the Anishinabek Police Service. In 1996, they signed a new three-year agreement, which allowed them to include 13 more First Nations in the agreement. In 1997, two more First Nations joined. As of June 2006, 17 communities (total population of 9000) were being served by 15 detachments. The force's headquarters is located in the Garden River (near Sault Ste. Marie), which is situated in the middle of the widespread participating communities that stretch from the northwest through central to southwestern Ontario. Currently working out of the headquarters is the police chief, an administrator, one staff sergeant for the north and one for the south, a court case manager, a financial assistant, a pay and benefits clerk, a computer systems manager, and an office assistant.

Table 22-1 charts the communities involved, their on-reserve population as of 1991, and the staff that works out of each detachment. The communities of Henvey Inlet, Magnetawan, and Wahnapitae are also served by the Anishinabek Police Service.

TABLE 22-1   The Anishinabek Police Service (2000)

First Nation	On-Reserve Population	Detachment Staff
North		
Fort William	506	1 commander, 2 constables, 1 court officer/secretary
Garden River	901	1 commander, 4 constables, 1 court officer/secretary
Heron Bay	378	1 commander, 2 constables, 1 court officer/secretary
Long Lake #58	321	1 commander, 4 constables, 1 court officer/secretary
Long Lake #77	179	combined with Long Lake #58
Pic Mobert	292	1 constable
Rocky Bay	240	2 constables, 1 court officer/secretary
South		
Christian Island	554	1 commander, 2 constables, 1 court officer/secretary
Curve Lake	751	1 commander, 3 constables, 1 court officer/secretary
Dokis	183	1 constable
Kettle Point	798	1 commander, 5 constables, 1 court officer, 1 secretary
Nipissing	539	1 commander, 3 constables, 1 court officer/secretary
Sagamok	993	1 commander, 3 constables, 1 secretary/court officer
Saugeen	651	1 commander, 1 detective sergeant, 5 constables, 1 secretary, and 1 court officer
Shawanaga	89	1 commander, 1 constable, 1 secretary/court officer
Wasauksing	259	1 constable

The First Nations Chiefs of Police Association

In 1992, the First Nations Chiefs of Police Association (FNCPA) was incorporated. It set the following objectives:

1. To encourage and develop establishment of First Nations Police Services to provide adequate police services to First Nations communities and territories throughout Canada.

2. To encourage, promote, and foster adequate and meaningful training programs to meet the needs of First Nations Police Services.

3. To encourage and establish liaison among all Canadian First Nations Police Services and other First Nation governments and organizations.

4. To encourage high efficiency in First Nations law enforcement.

5. To promote and maintain a high standard of ethics, integrity, honour, and conduct in the profession of First Nations policing, taking into account traditional values and First Nations traditional law.

6. To foster and encourage policing and other programs to ensure the safety and security of residents of First Nations communities and territories. (First Nations Chiefs of Police Association 1992)

In 1997, the FNCPA entered into partnership with Human Resources Development Canada (HRDC) to study the human resource needs and challenges facing First Nations policing services. They want to develop a concrete action plan for addressing those challenges. The report, which is still being written, is to have seven separate phases. The first phase, already completed, examined the historical background of First Nations policing in Canada. The title of this first phase publication is *Setting the Context: The Policing of First Nations Communities*. In 1998, along with the Department of the Solicitor General, the FNCPA sponsored a national conference on crime prevention in aboriginal communities.

Box 22-3 tells the story of the Garden River Aboriginal police force.

Box 22-3 — **An Aboriginal Policing Success Story: The Kitigan Zibi Anishinabeg First Nation Police Force**

Kitigan Zibi ("Garden River") is the largest of the nine communities that make up the Algonquin Nation in Quebec, with a registered population of 2648. It is located about 130 kilometres north of Ottawa. The people had lived in Oka up until the mid-1800s, when they left to form a community that used to be called Maniwaki ("Mary's country") because the people were Catholic.

The community first had its own policing services in 1981, through the ill-fated Amerindian Police Service in Quebec, allowing Natives to take on the limited role of Special Constables. Four years later, they moved to greater independence
(continued)

Box 22-3   (continued)

by transferring their policing to their own force. Following the introduction of the federal First Nation Policing Policy in April 1992, the community entered a three-year tripartite agreement, allowing the Kitigan Zibi Anishinabeg Police Department (KZAPD) to become a fully functioning force, the equivalent of any in Canada. This agreement was renegotiated in March 1995.

In a survey undertaken by the First Nations Chiefs of Police Association, web-posted in 2001, the KZAPD received a very high community satisfaction rate, one of a number of reasons why the KZAPD was one of two Native-run police services chosen by them to illustrate best practices (FNCPA 2001).

There are several keys to the success of this police service, only some of which can be exported to other Native communities. One of these is the stable political environment. At the time of the study, the chief councillor had been consistently elected to his position for 23 years, and there had been few other changes in the makeup of the band council. Also important was that there had been no major clashes between the Quebec provincial government and the Kitigan Zibi Anishinabeg First Nation, something that puts it in the minority in Quebec. Largely because of this lack of conflict, the relationship that the KZAPD had had with the Sûreté du Québec (SQ) had generally been positive.

One particularly strong aspect of policing at the Kitigan Zibi Anishinabeg First Nation is the relationship between the police and the youth of the community. In 1995, the KZAPD was one of four forces and the only Native-run force to be engaged in a pilot project mentoring Native youth. Aboriginal youths from 12 to 24 were paired with police officers, riding in cruisers, observing police duties first-hand, visiting the mentors' homes, and travelling together for outings. This program helped ensure a positive relationship between the KZAPD officers and the local youth as they grew to adulthood.

Dedication to training also seems to be an important aspect of the success of the KZAPD. One of the conditions of the signing of the first tripartite agreement in 1992 was that the constables already in the force's employ had to earn the basic training equivalency diploma as evaluated by the Institut de la Police du Québec. The officers would then have powers equivalent to those of any other officer in the province.

All the officers successfully completed the training, enabling them to conduct investigations throughout the province. The chief of police went beyond the qualifications required in the agreement, taking managerial courses for senior officers, following by additional courses offered at the Police College in Ottawa.

Source: *Adapted from Cummins and Steckley 2003:123–5.*

STARLIGHT TOURS IN SASKATOON

On May 22, 1976, three Aboriginal people, two men and one eight-months-pregnant woman who had been drinking, were taken by police beyond the outskirts of Saskatoon and left there to walk back home. Almost five months later, the police officer involved was charged by the Chief of Police with "Breaches of Discipline" and was fined $200.

Fourteen years later, in a chilling echo of these events, a 17-year-old Saskatoon Aboriginal named Neil Stonechild was looking for his ex-girlfriend, Lucille Neetz, on Saturday, November 24, 1990. He separated from a friend, Jason Roy, and knocked at the door of the apartment where Neetz was visiting her sister and her White boyfriend. The boyfriend called the police, and Stonechild disappeared. Some time later, Roy was stopped by the police and asked to identify Stonechild, who was in police custody in a cruiser. Not wanting to be arrested, Roy told police that he didn't know Neil Stonechild. Then on Thursday, Stonechild's frozen body was discovered on the northern outskirts of Saskatoon. He was wearing a light jacket, jeans, and only one running shoe, and there were parallel cut lines running across his face. An investigation into his death and treatment by police followed. A later public inquiry deemed this investigation "superficial and totally inadequate." No charges were ever laid.

These stories illustrate what have come to be known as **starlight tours**, a phrase coined by a veteran police office and journalist Brian Trainor in 1997. In the summer of 1997, Trainor, wrote his regular column "Tales from the Blue Lagoon" for the weekly newspaper the *Saskatoon Sun* about one night on the beat for two "fictional" officers. In the story, the officers pick up an Aboriginal man who is drunk and take him on a starlight tour by driving him outside of the city. The column ended as follows:

> Sensing that this wasn't the way home, the drunk began to demand he be taken to the highest power in the land. A few quick turns and the car comes to an abrupt stop in front of the Queen Elizabeth II Power Station. Climbing out and opening the rear door, he yelled for the man to get out, advising him that this was the place he had asked to go to. Quickly gathering his wits, the drunk tumbled out of the car and into the thickets along the riverbank, disappearing from view. One less guest for breakfast. (Reber and Renaud 2005:1999)

But fiction is much closer to fact than the readers may have realized. Another Aboriginal, Darrell Night, lived that very story. From the night of January 27 to early morning on January 28, 2000, the 33-year-old Aboriginal man was drunk. He was an unemployed bricklayer with a criminal record, a big, sturdy man at six feet, three inches and 260 pounds. While he was walking home, he saw two officers in a police car, lunged at the vehicle, flashed an obscene gesture at them, swore, and hit their car with his hands. They arrested him for causing a disturbance, handcuffed him, and put him in the vehicle. He became very nervous when they started driving him out of the city, rather than heading for the police station. Finally, they dropped him off by the Queen Elizabeth II Power Station, by the riverbank, just south of the city.

He was wearing no warm coat, just a denim jacket, and the temperature with wind chill was –22 degrees Celsius. Fortunately, he was able to catch the attention of a night watchman at the power station and called a cab. That may have saved his life.

Night did not tell his story to anyone in legal authority for a long time. He was Cree, and the officers were White. Who would be more likely to be believed? It was when two other cases came to light that he decided to speak to a sympathetic police officer who had stopped a car in which he was a passenger.

The day after Night's ordeal, Rodney Naistus was celebrating a reunion with his brother and cousin at a local bar. He was a 25-year-old Cree man with a muscular build, newly released from prison. Not much is known about the course of events that night. It is not clear when he became separated from his relatives. His body was found later in the Holiday Park industrial area, a short distance away from the power plant where Darrell Night had experienced the close call the night before.

The second case occurred the night after Naistus's death. Lawrence Kim Wegner, a 30-year-old Native university student who had recently been kicked out of a group home, left the new apartment he shared with two others. He was stoned and was having a panic attack. Despite the cold, he went outside in a t-shirt without a jacket or shoes. He headed for the nearby home of his mother's cousin and her daughter. A few minutes after midnight, he knocked on their door announcing pizza delivery. Not recognizing him, and worried that this stranger might freeze to death, they called the police. A passer-by later saw Wegner standing beside a police car. Wegner's body wasn't discovered until February 3, 2000, in a wheat-stubble field near the power plant. When this discovery was announced on the news, Darrell Night decided to tell his story to the police.

Investigations ensued. No one was charged with the deaths of Naistus and Wegner. The two officers who took Night on his starlight tour were convicted of unlawful confinement but were cleared of charges of assault. They were also fired by the Saskatoon Police Service. On October, 31, 2001, it was announced that the two officers had asked for a sentencing circle. Shortly afterwards, in an article in the *Globe and Mail*, John Stackhouse rightly described the request as "so bizarre that it prompted laughter in the courtroom and anger on the part of natives, who felt they were being mocked" (Stackhouse 2001:F2). The request was denied. Their conviction was upheld in March of 2003; but the next year, Maurice Vellacott, a Conservative MP, created a legal defence fund to have the decision appealed.

In 2000, in part the result of the publicity from the other cases, the Neil Stonechild case became the subject of an inquiry, headed up by RCMP Officers Ken Lyons and Jack Warner. They found that

> there is compelling independent evidence through CPIC records to show that [the constables involved] . . . did have Neil Stonechild in their custody. There is compelling evidence to suggest that Neil Stonechild had been struck on the face with a set of handcuffs and that he had handcuffs on his wrist prior to his death . . . . What we have not been able to determine is what transpired between the time that [the constables involved] . . . encountered Neil Stonechild and the date his body was discovered." (Reber and Renaud 2005:252)

These suspicions were repeated in the concluding statements of a judicial inquiry in October 2004. In 2005, authors Susanne Reber and Robert Renaud published *Starlight Tour: The Last, Lonely Night of Neil Stonechild*. The evidence it contained was very damning of the police involved. However, in March of 2006, the Saskatoon City Police Association applied to the Saskatchewan Court of Appeal to quash (i.e., set aside by judicial action) findings from the inquiry that suggested that the officers involved performed their jobs improperly. In December 2008, the Supreme Court of Canada decided that no appeal could be made concerning the judicial inquiry of 2004. Still, the police officers involved never faced criminal charges in the matter (Makin 2008).

Box 22-4 lists acronyms used in this chapter and elsewhere.

Box 22-4   Acronyms and Their Meanings

AFN = Assembly of First Nations

BCTC = British Columbia Treaty Commission

FNCPA = First Nations Chiefs of Police Association

FNPP = First Nations Policing Policy

HRDC = Human Resources Development Canada

NAPS = Nishnawbe-Aski Police Service

NWMP = North West Mounted Police

OPP = Ontario Provincial Police

RCMP = Royal Canadian Mounted Police

RCMP–FNCPS = Royal Canadian Mounted Police–First Nations Community Policing Service

SQ = Sûreté du Québec

UCCM = United Chiefs and Councils of Manitoulin

Native Individuals 22-1

Piapot (c. 1816–1908): A prominent Plains Cree leader.

J.J. Harper: A Native man living in Winnipeg who was killed by a policeman in March 1988 after refusing to stop for the officer.

Neil Stonechild: A 17-year-old Aboriginal youth whose death appears to have been the result of a starlight tour.

Darrell Night: An Aboriginal man whose testimony concerning a starlight tour helped to publicly expose the practice.

Rodney Naistus: A young Cree man whose death appears to have been the result of a starlight tour.

ENDNOTES

1. See website www.winnipeg.ca/census/2001/selectedtopics/datatables/AboriginalIdentity
2. See website www.winnipeg.ca/police/AnnualReports/2001/2001annual.pdf
3. See website www.rcmp-grc-ca/ccaps/fncps_e.htm
4. See website www.psepc-sppcc.gc.ca/pol/le/fnpp-en.asp

KEY TERMS

the confrontation
dkonwewnini (Ojibwe)
iyinnakiikoan (Blackfoot)

pass system
starlight tour

CONTENT QUESTIONS

1. What distorted image of Mountie/Native interaction is illustrated in the fictional Piapot story?
2. What is the First Nations Policing Policy and when was it initiated?
3. What three criteria must be met for a tripartite agreement to receive funding?
4. What are the keys to the success of the Kitigan Zibi Anishinabeg First Nation Police Force?

WEBLINKS

www.fncpa.ca
The website of the First Nations Chiefs of Police Association provides their mission statement and information about membership and their activities.

www.psepc-sppcc.gc.ca/prg/le/ap/1index-en.asp
This is a website on Aboriginal policing for Public Safety and Emergency Preparedness Canada.

www.apscops.org
The Anishinabek Police Services official website gives the history and organization of this unit.

chapter twenty-three

The Justice System and Natives

TRADITIONAL JUSTICE

Non-Natives often believe that prior to contact with Europeans, First Nations peoples lacked any system of justice or social control. This misrepresentation seems to be based primarily on one of two stereotypes. One is that Native peoples lived in some sort of idyllic Garden of Eden, where crime or aberrant behaviour was completely unknown. The second stereotype is based on the notion that they lived in a fierce and primitive world in which there were only the laws of the jungle, without social rules. Neither stereotype is true.

There were laws, recorded in oral tradition and interpreted by the elders. While these laws differed from nation to nation, it is a fair generalization to say that across cultures, these laws tended to emphasize social harmony and the restoration of peace over punishment or retribution (although the latter did exist). We will use the description of one culture to illustrate how this could function.

Traditional Native Justice for the Huron-Wendat

Restoring the community to the way it was before the crime was committed is a key element in **restorative justice**. The following illustration of how the seventeenth-century Huron-Wendat dealt with murder in their society shows the importance of restorative justice in Native traditions. The family or village of the murderer presented gifts to the family or village of the murder victim. These gifts were expensive, at least the value of a new beaver robe (JR10:215–7; cf. JR28:49). The number of gifts varied. If the victim was a man, the usual number was 30. For a woman, it was 40. It was said that the murder of a woman required more gifts as they peopled the country (JR33:243).

Each gift had a name, which informed those in attendance of its purpose. Each was presented with a long speech, probably of further explanation of the purpose. The judicial ceremony could last an entire day. What follows are the names of the first nine, the most important gifts, the only ones whose names survive. They illustrate Huron-Wendat notions of justice.

The first gift was named **condayee onsahachoutawas** (JR10:217), meaning "this is that which he uses to withdraw the axe" (authors' translation). The axe stood symbolically for all murder weapons. This is a statement of apology and regret on the part of the murderer and the murderer's family/village. Accepting the gift was probably a statement of accepting the apology.

The second gift was similar in purpose. It was named **condayee oscotaweanon** (JR10:217), meaning "this is that which he uses to wipe off the head" (i.e., of blood).

The third gift shifts the focus from the victim's family to the country generally. Its name was **condayee onsahondechari** (JR10:217), meaning "this is that which he uses to reunite the country" (see Chapter 1 for a discussion of the meaning and significance of -**ondech**-, "country"). This speaks to the mutual goal of all participants in restoring order to the society.

The fourth gift reiterates this important goal. It was named **condayee onsahondwaronti, etotonhwentsiai**, meaning "this is that which he uses to put a stone in the split in the earth or country."

In Huron-Wendat culture, vengeance was a respected aim in warfare with outside nations, but had to be held back within the circle of their own society so that social harmony would be maintained. The next three gifts all speak to the need to reduce the possibility of vengeance. The fifth gift was named **condayee onsahannonkiai** (JR10:219), meaning "this is that which he uses to clear away, cut down the brush" (i.e., from around the paths that people walk). It was a metaphorical statement of the shared goal of keeping people from hiding in the bushes beside the paths, ready to ambush those upon whom they wanted to exact revenge.

The sixth and seventh gifts related to the heart and mind. The Huron-Wendat believed that two souls/spirits existed within each individual: **yandiyonra**, "the mind," and **eiachia**, "the heart." The former was the spirit of peace and wisdom; the latter was the spirit of strong emotions such as sadness, anger, bravery, and vengeance. When the mind was at peace, feelings of vengeance were in check. The sixth gift was an offer of tobacco to smoke. Its name was **condayee onsahoheronti** (JR10:219), meaning "this is that which he uses to fill his stone" (i.e., his pipe bowl). The seventh gift was called **condayee onsahondionroenkha** (JR10:221), meaning "this is that which he uses to restore his mind" (i.e., after it has been driven away by the strong, negative emotions of the heart).

The last two gifts are directed to the mother of the person killed and thereby to the lineage and the clan, since Huron-Wendat society was matrilineal. The eighth gift was named **condayee onsaweannoncwa d'ocweton** (JR10:221), meaning "this is that which gives a medicinal drink to the one who gave birth to him/her." The ninth gift was **condayee onsahohiendaen**, meaning "this is that upon which she can lie on as a mat."

A FOREIGN SYSTEM

The British system of justice was and still is foreign to Native peoples. Prior to contact with Europeans, Natives had no jails, judges, juries, or lawyers. According to Mohawk lawyer and law professor Patricia Monture-Angus, some of the basic premises of the legal system are foreign. In an article about legal education for Natives, she takes issue with the writer of a then (1990) standard textbook who stated that conflicts between individuals and between individuals and the community were natural and universal, the fundamental core around which the legal system is based:

> To Aboriginal people, this ideology is nothing short of ridiculous. Harmony is the centre of our relations with the universe and all other beings, be they human, animal, or plant. Not only is this the basis of Aboriginal legal relations, but it is a total and integrated philosophy around which all social relations are constructed. (Monture-Angus 1995:101)

Further, as the highly technical, formal legal language of English and French is deeply embedded in a European social context, the terms used do not translate easily into Aboriginal languages.

To illustrate, let's take the word "guilty." It is loaded with meaning that comes from European cultures. According to Bernie Francis, a Mi'kmaq who was a Native courtworker in Nova Scotia, his people often used to misunderstand the word "guilty" because there was no such word in their language. The word closest to it meant "blame." So when some people were asked whether they were guilty, they answered "yes," as they felt that the question they were being asked was whether they were being blamed for the offence.

Other Algonquian languages seem to tell a similar story. In Rhodes' excellent dictionary of the Ojibwe language (often used in the instruction of the language), if you look up "guilty," the closest word you can find is **naammendaagzid**, "be considered guilty" (Rhodes 1985:269), derived from a verb root meaning "to accuse or to blame." In Frantz and Russell's dictionary of Blackfoot, there is no entry under the English word "guilty," but there is a verb **otóí'm**, meaning "accuse/blame" (Frantz and Russell 1995:176). In John O'Meara's extensive dictionary of Delaware, under "guilty" you will only find **maashiing-wéexiin**, meaning to "have a guilty look on one's face, look guilty of something" (O'Meara 1996:482). The literal meaning is "to have a strange face." Again, there is a verb **akwíi-meew**, meaning "blame" (O'Meara 1996:403). One might conclude that in Native culture, the issue to be resolved was less that a person was "guilty" of a "crime," and more that the harmony in society was disturbed (because something had happened that upset someone, and someone else had been blamed for it).

DEVELOPMENTS SINCE 1975

Prior to 1975, "[l]ittle attention was paid in any official or programmatic way to the distinctive problems, needs, and participation of Aboriginal people in the criminal justice system" (Clairmont and Linden 1998:4). In 1975, there was a three-day federal-provincial conference held in Edmonton, entitled "The National Conference on Native Peoples and the Criminal Justice System." More than 200 delegates attended this important conference and they came up with 58 specific guidelines. These included the need to hire more Native people throughout the criminal justice system and the need to teach non-Natives already working in that system about Aboriginal customs and values. Those and similar guidelines would be repeated over and again over the next 25 years. They still need to be addressed today. But, as is so often said, it was a beginning.

1988

In 1988, there was suddenly a coalescing focus on Native justice issues. In Manitoba, the outcry following the J.J. Harper (see Chapter 22) and Helen Betty Osborne (see Box 23-1)

Box 23-1 Helen Betty Osborne: Conspiracy of Silence

On November 12, 1971, four young White men who were drinking heavily in The Pas, Manitoba, went cruising for Native girls, a common practice in the area. They saw a 19-year-old Cree woman, Helen Betty Osborne, out walking. They tried to coax her into the car, but she refused. They grabbed her, forced her into the car, and drove out of town. They tore her clothes off and at least one of the men sexually assaulted her. She was eventually killed, stabbed 56 times with a screwdriver.

The identity of the guilty parties soon became public knowledge. One of the four men, Lee Colgan, described the slaying to friends, acquaintances, people he met in bars, even a local sheriff and a civilian employee of the RCMP. At a party in 1972, another of the four men, Dwayne Johnston, then around 17, described how he killed the Cree woman, boasting about the act. Yet nothing was done about it, even though there were physical clues linking the men to the scene of the crime.

The non-Native community protected the men. A friend threatened someone who wanted to tell. A local lawyer counselled the men to remain quiet.

Fourteen years passed before anything concrete was done about the crime. In 1985, the police put an ad in the local newspaper and received a response from a woman who had heard the story in 1972. Colgan then made a deal with the prosecution. He agreed to testify if all charges against him relating to the killing were dropped. Johnston and a third man, Jim Houghton, were arrested in 1986. The fourth man was not charged with anything as he claimed to have been too drunk at the time to remember any details.

One hundred and four prospective jurors were considered. Twenty of them were Aboriginal, but they were all rejected by the lawyers. The jury let Jim Houghton go free and convicted Dwayne Johnston. He served a 10-year sentence and was released on full parole in October 1997 to considerable protest from Native peoples across Canada.

That same year, the very conservative Canadian Bar Association issued a fairly radical 119-page report, *Locking Up Natives in Canada*, based on a two-year study and written by Professor Michael Jackson. This report became well known because of its suggestion that a separate, totally Native-run justice system might be one model for the future, a statement that ran into a lot of resistance from many non-Natives in the Canadian justice system. Jackson made an important observation concerning the inability of those non-Natives to consider such an option:

> Those in criminal justice typically see Native people at the worst part of their lives . . . Police, sheriffs, judges and prison staff don't see Native communities and their leadership solving their own problems. They see the people who have failed. They rarely come into contact with the Native leaders responding to problems in positive, effective ways. From that viewpoint, the response is predictable: "How can Native people do this when they can't stand up straight?" (Comeau and Santin 1990:132)

cases brought about the Manitoba Aboriginal Justice Inquiry. From September of that year to April 1989, two provincial judges, one a 37-year-old Saulteaux named Murray Sinclair, listened carefully to over 800 witnesses tell some unusually horrific stories about the sad state of justice for Natives in Manitoba. They heard of judges who were drunk when they sentenced Natives for drinking, of other judges who refused to go to a reserve to hear cases because there were no indoor washrooms—the band had to pick up the expensive tab for people to fly south where the conditions were more suitable for the judges. They listened to tales about gun-happy police officers and about one instance in which two Native teenagers sitting in a convertible were ordered by the police to stand up against a wall to be searched. It was assumed that they had stolen the car. A witness told the inquiry: "They said there's no way two Indian kids could own a car like that, it was too expensive" (York 1990:168–69).

The inquiry heard that for some young Native people in Manitoba at the time, crime was a way of getting out of isolated communities where there was nothing to do and no future in sight. In his book, *The Dispossessed*, Geoffrey York reports the story of Stan Sinclair, a 26-year-old Métis who had been in prison for 16 years of his life. He lived in a community in northwestern Manitoba where there was no running water, few jobs, and few recreational opportunities. In Sinclair's words:

> We have nothing to look forward to when we wake up in the morning. We get frustrated and scared. We don't give a damn what happens to anybody any more because nobody gives a damn about us. The only thing we know is to cause trouble and go to jail, where you have three meals a day and a place to sleep and a T.V. to look at. (York 1990:143)

Box 23-2 tells the story of Donald Marshall, a Mi'kmaq teenager who was wrongly convicted and imprisoned for murder.

As York points out, a sports and recreational program organized by a University of Manitoba professor, Neil Winther, was a factor in the 1987 drop of 17.4 percent in the crime rate in four Native communities where the program was in place. In contrast, in 26 other Native communities in the area, the rate increased by 10.6 percent (York 1990:143–44).

Another of the many justice system problems for Natives was the fact that money was a key factor in the disproportionately high number of Aboriginals in prisons. Making bail, even if the figure set was only for a few hundred dollars, kept more Natives in prison longer. Non-payment of fines is also a cause of incarceration. In one provincial jail in Manitoba, up to 60 percent of the Native inmates in 1987 were serving jail terms because they were unable to pay fines (York 1990:145). This was true even though Manitoba at that time had a kind of "fine option" program, in which people could perform community work if they could not afford to pay a fine, something 3700 Aboriginals did in that same year in Manitoba (York 1990:144). This seems to be a continuing problem, as Frideres reports in 1998 (with no date attached to the figures) that nearly one third of Aboriginal males and two thirds of Aboriginal females were sentenced to jail because of fine defaults (Frideres 1998:188).

The judges in the inquiry also looked at options for change. They studied the various traditional or customary forms of courts run by the Pueblo peoples (the Zuni, Hopi, Keresan, and Tanoan peoples) of the American southwest; the Courts of Indian Offences (set up in 1883); and, more extensively, the tribal courts, to which communities with a population as small as 500 could have access (sometimes by renting the tribal court officials of a larger Native community).

Box 23-2 The Donald Marshall Case: Justice Denied

On May 28, 1971, a 17-year-old Mi'kmaq named Donald Marshall Jr., along with a friend of his, Sandy Seale, were walking through a park in Sydney, Nova Scotia. They spotted two White men in the park and decided to ask them for some money. This led to a scuffle in which Seale was stabbed to death by one of the men, Roy Ebsary, who was carrying a large knife. There were no witnesses to the murder other than those who had been directly involved.

Marshall quickly became the prime suspect. Three teenagers who had been in the area but had not witnessed the stabbing testified to police that they saw very little. Gradually, they were coerced by the police into implicating Marshall. One of them, then 14 years old, eventually testified that he had been threatened with a jail sentence if he did not tell the story the Sydney police wanted to hear. In the trial that followed that November, the prosecutor, violating the ethics but not the letter of the law of his profession, refused to let the defence see the original versions of the teenagers' testimony. Marshall was convicted of murder by a jury of 12 White men. The judge sentenced him to life.

Ten days later, Jimmy MacNeill, who had been Ebsary's companion on the night of the stabbing, went to the Sydney police to tell them that Ebsary had committed the act. His description of the killing matched the one that Marshall had given during the trial. The police questioned Ebsary but accepted his protestations of innocence as truth.

Eleven years later, another man came forward to say that when he had lived in Ebsary's house, he had heard the man brag of killing someone in 1971. He knew Marshall, so he visited him in prison. They contacted Marshall's lawyer, and the RCMP reopened the case. They spoke with the three key witnesses, who then admitted that they had lied.

The case went to the Nova Scotia Court of Appeal in the spring of 1982. While the Crown prosecutor acknowledged that Marshall should be acquitted, he also asked the five judges involved to exonerate the criminal justice system of any blame on the grounds that its reputation must be upheld, that "[i]t seems reasonable to assume that the public will suspect that there is something wrong with the system if a man can be convicted of a murder he did not commit" (York 1990:161–62). The judges accepted this position and blamed Marshall more than the system for the lack of justice he received. They felt that he had initiated the series of actions that had led to his conviction and that he had been "evasive" in his answers during the trial.

Fortunately, the matter did not end there. A two-year study followed, revealing anti-Mi'kmaq prejudice deeply embedded in every aspect of the justice system. In the words of the three Nova Scotia judges who released their seven-volume report on January 26, 1990, "The criminal justice system failed Donald Marshall Jr. at virtually every turn" (Comeau and Santin 1990:126).

For more information, see Harris 1986.

Box 23-3 — Delayed Justice: The Lynching of Louie Sam

On February 27, 1884, roughly 120 members of a lynch mob rode from the then Washington Territory into British Columbia, took a 14-year-old boy out of protective custody, and hanged him. They claimed to be seeking justice for the murder of a Washington shopkeeper, James Bell.

The boy was Louie Sam, a Stó:lo. He was being held by a deputy pending investigation of the murder. The Stó:lo met and contemplated revenge for the hanging but decided to satisfy themselves with passing on the responsibility of justice to the British Columbia provincial police. Two police officers travelled south in an undercover operation.

They discovered what appears to have been the truth of the matter: that Louie Sam had been lured down to Washington with the promise of a non-existent job as a labourer on a telegraph line; that two of his accusers benefited from and were likely involved in Bell's death—the man who recruited Louie Sam and eventually took over Bell's business, and the man who eventually married Bell's widow.

Justice was long in coming. Thanks to the work of University of Saskatchewan historian Keith Thor Carlson, consultant for the Stó:lo, the story has recently come to light. The state of Washington drafted an official apology for not seeking justice for the illegal acts of the lynch mob, have offered an annual college scholarship to an Aboriginal student, and may return a Stó:lo sacred stone, the Tixwelatsa, now (June 2006) being held by a museum.

In April 1988, the Kainai, or Blood, were finally able to pressure the Alberta government into calling for an inquiry into police relations with the province's Native people. This inquiry would examine a claim that police had improperly conducted murder investigations concerning five band members. The inquiry lasted 11 months, involved more than 15,000 pages of transcripts, and cost about $2 million.

Box 23-3 gives the account of Louie Sam's lynching and murder.

STEPS FORWARD IN THE 1990s

In response to demands from Native communities and to recommendations of the inquiries and commissions of the late 1980s and early 1990s, the federal government, through the Department of the Solicitor General and through the Department of Justice, has initiated some changes. Under the sponsorship of the solicitor general, new Native-based penitentiaries have been constructed for both men and women in western Canada, supplementing existing policies and programs of penitentiary liaison and including Native counselling and spirituality (e.g., involving **sweatlodges** and **sweetgrass** ceremonies). The penitentiaries were developed in partnership with Native people and place an emphasis on healing.

In 1992, the federal government established the Aboriginal Justice Initiative in both the Justice and Solicitor General departments, renewed in 1996 as the Aboriginal Justice Strategy. Both departments have undertaken a number of initiatives (e.g., the Aboriginal Justice Learning Network and the Aboriginal Corrections Policy Unit) directed at such goals as supporting and evaluating Native community-based justice projects, getting Natives and non-Natives working together to improve justice institutions for Aboriginals, and generally moving toward greater self-sufficiency of Native communities in the area of justice.

Sentencing Circles

It is not so much what government initiates but what the people develop that will determine how well the justice system will serve Native people. One of the most promising developments in this area comes in the form of what are variously called youth justice committees, community peacemaking circles, or, more usually, **sentencing circles**. They provide alternatives to incarceration through adaptations of traditional notions of restorative rather than punitive justice. They typically involve community members such as Elders and Native social workers, lawyers, health care workers, and those affected by the crime, including both offender and victim(s) and their families. Guilt or innocence is not at stake; they follow guilty pleas. The circles are more informal than traditional courts. People sit in a circle, with no one above or "at the head of the table." Usually, those involved sit while speaking, and, instead of titles, personal names are used.

The participation in sentencing circles has been uneven in different parts of Canada. By the end of 1994, the Yukon had undertaken about 300 circle sentences, more than the rest of all of Canada at that time, with about 100 in Saskatchewan and a handful in Manitoba, British Columbia, and Quebec. The first case to use circle sentencing in the Yukon was *R. v. Moses* (1992), in which an offender with a long history of substance abuse, violent acts, and incarceration had committed an assault with a bat on an officer, had stolen something, and had breached his probation. His crimes had been more or less spontaneous acts of desperation.

Initial reports on the effectiveness of sentencing circles have been overwhelmingly positive, but during the last few years a few challenges have been made. In the 1998 paper, "Community Sentencing and Mediation in Aboriginal Communities," Gordon Green expresses concern for the victims, especially in cases of domestic violence. He worries how the emphasis on the healing of the offender might take away from supporting the victim and about whether there might be power imbalances between the victim's and the offender's "sides." The Native ideal is for there to be no such imbalance, but this remains a challenge that needs to be faced openly and honestly.

A more serious critique comes from Roberts and LaPrairie (1997) who point out that in Yukon and Saskatchewan from 1990 to 1995, the number of incarcerations increased among Native people—an indicator that sentencing circles might not be living up to what Roberts and LaPrairie term "extravagant claims." This critique generated many rebuttals. One is that the rate of incarceration might have gone up even more if not for the sentencing circles—it is hard to tell. Second, such a radically new form of justice requires time to mature before its effectiveness can truly be measured. Third, other benefits have to be considered when measuring the effectiveness of these circles. For example, greater community participation in justice has clearly been demonstrated.

The next section discusses two specific sentencing circle programs: the Hollow Water Community Holistic Circle Healing Program and the United Chiefs and Councils of Manitoulin Justice Project.

The Hollow Water Community Holistic Circle Healing Program

Hollow Water First Nation is a Saulteaux community of about 600, situated on the east side of Lake Winnipeg, some 190 kilometres north of Winnipeg. The sentencing circle program they developed in their community, called the Community Holistic Circle Healing (CHCH), has become a model for other Native communities interested in developing sentencing circles.

The CHCH began in 1984, when a group of people in the community who were involved with providing health and social services got together to discuss how they could create a more positive future for the youth of the community. They soon started to focus on ending the sexual abuse that had a negative impact on most of the people in their community, young and old. They developed a circle composed of a team of people (mostly women) who were involved in a wide spectrum of services, such as child protection, community health, nursing, policing, and spirituality, so that their approach would be holistic, not divided into separate aspects of the self.

They came up with a 13-step program promoting a kind of healing justice for sexual abuse "victimizers." The first step is Disclosure, where the victimizer admits the offence. For the team to support the victimizer, the individual must enter a plea of guilty rather than deciding to take the case to the courts and must express a willingness to accept full responsibility for what he or she has done. In Rupert Ross's brief analysis of CHCH in 1993, he noted that virtually all those accused of sexual abuse had requested the team's support in this matter, so that trials were rare.

The second step is the Healing Contract, designed by people who were affected by the offence, people who have to make commitments themselves to the healing process of the victimizer and others affected, including themselves. This contract is meant to last for more than two years. Special attention is given to the feelings and thoughts of the victim(s), the non-offending spouse of the victimizer, and the families of both victim(s) and victimizer. The team puts together a Pre-Sentence Report, which appraises the victimizer's chances of rehabilitation and what is required to effect that rehabilitation. An action plan is put together based on this report and on the Healing Contract. Upon completion of the Healing Contract, a Cleansing Ceremony is held to "mark a new beginning for all involved" and to "honour the victimizer for completing the healing contract/process" (Ross 1993).

A 1993 position paper gives some interesting insight into how the attitudes of CHCH workers have changed concerning the need for incarceration of individuals whose cases might be considered "too serious" for the CHCH process:

> In our initial efforts to break the vicious cycle of abuse that was occurring in our community, we took the position that we needed to promote the use of incarceration in cases which were defined as "too serious." After some time, however, we came to the conclusion that this position was adding significantly to the difficulty of what was already complex casework. (Position Paper in Ross 1993)

They have come to believe that:

> Removal of the victimizer from those who must, and are best able to, hold him/her account-able, and to offer him/her support, adds complexity to already existing dynamics of denial, guilt, and shame. The healing process of all parties is therefore at best delayed, and most often actually deterred. (Position Paper in Ross 1993)

The United Chiefs and Councils of Manitoulin Justice Project

The United Chiefs and Councils of Manitoulin (UCCM) Justice Project was first funded in 1994 by the federal Department of Justice and the Ontario Ministry of the Attorney General. However, it wasn't until January 1998 that the UCCM Justice Project began diverting cases from the courts to justice circles. The objective of the Justice Project is

> to contribute to building healthier communities by promoting Anishinabe values of healing, making amends and respect for self and others, and encouraging the active participation of community members in justice and expanding aboriginal control of criminal justice. (*Tribal Council News* 1999a)

From January 1, 1998, to the end of June 1999, the project diverted the cases of 87 people belonging to seven different communities. Seventy-seven justice circles were created, involving 110 members of the community. The kinds of cases involved were typically property offences (i.e., break and enter, theft, and vandalism) and relatively minor instances of assault, but did not include more serious crimes such as murder, manslaughter, sexual or spousal abuse, or impaired driving, which, in the words of one *Tribal Council News* article, "the government is intent on prosecuting." (*Tribal Council News* 1999b)

The wording of articles written by the UCCM Justice Project for the *Tribal Council News* indicates the positive approach that the people give to their work. The people whose cases they are diverting are referred to as "clients" rather than "offenders," and their "sentences" are referred to as "plans of action."

These plans of action are tradition-based, but are also creative and new. For instance, the clients make public apologies, not only to the victims involved but also to the police and others affected by the harmful actions. Some of the apologies have even been aired on a local cable TV station.

In the words of one writer, "since healing the community is as important as healing the victim and client, the plans of action often require some form of community service" (*Tribal Council News* 1999b). This community service has involved doing such things as cleaning up the results of vandalism, painting a new detox centre, and participating in a walk held annually to raise awareness of violence against women.

Making amends is a key feature of the plans of action. This has even involved assisting victims with their traplines. In one case, a woman had assaulted another woman, a close neighbour she had known for a long time. Had she decided to fight the charge, which had been her initial intention, she probably would have been put on probation and would have been told to stay away from the victim. Instead, with the apology, the two women have managed to remain on good terms. The benefits of making amends were articulated by the client when she stated: "They don't resolve anything in court. It wouldn't have been right if we had hated each other. In court, I would never have got the chance to apologize" (*Tribal Council News* 1999c).

The healing element has included referrals to drug and alcohol addiction treatment centres or mental health facilities, but it has also entailed some traditional activities. The intent of these traditional activities is to heal the clients "by enabling them to learn more about themselves and their culture, thereby raising their self-esteem and sense of identity" (*Tribal Council News* 1999b). Examples include helping to gather traditional medicines in the bush, participating in an arduous canoe trip around Manitoulin Island (the largest island in the world in a freshwater lake), and researching a family tree. Some clients have done more than was required of them because they felt rewarded by the activity.

An easy criticism of this system of alternative Native justice would be to say that the people get off lightly. A client of the Justice Project in one *Tribal Council News* article spoke of how it was more difficult to face people he knew, rather than a judge and jury, "a bunch of strangers. Who cares what they think?" (*Tribal Council News* 1999c).

Yet the program still faces difficulties. The staff of the Justice Project want to do more, but with only two lawyers and three court workers, they have had to cut back on the number of new cases they handle. Putting together reports and proposals for additional funding is time-consuming. Still, the outlook is positive. No victimizer has had to return to the court for non-compliance with their plans of action, and 41 files have been formally closed.

ABORIGINAL WOMEN AS VICTIMS OF MALE VIOLENCE

The case of Robert William "Willie" Pickton is perhaps Canada's most spectacular case of serial killing. He was arrested in 2002 and convicted in 2007 of the second-degree murders of six women. While he was charged with 20 more murders, these charges were stayed on August 4, 2010. The reluctance with which the murders were dealt with by the Vancouver police suggests that some women are valued less and are considered more disposable than others. Many of the women were sex-trade workers who lived and plied their trades in the notorious Downtown Eastside of Vancouver. In addition to being involved in prostitution, many were engaged in substance use. And, many were Aboriginal. We need only ask if the Pickton case would take so long to solve if the victims were White, post-secondary students from Point Grey, or Forest Hill, or Westmount. The answer is almost certainly "No, it would not." Drug-addicted Aboriginal prostitutes do not demand our attention the way that middle (or upper middle) class women do. Cameron (2010:213) quotes a police officer who was painfully honest: "The problem was that there was always a feeling within the organization [the Vancouver Police Department] that 'hypes' [prostitutes who sell sex to make enough money for their drugs] and whores are disposable." The idea that the victims were disposable made the force less interested in pursuing the women's disappearances and preventing future victimization, irrespective of the fact that each of the women was somebody's daughter, wife, sister, or mother—and as deserving of police attention as anybody else.

During the Pickton trial, the mainstream media never really focused on the Aboriginal identity of many of the victims, perhaps because they did not want to further perpetuate a negative stereotype of Native women. An exception is a 2006 documentary, *Finding Dawn*, produced by Métis filmmaker and university professor Christine Welsh. The central subject of the documentary is Dawn Teresa Crey, who was killed at 43, although the film also deals with the Highway of Tears victim Ramona Wilson (see below).

Robert Pickton is not alone in being a serial killer who preyed on Aboriginal women. In *Just Another Indian: A Serial Killer and Canada's Indifference* (2001) Goulding relates the story of Canada's least known serial killer, John Martin Crawford. Goulding's book not only profiles the murderer and his killings, but it also is critical of the media's lack of reporting on this serial killer.

In 1981, in Lethbridge, Alberta, Crawford, then 19 years old, brutally sexually assaulted, beat, and killed Mary Jane Serloin, a Sarcee from the Calgary area. For this, he received a 10-year sentence but was paroled in September 1987. He went back to jail in five months for violating the conditions of his parole but was out again in March 1989.

His next victim was Shelley Napone, a 16-year-old Cree whom he killed in 1991. He had driven her to her friend's place, offered her beer, had sex with her, and then killed her. Her body was not discovered until 1994. In that same year, the body of Eva Taysup, a Saulteaux mother of four, was discovered. She had disappeared in 1992. His fourth victim was 22-year-old Calinda Waterhen. Her body was found in 1994. It is believed she was killed two years earlier.

In 1994, during the four-month period in which he was under police surveillance, Crawford raped and beat another young Aboriginal woman, who was reluctant to press charges. Finally, in 1996, he was convicted of murder for the deaths of Napone, Taysup, and Waterhen. It was not nearly as big news as the Paul Bernardo conviction of the previous year, whose victims were White girls from southern Ontario.

There are three similar deaths in which Crawford is suspected. He had been charged with raping Janet Sylvestre, another Aboriginal woman, in 1992. The charge was stayed when she failed to show up for court, but he spent a month in jail before his mother put up the $4,000 in bail. Sylvestre disappeared, but her body was found in 1994. By 2001, the police still had not found her killer. Crawford had both motive and opportunity. The two other victims were Shirley Lonethunder (see below) and Cynthia Baldhead.

Goulding is quick to spot the bias of the press and the ways in which they appear to be blaming the victim. The following is an example:

> This injustice manifests itself in biased portrayals of women such as Eva, Calinda, and Shelley. Journalists seek out juicy quotes that carry sinister, unspoken messages. "Sometimes she would bring strangers home from the bar," was one such revelation. You can almost hear the tongues clucking and the heads shaking as readers absorb such comments. Was Eva Taysup the first young woman to bring a man home from a bar? Of course not. It occurs regularly in all sectors of society. But by exposing the imperfections in their lifestyles, the media assassinate the characters of the victims, rarely finding the positive aspects that are there if only they took the time to search for them. (Goulding, 2001:213–214)

One of the three women that Crawford is suspected of killing is Shirley Lonethunder, a Cree mother of two who disappeared late in 1991. She was 25 years old at that time and planning to go to university. In March 1992, her mother, Doris Lonethunder, who had been taking care of Shirley's children, filed a missing person report with the Saskatoon Police Service. The Amnesty International website that tells her story wrote the following about the police reaction to her disappearance:

> The Saskatoon Police Service's missing persons policy states that investigators have a responsibility to "liaise with complainants" and should request media assistance, if necessary, to

help locate a missing person. According to Doris Lonethunder, the police investigator was in regular contact with her at first, phoning every week for approximately a month, and then phoning every two weeks. However, the police did not make any public appeals for assistance on the case and the family members felt the police were not very supportive. After about three months, the investigator stopped phoning. Approximately six months after having filed a Missing Person report, Shirley Lonethunder's brother contacted the Saskatoon Police to enquire about any progress in the case. He says that he was told there was no record of the Missing Person report. (www.amnesty.ca/campaigns/sisters_shirley-lonethunder.php)

The infamous Highway of Tears is another terrible example of the failure of the authorities to address a lengthy history of the disappearance of women, many of them Native. The 720-kilometre-long stretch of Highway 16 in northern British Columbia, linking Prince George and Prince Rupert, has been deemed the "Highway of Tears" because a number of young women, most of them Aboriginal, have been murdered or disappeared along its route.

On September 25, 2012, an announcement was made by officials from Project E-PANA (an RCMP initiative named after an Inuit goddess in charge of the recently dead), a task force that began in the fall of 2005. The goal of this task force is "to determine if a serial killer, or killers, is responsible for murdering young women traveling along major highways in BC (www.highwayoftears.ca). They investigated 18 murders or disappearances, not just on Highway 16, but on other highways in the area as well. A DNA analysis related to a 1974 murder case was undertaken in 2007, with no matches with known suspects. However, in 2012, with the improvement of DNA techniques, the analysis qualified to be sent to INTERPOL. A match was found with a US citizen, Bobby Jack Fowler, who died in 2006 after serving 10 years for a violent attack on a woman in Oregon. He had a history of casual employment in British Columbia. He is still a person of interest with respect to some of the killings of women in the area, but the murders of most of the Aboriginal women remain unsolved.

So notorious is the Highway of Tears that the July 2012 edition of the multi-award-winning outdoors and adventure magazine *Outside* (an American publication) included an article, appropriately enough titled "Highway of Tears," thereby bringing the tragedy to the world's attention (and, perhaps, focussing international attention on Canada's shame in failing to address it).

We should not assume that Aboriginal women are solely the victims of non-Aboriginal men. They are abused by Aboriginal men as well and in horrific numbers. Aboriginal male spousal abuse of Aboriginal girls and women has reached what sociologists James Frideres and others refer to as "epidemic proportions." He sums this up succinctly in the following quotation:

> Aboriginal women [in 2004] report spousal assault at a rate (21 percent) that is three times higher than that for non-Aboriginal women. Research shows that women are, on average, abused 35 times before they leave the relationship and seek help. Aboriginal women only report the most severe and potentially life-threatening forms of violence . . . and this rate (54 percent) has been consistent over the past decade; yet for non-Aboriginal women, the rate of severe violence has decreased to nearly 35 percent. Overall homicide rates for Aboriginal women are about eight times the rate for non-Aboriginal women. (Frideres, 2012:152)

In *First Nations, Métis and Inuit Women*, published in 2011, we have the following statistics:

Self-reported Spousal Violence for Aboriginal and Non-Aboriginal Populations, aged 15 and over (Canada, 2009)

	Aboriginal Women	Non-Aboriginal Women
Percentage who reported being physically or sexually victimized by a spouse in the previous 5 years	15%	6%
Of those who had been physically or sexually victimized by a spouse in the previous 5 years, percentage who reported that they:		
had been sexually assaulted, beaten, choked, or threatened with a knife	48%	32%
sustained an injury	58%	41%
feared for their lives	52%	31%

(O'Donnell and Wallace, 2011:41)

Aboriginal women are sometimes vulnerable to discretionary abuse by the policing system. For example, on reserves, the dispute might not be just between the man and the woman but between their families as well. If a woman accuses a man of spousal abuse, she might have to contend with his family, which may include the band chief, band councillors, social workers, or even the police.

We must also consider alternative sentencing practices in Native communities. These typically involve diversion from prison. Generally, this may be viewed in a positive light. However, a problem arises when the "diverted" potential prisoner has committed spousal abuse and is returned to his reserve community. In such a situation, reserve-based alternatives to prison can easily put the woman in a dangerous position.

The Aboriginal women who speak out in McGillvray and Comaskey's *Black Eyes All of the Time: Intimate Violence, Aboriginal Women, and the Justice System* (1999), which is based on the authors' analysis of interviews with 26 women in Winnipeg in the summer of 1995, argue that the women can only feel safe if those who abused them serve jail time. Otherwise, they might have to leave the reserve and be exposed to the dangers of urban Aboriginal life.

Amidst these horror stories of abused, killed, and vanished Aboriginal women there are some glimmers of hope. In 2004, Amnesty International in Canada published *Stolen Sisters: A Human Rights Response to Discrimination and Violence Amongst Indigenous Women in Canada*. Hopefully, it has drawn attention to the plight women face. Nonetheless, the problem has yet to go away even while more efforts are being made to eradicate abuse.

In recognition of the fact that Aboriginal women are often abused, murdered, and disappear, in 2005 the Sisters in Spirit Initiative, a joint effort of the federal government and the Native Women's Association of Canada (a coordinated network of smaller Native Women's Associations), began. There was a felt need to draw attention to the problem and to initiate action to lessen it. Five years' funding produced, among other gains, in 2010, the important publication, *What Their Stories Tell Us: Research Findings from the Sisters in Spirit Initiative.* Among their research findings were the following:

(1) Between 2000 and 2008, there were 153 cases of murdered Aboriginal women in Canada, representing 10 percent of homicides of women, an overrepresentation.

(2) Some 115 Aboriginal women were still missing.

(3) Most of the murdered and missing were young, under 31 years of age (2010:10).

On December 13, 2011, the United Nations Committee on the Elimination of Discrimination Against Women reported that, after what it felt was inadequate response to earlier questions concerning this situation, it had decided to conduct an inquiry into the murders and disappearances of Aboriginal women and girls across Canada. The committee comprises 23 independent experts from around the world and is the UN's main authority on women's human rights.

ABORIGINAL GANGS

The last three decades or so have seen a disturbing new phenomenon in crime in Canada, particularly on the Prairies. Aboriginal gangs are now one of the major forms of organized crime. The three largest are the Indian Posse, the Manitoba Warriors, and the Native Syndicate. While the numbers of gang members are unknown because of the inherent fluidity of the gangs, it is believed that the Indian Posse—with members from Ontario to British Columbia (but primarily in the Prairies)—had no fewer than 1,000 and possibly as many as 3,000 members by the end of the 1990s. The Native Syndicate (primarily in Saskatchewan) and the Manitoba Warriors (in all three Prairie provinces) had several hundred members each (Friesen, 2011).

Joe Friesen of the *Globe & Mail* wrote an extensive article about the Indian Posse, the largest and most powerful of the Native gangs. The article was based on more than two dozen interviews with gang members, relatives, lawyers, and police, as well as court transcripts and Daniel Wolfe's letters from prison. Most significant, however, is that he also interviewed Richard Wolfe, Daniel's older brother (by a year), who had recently been released from prison. Much of what follows below comes from Friesen's article (2011).

Native gangs began in 1988 in a Winnipeg basement with two brothers, Daniel and Richard Wolfe, and five others, all Native from impoverished backgrounds. The Wolfe brothers came from a family and background that, tragically, was conducive to crime. They were sons of residential school survivors who had their own demons including substance abuse and violence. Taken away at age five, their mother had suffered both physical and sexual abuse while in school. Susan Creeley, the boys' mother, was only 18 years old when she had Daniel, her second son. She claims she consumed a full bottle of whisky before checking into a Regina hospital before giving birth to her second child. He was three months premature. She would later say that her son almost certainly suffered from fetal alcohol spectrum disorder, which impairs judgment and impulse control. And always there was violence: An indelible memory was the sight of their mother in a hospital bed, beaten black and blue by their father, who vanished after the assault. Years later, Richard Daniel Wolfe—whose names were passed on to his sons—wound up in prison for stabbing a man to death after drinking hairspray all day. It was his 55th conviction.

The boys had virtually no supervision growing up and little formal education. Daniel barely had grade six, but he had leadership qualities. Inseparable, the boys roamed the streets all night and sometimes ended up in foster homes, only to run away. At the age of ten and eleven, the brothers stole a van and drove from Winnipeg to Regina with Richard at the wheel and younger brother Daniel on the floor, controlling the gas pedal. It took the police a week to find them. By the time he was 12 years old, Richard had been arrested 20 times. Daniel first went to jail at the age of 13 and averaged almost a sentence a year until he was 19 years old. Clearly jail did not deter him from crime, but the force of his character did draw more people whom he met in jail into the Indian Posse.

When they were 12 and 13 years old the Wolfe brothers founded the Indian Posse. The name is intriguing and not without meaning; it also suggests the pervasiveness of popular culture. They found "posse" in a hip-hop magazine. "Indian," as opposed to "Native" or any other term, was deliberately chosen. They reclaimed the word in much the same way that Blacks have taken back the (infamous and notorious) "n-word." As Richard Wolfe explained it to Friesen:

> It was about us Indians sticking together at the time. Because we were looked down. We were living under the same roofs, had the same struggles: no food in the fridge. Empty beer bottles in the house. People coming over for hours at a time at night and you don't even know who the hell they are.

Richard Wolfe acquired his first handgun when he was 13 years old. Frighteningly, he carried it to school, tucked into the back of his pants. Shortly thereafter, he had an AK-47—an assault weapon capable of firing 40 rounds a minute in semi-automatic form or 100 rounds a minute in fully automatic—that he kept in a heating vent at home.

The Indian Posse began with stealing car stereos, which they could sell for $100, but quickly graduated to break-ins and armed robbery, hitting bingo halls, convenience stores, service stations, and even banks. According to the Winnipeg police, they were very violent, even by street gang standards. Within three years—in 1991, when Richard was 15 and Daniel a mere 14 years old—they moved into the lucrative drug market. As Daniel explained it to Friesen, money from the sale of stolen car stereos was adequate for buying trendy items such as name-brand running shoes, but it wouldn't pay the rent. Drug money allowed them to move into a rented house away from their mother, who admits today that she was lost in a fog of alcohol and drugs. Meanwhile, her sons very quickly, and while still teenagers, were earning—and spending—hundreds of thousands of dollars.

The Indian Posse was clearly, and admittedly, influenced by Black gangs of the period but they also learned from outlaw motorcycle clubs. As the Indian Posse started to prosper, rivals increased. Taking a cue from an outlaw bike gang that employed the same intimidation strategy, they picked up a rival, drove him far out of town and into the woods, gave him a shovel, and told him to dig his own grave. As Richard Wolfe told Friesen, "That really works." They spared the man's life, but his gang became part of the Posse. Daniel likewise found drive-by shootings too "soft," so they began "walk-by shootings," a clear statement that the Indian Posse was not afraid of potential witnesses to their crimes.

After taking over Winnipeg, it was not long before the Indian Posse went back to the reserves, where there was a ready market for drugs, even though they sold for three to five times more than they sold for in the city. For the gangs, this was a profitable and steady market. Moreover, the reserves were fertile grounds for recruiting new gang members seeking a way out of northern poverty. A Royal Canadian Mounted Police (RCMP) report, *First Nations and Organized Crime,* examined the reasons why people joined gangs. Protection and support were the main reasons. Stability and the structure of gangs were other reasons, in other words, an alternative to the family dysfunction that many young people experience (http://www.rcmp-grc.gc.ca/pubs/abo-aut/firstnat-premnat-eng.htm). To this we might add that, for many young people seduced by popular media, there very well might be a "glamour" attached to the gang lifestyle with its attendant apparent wealth, power, and status.

Recruitment to the gangs is not difficult, as we might expect, but getting the right people is. It is neither coercive nor obligatory but follows what the RCMP call a "fraternity" type of recruitment. Young men perceived to have the desired attributes are invited to a gang party where they are exposed to illicit substances, money, women, and the alleged benefits and attractions of the gang (presumably, the same money, women, and illicit substances that they are witness to at the party). Predictably, some may seek to join right away but potential members are not allowed to engage in any criminal activities for a while, possibly to assess their mettle. Later, if they are still affiliated with the gang, they are asked to perform some criminal task such as selling drugs or partaking in a violent act (http://www.rcmp-grc.gc.ca/pubs/abo-aut/firstnat-premnat-eng.htm). Richard Wolfe told Friesen that recruitment of suitable members—even for Daniel, who was a good recruiter—was a challenge. Often those seeking to join came from disastrous homes and were looking for any place to which they could belong. They were tough enough but had "baggage." As Richard Wolfe explains, it was better to get a smart kid than a tough kid because "the smart guy can be a tough guy when the time comes, but not vice versa. The smart guys usually stay out of gangs, though." And, it should be noted, kinship was insignificant relative to gang membership. The RCMP's *First Nations and Organized Crime* refers to families in which visits to the familial home by brothers had to be staggered to avoid a blood bath because they belonged to different gangs.

This rapid expansion of the Wolfe brothers' criminal empire meant that by the age of 19, Richard Wolfe was making $15,000–$30,000 a week, or approximately $1 million a year. Those who worked for him peddling drugs paid him 35% of what they made. After they muscled out Winnipeg's other pimps, they took over prostitution and increased the women's take to 40% from 25% and were able to make $3,000–$5,000 a night from 10 prostitutes. But, according to the police, unlike old, more established, traditional organized crime organizations, there is little discipline or financial planning with Native gangs. There is no drive to save or accrue assets, no Swiss bank accounts, no investments. As a Winnipeg police officer told Friesen, "You might pull them over and they'll have $10,000 or $15,000 on them, but at the end of the day that's money already spent. . . . We haven't seen anyone moving up into buying large condos or anything like that. They still live in the neighbourhoods they always lived in."

It was all but inevitable that when others saw the success that the Indian Posse had with robberies, drugs, and prostitution that other gangs would form. The federal government's *Annual Report 2004* addressed the issue of Aboriginal based organized crime (ABOC) and noted that in the Prairies, ABOC was almost exclusively composed of street gangs, whereas in Ontario and Québec, criminal activities were concentrated along the international border and involved smuggling and inter- and intra-provincial distribution of contraband (http://www.cisc.gc.ca/annual_reports/annual_report_2004/aboriginal_2004_e.html).

The influence of the Indian Posse was such that it was the most important Native gang in all three Prairie Provinces. It Alberta, Redd Alert, and the Alberta Warriors were also prevalent. All three were operating mainly out of Calgary and Edmonton. In Saskatchewan, Native Syndicate operated out of Regina while Indian Posse was the main gang in Saskatoon. The Manitoba Warriors, Native Syndicate, and Indian Posse were the main gangs in Manitoba. Violence among gangs as they competed for turf and business was unavoidable.

There were perpetual skirmishes between and among the various gangs. In 2008, Daniel Wolfe went to prison for a home invasion he committed in 2007 in Fort Qu'Appelle, Saskatchewan, his mother's home reserve but also Native Syndicate territory. After a dispute in a bar, he, along with an accomplice, smashed open the door of an elderly woman in search of the man with whom he had argued. When they left, two people were dead and three injured. He would be arrested and sent to prison, but would escape. Arrested again, he was killed in a prison brawl in 2010. Violence begets violence. His brother Richard had also been sentenced to 19 years for the attempted murder of the owner of a pizza restaurant who owed him $60,000. Feeling he was being "disrespected" and starting to lose credibility, he opened fire. Like Daniel, he attempted to murder somebody over perceived lack of respect and ended up in prison. More recently, six men were arrested in the beating death of a 16-year-old boy who was a member of a rival gang, MOB Squad. Beaten on the street September 4, he died three days later. Members of the Indian Posse, including the leader, Michael Guimond, were charged. With the exception of an 18-year-old, all the suspects were in their 20s or 30s. It was the third time Guimond was charged with gang-related murder. In 2000, he was charged with second-degree murder of an 18-year-old, but when witnesses recanted or refused to testify, he pleaded to assault causing bodily harm. In 2006, he was charged with second-degree murder and two counts of attempted murder after a shotgun was fired at a New Year's Eve party. A 20-year-old was killed and two teens injured. The charges were later stayed (Santin, 2012; Turner, 2012). And so the violence continues.

The Aboriginal gangs are not going to disappear. The RCMP's report on Aboriginal organized crime notes that children as young as 10 are being recruited. The original members of the Indian Posse now have grandchildren in the gang. Attempts to move Indian Posse gang members to correctional facilities out of province only resulted in expanding the gang nationally to British Columbia and Ontario.

There are some other important points that need stressing. The first is that there is nothing glamorous or attractive about gangs. The RCMP's *First Nations and Organized Crime*, which was based on interviews with RCMP and municipal police officers, elders, Aboriginal Justice personnel, community leaders, and community residents, all agreed that Aboriginal gang activity is both serious and potentially destructive to communities. The government's *Annual Report 2004* agreed, stating that while the gangs' capabilities for sophisticated or large-scale criminal activities are low, their propensity for violence is high, posing a threat to public safety. Their willingness to use firearms, especially handguns, is especially disturbing. Friesen probably stated it best:

> The cost of what [the Wolfe brothers] started is almost incalculable. It's a plague that stalks neighbourhoods west from Winnipeg to B.C. and north to the most remote and desolate reserves. . . . The direct, measurable impacts . . . are mostly financial: the gang's presence, or perceived presence, drives down property values, boosts insurance costs, and generally diverts resources to crime prevention.

The gang also erodes confidence in public institutions—not only in police and the courts, but in schools and the general possibility of making a living legitimately. It preys on poor people by getting them hooked on drugs or the fast money of prostitution.

And then there are the immense indirect costs, the wasted potential of so many young people who end up dead or in prison when they are capable of so much more—including, no doubt, the Wolfe brothers themselves.

Finally, we need to look at the gangs in the context of their time. Friesen acknowledges that, perhaps, there is a connection between the emergence of the gangs and Native activism and events such as Oka, Ipperwash, the shooting of J. J. Harper, Oldman Dam, and the standoff at Gustafsen Lake. It is an easy connection to make—i.e., Native youth rebelling against the State that oppresses them. However, Richard Wolfe admitted that the "vague political ideas" that might have existed took a backseat to "basic survival" and have no role today. Furthermore, as noted by a police spokesperson, the victims of the gangs are all Native: those who are killed in intergang warfare, those to whom they sell drugs, and the women who are forced into prostitution. As a police officer says, "There is nothing cultural about the Indian Posse. The only cultural thing is a gang subculture." With that being said, however, we must never forget that, at its base, the Aboriginal gangs are the result of colonialism, in particular the residential schools and their horrors.

Native Individuals 23-1

Donald Marshall Jr.: A Mi'kmaq who was falsely imprisoned for 11 years for the murder of his friend.

Helen Betty Osborne: A young Cree woman who was killed by young White men in northern Manitoba in 1971. Her murderers were not apprehended until 1986.

Murray Sinclair: A Saulteaux who was one of two provincial court judges who led the Manitoba Aboriginal Justice Inquiry of 1988–89.

KEY TERMS

naammendaagzid (Ojibwe)

sweatlodge

restorative justice

sweetgrass

sentencing circle

CONTENT QUESTIONS

1. How did the Huron-Wendat deal with murder in the seventeenth century?

2. How do the expressions relating to guilt in the four Algonquian languages differ from the English justice notion of "guilty"?

3. What reasons have proven to be a factor in the disproportionately high number of Aboriginals in prison?

4. What important observation did Professor Jackson make concerning the inability of non-Natives to consider a Native-run justice system as an option?

5. Why is it important to perform delayed acts of justice, such as the apology for Louie Sam's lynching?

6. What are sentencing circles?

WEBLINKS

www.uccm.ca/viewreport.php?sesid=&id=27
This website presents a recent report by the United Chiefs and Councils of Manitoulin on the Justice Project.

www.psepc.gc.ca/prg/cor/ac/index-en.asp
This website presents the "Aboriginal corrections" part of the Public Safety and Emergency Preparedness Canada website. Particularly useful is the section on successful projects.

http://ww2.psepc-sppcc.gc.ca/publications/abor_corrections/199703_e.pdf
This website presents the 1997 publication *The Four Circles of Hollow Water*.

www.ajic.mb.ca/volume.html
A detailed examination of the justice system's treatment is provided in the Report of the Aboriginal Justice Inquiry of Manitoba. The report contains Aboriginal concepts of justice, a discussion of over-representation of Natives in jails, and the justice system's treatment of Aboriginal women.

www.usask.ca/nativelaw/publications/jah/scircle.html
The University of Saskatchewan maintains an excellent website on sentencing circles.

chapter twenty-four

Native Governance

EARLY POLITICAL LEADERS

Native political activism is not a recent phenomenon. Throughout the nineteenth and twentieth centuries, Native political leaders have risen to the huge challenges involved with governance issues. The following are five examples.

Nahne's Trip to Meet the Queen

Nahne was born in 1824 beside the Credit River, which flows south into Lake Ontario. Her Mississauga name was **Nahnebahwequay** ("Upright Standing Woman"), but many people just called her Nahne. She married at 15 and eventually had six children. In 1845, Nahne, her family, and all of the other Mississauga in her community were forced to move from their Credit River home because their rights to the reserve there were not guaranteed. They accepted an invitation from another Ojibwa community that lived near the shores of Lake Huron. In 1857, however, Nahne and her new community were forced to auction off their new land. Nahne was determined to buy some of this land. Initially, all went well. Nahne's bids were the highest. But government bureaucrats opposed her, telling her she could not buy the land because she was an Indian. Appeals failed. What could she do?

When Canadian First Nations signed treaties, the government officials signed them in the name of the "Great White Mother," or Queen Victoria. So when her people selected Nahne to speak about the problems they were having, it seemed right for her to go to meet the Queen. This would not be easy. She had neither the money for the trip nor the contacts to get her an appointment with the Queen. That did not stop her. She went to New York to raise funds for her trip. While there, she met some influential Quakers who saw the rightness of her cause and who had friends in high places. Money and contacts became available. The date arranged was June 19, 1860. Many questions and worries must have rushed through her mind: What do you say to the Queen? How do you curtsy when you are eight months pregnant?

Nahne's thoughts are recorded in a letter she wrote:

> So you see I have seen the Queen. The Duke went before us, and he made two bows, and then I was left in the presence of the Queen; she came forward to meet me, and held out her hand for me to kiss, but I forgot to kiss it, and only shook hands with her. The Queen asked me many questions, and was very kind in her manners and very friendly to me. . . (Sutton 1860)

The Queen was favourably impressed. When Nahne returned home, she was able to buy the land for her family despite government resistance.

The Wyandot Council of Elders in 1747: The Traditional Role of Women in Aboriginal Governance

Written primary documents used as sources of historical knowledge are typically inadequate for talking about the traditional role of women in Aboriginal governance. One exception is the census of the Wyandot of the Detroit/Windsor communities in 1747, an Iroquoian matrilineal society. The person recording the census, Jesuit Father Pierre Potier, recorded not only the people living in each longhouse, but also wrote down who were "Leurs anciens et Leurs anciennes"—in other words, their council of elders (whether old or young) (Toupin 1996:227). The census referred to clan leaders and chief of the three phratries, or groupings of clans. There were 60 members of the council of elders, approximately one member for every 10 Wyandot in the area. All phratries were represented as well as almost every clan.

What is most significant about this document is that of the 60 people in the council, 29 were women. Also, the youngest males in the council (aged 28, 29, and 32) also had their mothers on the council. This suggests that women had authority in Wyandot society.

Deskahe ("More Than Eleven"), a Cayuga Sachem

The name Deskahe was held by **Levi General** (1873–1925), who became the official speaker of the Six Nations Iroquois in 1922. At that time, the community was still governed by hereditary sachem government that had been set down through the Great Law of Peace. The community was also fighting with the federal government and decided to seek sovereignty. In 1923, Deskahe went to the League of Nations headquarters in Geneva to plead the Six Nations Iroquois's cause. He received the support of nations that knew what outsider control was like—Estonia, Ireland, Panama, and Persia—but Britain intervened, and the proposal was dropped. Deskahe also went the next year to talk to the King of England, but with no effect.

While Deskahe was away in England, the federal government struck. It ruled that the Six Nations must be governed by elected council, not by the system that had been serving them well for hundreds of years. The people of the community were not consulted. The RCMP changed the locks of the council house so the sachems could not get in. An election was staged on October 21, 1924. Out of a population of 4615 (as recorded in 1920), only 52 people voted. The community has been divided on that issue ever since.

Levi General died the next year, but named his brother Alexander (1889–1965) to replace him before his death. Alexander then bore the name Deskahe well. In 1928, as a guiding influence on the Indian Defense League of America, he helped gain legal recognition in the United States for the part of the **Jay's Treaty** that permitted Natives to cross the border between Canada and the United States without paying customs. In 1930, on a Six Nations–issued passport, he went to see the King of England. England recognized his passport, but King George V did not accept Deskahe's appeal for sovereignty.

After that time, Deskahe became an important anthropological informant, teaching the famous anthropologist Frank Speck and others about the traditional customs of his people.

Andy Paull: The Last of the "One Man Shows"

Squamish leader **Andy Paull** (1892–1959) was an early political activist that George Manuel referred to as the last of the "one man shows." In 1916, he was one of the founding members of the Allied Tribes of British Columbia, working extensively on the "Indian Land Question" that was unique to that province. It was difficult work, because from 1927 to 1951, it was illegal to "receive, obtain, solicit, or request from any Indian any payment or contribution for the purpose of raising a fund or providing money for the prosecution of any [land] claim" (Indian Act, Section 140, 1927 Amendment) without the consent of the superintendent general of Indian Affairs. His train trips to and from Ottawa were dramatic affairs. He would get off the train to meet with other activists and would dress up in formal suits to meet with federal officials in the country's capital. Having worked for four years as a legal assistant, he had good legal training for dealing with those officials. While he had the knowledge and experience to become a lawyer, he was ineligible to become one because he was a Status Indian and, therefore, legally only a minor and not able to vote or practise law.

Paull was considered a radical, even by other Native leaders, but most of what he fought for seems reasonable today. He advocated such measures as the right to vote in federal elections (this didn't happen until 1960), the abolition of the culturally destructive residential schools (this took place in the 1960s and 1970s), and the end of the federal power to determine band membership (this took place in the 1980s). He also advocated giving Indian bands the power of local, municipal governments (the Sechelt achieved this in 1986) and hiring more Natives in administrative positions in the Department of Indian Affairs (this has been gradually taking place recently). Paull was ahead of his time.

Frank Calder: Nisga'a Leader

Frank Calder, the man who initiated the procedure that eventually led to the Nisga'a treaty, was born in 1915. He was adopted by his mother's older sister, Louisa, for traditional Nisga'a reasons. Because Louisa was the eldest daughter of a prominent lineage, her son was supposed to become the chief of the clan. But her son died in childhood, so she adopted Frank from her sister.

Calder often tells the story of how he was formally introduced to the land question when he was 12. It was 1927, the year the fundraising for claims issues was declared illegal. His father placed a box of claims-related documents down in front of him, telling Frank that he had to learn their content.

He was fortunate enough to attend the University of British Columbia, something very few of his Native contemporaries were in a position to do. Initially, he studied theology, but he later became involved with the politics of getting his people the right to vote. In 1949, when the British Columbia government finally gave Aboriginal people the vote in the provincial election (they wouldn't get the federal vote until 1960), he was elected as candidate for the Co-operative Commonwealth Federation (CCF, the forerunner of the NDP) in the predominantly Aboriginal riding of Atlin, where he served for 26 years. That made him a groundbreaker, as he was the first Native to be elected to the provincial legislature and was, in fact, the first Native to be elected to any Canadian legislature. Interestingly, he had not been given the endorsement of the Native Brotherhood of British Columbia, who supported the Liberal-Conservative coalition candidate out of appreciation for giving them the vote.

In 1955, Frank Calder founded the Nisga'a Tribal Council from the four traditional clans. He was its president from that year to 1974, holding the position very much like the hereditary chief he would have been at an earlier time in Nisga'a history.

In 1967, he brought the Nisga'a land claim to the British Columbia court system. This did not receive the unanimous support of his people, because some held the very realistic fear that if they lost in the courts, they would lose their rights forever.

In 1972, Calder became a cabinet minister in the British Columbia NDP government, but that didn't work out for him, in part because he was a minister without a portfolio and so had no readily defined tasks to perform. Curiously, another cabinet minister handled Native matters. In 1973, the year when the Supreme Court handed down its decision about the Nisga'a land claim, he was held by the police for being found drunk in a public place. One wonders if a non-Native cabinet minister would have been apprehended in the same way. He was not formally charged with a crime, but ended up being kicked out of the cabinet in disgrace. He quit the NDP, but ran as a Social Credit candidate in 1975 and won.

In an interview held shortly after the passing of the treaty through parliament, Calder said the following:

> We've been liberated, that's what's going on here . . . Now we're free to exercise what we wanted to do, instead of remaining under the confinement of the reservation. The reservation and to get out of it, that's the main theme of what we're doing. (Matas 1999)

NATIVE GOVERNANCE

Nunavut

On April 1, 1999, Canada created its third territory: **Nunavut**. This was a major political event, as it redrew our map for the first time since Newfoundland had joined in 1949. For the Inuit of the Eastern Arctic, it had a greater significance, changing their relationship with the Canadian government and with other Canadians.

The land mass involved is huge. It is larger than any other Canadian province or territory, roughly twice the size of British Columbia, and about one-fifth of Canada's geographic size. It covers roughly everything north of the treeline in the old Northwest Territories, stretching from a line north of the Manitoba border east and north. It includes half of Victoria Island and all of the big islands of Ellesmere, Southampton, Baffin, and Devon. Its population is small, about 25,000; the caribou (about 750,000 of them) outnumber the humans by about 30 to 1. There are 28 communities in Nunavut.

The word Nunavut (pronounced noo-nah-voot) means "our land" in Inuktitut. There are several important reasons why the Inuit can name it so. They have been on the land for thousands of years. Inuit are, as well, usually estimated as making up between 82 percent to about 85 percent of the population, numbering 17,500. And prior to the signing of the Nunavut agreement, the Inuit still had Aboriginal rights to the land, having never been conquered, and having never put pen to any treaties.

The agreement involves in part the settlement of the largest and richest land claim in Canadian history. In this settlement, the Inuit retain a number of rights. First is the right to hunt, fish, and trap throughout Nunavut. While the number of hunters is not as great as it used to be, nearly 60 percent of all Inuit households still rely upon the land for their meat. Nearly 85 percent of households are still involved in hunting and fishing to some extent, and over 15 percent still trap. Inuit will not require any licence to hunt for basic needs. In addition, the Inuit will retain outright ownership of 353,610 square kilometres of land, about 18 percent of Nunavut.

In a move unusual in the signing of treaties, and unlike other agreements by Native people, the Inuit got to choose which lands they desired. The remaining 82 percent remains Crown land, but the people will have joint control with the federal government over land use planning, wildlife, environmental protection, and offshore resources. On 36,257 square kilometres, or 10.5 percent of Inuit-owned land (about 2 percent of Nunavut), the Inuit will own subsurface rights to oil, gas, and minerals. It is believed that the land over which the Inuit hold rights contains as much as 80 percent of Nunavut's mineral resources. Of equal importance, the Inuit will receive a royalty from the government on any oil, gas, or mineral development on Crown land within Nunavut. This amounts to 50 percent of the first $2 million and 5 percent thereafter. In terms of cash, the Inuit receive $1.15 billion over 14 years—at least in theory, since monetary amounts in agreements have a way of diminishing. The Nunavut Trust will be set up by the Inuit to receive the money and to manage and invest it. The money will be put into such concerns as Inuit-owned businesses, a scholarship program for Inuit students seeking post-secondary education, and an income support program for hunters, similar to what was developed for the Cree of James Bay.

A number of boards have been or will be established to help govern the new territory. The land claim agreement requires the relevant governments to negotiate a political accord (the Nunavut Accord), which would establish Nunavut as a new territory. In practice, this means that the territory, under the Nunavut Legislative Assembly, would have the same powers as those held by the Northwest Territories. The Nunavut Implementation Commission designed the new government, prepared for the first election, determined the capital, and began training the territory's new leaders. The Inuktitut language was recognized as official, the first Native language to receive such recognition in Canada (although this practice is not unusual in South America). Having Inuktitut as the official language means having legal documents published in the language, having the right to be tried in court in the language, and having the language taught in schools.

The choice of capital city was an issue of many debates. There are only 20 kilometres of highway in Nunavut, so for the most part travel is by plane. Nunavut residents use aircraft five or six times as often as do other Canadians. Because there are almost 30 communities throughout the territory, accessible only by air, the choice of capital was a touchy subject. The contenders were Rankin Inlet (on the west coast of Hudson Bay), Iqaluit (on Baffin Island), and Cambridge Bay (on Victoria Island, at the extreme west of Nunavut).

In 1995, Iqaluit (known as Frobisher Bay until 1987) was chosen at a plebiscite, with 60 percent of the 79 percent who voted choosing it. The choice is not surprising. It is the largest community in Nunavut, with a population of about 4500, and it is far removed from Yellowknife, which has been vilified in Inuit country in the same way that Ottawa has sometimes been vilified in western and eastern Canada.

A number of boards and commissions have been established to oversee crucial social and environmental concerns. The Nunavut Wildlife Management Board has responsibility for management of the wildlife throughout Nunavut. The Inuit are a majority on the board. Five of the nine members are to be appointed from either the regional Inuit organization or the Nunavut government. Current quotas and restrictions remain in effect until this new board changes them.

The Nunavut Impact Review Board (NIRB), Nunavut Planning Commission (NPC), and Nunavut Water Board (NWB) are all essentially Inuit-controlled. The NIRB has the mandate to review and assess all projects throughout the territory to determine their impact on the environment or on socioeconomic conditions. The NPC reviews land use plans and identifies cleanup requirements. The NWB works in association with the other two boards, but its mandate is to license the use of water for purposes other than navigation, and to approve the disposal of waste into waterways and water systems.

The Inuit have a say in all future developments before projects begin. This applies to such concerns as parks (three of which are planned) and, of course, hydroelectric projects. Any developer must negotiate impact and benefit agreements with the Inuit before beginning such projects The Inuit are especially concerned with the hiring and training of local Inuit and with the potential social and economic gains to be had.

A lot, then, has been planned. And this has been done without a great deal of awareness in the south. We need to address the question, then, of what led to the creation of Nunavut.

The Road to Nunavut

The road to Nunavut can be said to have begun in 1969 when then-Minister of Indian Affairs Jean Chrétien introduced his infamous "White Paper" on Indian policy. Among other things, it proposed doing away with special status for Native people, doing away with treaties, denying the existence of Aboriginal rights, and making the provinces responsible for Natives.

The reaction was loud, sometimes confrontational, but not in the north. The Inuit quietly chose a peaceful political route. In 1971, they formed the **Inuit Tapirisat** of Canada, an organization with representation from the four corners of the Northwest Territories, along with Labrador and Quebec. It became the prime political vehicle for the Inuit. In 1976, the Inuit Tapirisat published a 60-page document entitled *Nunavut: A Proposal for the Settlement of Inuit Lands in the Northwest Territories*.

The document was received very coolly by the Trudeau government, ostensibly on the basis of its "racial bias." The government contended that it assigned legislative and governmental jurisdiction based on racial differentiation, something out of place in democracy as the government saw it. However, Liberal MP Bud Drury was appointed to conduct a study on the subject. He talked with recognized Native leaders and attempted to get a consensus from Native people. While not supportive of division of the Northwest Territories, he did not reject the idea outright. He concluded that Native aspirations could be met merely by settling land claims and setting aside land for Native peoples. However, the Inuit Tapirisat rejected his plan.

In 1979, three major developments took place in Inuit country. First, the Inuit of Baker Lake appealed to a federal court judge, claiming that 78,000 square kilometres in the area was theirs. They were protesting prospecting that was being conducted by uranium companies. They sought a court order prohibiting further exploration because the helicopters and prospecting camps were frightening the caribou.

For the first time, Inuit went to court suing for Aboriginal title. Testimony went on for weeks, with Elders demonstrating their knowledge of the land. The federal court judge demanded that four criteria be satisfied to determine Aboriginal title. The Inuit had to prove that their ancestors formed an organized society, that they occupied the claimed land, that all other organized societies were excluded, and that the occupation was a fact at the time that Britain asserted sovereignty over the land. The Inuit were able to satisfy these four criteria, so the judge declared that Inuit title did exist in the lands surrounding Baker Lake. However, he refused to stop the prospecting. While acknowledging that the caribou herds had declined, he failed to recognize that mining was a significant factor in that decline. He also stated that federal and territorial mining legislation could abrogate Aboriginal title. It was a partial victory. While recognizing Inuit Aboriginal rights, it still allowed that governments were within their legal rights to issue exploratory permits to mining companies on Inuit land.

The second event of 1979 was the Inuit Tapirisat adoption of a position paper entitled *Political Development in Nunavut*, which proposed a three-stage, 15-year period during which the Eastern Arctic would grow into provincehood. The first stage would be the recognition of Nunavut. The second would be the transfer of territorial powers to the new territory and finally would be the achievement of provincial status.

The third event was political: rather than following the usual practice of boycotting territorial elections because they were irrelevant to their needs, the Inuit and Dene voted in large numbers, with the result that a majority of Members of Legislative Assembly were Native. For the first time, First Nations issues became a priority. Territorial division was then put on the table. A vote was called for and a plebiscite was held in 1982. The voters were asked whether they thought that the Northwest Territories should be divided. Over half the eligible voters turned out, with 56.5% percent voting "yes." The demographics tell an interesting story. Voter turnout in the Inuit east was 76 percent, with 82 percent supporting division, compared to a turnout of 45 percent in the west, where only 44 percent supported it. In western Inuit and Dene communities, support was 60 percent; in non-Native communities, it was 25 percent. After the plebiscite, the Assembly voted 19–0 in favour of division and asked the federal government to recommend the new boundaries after consultation with the people of the Northwest Territories.

A group called the Constitutional Alliance, which had lobbied for division, set up two forums, one for the east (the Nunavut Constitutional Forum, or NCF) and one for the west (the Western Constitutional Forum, or WCF). The NCF became very active in consulting communities and elders, publishing widely in newspapers, broadcasting through television and radio, and producing position papers. In 1987, the Iqaluit Agreement was signed by the NCF and the WCF. It set the tentative boundaries and the principles under which the territories would operate.

Support for the division continued. In 1989, the Legislative Assembly again affirmed its support for Nunavut by a vote of 20–0, with one abstention. This was reaffirmed two years later by Territorial Commissioner Dan Norris. In November 1992, a plebiscite was held, with 69 percent of voters in favour of division.

Nunavut has not been without its detractors within the Inuit community, particularly concerning the signing away forever of any future claim to Aboriginal title. Some have felt that the loss of so much land involves the severing of the spiritual connection between the Inuit, their ancestors, and the land. Opposition to the surrender took on a very public face, when the lone Inuit Member of Parliament, **Jack Anawak**, questioned whether the Inuit were being asked to pay too high a price for Nunavut.

On the other side was **John Amagoalik**, referred to as the "father of Nunavut." His passion is inflamed by the fact that his family and community faced hunger and deprivation after being forcibly removed from Inukjuak in northern Quebec to Ellesmere Island in 1953 (see Chapter 5). He is co-chair of the Inuit Committee on National Issues and has been involved with the issue for 20 years. While battling for Nunavut and for a capital far removed from Yellowknife, he has also demonstrated that he has a more-than-local perspective, supporting the notion of a Dene and Métis homeland in the west. On a global scale, he sees his struggle as not only one for the Inuit, but perhaps as a model for other indigenous peoples worldwide. At the same time, he sees Nunavut as providing an education for non-Natives, reducing the fears that the term "self-government" brings to the uninformed.

The First Nunavut Election

On February 15, 1999, Nunavut held its first election. The voter turnout was incredibly high, with 88 percent of eligible voters showing up at the polls. One unusual feature of the Nunavut Legislative Assembly is that no political parties are represented, making it more like a municipal than a provincial political body. Several names were proposed for the first premier, **Paul Okalik** and Jack Anawak being the finalists. Okalik, a 34-year-old lawyer, was voted in. He remains premier in 2006.

The elected candidates, called MLAs, included 17 men and one woman. In 1997, showing how willing the Inuit are to at least entertain issues of equity unheard of in the rest of Canada, the people of Nunavut held a plebiscite concerning whether each riding would have both a male and a female MLA. It had some support, losing only by 2662–1978. In 2006, two women were MLAs.

Interestingly, four of the MLAs were non-Inuit, slightly more than their percentage of the population. Jack Anawak has expressed his concern about the future of non-Inuit in Nunavut, particularly those resident in the area for the long-term. His worry is that there are no legal mechanisms in place to respect their rights. Of the many challenges that the leaders of Nunavut face, this is one that many people from outside Nunavut will be looking at closely.

Westbank First Nation Self-Government

The Westbank First Nation (with a registered population of 643 in June 2006) owns five reserves on the west shore of Okanagan Lake, across from the city of Kelowna, British Columbia. It began self-government negotiations with the federal government in 1990, through the Inherent Right to Self-Government Policy. The Westbank Self-Government Agreement became law on May 6, 2004. The powers given to them through this Agreement are reflected in the laws that the Westbank community passed in 2005, which show that the band attained an authority much like that of a non-Aboriginal municipality.

2005-01 Long-Term Debt Liability and Guarantees Law
2005-02 Noxious Weeds and Grass Law

2005-03 Noxious Insect Control Law
2005-04 Dog and Cat Control Law
2005-05 Animal Control Law
2005-06 Garbage Collection Law
2005-07 Unsightly Premises Law
2005-08 Noise and Disturbance Control Law
2005-09 Second-hand Dealers and Pawnbrokers Law
2005-10 Discharge of Firearms Law
2005-11 Fire Protection Law
2005-12 Fireworks Law
2005-13 Traffic and Parking Control Law
2005-14 Building Law
2005-15 Subdivision, Development and Servicing Law
2005-16 Waterworks Law
2005-17 Business Licence Law
2005-18 Sanitary Sewer Systems Law
2005-19 Disorderly Conduct and Nuisances Law
2005-20 Outdoor Events Law
2005-21 Residential Premises Law
2005-22 Advisory Council Law
2005-23 Immunity and Indemnity Law

One can imagine from this how often the band council had had to go to the federal government for approval of its acts before self-government.

The one contentious part of the Agreement comes from the fact that about 7500 non-Aboriginal people live or own businesses on the five reserves belonging to the Westbank First Nation. The ultra-conservative Canadian Taxpayers Federation criticized the Westbank First Nation Self-Government Agreement because it would deny non-Aboriginals who are taxed on their property on this land the right to vote in band council elections, in their view amounting to taxation without representation. The band pointed out that Section 54 of the Agreement requires the Westbank First Nation to pass a law providing non-members living on their lands or having an interest on their lands legal mechanisms through which they can have input into proposed laws or their amendments. It remains to be seen how this turnaround situation will work itself out.

Tlicho Land Claims and Self-Government Act

On February 15, 2005, Royal Assent was given to the Tlicho Land Claims and Self-Government Act, creating a new level of government in the Northwest Territories. The Tlicho Government represents the four bands of the Tlicho or Dogrib, which will no longer be politically separate. Among the legal rights now held by the Tlicho Government are those of what is termed a "natural person." These include the ability to enter into contracts or agreements, acquire and own property, raise, invest, expend, and borrow money, sue or be sued, and form corporations. The band councils did not have that set of rights before 2005. They also have the power to enact laws concerning adoption of a Tlicho by a Tlicho, as well as that of determining custody, and the protection and promotion of the Tlicho language and culture, which includes the certification of teachers and of traditional medicine practitioners.

They were also given a strong measure of control of the surface and subsurface rights of some 39,000 square kilometres of land, a block of land that includes two diamond mines.

Clan Principles and Aboriginal Self-Government: An Anishinabek Example

A number of the proposals for Aboriginal self-government that have been made attempt to use traditional principles and practices of governance. In the June 2006 edition of *Anishinabek News*, an article entitled "Anishinaabe Gchi-Naaknigewin" discussed proposals for the content of the Anishinabek Nation Constitution. Several proposals were put forward that made use of the traditional system of seven dodems or clans of the people. The discussion of the governing principles of the proposed Anishinabek Nation Government contained the following statement:

> The Anishinabek believe that the Dodem System is a truly democratic form of governing where each Dodem leader advances the voice of the dodem membership rather than speaks on behalf of it. The Dodemaag Giimaag (Dodem Leaders) function as advocates by becoming knowledgeable of the wishes and directives of the people through dodem gatherings and through continual contact and communication with individuals and families of the dodems. The system is based on a cooperative and integrative working relationship between all of the dodems in an interdependent fashion. (Anishinaabe Gchi-Naaknigewin 2006)

Two points should be made in conclusion here. First, plans for Aboriginal self-government do not threaten to tear the country apart; they fit well into the Canadian political system. Second, there is not just one path to Aboriginal self-government; there are several.

Native Individuals 24-1

John Amagoalik: Called the "father of Nunavut," Amagoalik is a long-time Inuk activist promoting Nunavut.

Jack Anawak: An Inuk MP who questioned whether the gains of Nunavut were worth giving up aboriginal title forever.

Senator Patrick Brazeau: Patrick Brazeau, born in 1974, is an Algonquin from the Kitigan Zibi reserve in Québec. In 2009, at the incredibly young age of 34, he was made the youngest senator in Canada. Prior to that, from 2006 to 2009 he was national chief of the Congress of Aboriginal Peoples, which represents Métis, southern Inuit, and non-status Natives living off-reserve.

In March 2012, Brazeau fought Member of Parliament Justin Trudeau in a charity boxing match to raise money for cancer research. Although the tattooed Brazeau was the more intimidating looking opponent, he lost to Trudeau (whose father, former Prime Minister Pierre Trudeau, was an accomplished martial artist) via a technical knockout in the third round.

As a senator, Brazeau has been surrounded with controversy. He has a low attendance record at meetings, missing about 65% of the Standing Senate Aboriginal Peoples Committee. As well, as a senator he can claim $20,000 if his primary residence is more than 100 kilometres away from Ottawa. He asserted

(continued)

Native Individuals 24-1 (continued)

that his father's house in Maniwaki, 130 kilometres from the national capital, is his primary residence, an assertion that has been challenged and may be investigated.

Brazeau was also criticized by some people for his opposition to Idle No More. In the eyes of his critics, he appeared to be speaking from a position of privilege. On Thursday, February 7, 2013, he was removed from the Conservative caucus and was put on leave of absence from the Senate, following an arrest for alleged incidents of domestic violence. He spent the night in jail. He has since pleaded not guilty.

Frank Calder: Nisga'a activist and provincial cabinet minister, he started the land claims case in 1967 that ended up with the Nisga'a treaty.

Deskahe ("More than eleven"): A Cayuga sachem title. It was held by Levi General (1873–1925) who went to the League of Nations to try to gain sovereignty for his people. The title was then held by Alexander General (1889–1965), who helped gain recognition for the Native rights that came from the Jay's Treaty.

Nahnebahwequay: A nineteenth-century Mississauga woman who had to speak with Queen Victoria in order to buy land.

Paul Okalik: Inuk, the first premier of Nunavut.

Andrew Paull (1892–1952): Squamish leader, one of the founding members of the Allied Tribes of British Columbia in 1916.

Timeline 24-1

1969: Minister of Indian Affairs Jean Chrétien tables the "White Paper."

1971: The Inuit Tapirisat is formed.

1976: The Inuit Tapirisat puts forward its first proposal for Nunavut.

1979: The Inuit of Baker Lake put forward their first land claim proposal.

1982: A plebiscite is held in which the division of the Northwest Territories is approved.

1987: The Iqaluit Agreement is signed by Inuit from the west and east.

1999: February 15: Nunavut holds its first election.

1999: April 1: Nunavut is officially born.

KEY TERMS

Inuit Tapirisat

Jay's Treaty

CONTENT QUESTIONS

1. Why was Nahnebahwequay not allowed to buy land in 1857?
2. How did the federal government take authority away from the traditional sachems of the Iroquois?
3. What are the terms of the Nunavut agreement?
4. What percentage of the population of Nunavut is Inuit?
5. What is unusual about how the Legislative Assembly of Nunavut is composed?

WEBLINKS

www.tlicho.com

This website contains the Tlicho Land Claims and Self-Government Act, as well as a discussion of its history.

http://wfn.ca

This is the Westbank First Nation website, with information about its administration, local government, and economic development.

www.gov.nu.ca

The official website for Nunavut.

www.afn.ca

This is the website of the Assembly of First Nations, the leading political body for status Indians in Canada.

chapter twenty-five

Undoing the Past

A REASON TO HOPE: ALKALI LAKE, POUNDMAKER'S LODGE, AND THE NECHI INSTITUTE

Alcoholism

The federal and provincial legal systems, somewhat ironically, lent alcoholism a hand by giving Natives equal rights in access to alcohol. In 1951, the Indian Act was amended so that it was legal for Status Indians to drink alcohol in licensed bars. A British Columbia provincial law passed in 1962 allowed Status Indians to purchase alcohol outside of bars. By the end of that decade, Section 94 of the Indian Act had been successfully challenged in the *Regina v. Drybones* case. Joseph Drybones, a Dene, had been charged under Section 94(b) for being intoxicated in a hotel bar in Yellowknife, Northwest Territories, on April 8, 1967. As Section 94(b) differed significantly from the territorial Liquor Ordinance, Drybones' lawyers argued that this contravened the 1960 Canadian Bill of Rights. They won the case in 1969, liberalizing alcohol-related laws concerning Status Indians across the country.

The Native battle against alcohol began to turn around during the 1970s. The major hot spot for the turnaround was in the area of Alberta and the interior of British Columbia. We can start this story with Alkali Lake.

Alkali Lake

Alkali Lake is a community of the Shuswap, or Secwepemc people. Their battle with alcohol is said to have begun when their hereditary chief, Sxoxomic, died in 1940, after decades of his tough anti-alcohol leadership. He had developed a policy of imposing harsh penalties on anyone who was found drinking on the reserve. After his death, alcoholism rates in the community soared.

Another factor that helped earn Alkali Lake the local nickname of "Alcohol Lake" is the influence of the nearby Williams Lake residential school. Throughout the 1950s and 1960s, Native children at that school were sexually and physically abused. (A priest was convicted in 1989.) Alcohol was a way of trying to escape that pain.

By the late 1960s, Alkali Lake existed in an alcoholic haze. Although alcohol could not be purchased legally on the reserve, taxis and buses brought in a great supply, and there were always the local makers of homebrew. Drinking parties lasted several days, women and children were beaten and raped, and people died due to alcohol and alcohol-related incidents. Francis Johnson described the following recurring incident of his childhood:

> Many times our parents left us children alone when they went to town. When they went in the bar, we would spend hours waiting in the truck, not knowing when they would be back. Many times we went to bed hungry and without knowing when our parents would get back. (York 1990:178)

The turnaround began in 1972 with one family, the Chelseas. Phyllis Chelsea stopped at her mother's to pick up her seven-year-old daughter but the girl refused to go, saying: "You and Daddy drink too much" (York 1990:179). Phyllis Chelsea poured her bottle of liquor down the sink, becoming sober from that day on, the first in her community to walk down that path. A strong sense of family would also help others, later, to walk that same path (Johnson and Johnson 1993:228–29).

A few months later, Phyllis's husband, Andrew, joined her on the road to recovery. He saw a group of children with bruised faces walking to school after their parents had been drinking all night. When he asked them whether they had had anything to eat that morning, and they replied "no," he decided to stop drinking. The place on the road where he saw the children became a sacred place to him. He would revisit it to remind himself why he had quit drinking.

Andrew Chelsea was elected chief in 1973 and quickly took action against the local bootleggers, arranging a sting operation with the local RCMP and banning from the reserve a bus driver who made runs carrying thousands of dollars of alcohol. His wife became the welfare supervisor and arranged to have welfare cheques replaced with food and clothing vouchers.

The next big step came from the community, which developed a supportive series of Alcoholics Anonymous-style "Alcoholism Awareness" meetings. When people went away to treatment centres, they received a constant flow of cards and letters of support, and the community painted and repaired their houses.

In 1985, more than a thousand Native people and addiction counsellors from Canada and the United States came to Alkali Lake to attend an international conference on alcohol abuse. That same year they made a video entitled *The Honour of All: The Alkali Lake Story*, which has since been used effectively to teach other Native communities that such a change is possible. By 1988, three quarters of the band members (in a community of over 400) had completed an alcohol treatment program. By 1989, more than 90 percent of band members were sober.

Spiritual revival played a very important role. When members of the community of Alkali Lake began their struggle against alcoholism, there was almost no practice of traditional spiritual ceremonies. With the help of Shuswap Elders from other communities, reviving spiritual practices such as the sweat lodge, sweetgrass, and pipe ceremonies played a key role in the rehabilitation of the community. A 1992 study of the success of Alkali Lake's fight with alcohol, conducted by drug and alcohol counsellors Jean and Fred Johnson, demonstrated the importance of spirituality in the recovery process. When the people were asked "What significant event or thing caused you to want to be sober?" 31 percent responded "spiritual support." When asked "What have been the most effective factors in your after-care programs?" 34 percent also answered "spiritual support" (Johnson and Johnson 1993:229).

The effectiveness of traditional spiritual ceremonies and a consequent strengthening of cultural identity in helping Native people fight alcohol is not confined to Alkali Lake. A 1995 study sponsored by the Department of the Solicitor General of Canada and researched by the Nechi Institute and KAS Corporation Limited found similar stories in other communities. For example, twenty Native people who had come into serious conflict with the law and served time in Canadian penal institutions had subsequently turned their lives around using traditional cultural means. In the words of one of these former prisoners:

> What helped me into sobriety was the spiritual part this program offered—the Sweat Lodge and the sweetgrass and the stories the Elder used to share with me. Some stories I already heard from my late grandfather. I was amazed those stories were even over here [in prison]. . . [T]hat brought back a lot of strength with me again. I grew up as a little spiritual person and bringing that back to me was welcoming. It hit home. In a spirituality sense, I knew now that I found myself. This is me and I knew then, too, that I will never drink again. (Nechi Institute and KAS Corp. 1994)

This change was also made possible through the development in the area of Native-run alcohol treatment centres such as Poundmaker's Lodge (named after Pitikwahanpiwiyin or Poundmaker, a Plains Cree leader of the nineteenth century), and the Hobbema Centre in the early 1970s, both in Alberta. They were the first such institutions that were run by Natives. Their success rate soon surpassed comparable institutions that were run and staffed by non-Natives.

What the people running these centres quickly found was that they needed Native people with special training as alcohol and drug counsellors. On October 15, 1974, the Nechi Institute was incorporated as a non-profit society to train counsellors. It provided the first Addictions Diploma in Alberta. The following are the founding principles of the Nechi Institute:

1. Native alcohol and drug abusers can be most effectively counselled and rehabilitated by our Native people.

2. Native people can best manage and direct their own community programs and businesses.

3. Native people will research the most effective methods of dealing with community problems (i.e., employee assistance).

Since its inception, the Nechi Institute has trained over 1500 counsellors. It currently shares its facilities (which include training rooms, a gymnasium, a large ceremonial room, three sweat lodges, and residences for 44 training program participants and 54 treatment clients) with Poundmaker's Lodge and has over 30 staff members.

For a good example of the impact of Poundmaker's Lodge, read Herb Nabigon's *The Hollow Tree: Fighting Addiction with Traditional Native Healing* (McGill-Queens, 2006).

Herb Nabigon is Ojibwa. His walk down his first path of life, alcoholism and despair, began when he was taken to the residential school in Spanish, Ontario, at age nine. Alcoholism took his right arm one drunken night when he was struck by a train. With several stops, he slowly pursued a career in social work at college and at university, but didn't really seem to be going anywhere.

The turning point in his life occurred when his Aboriginal employer pressed him into going to Poundmaker's Lodge. There he was exposed to the teachings of several Cree Elders (including Eddy Bellerose and Abe Burnstick) and Elders who have touched many lives—Native and non-Native. They guided him to his second path of life, a spiritual one. Herb Nabigon now teaches in the Native Social Work program at Laurentian University in Sudbury, Ontario.

TAKING OVER THE SCHOOLS

In September 1970, after a month-long sit-in by about 300 people, Blue Quills (situated on the Saddle Lake Reserve, in northeast Alberta) changed from residential school (which it had been since 1931) to the first Native-run school in Canada. This event marked an important beginning in Native education in Canada, the beginning of Native control over their own education. In 1973, the National Indian Brotherhood produced a document entitled *Indian Control of Indian Education*, which set forth a plan for the gradual takeover of Native education by the parents and local Native communities.[1] It was later accepted by the federal government and adopted as official educational policy. Box 25-1 discusses a Montagnais Elder's views of the importance of including Native culture in the curriculum at the local school.

The changes in Native education can be documented by the numbers. By 1980, there were well over 100 band-operated schools. Ten years later, there were about 300. In 1975–76, only 2842 of the 71,817 on-reserve Indian children enrolled in schools went to band-operated schools, roughly 5 percent of all Native children (Frideres 1998:153). By 1989–90, the number was 34,674 of 88,158, slightly less than 40 percent (Frideres 1998:153).

BOX 25-1   A Montagnais Elder Talks About Young People and Education

Julienne Malec, a Montagnais Elder in the community of Natashquan, actively promotes the inclusion of Montagnais culture in the local school. She believes the following:

> [c]ulture has to be taught like other school subjects. Otherwise, how will the children remain Innuat? Both cultures must be passed on for the well-being

of young people, so that we can communicate with them . . . Ten years ago, suicide was unknown here. Now, not a year goes by without a young person killing himself. I don't know why they do it, but perhaps if they felt more strongly that they were Innuat, proud of their culture, they would feel better. (Chaumel and Mesténapéo 1995–1996)

Several positive statistics go along with these changes. The enrollment rate of school-age (i.e., age 4 to 18), on-reserve Natives rose about 8 percent, from 81 percent to 90.2 percent between 1975 and 1990 (Frideres 1998:155). Likewise, over the same years, the number remaining in school continuously until grade 12 or 13 rose significantly, from 15.8 percent to 41.6 percent (Frideres 1998:158). Similarly, the number of Native students in high school, as a percentage of total school enrollment, rose from 17.1 percent to 22.4 percent between 1975 and 1990 (Frideres 1998:159).

The Challenge of Native Post-Secondary Education

There has been a similar rise in the number of Native students involved with post-secondary education. For example, from 1975 to 1990, the number of Native students enrolled in university climbed from 2071 to about 23,000 (Frideres 1998:159). However, some real problems are occurring at the post-secondary level, as Frideres points out:

> Today [1995] 40,000 Aboriginals are enrolled in post-secondary educational institutions. Of these about 9 percent graduate, compared to a graduation rate of well over 18 percent for non-Aboriginals. Clearly, an Aboriginal student's chances of finishing university are still quite small. For individuals having attended university, non-Indians are about 2.4 times as likely as Indians to earn a degree. (Frideres 1998:165)

Native students, then, are having difficulties adapting to post-secondary institutions. One solution is Native-run colleges and universities (see Box 25-2). Institutions called "tribal colleges" exist in the United States. Although they operate under less secure funding formulas than most other post-secondary institutions in the United States, enrollment figures suggest that Native students increasingly want to attend these schools.

BOX 25-2   Yellowquill College Philosophy

The Dakota-Ojibway Tribal Council believes that education of Native people is both the right and responsibility of Native people as they are capable of determining their own educational needs. Education and training are seen as an integral part of the process of Indian self-government and economic and social development. Native people have the leadership and knowledge needed to implement and maintain an effective post-secondary institution.

Philosophy

The mandate of Yellowquill College is to provide learning experiences that are relevant and appropriate for First Nations and their members. The College operates on the philosophy that:

1. Education of First Nation people is both the right and responsibility of First Nation people as they are capable of determining their own educational needs.
2. Education and Training are seen as an integral part of the process of First Nation self-government, economic and social development.
3. First Nations people have the leadership knowledge needed to implement and maintain an effective post-secondary institution.

(Yellowquill College 2006)

In Canada, many leading Native educators do not believe that non-Native post-secondary institutions can provide a suitable education for Native students. Doctor Vivian Ayoungman, a prominent Blackfoot educator in Canada, states the following in the "Proceedings of the Standing Senate Committee on Social Affairs, Science, Technology: Subcommittee on Post-Secondary Education":

> It is our opinion that after more than 100 years of ignoring its obligations, Canada and its post-secondary institutions are no longer in a moral position to affirm that they will eventually do the right thing. (Standing Senate Committee 1997)

Credentials and accreditation concerning who can teach Native courses and what those courses should contain are currently sore spots for educators with views similar to those of Ayoungman and Don Fiddler. Fiddler is the executive director of the En'owkin Centre in the interior of British Columbia. It is a reasonably successful, Native-run educational institute that offers courses in the Okanagan language, as well as Adult Basic Education, pre-college, and university transfer programs. For funding and accreditation purposes, it is affiliated with Okanagan University College. It is not on par with colleges or university colleges in British Columbia. Fiddler expresses frustration with that situation, with the system as it is, even with the successes:

> What we are saying, when we talk about accreditation of those issues, is that we have the expertise. In our communities throughout North America, we have many scholars who have already been educated in mainstream universities and have recognized that if we wish to pursue aboriginal education we need to take radical alternatives . . . . We are talking about the freedom to develop education that is particular to our own people and whose direction may differ very widely from what is commonly called education. (Standing Senate Committee 1997)

Elders in Post-Secondary Education

Most Native post-secondary educators work in non-Native institutions and have been trying to find ways in which they can reach out to Native students. One of the most innovative ways is the use of Elders. What is an Elder? The following definitions are useful in establishing this important concept:

> [Elder is] a label given to men or women who, recognized by others, possess knowledge of Aboriginal stories, values, and the history of communities and nations. (Ontario Ministry of Education 1999:69)

> Elders are repositories of cultural and philosophical knowledge and are the transmitters of such information. (Medicine 1987:142)

> [Elders are] those people who have earned the respect of their own community and who are looked upon as Elders in their own society. (Mark, cited in Medicine 1987:146)

Taken together, then, we can say that, for purposes of education, Elders are people who:

1. have significant wisdom in areas of traditional aboriginal knowledge.
2. are recognized as having that wisdom by their community, their Nation.
3. have the capacity to transmit this knowledge to others.

What Roles Should Elders Play?

It is vitally important that Elders as leaders in post-secondary education are not decorative or symbolic, but are deeply entrenched in the workings of the post-secondary institution.

Two ways in which this is done are programs of Elders-in-Residence and Visiting Elders. Some institutions, particularly those with a significant percentage of Native students and those with Native stream programs, offer both. Others, with a lower percentage of Native students and fewer programs, opt for just the Visiting Elders. A good example of an Elder-in-Residence program is at Lakehead University in Thunder Bay in northwestern Ontario, deep in the traditional country of the Ojibwa or Anishinabe people. In addition to the Elders-in-Residence Program, Lakehead also has a Visiting Humanities Fellowship in Native Philosophy, an Annual Elders Conference, and Elder/Healing Circles.

Visiting Elders programs are useful at community colleges, where Native students study at different campuses, such as at Georgian College in Ontario.

TAKING BACK THE CHILDREN

The Spallumcheen Story

Spallumcheen, a Shuswap community, is one that was particularly hard hit by the Sixties Scoop. It would be little exaggeration to say that Aboriginal people lost almost an entire generation to overzealous non-Native social workers in the 1960s. Imagine the impact of losing 50 children in one year on a community of about 300, of having a social worker rent a bus one weekend to take away 38 of their children, to be deposited among non-Native Mormon families in southeastern British Columbia and the United States.

This story turned around in 1979 when Wayne Christian, himself an adult survivor of the child welfare system, was elected chief. In 1980, the band council passed a by-law that seems to have been modelled after the Indian Child Welfare Act in the United States. The by-law proposed the takeover of Spallumcheen's own child welfare from the British Columbia Ministry of Children and Families. The by-law reflected the community's recognition of and support for the traditional role of the extended family. The by-law proposed that if a child had to be taken away from its home, he or she be placed according to the following priorities of placement:

1) a parent
2) a member of the extended family living on the reserve
3) a member of the extended family living on another reserve, although not a reserve to the Indian Band
4) a member of the extended family living off the reserve
5) an Indian living on a reserve
6) an Indian living off a reserve
7) a non-Indian living off the reserve

Remarkably, the minister of the Department of Indian Affairs approved this by-law. The success of this policy was soon evident. The Spallumcheen by-law reduced the number of children taken into care and ensured that the children taken from their homes were often kept within the social circle of the community. It wasn't until the 1990s that other Aboriginal communities in British Columbia were able to introduce similar plans.

In a high-profile case in 1998, the Spallumcheen Band Council had to fight to protect their authority over band children. The case involved a girl who was born to a young Spallumcheen woman on October 27, 1996. The mother, who felt unable to take care of her child at that time, asked a non-Native couple to act as foster parents. The agreement was formalized through the provincial ministry, as the child had not yet been registered as a member of the band. When the girl was later registered, in 1998, the responsibility for her welfare passed to the band. Initially, the band was content to leave the child with the foster parents, but it entered into an agreement with them that would eventually see the child reunited with her mother. The agreement required an increasing number of parental visits, initially supervised, and then unsupervised.

In the spring of 1998, the relationship between the foster parents and the band began to deteriorate. In June, the band council decided to place the girl with her mother's sister living off the reserve. As a result, the foster parents no longer had access to the child, so they applied to the court for access and also applied for custody. They wanted a ruling that said that the by-law was discriminatory in not allowing them to adopt the child. The court case was picked up by the British Columbia media, which, rather than clarifying the situation, muddied the waters.

The band admitted it had been too abrupt in taking the child from the non-Native foster home, but felt that the foster parents' antagonism to the band would become apparent to the child, which would not be in the child's best interests. The judge ruled in favour of the band council, reaffirming the authority of their child welfare by-law.

A Troubled System: Xyolhemeylh Family and Child Care Services

Aboriginal child welfare organizations run by an Aboriginal community can run into problems. The story of the **Xyolhemeylh** Family and Child Care Services (XFCCS) of the Stó:lo Nation, a British Columbia Aboriginal child care agency, is an example.

Xyolhemeylh (pronounced, roughly, "yoth-meeth") means "the special relationship of caring, respect, and love that exists between a caregiver and a child" (Fournier and Crey 1997:233). The agency was first formed in 1994 and then achieved a breakthrough deal in 1997 in which Aboriginal families of a nation living inside Stó:lo traditional territory could choose to be served by them rather than by the British Columbia Ministry for Children and Families. At its peak, XFCCS ran 100 foster homes, 60 of which were Native and 40 non-Native; three group homes for high-risk teens and youths; a repatriation program; and a wide variety of preventive and remedial programs, ranging from camps for children to parenting education to sweat lodges. The agency also had a connection with street kids, acting as a liaison between the youth and non-Native institutions and agents (e.g., social workers, school staff, and probation officers).

Despite these successes, the XFCCS has faced some challenges recently. On September 21, 2002, a two-year-old girl was found in a shallow grave on a reserve of the Leq'a:mel First Nation. The child's father was charged and convicted of manslaughter, indignity to human remains, and assault causing bodily harm. In 2003, XFCCS was found by independent investigators to have been negligent in their assessment of the risk involved in placing the little girl with her father. Around the same time, eight of the 19 Stó:lo bands within the Stó:lo Nation, including the five largest bands, separated to form the Naut'sa Mawt Tribal Council. Among other complaints, they did not feel that the XFCCS served the child care needs of the Stó:lo or Coast Salish people adequately and lobbied for a separate child care agency.

By 2005 there were 24 approved agreements with First Nations in British Columbia, covering somewhere over 50 percent of the bands in that province.

ABORIGINAL ARTS

Music is one way in which Aboriginal people are undoing the past and strengthening their identity. The following story was written in 2006 by a young Anishinabe woman currently working for the Inuit singer/songwriter Susan Aglukark.

"Being on the Dial"

By Kerry Potts

When I was younger, Aboriginal musicians were significant to my own identity, because they made public the identity of Aboriginal people. They took it off the reserve, outside of the arctic tundra, and made it accessible to a larger public. They created an image that I, as an urban Aboriginal person, could grasp onto and try to better understand what being Aboriginal was all about.

When I was sixteen, I recall Canada Day celebrations that featured an Innu group by the name of Kashtin. My friends would tease me by serenading me with the chorus from Kashtin's hit "Tshinanu" ad nauseam. Even though they made fun, it is still so noteworthy that my white friends could connect to a real image about Aboriginal people that was generated by an Aboriginal person. The fact that it was even on the radars of fifteen- and sixteen year-old city kids spoke volumes to me about the potential of music to reach far and wide. You did not have to read a book to find out about Aboriginal peoples. You could turn on your radio and hear them. You were exposed to Aboriginal sounds, languages, stories and aesthetics without even seeking it out. We were there, on the radio dial.

Regardless of my youthful enthusiasm about visible Aboriginal identity, it isn't enough to simply insert ourselves into the conduits of Canadian culture. Just because Aboriginal people are now visible as musicians and actors, [that] does not necessarily dismantle any of the racist assumptions made about us. Even if we are recognized as Aboriginal, even if we are seen as cool, beautiful and alive, there is still a racist lens through which the mainstream often sees us that remains intact. Let me give you a recent example:

In May 2005, Red Sky, a contemporary Indigenous performance company put to stage, at the CBC's Glenn Gould Studio, a contemporary version of the Ojibway story of Cheeby-Aub-Oozoo, "whose mythic descent to the underworld bequeaths music and dream quests to the land of the living."[2] This adaptation combined dramatic storytelling with both traditional and contemporary music. A key element to this performance was the presence of two hand-drummers, Eddy Robinson and Derrick Bressette. An online music magazine in Toronto reported, ". . . traditional singers Eddy Robinson and Derrick Bressette drum a heart-beat as their war-like cries pass back and forth." Though the reviewer shared appreciation for the performance, the interpretation reflects an uneducated description that draws upon a racist stereotype. The image of the savage, war-like Indian was projected upon an Aboriginal performance that was attempting to relay a story of great depth and resonance for the Anishinabe nation. As Eddy Robinson explains, "the purpose of the play was about the gift of song brought to us by Cheeby-Aub-Oozoo. So, for us to just shout out war cries is just ridiculous. Singing is about celebrating life. It's about being in the spirit. It's that universal language—it's the heart—the heart speaks the truth. It's the language of the spirits" (Personal Communication, October 1, 2005). As Sandra Laronde, Founder and Artistic Director of Red Sky Performance, further elaborates, "We definitely had war cries as Aboriginal people, and we did have songs before battle; the problem is that everything we sing, even the most beautiful song, is interpreted as a war cry" (Personal Communication, October 1, 2005; used with permission).

When this is the interpretation of our arts and music by audiences and media, how do we dismantle the Imaginary Indian construct? It is discouraging, to say the least, but we have to look on the positive side. Fifty years ago, such a production likely would not have been allowed to exist. Even twenty years ago, would Aboriginal people have thought that they could be performing at such a distinguished venue as the Glenn Gould? Would a mainstream paper have even been interested in covering such a performance? I want to be clear that the vision of Red Sky Performance, and the calibre of its work, have a lot to do with making this happen. However, it is important to note that Aboriginal artists are starting companies and organizations, securing some financial backing, and starting to develop an audience base that reaches beyond Aboriginal communities. Things have improved, and we have to be mindful of such improvements in order to not feel defeated.[3]

IDLE NO MORE

The Idle No More (INM) movement might seem to have appeared spontaneously but, in fact, it was the result of the lengthy history of suppression (as suggested by the name), albeit sparked by the federal government's Bill C-45 (or Second Omnibus Budget Bill). The movement was initiated by four Saskatchewan women who coined the term "Idle No More" as a motivational slogan. It was their belief that they had to be active and challenge the government's omnibus bill, specifically parts thereof perceived to be anti-environment and anti-Aboriginal. In November, 2012, Sylvia McAdam, a Cree lawyer and author; Jessica Gordon, also Cree; Nina Wilson, Nakota (Assiniboine) and Cree; and Sheelah Mclean, a non-Native, decided to be "idle no more." The term "Idle No More" was first used in a tweet on November 4 by Jessica Gordon. The movement is reminiscent of the 1960s in that it uses civil disobedience, rallies, hunger strikes, non-violent protest, and teach-ins to spread its message. However, it is also very much 21st century in that it employs flash mobs, cyber-activism, and social media. These strategies, along with its causes—i.e., acknowledgment of and respect for the rights of Aboriginal peoples, respect for the environment and opposition to its wanton destruction, and opposition to social and economic inequality—help to explain its rapid spread.

The women started with a series of teach-ins, first in Saskatoon on November 10, 2012, and within a week expanded to Regina, Prince Albert, North Battleford, and Winnipeg. Through the magic of modern technology and social media, the movement spread quickly. A month after the first event in Saskatoon, Idle No More held a National Day of Action in locations across the country. Throughout December, and in particular during the Christmas shopping spree, INM "flash mob" protestors performed round dances in some of the country's—indeed, the world's—largest shopping malls including the West Edmonton Mall, Ottawa's Rideau Centre and—indicating rapid international spread—the Mall of America in Minneapolis/St. Paul.

More protests followed in the new year, with rail and road blockades occurring across the country. On January 16, 2013, the Ambassador Bridge, the main link between Windsor and Detroit and one of the busiest border crossings in the country, was blocked by protestors. Another border crossing in Sault Ste. Marie was blocked. In Manitoba, protestors claiming to represent the American Indian Movement (AIM) blocked the CN rail line.

Overall, there were protests from New Brunswick to British Columbia on January 16. Minister of Finance Jim Flaherty voiced concern that the protests threatened the economy.

Idle No More is most concerned with three aspects of the omnibus bill: those pertaining to the Indian Act, the Navigation Protection Act (formerly known as the Navigable Waters Protection Act), and the Environmental Protection Assessment Act. These three Acts, of course, have direct implications for Aboriginal people. In particular, INM fears that changes to the Indian Act will erode indigenous rights and exploit treaty lands and territory. How can this happen? First Nations communities can, as a result of Bill C-45, lease designated reserve lands *if a majority attending a meeting called for that purpose vote to do so, regardless of how many people show up.* Prior to Bill C-45, approval required the support of a majority of eligible voters. Moreover, the minister of Aboriginal Affairs can now call a meeting to address the surrender of band territory *and* the minister can choose to ignore a resolution from the band council that's in opposition to a decision at the meeting. Briefly stated, the community has virtually no say and all the power resides with the government.

The Conservative government, in a number of areas, has demonstrated considerable lack of interest in protecting the environment, for example, pulling out of the Kyoto Accord in 2011 and, in March 2013, closing the internationally renowned freshwater research station Experimental Lakes Area in northern Ontario and pulling out of the United Nations Convention to Fight Desertification, which fights droughts globally. This move makes Canada the only country in the world outside the agreement (despite the fact that, with our Prairie Provinces subject to drought, 60% of our cropland is in dry regions).

With Bill C-45, there are additional threats to the environment. Under the Navigation Protection Act, major pipeline and power line project advocates are not required to prove that their mega-projects will not damage or destroy navigable waterways that they cross unless those waterways are on a list prepared by the transportation minister. Given what is perceived by some people to be an anti-science and anti-environment government, that list is likely to be seen as brief and favourable to project developers. Idle No More argues that the bill's amendments remove environmental protection for 99.9% of lakes and rivers in Canada. Likewise, the Environmental Protection Assessment Act reduced the number of projects that would require an environmental impact assessment before any work could begin. Idle No More, not surprisingly, objected to the expedited process for mega-project developers. However, it was not simply the perceived insensitivity of the federal government in dealing with these issues to which INM objected. It was also the lack of consultation with indigenous peoples. Such has usually been the case, of course, when it has come to First Nations and the federal government.

Attawapiskat Chief Theresa Spence quickly became the public face of INM although she was not a founder of the movement. On the initial National Day of Action on December 11, she announced that she would begin a hunger strike the next day to draw attention to the wretched conditions found on so many reserves, particularly those in remote and/or rural areas and, specifically, her own James Bay community. In the autumn of 2011, Spence had drawn worldwide attention to Attawapiskat when she declared a state of emergency over the housing crisis and other deplorable conditions. Appropriately, she settled on Victoria Island in the Ottawa River, near the nation's capital, drinking only lemon water, medicinal teas, and fish broth. She intended to continue her hunger strike until she had a meeting with Prime Minister Stephen Harper and Governor-General David Johnston to discuss how to improve the conditions on native reserves. She ended her 43-day strike on January 24 and, while she did not exactly get what she wanted, she became a symbol of the INM movement and focussed attention on Native issues in Canada. During her hunger strike she had visits from two former prime ministers but not Prime Minister Harper.

Neither Spence nor INM had unanimous support from the Aboriginal community. Patrick Brazeau, a Conservative senator and an Algonquin, was critical of both. He is quoted as saying that some Aboriginal people expect to live on government money, "To sit back, wait for the government to give me handouts. Maybe be on welfare, maybe drink, maybe take up drugs." His attacks on Theresa Spence were perceived by some observers as misogynist. He also noticed that some of her supporters were "White," the implication of which is unclear (http://www.ctvnews.ca/canada/sen-brazeau-mocks-chief-spence-idle-no-more-movement-1.1138545). Conversely, while there is no connection between INM and the Assembly of First Nations, Shawn Atleo, grand chief of the Assembly of First Nations, publicly offered his support for the movement. Out of concern for her health, he urged Theresa Spence to end her hunger strike.

For a number of reasons Idle No More may be deemed a success. It focussed media and public attention on Aboriginal (and environmental) issues in a way that few other events have. The movement was a grassroots, volunteer endeavour with no financial backing but managed to garner global attention. Public awareness and consciousness were hopefully raised in a positive way. The attention INM and Theresa Spence attracted was international, with solidarity protests in Cairo, Auckland, London, Stockholm, and Berlin. That is success. While largely an Aboriginal movement, Aboriginals and non-Aboriginals demonstrated and protested together in a shared cause (or causes). It spread rapidly, and the means by which people displayed their displeasure with the government were non-violent. And, consistent with other movements, such as the Arab Spring, INM showed the power of social media in fostering social action.

Perhaps the greatest success of Idle No More, however, is the inspiration it provided for others. A perfect example of this inspiration comes from Québec's James Bay. A group of seven young Cree left Whapmagoostui in January, 2013, and walked and snowshoed an incredible 1,600 kilometres to Parliament Hill in an effort to raise awareness of Aboriginal issues. By the time they arrived at the end of March, the group numbered nearly 400 as other Cree and some Algonquin had joined the walk, which the Cree called "The Journey of Nishiyuu" ("The Journey of the People"). As they arrived at Parliament Hill on March 25, there were thousands more cheering their arrival. Conspicuously absent was Prime Minister Harper, who had chosen instead to be in Toronto to greet the arrival of two giant pandas from China.

Native Individuals 25-1

Andrew and Phyllis Chelsea: Shuswap couple who spearheaded the Alkali Lake community's successful fight against alcohol.

Joseph Drybones: Dene man whose court case liberalized the liquor laws concerning Status Indians.

Timeline 25-1

1951: The Indian Act is changed to allow provincial child welfare agencies to deal with Status Indians.

1978: Indian Child Welfare Act is passed in the United States.

1979: The Secwepemc, or Shuswap, community of Spallumcheen passes a

by-law taking responsibility for child welfare away from the province.

1981: Dakota Ojibway Child and Family Services becomes the first Native-run child welfare agency.

1994: Xyolhemeylh Family and Child Care Services is formed.

ENDNOTES

1. See website http://web.uvic.ca/ablo/documents/IndianControlofIndianEducation.pdf.
2. Retrieved October 30, 2006 from www.redskyperformance.com.
3. I should note that many Aboriginal artists involved in Canada's arts world may not necessarily share my perspective. Sandra Laronde shared with me that she feels there are very few Aboriginal organizations and artists who are securing adequate financial backing and whose art forms are reaching beyond Aboriginal communities (Personal Communication, October 1, 2005).

KEY TERM

xyolhemeylh (Stó:lo)

CONTENT QUESTIONS

1. What is the Nechi Institute?
2. What has played a significant role in the rehabilitation of Native alcoholics at Alkali Lake and elsewhere?
3. What roles do Elders play in post-secondary education?
4. What did the Spallumcheen band do to change child welfare in its community?
5. What services are provided by Xyolhemeylh Family and Child Care Services among the Stó:lo?

WEBLINKS

Alcohol Programs

www.nechi.com
The website of the Nechi Institute, based in Edmonton, has useful information about their training, research, and health promotions programs.

www.4worlds.org/4w/ssr/Partiv.htm
This website tells the Alkali Lake community's story.

Education

www.firstnationsuniversity.ca
This is the website for the First Nations University of Canada.

www.redcrowcollege.com
This is the website for Red Crow Community College in Alberta.

www.ankn.uaf.edu
The Alaska Native Knowledge Network website provides resources related to Alaskan Native systems of knowledge.

www.yellowquillcollege.mb.ca
The website for Yellowquill College, a Native-run post-secondary institution, has useful information on their programs.

Child Welfare

www.turtleisland.org/discussion/viewtopic.php?t=1306
This website provides a discussion of the difficult situation faced by Xyolhemeylh Family and Child Care Services.

Glossary

Note on Languages

Both authors of this book have the strongly held belief that in order for non-Natives to be able to understand Native culture and Native people, non-Natives should learn at least a few words from Native languages, in part because such words have no equivalent terms in English or French. The Native words presented here have equal value to the more technical English terms in the comprehension of the material of this textbook.

Aboriginal rights As originally used, "aboriginal rights" referred only to land; in 1972 it was defined as "those property rights which inure to Native peoples by virtue of their occupation upon certain lands from time immemorial." Today, most Native speakers use the term to include rights to self-determination and self-government. (Dickason 1997:366)

Ahayuda A Zuni word for sacred wooden carvings that represent spirits associated with war. Ahayudas are carved in ceremony every year. The Zuni people have had a good deal of success in retrieving the Ahayuda from museums and private collections.

Algon(qu/k)ian The largest Native language family in Canada. Algonquian includes Mi'kmaq, Maliseet, Innu, Attikamek, Cree, Delaware, Ojibwe, Blackfoot, Peigan, and Kainai. The word is based on "Algonquin" (possibly derived from a Maliseet term meaning "they are relatives or allies"), which refers to only one group.

angajuqqaq An Inuktitut term for a relatively hierarchical leader, that is, one who has the capacity to give orders to another.

Anishinabe An Ojibwe term for themselves, often translated as "real people" or "original people."

annen-en A Huron/Wendat word meaning "my mother." Annen-en could be used to address or refer to both one's biological mother and her sister(s).

annuities Small, yearly payments that came with treaties.

âtalohkâna A Cree term referring to stories about events supposed to have taken place at a time when the world was being transformed into what it is today.

Atha(b/p)aska(n) A Woods Cree word usually translated as "[where] there are plants one after the other" or as "there are reeds here and there," referring to the lake of that name. From that word is derived Athapaskan, which refers to languages spoken by the Dene peoples.

atlatl A Nahuatl or Aztec word referring to the spearthrower, a device that creates an extension of the arm, thus enabling the person using the device to throw the spear harder and farther than would otherwise be possible.

awokanak A Cree word referring typically to domesticated animals, which came to be translated as "slaves" when referring to Dene peoples whom the Cree were fighting in the eighteenth century.

band In Dickason's words interpreting the legal definition of "band" as set down in the Indian Act: "According to the Act, a band is a body of Amerindians for whom the government has set aside lands for their common use and benefit; or which has been declared a band by the governor-in-council for the purposes of the Act" (Dickason 1997:259).

This legal entity differs from the anthropological definition of a band, which refers to a socio-political unit in traditional cultures. (See use of the terms **microband** and **macroband** in the text.) Kottak supplied the following typical anthropological definition of the term "band": "Basic unit of social organization among foragers [i.e., those that live by hunting and gathering]. A band includes fewer than 100 people; it often splits up seasonally" (Kottak 2000:501).

bilateral An anthropological term referring to "[a] system in which kinship ties are calculated equally through both sexes: mother and father, sister and brother, daughter and son, and so on" (Kottak 2000:501).

bitterroot This plant (Lewisia rediviva) has a pink or white flower, short stems, and a starchy root that looks like a forked radish. The root is sweet (and edible) in the spring, but becomes bitter by the summer.

camas The word for this plant (Camassia quamash) comes from a Nootka word, "chamas," meaning "sweet." The Camas is a member of the lily family and has a large, edible underground bulb, narrow leaves, purplish flowers, and a long stem (up to 90 cm).

Category 1 According to the James Bay and Northern Quebec Agreement, this category of land (amounting to 5543 square kilometres) was kept in Cree possession.

Category 2 According to the James Bay and Northern Quebec Agreement, on this category of land (amounting to 62,160 square kilometres) the Cree had exclusive rights to hunt, fish, and trap.

Category 3 According to the James Bay and Northern Quebec Agreement, this category of land, by far the greatest amount, was surrendered by the Cree, but would have special consideration in terms of their traditional activities.

Clovis points These are fluted or grooved spear points that were used for hunting big game from roughly 11,600 to 10,200 years ago. Clovis points have been found from the extreme north to the extreme south of the Americas.

cognates These are words, or parts of words, that sound alike, have similar meaning, and ultimately come from the same word (e.g., chant, enchantment, and incantation in English, and chanter in French, ultimately derive from the Latin cantare, a form of the verb "to sing").

confrontation, the A mythologized encounter between a non-Native official (typically an RCMP officer) and a Native who is "in trouble with the law." The non-Native triumphs through sheer heroism, typically without the use of arms.

copper A copper shield (from copper traditionally mined in Alaska) that bears a personal name and is given away in a potlatch ceremony as a highly valued item.

Dene A term in Athapaskan languages meaning "people." Often the names that Athapaskan-speaking First Nations give themselves have some form of this word in them. This includes the following from the text:

Dunne-za	"Real People," the Beaver
Kawcho *dinneh*	"Hare Big People," the Hare (term given to them by other Athapaskan speakers)
K'ashogo *tine*	"Willow Big People," the term used by the Hare to refer to themselves
Sahtú *Dene*	"Bear Lake People"
Thlingcha-*dinneh*	"Dog Side People," Dogrib term for themselves

dialect A version of a language, differing somewhat in pronunciation (i.e., accent), in grammar, or in words used in other versions of the language.

Diabetes type II Non-insulin-dependent diabetes is the most common form of diabetes, accounting for 90 to 95 percent of all diabetics.

dkonwewnini An Ojibwe term for police officer, meaning "a man who captures, grabs, or seizes something living."

Elder This term is used to refer to Native people recognized as having grown to wisdom over a relatively long life. Typically this growth to wisdom has been nurtured by areas of traditional Aboriginal knowledge.

enfranchisement This term refers to losing the status of being legally "Indian." In some ways it is like having a contract one has signed declared no longer legally binding. It was called "enfranchisement" because prior to 1960, the individual, upon losing Indian status, was then legally enfranchised to vote in elections.

epicanthic fold Driben and Herstein define this feature in the following way: ". . . a fold of skin on the upper eyelids that droops down over one or both corners of the eyes and makes them appear to be almond shaped" (Driben and Herstein 1994:422).

While this feature is not unique to Asia (e.g., it is found among the San [bushmen] of the Kalahari Desert in Africa and among some Native peoples), and not all Asians have this feature, for many, this feature is associated with "looking Asian."

Gaiwi:yoh A Seneca term meaning "it is a good, great, or beautiful matter." It refers to the teachings that sprang from the visions of the Seneca prophet, Handsome Lake, around the beginning of the nineteenth century. (The ":" after the "i" means that the vowel is long.)

Gayanerengo:wa A Mohawk word meaning "it is a great good," but typically referred to in English as "the Great Law of Peace." It refers to the story of how the five nations of the Iroquois came together, the rules they set in place, and the teachings that come from both these components.

hereditary chief Someone whose lineage provides the leader of a particular group. Usually this term is used when speaking about the more hierarchical First Nations, such as the Iroquoians and the peoples of the Northwest Coast.

hierarchical A people who have relatively clear distinctions among different ranks or classes of peoples within their society. These distinctions relate to a greater number of privileges of authority, and the use or ownership of

material and non-material (e.g., songs, dances, or stories) possessions. The opposite of this term is "egalitarian."

hierarchy of person An Ojibwe pronominal feature in which the morpheme or word part for "you" is always placed before the morpheme for "I" or "we."

hominids This term refers to the family of primates to which, today, only humans (e.g., homo sapiens) belong. The australopithecines, who lived until about one million years ago, and Neanderthal, who lived until about 30,000 years ago, were also hominids.

hunter's response A physical adaptation of Inuit and other Northern peoples in which the hands warm up quickly after being exposed to the cold.

ice creepers Pieces of ivory attached to footwear. The ivory is notched to form treads that grip the ice.

Indian agent An official of the federal government that was typically assigned to administer several bands. This official had great power over the bands, more than that held by the chief and council.

iniskim A Blackfoot term meaning "buffalo stone." It refers to a sacred rock, usually one containing fossils bearing a spiral shell.

Innu An Innu (i.e., Montagnais or Naskapi) word meaning "person." It is used to refer to the people generally. It appears in the words mushuau-innu ("barren ground person") and Sheshatsiwinnu ("great inlet person").

Interim agreement An agreement between a government body and a Native group that lasts for a fixed period of time. Sometimes it leads to a more permanent agreement, but that certainly is not always the case.

Inuit Tapirisat An Inuit political group, formed in 1971, that provided the primary push for the development of Nunavut. In Hugh Brody's words, Tapirisat is an Inuktitut word meaning, "literally 'the people's team' or 'collaboration' " (Brody 1987:233).

i(s/h)umataq An Inuktitut term roughly translated as "one who thinks." It refers to a type of egalitarian leader who leads by suggestion rather than by giving orders. In order to understand what the root **-ihuma-** means in Inuktitut, see Jean Briggs' important discussion on the subject (Briggs 1970:358–64).

iyinnakiikoan A Blackfoot term for police officer. It is derived from the verb stem yinnaki, which means "to grab, seize, hold, capture something living" (Frantz and Russell 1995:266).

Jay's Treaty This was an agreement, concluded on November 19, 1794, between U.S. Chief Justice John Jay and British Foreign Minister Lord Grenville, in which issues were settled that had not been resolved after the end of the American Revolution in 1783. Some of the issues related to border crossing between what would become Canada and the United States.

language family A group of languages that have been demonstrated to be related. English, for example, is in the Indo-European language family, related to such diverse languages as French, Russian, Greek, and Hindi.

language isolate A language that has no known relatives.

macroband A relatively large Subarctic group made up of several microbands gathered together during the summer for communal activities such as fishing. The macroband typically numbers from 75 to 150 people.

manly-hearted-woman See ninauposkitzipxpe.

matrilineal A way of determining kinship following the line of the mother. If, for example, a father belongs to the Bear clan and a mother belongs to the Turtle clan, then their children are of the Turtle clan.

microband A Subarctic hunting group made up of several linked families, typically numbering from 10 to 20.

microblades Small pieces of rock that have been flaked off a rock core and then fashioned to work as tools (e.g., scrapers) or as attachments in other tools (e.g., lances).

miksísstsiksi This word means "my mothers" in Blackfoot, and refers, collectively, to a person's mother and her sisters.

moiety Derived from a French term meaning "half," it refers to two social groups that a society is divided into, typically for burial, ritual, and political purposes. These groups can be subdivided into clans.

morpheme A part of a word that has meaning or grammatical function. For example, in the term "words," there are two morphemes, the noun "word" and the plural marker "-s."

mothers See annen-en and miksísstsiksi.

Mushuau-Innu An Innu term meaning "barren ground person," referring to Innu peoples who live in the barrens area of Labrador.

muyine' A Dunne-za or Beaver term meaning "his/her song," referring to a person's spiritual power or medicine bundle (i.e., collection of sacred items that connect a person with the spiritual).

myth of Native biological helplessness The belief that Native people generally have no physical resistance to alcohol and cannot control how much they drink.

myth of Native cultural helplessness This belief portrays Aboriginal people as victims of disease and ill-health, unable to help themselves.

naammendaagzid An Ojibwe verb meaning "to be considered guilty." This is the closest term in the traditional language to the European legal sense of someone "being guilty."

Na'pi A Blackfoot term meaning "Old Man," referring to the cultural hero of the Blackfoot.

nimass aksiwin A Cree term meaning "fish disease," referring to mercury poisoning. The Cree use this term because the fish in the East James Bay area have dangerously high amounts of mercury in their system.

ninauposkitzipxpe A Blackfoot term meaning "manly hearted woman." It refers to women who take on roles usually associated with men.

Ni'taiitsskaaiks A traditional Peigan warrior society that was reactivated to protest the damming of the sacred Oldman River.

nitapiksisako A Blackfoot term meaning "real meat." It refers to buffalo meat, showing the significance of buffalo to the traditional diet of the Blackfoot.

notka The standard derivation of the term Nootka states that it came from an instruction by the Nuu'chah'nulth to Captain James Cook to "circle around" the area of what is now Nootka Sound.

nutshimit An Innu word sometimes translated as "the bush" or "the country" in English. Its significance is hard to translate. A good English translation would also have to incorporate such diverse notions as: "(at) home," "my country," "my homeland," "the cottage," "where I can be myself." Some further sense of this term can be seen in the following East Cree cognates that, with a slightly different spelling, incorporate the same morpheme:

nuuhchimiiuiinuu	"inland hunter, trapper" (with -iinuu- "person")
nuuhchimiiunitunkuin	"bush medicine" (with -nitunkuin- "medicine")
nuuhchimiiumaakusuu	"s/he smells like the bush"
nuuhchimiiumaakusuu	"s/he looks like someone from inland, from the bush.

(Cree School Board 1987:406)

okan A Peigan word referring to the centre pole of the Sun Dance lodge (the most sacred object of the ritual) and to the Sun Dance itself. In Blackfoot, the cognates are the following:

ookaa: [to] sponsor the primary religious ceremony associated with the Sun Dance

áakookaawa: she [/he] will sponsor a Sun Dance

ookáán: the primary religious ceremony associated with the Sun Dance. (Frantz and Russell 1995:168)

-ondech(r)- A Huron noun stem referring to "country" in the physical, social, and spiritual senses of the word.

on,8e n'on,8e (Huron) or **Ongwehon:we** (Mohawk) Loosely translated, this term means "humans who are humans." The Huron term referred to Native peoples, and the Mohawk term can be used to refer to Six Nations peoples or Natives in general.

oolichan (also eulachon, oolakan, or oulakan) A Chinook word referring to the candlefish (Thaleichthys pacificus), a fish related to the smelt. When it goes on its spawning run, this fish is so oily that it can be used to make an oil that was an important food item for Northwest Coast peoples. It got its name "candlefish" because when it is dried, a wick can be stuck in it and the fish can be used as a candle.

pass system Introduced in 1885 and lasting until the 1930s, a legally questionable practice of not allowing Natives in prairie reserves to leave the reserve without a pass issued by their non-Native farming instructor or Indian agent.

pâstâmowin A Cree word referring to stories in which something bad happens after someone breaks the rules.

patrilineal Reckoning kinship along the husband's or father's line.

pemmican A Cree word referring to buffalo jerky, made from dried buffalo meat, rendered fat, and saskatoon berries. Pemmican was a staple of the fur trade in the eighteenth and nineteenth centuries.

Pine Tree Chiefs A term used to refer to members of the Iroquois Confederacy who take on leadership roles, not because they hold one of the 50 chiefly titles, but solely because they have made a name and role for themselves.

potlatch Based on a Chinook trade jargon term meaning "to give." Because of the importance of generosity and giveaway in the ceremony, potlatch refers to the most important ceremony of most of the Northwest Coast peoples. It was banned from 1884 to 1951.

phratries A way of dividing up society for social, political, and ritual purposes, similar to moieties. Phratries typically contain clans. The eighteenth-century Wyandot of the Windsor/Detroit area had three phratries: Deer, Turtle, and Wolf. Each phratry had a chief and various member clans:

Deer phratry—Deer, Bear, and Snake clans

Turtle phratry—Porcupine, Large Turtle, Striped Turtle, and Prairie Turtle clans

Wolf phratry—Wolf, Hawk, and Sturgeon clans

public purchase Government acquiring ownership of land by entering into a treaty or other formal agreement with a Native group.

reserves Called "reservations" in the United States, reserves are plots of land reserved to particular Native bands.

residential schools Boarding schools for Native students financed by the federal government and run by various churches. Not only did these schools have a lower standard of education than schools intended for non-Native children, but they were also places where a significant number of Native children were abused—physically, emotionally, and sexually.

restorative justice The principle of justice that stresses that the offender, the victim, and the general community need to be "healed" or restored to a healthy state. It is in contrast to retributive justice, in which the main idea is that someone gets punished.

root The central part of a word, the main building block upon which other parts (e.g., prefixes or suffixes) are added. For example, in the word "building", -build- is the root.

sachem Derived from an Eastern Algonquian word for "leader" (see **saqmaw**). This term is often used to refer to the 50 chief titles of the League of the Iroquois.

saqmaw A Mi'kmaq word for "leader." Cognates have entered English as **sachem** and **sagamore**.

saskatoon Derived from the Cree word "misaskwatomi" (lit. much-wood-berry), referring to the service or saskatoon berry, which is used in the making of pemmican and on its own as a sacrament in the Sun Dance.

sentencing circle A tradition-based restorative Aboriginal justice practice in which offenders face community members (including the victim[s]), their own family members, Elders, and victim's family members), who discuss how a criminal act will be dealt with.

Sheshatshit An Innu word meaning "Great Inlet," the name of the community in Labrador known in English as Northwest River.

sheshatsiwinnu An Innu word meaning "Great Inlet Person."

Sixties Scoop A term coined by writer Patrick Johnston that refers to the taking of thousands of Native children from their families, communities, and peoples during the 1960s to early 1980s.

starlight tours The policing practice of driving Native people who have been drinking to isolated locations outside of a city or town, forcing them to walk back home.

Status Indian Term used to refer to someone who is recognized by the federal government as having the status of being an "Indian" under the Indian Act.

Suyitapis A Peigan word meaning "Underwater People." It refers to the spirit figures who live in the water and who gave the Peigan people sacred images and items.

sweatlodge A ceremonial building (and the ceremony itself) in which water is poured over hot rocks, producing cleansing steam. An Elder or some other spiritual leader typically directs people in their own experience of the sweatlodge.

sweetgrass A plant that is burned so that the smoke can ritually purify the place.

thrifty gene A gene that enables the body to hold onto or "save" blood sugars longer. The ability to hold onto blood sugars gave people of certain families in the Eastern Subarctic an advantage in being able to deal with periodic famine.

tipâcimôwina A Cree word typically translated as stories, news, historical narratives, or personal experiences.

totem An Ojibwe word for "clan." It has come to be associated in English with the Northwest Coast poles, which have carved symbols of clans or moieties.

tribal council Aboriginal organization that includes more than one band. They are usually dominated by or are exclusively of one cultural or "tribal" tradition.

Tun(n/r)it A gentle, seal-hunting people in traditional Inuit stories, thought to be the Dorset people.

umiak An Inuit word referring to a large seal-skin boat that could hold 12 people and could be over nine metres in length.

u'mista A Kwakwaka'wakw word meaning "special return." It is used in the name of the U'mista Cultural Centre, constructed in 1980 to receive the special return of the sacred potlatch items.

urban reserve Land that has received official Indian reserve status from the federal government and is located within a municipality or, in Saskatchewan, a Northern Administrative District.

victimology The study of why people are victims of crime, including lifestyles and social perceptions that contribute to Aboriginals being seen as victims and unable to help themselves.

War Measures Act An act that the federal government can invoke to suspend the usual rights of the people in order to serve the needs of war or a special emergency.

weir A trap, typically constructed out of poles or rocks, that gathers fish together in one spot where they can be easily speared.

xyolhemeylh A Stó:lo or Halkomelem word referring to the special relationship of caring, respect, and love that exists between a caregiver and a child.

[y]andarachrio Originally spelled **andarachrio**, a seventeenth-century Huron word meaning "it is great in existence." It refers to a people as the original or First Nation in a particular place.

References

Abel, Kerry. 1993. *Drum Songs: Glimpses of Dene History.* Montreal: McGill-Queen's University Press.

Act to Further Amend the Indian Act. 1880. S.C. 1884, c.27 (47 Vict.), Section 3.

Albers, P., and B. Medicine. 1983. *The Hidden Half.* Lanham, MD: University Press of America.

Anishinaabe Gchi-Naaknigewin. 2006. *Anishinabek News,* June 29, p.18.

Anti-Colonial Action Alliance. 1996. "Justice for the Stoney Point People." Info-Leaflet #4. Retrieved November 9, 2006 from www.execulink.com/~hkoehler/stonsups. htm.

Assu, Harry, and Joy Inglis. 1989. "Assu of Cape Mudge: Recollections of a Coastal Indian Chief." Vancouver, BC: University of British Columbia Press.

Barbeau, Marius. 1915. *Huron and Wyandot Mythology.* Memoir 80, No. 11, Anthropological Series. Ottawa: Dept. of Mines Geological Survey.

Barman, Jean. 1986. "Separate and Unequal: Indian and White Girls at All Hallows School, 1884–1920." In J. Barman, Y. Hébert, and D. McCaskill, eds. *Indian Education in Canada: Vol. 1. The Legacy,* pp. 110–127. Vancouver: University of British Columbia Press.

Barman, Jean, Yvonne Hébert, and Don McCaskill. 1986. "The Legacy of the Past: An Overview." In J. Barman, Y. Hébert, and D. McCaskill, eds. *Indian Education in Canada: Vol. 1. The Legacy,* pp. 1–22.

Barman, J., Y. Hébert, and D. McCaskill, eds. *Indian Education in Canada: Vol. 1. The Legacy,* pp. 1–22. Vancouver: University of British Columbia Press.

Benton-Banai, Edward. 1988. *The Mishomis Book: The Voice of the Ojibway.* Saint Paul, MN: Red School House.

Bergman, Brian. 1996. "Dark Days for the Inuit." *Maclean's,* March 4, p. 67.

Blondin, George. 1996. "When the World Was New: Stories of the Sahtú Dene." In K. Coates and R. Fisher, eds., *Out of the Background: Readings on Canadian Native History,* 2nd ed., pp. 245–278. Toronto: Copp Clark.

Born With a Tooth, M. 1994. Statement. *Windspeaker,* October 9.

Briggs, Jean. 1970. *Never in Anger: Portrait of an Eskimo Family.* Cambridge, MA: Harvard University Press.

Brizinski, P. 1993. *Knots in a String: An Introduction to Native Studies in Canada.* Saskatoon: University Extension Press.

Brody, Hugh. 1987. *Living Arctic: Hunters of the Canadian North.* Vancouver: Douglas & McIntyre.

Brownlie, Robin. 2003. *A Fatherly Eye: Indian Agents, Government Power, and Aboriginal Resistance in Ontario, 1918–1939.* Toronto: Oxford University Press.

Burch, Ernest S., Jr. 1995. "The Caribou Inuit." In R.B. Morrison and C.R. Wilson, eds., *Native Peoples: The Canadian Experience,* pp. 115–142. Toronto: McClelland & Stewart.

Burke, Marie. 1999. "It's How a Foster Family Works." *Alberta Sweetgrass,* Oct. 11.

Cameron, S. 2010. *On the Farm: Robert William Pickton and the Tragic Story of Vancouver's Missing Women.* Toronto: Knopf Canada.

Canada, Dominion of. 1920. *Sessional Papers, LVI*(27) 13–14. In *Northern Blue,* Jan 27. 2005. Retrieved November 14, 2001, from http://northernblue.ca/ablog/index.php?/categories/7-Warriors.

Canada, Solicitor General. 1996. *Crime Prevention in First Nations Communities: An Inventory of Policing Initiatives.* Ottawa: Author.

Carl, Julie. 1999. "Ipperwash Conviction, Sentence Appealed." *London Free Press,* Sept. 15.

Chaumel, Gilles, and Mesténapéo, Germaine. 1996. "The Four Seasons of Julienne." *Rencontre, 17*(2), 4–5.

Clarkson, Betty. 1967. *Credit Valley Gateway: The Story of Port Credit.* Toronto: University of Toronto Press.

Clairmont, Don, and Rick Linden. 1998. *Developing and Evaluating Justice Projects in Aboriginal Communities: A Review of the Literature.* Ottawa: Solicitor General Canada.

Clutesi, George. 1969. *Potlatch.* Victoria, BC: The Morris Printing Company.

Coccola, Raymond de, and Paul King. 1986. *The Incredible Eskimo: Life among the Barren Land Eskimo.* Surrey, B.C.: Hancock House.

Comeau, Pauline. 1993. *Elijah: No Ordinary Hero.* Vancouver: Douglas & McIntyre.

Comeau, Pauline, and Santin Aldo. *The First Canadians: A Profile of Canada's Native People Today.* Toronto: James Lorimer.

Copway, George (Kahgegagahbowh). 1972. *The Traditional History and Characteristic Sketches of the Ojibway.* Toronto: Coles Publishing Ltd. Originally published 1850.

Cree School Board. 1987. *Cree Lexicon: Eastern James Bay Dialects.* Author: Baie-de-la-Poste, Mistassini Lake.

Crowe, Keith. 1974. *A History of the Original Peoples of Northern Canada.* Montreal, Arctic Institute of North America. McGill-Queen's University Press.

Cruikshank, Julie. 1990. *Life Lived Like a Story: Life Stories of Three Yukon Native Elders.* Vancouver: University of British Columbia Press.

Cummins, Bryan. 2002. *First Nations, First Dogs: Canadian Aboriginal Ethnocynology.* Calgary: Detselig Enterprises Ltd.

Cummins, Bryan, and John Steckley. 2003. *Aboriginal Policing: A Canadian Perspective.* Toronto: Pearson Education Canada.

Curnoe, Greg. 1996. *Deeds/Nations.* London: London Chapter, Ontario Archaeology Society.

Day, Gordon M. 1978. "Western Abenaki." In B.G. Trigger, ed., *Handbook of North American Indians: Vol. 15. Northeast,* pp. 148–159. Washington: Smithsonian Institute.

Day, Gordon M. 1994. *Western Abenaki Dictionary: Vol. 1. Abenaki-English.* Hull, PQ: Canadian Museum of Civilization.

Dempsey, Hugh. 1972. *Crowfoot, Chief of the Blackfeet.* Norman: University of Oklahoma Press.

Dempsey, Hugh. 1995. "The Blackfoot Indians." In R.B. Morrison and C.R. Wilson, eds., *Native Peoples: The Canadian Experience,* 2nd ed, pp. 381–413. Toronto: McClelland & Stewart.

Dick, Lyle. 1995. "'Pibloktoq' (Arctic Hysteria): A Construction of European-Inuit Relations?" *Arctic Anthropology 32*(2) 1–42.

Dickason, Olive. 1992. *Canada's First Nations: A History of Founding Peoples from Earliest Times.* Toronto: Oxford University Press.

Dickason, Olive. 1997. *Canada's First Nations: A History of Founding Peoples from Earliest Times.* 2nd ed. Toronto: Oxford University Press.

Dickason, Olive. 2002. *Canada's First Nations: A History of Founding Peoples from Earliest Times.* 3rd ed. Toronto: Oxford University Press.

Douglas, Mark. *Mnjikaning: The Fish Fence at the Narrows.* Pamphlet.

Driben, Paul, and Harvey Herstein. 1994. *Portrait of Humankind: An Introduction to Human Biology and Prehistoric Cultures.* Scarborough: Prentice-Hall Canada.

Dumont, G. 1993. *Gabriel Dumont Speaks.* Trans. M. Barnholden. Vancouver: Talonbooks. Originally published 1903.

Duuren, Ed van. 1994. *Hunstville Forester,* May 25.

Edwards, Peter. 2003. *One Dead Indian, The Premier, The Police and the Ipperwash Crisis.* Toronto: Stoddard Publishing.

Ellis, Douglas C. 1995. *Âtalohkâna nêsta Tipâcimôwina: Cree Legends and Narratives from the West Coast of James Bay.* Winnipeg: University of Manitoba Press.

Ezzo, David. 1988. "Female Status in the Northeast." In W. Cowan, ed., *Papers of the Nineteenth Algonquian Conference.* Ottawa: Carleton University Press.

"Fishing rights." 1999, 29 September. Retrieved November 1, 2000, from *Disparities in law and power,* www.rism.org/isg/dlp/bc/news/bc_ts_19990929_1.htm.

FH1693 ca1693. *French-Huron Dictionary,* ms., Archive Séminaire de Québec.

FH1697 ca1697. *French-Huron Dictionary,* ms., John Carter Brown Library, Brown University, Providence, Rhode Island.

First Nations Chiefs of Police Association (FNCPA). 1992. "About FNCPA." Retrieved November 4, 2006, from www.fncpa.ca/About_Fncpa.htm.

Fisher, Robin. 1977. *Contact and Conflict: Indian-European Relations in British Columbia, 1774–1890.* Vancouver: University of British Columbia Press.

Fournier, Suzanne, and Ernie Crey. 1997. *Stolen from Our Embrace: The Abduction of First Nations Children and the Restoration of Aboriginal Communities.* Vancouver: Douglas & McIntyre.

Francis, Daniel. 1992. *The Imaginary Indian: The Image of the Indian in Canadian Culture.* Vancouver: Arsenal Pulp Press.

Franklin, John. 2005. *Narrative of a Journey to the Shores of the Polar Sea: In the Years 1819, 20, 21 and 22.* New York: Cosimo Books.

Frantz, Donald G., and Norma Jean Russell. 1995. *Blackfoot Dictionary of Stems, Roots and Affixes.* 2nd ed., Toronto: University of Toronto Press.

Frideres, James S. 1998. *Aboriginal Peoples in Canada: Contemporary Conflicts,* 5th ed. Scarborough: Prentice Hall Allyn and Bacon.

Frideres, James S., & R. R. Gadacz. 2012. *Aboriginal Peoples in Canada* 9/e. Toronto: Pearson Canada.

Friesen, Joe. 2011. The Ballad of Daniel Wolfe. *The Globe & Mail.* June 11, 2011.

Friesen, John W. 1997. *Rediscovering the First Nations of Canada.* Calgary: Detselig Enterprises Ltd.

Gordon, Tariq Hassan. 1996. "Trial Date Set for Stoney Point Members Charged in Defence of Traditional Territory." *Prison News Service* 54, Spring. Retrieved November 15, 2006, from http://sisis.nativeweb.org/ipperwash/may96.html.

Goulding, W. D. 2001. *Just Another Indian: A Serial Killer and Canada's Indifference.* Markham, ON: Fifth House.

Great Britain. 1824. "By the King: A Proclamation." In *A Collection of the Acts Passed in the Parliament of Great Britain and of Other Public Acts Relative to Canada.* Quebec: P.E.

Desbarats. Retrieved October 26, 2006, from www.bloorstreet.com/200block/rp1763.htm. Originally published in 1763.

Green, Gordon. 1998. "Community Sentencing and Mediation in Aboriginal Communities." *Manitoba Law Journal.*

Gryier, Pat. 1994. *A Long Way from Home: The Tuberculosis Epidemic and the Inuit.* Montreal: McGill-Queen's Publishing.

Hamilton, John. 1998. "Ipperwash Protester Sent to Jail, Natives Angered over 'Injustice.'" *London Free Press*, April 4. Retrieved November 15, 2006, from http://sisis.nativeweb.org/ipperwash/tapr0498.html.

"Harris Denies Ever Using Profane Slur against Natives." 2006, Feb. 15. Retrieved November 15, 2006, from www.cbc.ca/canada/story/2006/02/15/newipperwashl.060215.html.

Harris, Michael. 1986. *Justice Denied: The Law Versus Donald Marshall.* Toronto: Macmillan.

Heartfield, Kate. 1998. "Aboriginal Elder visits U of O Campus." *Fulcrum Online* Issue 59-09, October. Retrieved November 16, 2000, from www.thefulcrum.com/98-99/59_ 09_05.html.

Helm, June, and Vital Thomas. 1991. "The Bewitched Pale Man from 'Tales of the Dogribs.'" Originally published in 1966. In Peter Nabokov, ed., *Native American Testimony: A Chronicle of Indian-White Relations from Prophecy to the Present, 1492–1992*, pp. 47–48. Toronto: Penguin Books.

Hodge, F.W. (Ed.). 1971a. *Handbook of Indians of Canada.* Toronto: Coles Ltd. Originally published 1913.

Hodge, F.W. 1971b. *Indian Treaties and Surrenders.* (Vols. 1–3). Toronto: Coles Ltd. Originally published 1891 and 1912.

Hopkins, Grant. 1993. *Ottawa Citizen*, August 8.

http://www.aadncaandc.gc.ca/eng/1100100013791/1100100013795

http://www.cccb.ca/site/eng/media-room/files/2630-apology-on-residential-schools-by-the-catholic-church

http://www.cisc.gc.ca/annual_reports/annual_report_2004/aboriginal_2004_e.htm

http://www.ctvnews.ca/canada/sen-brazeau-mocks-chief-spence-idle-no-more-movement-1.1138545

http://www.hc-sc.gc.ca/fniah-spnia/diseases-maladies/aids-sida/index-eng.php

http://www.hc-sc.gc.ca/fniah-spnia/diseases-maladies/tuberculos/index-eng.php

http://www.phac-aspc.gc.ca/aids-sida/publication/ps-pd/aboriginal-autochtones/index-eng.php

http://www.rcmp-grc.gc.ca/pubs/abo-aut/firstnat-premnat-eng.htm

Hudson, D. 1989. *Overlap Report. Prepared for the Taku River Tlingit First Nation.* Retrieved November 3, 2006, from www.eao.gov.bc.ca/epic/output/documents/p11/1036627042573_424b8b884aaf491991579 45afb126fc6.pdf.

Hungry Wolf, Adolph, and Beverly Hungry Wolf. 1991. *Indian Tribes of the Northern Rockies.* Skookumchuck, BC: Good Medicine Books.

Indian and Northern Affairs Canada. 1996a. *Royal Commission on Aboriginal Peoples. Volume 1: Looking Forward, Looking Back.* Part 2, Chapter 12, Section 4.5. Retrieved October 29, 2006, from www.ainc-inac.gc.ca/ch/rcap/sg/sg48_e.html.

Indian and Northern Affairs Canada. 1996b. *Royal Commission on Aboriginal Peoples. Volume 1: Looking Forward, Looking Back.* Part 2, Chapter 11, Section 3. Retrieved October 29, 2006, from www.ainc-inac.gc.ca/ch/rcap/sg/sg39_e.html#114.

Indian and Northern Affairs Canada. 1996c. *Royal Commission on Aboriginal Peoples. Volume 3: Looking Forward, Looking Back.* Chapter 2, Section 4. Retrieved October 29, 2006, from www.ainc-inac.gc.ca/ch/rcap/sg/si5_e.html.

"Indian Murders." 1864. *Victoria Daily Colonist.* Retrieved November 2, 2006, from www.canadianmysteries.ca/sites/klatsassin/archives/indexen.html.

Indian Residential Schools Resolution Canada (IRSRC). 2006a. Retrieved May 10, 2006, from www.irsr-rqpi.gc.ca/english/news_10_05_06.

Indian Residential Schools Resolution Canada (IRSRC). 2006b. Retrieved May 10, 2006, from www.irsr-rqpi.gc.ca/english/statistics.

Jaenen, Cornelius J. 1986. "Education for Francization: The Case of New France in the Seventeenth Century." In J. Barman, Y. Hébert, and D. McCaskill, eds., *Indian Education: Vol. 1. The Legacy,* pp. 45–63.

Jenness, Diamond. 1932. *The Indians of Canada.* Ottawa: King's Printer.

Jenness, Diamond. 1937. *The Sekani Indians of British Columbia.* Ottawa: Dept. of Mines. National Museum of Canada. Bull. 84, Anthropological Series No. 20.

Jesuit Relations and Allied Documents: Travels and Explorations of the Jesuit missionaries in New France, 1610-1791 (JR). 1959. Ed. Reuben Gold Thwaites, Jr. (Vols. 1–73). New York: Pageant Book Company.

Johnston, Basil. 1991. "One Generation from Extinction." In W.H. New, ed., *Native Writers and Canadian Writing,* pp. 10–15. Vancouver: University of British Columbia Press.

Johnston, Patrick. 1983. *Native Children and the Child Welfare System.* Ottawa: Canada Council on Social Development.

Johnson, Joyce, and Fred Johnson. 1993. "Community Development, Sobriety and After-Care at Alkali Lake Band." In *The Path to Healing: Report on the National Round Table on Aboriginal Health and Social Issues.* Ottawa: Royal Commission on Aboriginal Peoples.

Justice Canada. 1998, July 8. "Dena Keh community justice program now under way." Retrieved October 26, 2006, from http://justice.gc.ca/en/news/nr/1998/denake.html.

Kehoe, Alice. 1992. *North American Indians: A Comprehensive Account.* Englewood Cliffs, NJ: Prentice Hall.

Kehoe, Alice. 1995. "Blackfoot Persons." In L. Klein and L. Ackerman. *Women and Power in Native North America.* Norman, OK: University of Oklahoma Press.

Kelsay, Isabel Thompson. 1984. *Joseph Brant 1743–1807: Man of Two Worlds.* Syracuse, NY: Syracuse University Press.

Kipp, Darrell Robes. 1996. "Blackfoot." In Frederick E. Hoxie, ed., *Encyclopedia of North American Indians,* pp. 75–76. Boston/New York: Houghton Mifflin Co.

Knockwood, Isabelle. 1992. *Out of the Depths: The Experiences of Mi'kmaw Children at the Indian Residential School at Shubenacadie, Nova Scotia.* Lockeport, NS: Roseway Publishing.

Koehler, H.P. 1996, March 26. "Stoney Point People's Support." Retrieved November 15, 2006, from www.execulink.com/~hkoehler/stonsups.htm.

Kottak, Conrad Phillip. 2000. *Cultural Anthropology,* 8th ed., Boston: McGraw-Hill.

Kulchyski, Peter, ed. 1994. *Unjust Relations: Aboriginal Rights in Canadian Courts.* Toronto: Oxford University Press.

Land O'Lakes Tourist Association. 1994, January 25. *North Frontenac News.* Editorial.

Lil' Wat Nation. 1911. Retrieved November 2, 2006, from http://sisis.nativeweb.org/lilwat/pam.html.

MacGregor, Roy. 1989. *Chief: The Fearless Vision of Billy Diamond.* Toronto: Penguin Books.

Mackenzie, William Lyon. 1960. In M. Fairley, ed., *The Selected Writings of William Lyon Mackenzie, 1824–1837.* Toronto: Oxford University Press.

Maclean, John. 1970. *The Indians of Canada: Their Manners and Customs.* Toronto: Coles Ltd. Originally published 1889.

Manuel, George, and Michael Posluns. 1974. *The Fourth World: An Indian Reality.* Don Mills: Collier-Macmillan Canada.

Matas, Robert. 1999. "He Carried the Torch for the Nisga'a." *The Globe and Mail,* Dec. 14, 1999, p.A18.

Matthiasson, John S. 1992. *Living on the Land: Change Among the Inuit of Baffin Island.* Peterborough: Broadview Press.

Matthiasson, John S. 1995. "The Maritime Inuit: Life on the Edge." In R.B. Morrison and C.R.Wilson, eds., *Native Peoples: The Canadian Experience,* pp. 78–114. Toronto: McClelland & Stewart.

May, Philip A. 1998. "The Epidemiology of Alcohol Abuse Among American Indians: Mythical and Real Properties." Originally published 1994. In Susan Lobo and Steve Talbot, eds., *Native American Voices: A Reader,* pp. 388–399. Don Mills: Longman.

McGillvray, A., & B. Comaskey. 1999. *Black Eyes All of the Time: Intimate Violence, Aboriginal Women, and the Justice System.* Toronto, ON: University of Toronto Press.

Medicine, B. 1983. "My Elders Tell Me." In Don MacCaskill and Yvonne Hebert, eds., *Native Education: Volume 2,* pp. 142–51. Toronto: University of Toronto Press.

McGhee, Robert. 1978. *Canadian Artic Prehistory.* Chicago: University of Chicago Press.

Mercredi, Ovide, and Mary Ellen Turpel. 1993. *In the Rapids: Navigating the Future of First Nations.* Toronto: Penguin Books.

Miller, J.R. 1996. *Shingwauk's Vision: A History of Native Residential Schools.* Toronto: University of Toronto Press.

Miller, Virginia P. 1995. "The Micmac: A Maritime Woodland Group." In R.B. Morrison and C.R. Wilson, eds., *Native Peoples: The Canadian Experience,* pp. 347–374. Toronto: McClelland & Stewart.

Milloy, John. 1988. *The Plains Cree: Trade, Diplomacy and War, 1790–1870.* Winnipeg: University of Manitoba Press.

Minthorn, Armand. 1996, September. "Human remains should be reburied." Retrieved October 1, 2006, from www.umatilla.nsn.us/kman1.html.

Monture-Angus, Patricia. 1995. *Thunder in My Soul: A Mohawk Woman Speaks.* Halifax: Fernwood Publishing.

Moran, Bridget. 1996. "Justa: A First Nations Leader" ("Dakelhne butsowhudilhulh'un"). In Coates and Fisher, eds., *Out of the Background: Readings on Canadian Native History,* pp. 297–309. Toronto: Copp Clark Ltd.

Morehead, Albert, and Loy Morehead. 1972. *The New American Webster's College Dictionary.* New York: Signet.

Morrison, R. Bruce, and C. Roderick Wilson, eds. 1995. *Native Peoples: The Canadian Experience.* 2nd ed. Toronto: McClelland & Stewart.

Nabokov, Peter, ed. 1991. *Native American Testimony: A Chronicle of Indian-White Relations from Prophecy to the Present, 1492–1992.* Toronto: Penguin Books Canada.

"National Defence Documents." 1995. Retrieved November 15, 2006, from http://sisis.nativeweb.org/ipperwash/sep0795dis.html.

"Native Veterans." In *Courage Remembered: The world wars through Canadian Eyes.* Retrieved October 29, 2006, from http://northernblue.ca/ablog/index.php?/categories/7-warriors. *Cape Breton's Magazine,* No. 52, p.58.

Native Women's Association of Canada. 2010. *What Their Stories Tell Us: Research Findings from the Sisters in Spirit Initiative.* http://ywcacanada.ca/data/research_docs/00000136.pdf.

Nechi Institute and KAS Corporation Limited. 1994, December. *Healing, Spirit and Recovery: Factors Associated with Successful Integration.* Ottawa: Solicitor General Canada. Retrieved October 30, 2006, from www.sgc.gc.ca/epub/Abocor/eAPC11CA/eAPC11CA_e.pdf

Neves, Walter, and Mark Hubbe. 2005, December 20. "Cranial morphology of early americans from Lagoa Santa, Brazil: Implication for the settlement of the New World." Proceedings of the National Academy of Sciences. Retrieved October 1, 2006, from www.pnas.org/cgi/full/102/51/18309.

Nihmey, John. 1998. *Fireworks and Folly: How We Killed Minnie Sutherland.* Ottawa: Phillip Diamond Books.

Niquay, Marie-Louise. 1995/1996. "Kokomino Judith Kawiasiketct, Preserving the Atikamekw Soul." *Rencontre, 17*(2) 8–9.

Nowell, Charles James. 1968. In Clellan S. Ford, ed., *Smoke from Their Fires: The Life of a Kwakiutl Chief.* Hampden, CT: Archon Books. Originally published 1941.

O'Donnell, V., & S. Wallace. 2011. First Nations, Métis and Inuit Women. In *Women in Canada: A Gender-Based Statistical Report.* Ottawa, ON: Social and Aboriginal Statistics Division, Statistics Canada.

O'Hara, Jane. 1999. "Trade Secrets." *Maclean's*, October 18, pp. 20–29.

O'Meara, John. 1996. *Delaware-English/English-Delaware Dictionary.* Toronto: University of Toronto Press.

Ontario Ministry of Education. 1999, January. *Draft Proposal, The Ontario Curriculum, Grades 11 and 12, Native Studies.* Toronto: Author.

Paradis, Melanie. 2013. For the Métis, Justice Had No Expiry Date. *The Globe & Mail.* March 13, 2013.

Pelletier, Wilfred, and Ted Poole. 1973. *No Foreign Land: The Biography of a North American Indian.* New York: Pantheon Books.

Pine Tree Legal Assistance. 2002, January. "Indian Child Welfare Act Update." *Wabanaki Legal News.* Retrieved November 3, 2006, from www.ptla.org/wabanaki/icwa.htm.

"Plainspeak." 2000. *The Métis Hunt for Justice: A Plainspeak of the Powley Decision.* Pamphlet.

Potier, Pierre. 1920. *The Fifteenth Report of the Bureau of Archives for the Province of Ontario.* Toronto: C.W. James.

Priest, Lisa. 1989. *Conspiracy of Silence.* Toronto: McClelland & Stewart.

Rajotte, Freda. 1998. *First Nations Faith and Ecology.* Toronto: Anglican Book Centre.

Reber, Susanne, and Robert Renaud. 2005. *Starlight Tour: The Last, Lonely Night of Neil Stonechild.* Toronto: Random House Canada.

Red Crow, Jackie. 1990. "Council Opposed to Peigan Diversion." *Windspeaker*, August 17.

Regina v. White and Bob, 52 *Dominion Law Reports* (2d.) 481 (1965).

Rex v. Syliboy, 1 *Dominion Law Reports* (307) (1929).

Rhodes, Richard. 1985. *Eastern Ojibwa-Chippewa-Ottawa Dictionary.* Amsterdam: Mouton Publishing.

Richardson, Boyce. 1991. *Strangers Devour the Land.* Vancouver: Douglas & McIntyre.

Ridington, Robin. 1982. "Technology, world view and adaptive strategy in a northern hunting society." *Canadian Review of Sociology and Anthropology, 19*(4) 46–67.

Roberts, Julian, and Carol LaPrairie. 1996. "Raising Some Questions About Sentencing Circles." 39 *Criminal Law Quarterly* 69.

Robinson, Carla. 1999. *Aboriginal Voices, 6*(3). Retrieved November 1, 1999, from www.aboriginalvoices.com/1999/06-03/robinson.html.

Rose, Alex. 2000. *Spirit Dance at Meziadin: Chief Joseph Gosnell and the Nisga'a Treaty.* Maderia Park, B.C.: Harbour Publishing.

Ross, R. 1993. "Aboriginal Community Healing in Action: The Hollow Water Approach." Retrieved March 1, 2000, from www.usask.ca/nativelaw/publications/jah/ross.html.

Ross, R. 1996. *Returning to the Teachings: Exploring Aboriginal Justice.* Toronto: Penguin.

Rudes, Blair. 1987. *Tuscarora Roots, Stems and Particles: Towards a Dictionary of Tuscarora.* Memoir 3. Winnipeg: Algonquian and Iroquoian Linguistics.

Sanders, Thomas, and Walter Peek. 1973. *Literature of the American Indian.* Beverly Hills, CA: Glencoe Press.

Santin, Aldo. 2012. Police Lay Charge in Beating Death. *The Winnipeg Free Press.* September 28, 2012.

Sarazin, Greg. 1989. "220 Years of Broken Promises." In Boyce Richardson, ed., *Drumbeat: Anger and Renewal in Indian Country,* pp. 139–166. Toronto: Summerhill Press.

Schmalz, Peter S. 1991. *The Ojibwa of Southern Ontario.* Toronto: University of Toronto Press.

Sewid, James. 1969. *Sewid: A Kwakiutl Indian.* New Haven and London: Yale University Press.

Siggins, M. 1994. *Riel: A Life of Revolution.* Toronto: HarperCollins.

Simon v. The Queen. 1985. 2 S.C.R. 387. Retrieved November 1, 2006, from http://scc.lexum.umontreal.ca/en/1985/1985rcs2-387/1985rcs2-387.pdf.

Sioui, Georges E. 1999. *Huron-Wendat: The Heritage of the Circle.* Trans. Jane Brierley. Vancouver: University of British Columbia Press.

"Sir James Douglas and the Indians." 1864. *The British Columbian,* June 8. Retrieved November 15, 2006, from www.mysterescanadiens.ca/sites/klatsassin/murdersorwar/deathofaroadcrew/255en.html.

Slinger, Joey. 1991. "Province selling off our Algonquin Park birthright." *Toronto Star,* September 28.

Smith, Donald. 1979. "Kineubenae." In *Dictionary of Canadian Biography: Volume 5,* p. 467. Toronto: University of Toronto Press.

Smith, Donald. 1979. "Wabakinine," *Dictionary of Canadian Biography: Volume 4,* pp. 755–756. Toronto: University of Toronto Press.

Smith, Donald. 1987. *Sacred Feathers: The Reverend Peter Jones (Kahkewaquonaby) and the Mississauga Indians,* Toronto: University of Toronto Press.

Smith, James G.E. 1981. "Chipewyan." In *The Handbook of North American Indians: Volume 6. Subarctic,* pp. 271–284. Washington: Smithsonian Institute.

Speck, Frank. 1977. *Naskapi.* Norman: University of Oklahoma Press. Originally published 1935.

Spielmann, Roger. 1998. *You're So Fat: Exploring Ojibwe Discourse.* Toronto: University of Toronto Press.

Spradley, James P. 1969. *Guests Never Leave Hungry: The Autobiography of James Sewid: A Kwakiutl Indian.* New Haven and London: Yale University Press.

Stackhouse, John. 2001. "Welcome to Harlem on the Prairies." *Globe and Mail,* November 3, F2–F4.

Standing Senate Committee on Social Affairs, Science, Technology. Proceedings, Subcommittee on Post-Secondary Education. 1997, February 11. Retrieved October 30, 2006, from www.parl.gc.ca/35/2/parlbus/commbus/senate/com-e/educ-e/06evb-e.htm?Language=E&Parl=35&Ses=2&comm_id=28.

Steckley, John L. 1993. "Leaders, Origins, Customs and Unity: Traditional Huron Notions of Country," *Arch. Notes,* 4, 18–21.

Steckley, John L. 1997. "Aboriginal Peoples." In Paul Angelini, ed., *Our Society:*

Human Diversity in Canada, pp. 131–158. Toronto: ITP Nelson.

Steckley, John L. 2003. *Aboriginal Voices and the Politics of Representation in Canadian Sociology Textbooks*. Toronto: Canadian Scholars' Press.

Stevenson, Marc. 1997. *Inuit Whalers and Cultural Persistence: Structure in Cumberland Sound and Central Inuit Social Organization*. Toronto: Oxford University Press.

Stewart, Hilary, ed. 1987. *The Adventures and Sufferings of John R. Jewitt, Captive of Maquinna*. Vancouver: Douglas & McIntyre.

Stymeist, David. 1977. *Ethnics and Indians: Social Relations in a Northwestern Ontario Town*. Toronto: Peter Martin Associates.

Sutton, Catharine. 1860. "An Indian Woman's Audience with Queen Victoria." *Brantford Courier,* August.

Sutton, Catharine. 1862. "Is There Hope for the Indians?" *Christian Guardian,* May 28.

Talbot, Francis X.S.J. 1956. *Saint Among the Hurons: The Life of Jean de Brébeuf.* New York: Image Books.

Teichroeb, Ruth. 1998. *Flowers on My Grave: How an Ojibwa Boy's Death Helped Break the Silence on Child Abuse*. Toronto: HarperCollins.

Tooker, Elisabeth. 1978. The league of the Iroquois: Its history, politics, and rituals. In Trigger, B.G., ed. *Handbook of North American Indians: Volume 15. Northeast,* pp. 418–41. Washington, Smithsonian Institute.

Toupin, Robert S.J. 1996. *Les Écrits de Pierre Potier: Collection Amérique Française No. 3.* Ottawa: Les Presses de l'Université d'Ottawa.

Tribal Council News. 1999a, February. *Tribal Council News, 2*(6). Retrieved November 16, 2000, from www.uccm.on.ca/Archive/February1999/feature3.htm.

Tribal Council News. 1999b, April. *Tribal Council News, 2*(8). Retrieved November 16, 2000, from www.uccm.on.ca/Archive/April1999/web2.8.5.htm.

Tribal Council News. 1999c, June. *Tribal Council News, 2*(10). Retrieved November 16, 2000, from www.uccm.on.ca/Archive/June%201999/ feature2.htm.

Turner, James. 2013. Cops Take on Indian Posse for Fatal Beating of Paris Bruce. *Winnipeg Sun.* March 13, 2013.

Upton, L.F.S. 1979. *Micmacs and Colonists: Indian-White Relations in the Maritimes, 1713–1867.* Vancouver: University of British Columbia Press.

Veteran Affairs Canada. 2005, June 30. "Native Soliders–Foreign Battlefields: A Peaceful Man." Retrieved October 26, 2006, from www.vac-acc.gc.ca/general/sub.cfm?source=history/other/native/peaceful.

Wadden, Marie. 1996. *Nitassinan: The Innu Struggle to Reclaim Their Homeland.* Vancouver: Douglas & McIntyre.

Wallace, Bruce. 1999. "Move Over: A New Generation of Younger Natives Is Coming into Its Own—and Flexing Its Powerful Muscles," *Maclean's, 112*(39), Sept 27, 20–30.

Walmsley, Christopher, 2005. *Protecting Aboriginal Children.* Vancouver: UBC Press.

Watkins, Mel, ed. 1977. *Dene Nation: The Colony Within.* Toronto: University of Toronto Press.

Western Economic Diversification Canada. 2005, April. "Urban Reserves in Saskatchewan." Retrieved November 1, 2006, from www.wd.gc.ca/rpts/research/urban_reserves/intro_e.asp.

Western Report, 10(3). 1995.

Whitehead, Paul C., and Michael J. Hayes. 1998. *The Insanity of Alcohol: Social Problems in Canadian First Nations Communities.* Toronto: Canadian Scholars' Press.

Whyte, Kenneth. 1990. *Alberta Report*, September 17.

Woodbury, Hanni, Reg Henry, and Harry Webster. 1992. *Concerning the League: The Iroquois League Tradition as Dictated in Onondaga by John Arthur Gibson.* Memoir 9. Winnipeg: Algonquian and Iroquoian Linguistics.

Wright, James V. 1995. *A History of the Native People of Canada, Volume 1 (10,000–1000 B.C.)* Ottawa: Canadian Museum of Civilization.

Wright, Ronald. 1988. "Beyond Words." *Saturday Night, 103*(4), April, 38–48.

www12.statcan.gc.ca/census-recensement/2006/as-sa/97-558/p2eng.cfm

www.amnesty.ca/campaigns/sisters_shirley-lonethunder.php

www.highwayoftears.ca

Yellowquill College. 2006. "White Paper." Retrieved October 30, 2006, from www.yellowquillcollege.mb.ca/.

York, Geoffrey. 1990. *The Dispossessed: Life and Death in Native Canada.* London: Vintage Books.

Index